Lecture Notes in Computer Science 11546

More information about this series at http://www.springer.com/series/7407

Simon K. S. Cheung · Lap-Kei Lee ·
Ivana Simonova · Tomas Kozel ·
Lam-For Kwok (Eds.)

Blended Learning

Educational Innovation for Personalized Learning

12th International Conference, ICBL 2019
Hradec Kralove, Czech Republic, July 2–4, 2019
Proceedings

Springer

Editors
Simon K. S. Cheung
The Open University of Hong Kong
Hong Kong, China

Lap-Kei Lee
The Open University of Hong Kong
Hong Kong, China

Ivana Simonova
Jan Evangelista Purkyne University
Ústí nad Labem, Czech Republic

Tomas Kozel
University of Hradec Kralove
Hradec Kralove, Czech Republic

Lam-For Kwok
City University of Hong Kong
Hong Kong, China

ISSN 0302-9743 ISSN 1611-3349 (electronic)
Lecture Notes in Computer Science
ISBN 978-3-030-21561-3 ISBN 978-3-030-21562-0 (eBook)
https://doi.org/10.1007/978-3-030-21562-0

LNCS Sublibrary: SL1 – Theoretical Computer Science and General Issues

This Springer imprint is published by the registered company Springer Nature Switzerland AG
The registered company address is: Gewerbestrasse 11, 6330 Cham, Switzerland

Preface

Welcome to the proceedings of the 12th International Conference on Blended Learning (ICBL 2019). This year, ICBL 2019 was held at the University of Hradec Kralove in Hradec Kralove, Czech Republic, during July 2–4, 2019.

Blended learning is one of the promising approaches to teaching and learning. It integrates traditional learning with innovative means to create a new learning environment conducive to effective learning. Like the previous conferences in the series, ICBL 2019 provided a platform for knowledge exchange and experience sharing among researchers and practitioners in this field.

The theme of ICBL 2019 was "Educational Innovation for Personalized Learning." Our focus was on new and innovative practices of blended learning that can enable personalized learning, enhance learning effectiveness, and enrich the learning experience. ICBL 2019 attracted a total of 80 paper submissions. After a rigorous review process, 28 papers were selected for inclusion in this volume. The selected papers cover various areas in blended learning, including personalized learning, adaptive learning, content development, analytics and evaluation for blended learning, experience in blended learning, open educational resources, and pedagogical and psychological issues.

We would like to take this opportunity to thank the following parties who made the conference a success: (a) the conference Organizing Committee; (b) the International Program Committee; (c) the conference organizers and co-organizer; (d) the conference sponsors, and (e) all the conference participants.

We trust you will enjoy reading the papers.

July 2019

Simon K. S. Cheung
Lap-Kei Lee
Ivana Simonova
Tomas Kozel
Lam-For Kwok

Preface

[illegible] 2019.

[illegible] among researchers [illegible] of this field.

The theme of ICBL 2019 was [illegible] Our [illegible] blended learning [illegible] experiences. ICBL 2019 [illegible] After a rigorous review process, 28 papers were selected for inclusion in this volume. These selected papers cover [illegible] in blended learning [illegible] and pedagogical and psychological issues.

We would like to take this opportunity to thank the following parties who made the conference a success: [illegible] the conference organizing committee; [illegible] Program Committee, for the conference [illegible] and [illegible] all the conference participants.

[illegible]

[illegible]

Organization

Organizing Committee

Honorary Chairs

Horace H. S. Ip	City University of Hong Kong, SAR China
Kamil Kuca	University of Hradec Kralove, Czech Republic

Conference Chairs

Lam-For Kwok	City University of Hong Kong, SAR China
Petra Poulova	University of Hradec Kralove, Czech Republic

Program Chairs

Simon K. S. Cheung	The Open University of Hong Kong, SAR China
Lap-Kei Lee	The Open University of Hong Kong, SAR China
Ivana Simonova	Jan Evangelista Purkyne University, Czech Republic
Tomas Kozel	University of Hradec Kralove, Czech Republic

Organizing Chairs

John Hui	Education University of Hong Kong, SAR China
Miloslava Cerna	University of Hradec Kralove, Czech Republic

Finance and Registration Chairs

Steven Ng	University of Sunderland, UK
Hana Sramkova	University of Hradec Kralove, Czech Republic

Publicity Chairs

Jana Rubackova	University of Hradec Kralove, Czech Republic
Kristyna Jandova	University of Hradec Kralove, Czech Republic
Morris Jong	The Chinese University of Hong Kong, SAR China
Yinghui Shi	Central China Normal University, China

Web Masters

Richard Li	City University of Hong Kong, SAR China
Vera Palanova	University of Hradec Kralove, Czech Republic

Program Committee

Chairs

Simon K. S. Cheung	The Open University of Hong Kong, SAR China
Lap-Kei Lee	The Open University of Hong Kong, SAR China
Ivana Simonova	Jan Evangelista Purkyne University, Czech Republic
Tomas Kozel	University of Hradec Kralove, Czech Republic

Members

Oliver Au	The Open University of Hong Kong, SAR China
Jan Beseda	Centre for Higher Education Studies, Prague, Czech Republic
Pavel Brebera	University of Pardubice, Czech Republic
Jana Burgerova	University of Presov, Slovakia
Jinnong Cao	The Hong Kong Polytechnic University, SAR China
C. S. Chai	The Chinese University of Hong Kong, SAR China
Keith Chan	The Hong Kong Polytechnic University, SAR China
Peter Chan	Brigham Young University, USA
Chih-Tsan Chang	National Chung Cheng University, Taiwan, China
Wei Chen	Chinese Academy of Agricultural Sciences, China
Guo-Li Chiou	National Taiwan Normal University, China
Giuliana Dettori	Istituto di Tecnologie Didattiche del CNR, Italy
Ludvík Eger	University of West Bohemia, Czech Republic
Zbynek Filipi	University of West Bohemia, Czech Republic
Rostislav Fojtík	University of Ostrava, Czech Republic
Yoshiko Goda	Kumamoto University, Japan
Radomira Greganova	Slovak University of Agriculture, Slovakia
Owen Hall Jr.	Pepperdine University, USA
Andreas Henrich	University of Bamberg, Germany
Dagmar Hillova	Slovak University of Agriculture, Slovakia
Yoko Hirata	Hokkai-Gakuen University, Japan
Yoshihiro Hirata	Hokkai-Gakuen University, Japan
Wai Shing Ho	Caritas Institute of Higher Education, Hong Kong, SAR China
Norio Hosaki	Waseda University, Japan
Jenq-Muh Hsu	National Chiayi University, Taiwan, China
Ronghuia Huang	Beijing Normal University, China
John Hui	Education University of Hong Kong, SAR China
Josef Hynek	University of Hradec Kralove, Czech Republic
Geng Jie	The Chinese University of Hong Kong, SAR China
Morris Jong	The Chinese University of Hong Kong, SAR China
Jacky Keung	City University of Hong Kong, SAR China
Blanka Klimova	University of Hradec Kralove, Czech Republic
Reggie Kwan	The Open University of Hong Kong, SAR China
Lam-For Kwok	City University of Hong Kong, SAR China

Chiu Lin Lai	National Taiwan University of Science and Technology, Taiwan, China
Ivan Lai	City University of Macau, SAR China
Jeanne Lam	University of Hong Kong, SAR China
Jun Le	Guangdong Radio and TV University, China
Min Hsien Lee	National Taiwan Normal University, Taiwan, China
Victor Lee	City University of Hong Kong, SAR China
K. C. Li	The Open University of Hong Kong, SAR China
Yan Li	Zhejiang University, China
Yi Li	Nanjing University, China
Heng Luo	Central China Normal University, China
Will Ma	Technological and Higher Education Institute of Hong Kong, SAR China
Jason MacLeod	Central China Normal University, China
Martina Manenova	University of Hradec Kralove, Czech Republic
Jaroslava Mikulecka	University of Hradec Kralove, Czech Republic
Kousuke Mouri	Kyushu University, Japan
Masayuki Murakami	Kyoto University of Foreign studies, Japan
Junko Nemoto	Ehime University, Japan
Steven Ng	University of Sunderland in Hong Kong, SAR China
Diana Perez-Marin	Universidad Rey Juan Carlos, Spain
C. K. Poon	Caritas Institute of Higher Education, SAR China
Linda Pospíšilová	University of Pardubice, Czech Republic
Petra Poulova	University of Hradec Kralove, Czech Republic
Yanghui Rao	Sun Yat-sen University, China
Lucie Rohlikova	University of West Bohemia, Czech Republic
Junjie Shang	Peking University, China
Yinghui Shi	Central China Normal University, China
Ju Ling Shih	National University of Tainan, Taiwan, China
Raymond So	The Open University of Hong Kong, SAR China
Yanjie Song	Education University of Hong Kong, SAR China
Niwat Srisawasdi	Khon Kaen University, Thailand
Liana Stanescu	University of Craiova, Romania
Cai Su	Beijing Normal University, China
Hana Svobodova	Masaryk University, Czech Republic
Libuse Svobodova	University of Hradec Kralove, Czech Republic
Jeff Tang	The Open University of Hong Kong, SAR China
Jay Tashiro	University of Ontario Institute of Technology, Canada
Jumpei Tokito	Kwansei Gakuin University, Japan
Shikui Tu	Shanghai Jiao Tong University, China
Olga Vrastilova	University of Hradec Kralove, Czech Republic
Aihua Wang	Peking University, China
Cong Wang	City University of Hong Kong, SAR China
Fu Lee Wang	The Open University of Hong Kong, SAR China
Shu Ming Wang	Chinese Culture University, Taiwan, China
Shudong Wang	Shimane University, Japan

Billy Wong	The Open University of Hong Kong, SAR China
Crusher Wong	City University of Hong Kong, SAR China
Gary Wong	University of Hong Kong, SAR China
Raymond Wong	City University of Hong Kong, SAR China
T. L. Wong	Douglas College, Canada
Di Wu	Central China Normal University, China
Haoran Xie	Education University of Hong Kong, SAR China
You Ru Xie	South China Normal University, China
Toshiyuki Yamamoto	Kansai University, Japan
Harrison Yang	State University of New York at Oswego, USA
Y. T. Yu	City University of Hong Kong, SAR China
Tomáš Zeman	Masaryk University, Czech Republic
Liming Zhang	University of Macau, SAR China
Guodong Zhao	Peking University, China
Jianhua Zhao	South China Normal University, China
Yunxiang Zheng	South China Normal University, China
Ying Zhou	Beijing Normal University, China
Sha Zhu	Central China Normal University, China

Organizers

University of Hradec Kralove

City University of Hong Kong

Co-organizer

Hong Kong Society for Multimedia and Image Computing

Sponsors

Hong Kong Pei Hua Education Foundation

Springer Science+Business Media

Keynote Speakers and Panel Chairs

Keynote Speakers

Andrea Benn	University of Brighton, UK
Harrison Yang	State University of New York at Oswego, USA
Shengquan Yu	Beijing Normal University, China
Miloslava Cerna	University of Hradec Kralove, Czech Republic

Panel Chairs

Horace H. S. Ip	City University of Hong Kong, SAR China
Naraphorn Paoprasert	Kasetsart University, Thailand

Contents

Open Educational Resources

Pedagogical and Psychological Issues

Keynotes

Pedagogic Practice in Blended-Learning

Andrea Benn(✉)

Brighton Business School, University of Brighton,
Brighton, E Sussex BN2 4AT, UK
a.benn@brighton.ac.uk

Abstract. Pedagogues are the architects of their own classroom settings. Each teacher will bring something of themselves into that environment, their values, their beliefs and above all their knowledge. All of these should underpin the learning that will take place and in turn should support the design of the lesson, the workshop, the seminar, the lecture. At the end of day, traditional education is a social occasion: an interaction between everybody in the class. Even in a one-directional lecture theatre environment, the lecturer will always bring their own personality, their idiosyncrasies, themselves. So how can we replicate this in a fairly static online environment? This has been my challenge as I have embraced the new arena of the online classroom. My paper will focus on us as individuals and pedagogues and the importance of ensuring that we remain pivotal in the design and delivery of the online element of blended learning.

Keywords: Curriculum design · Blended Learning · Instructional teaching

1 Introduction

Before understanding how to develop an online pedagogy or complementary blended pedagogy, this paper explores the role of the pedagogue in an attempt to realise how this role is adapting and whether technology is getting in the way.

"Teachers communicate much more than content to students. They share values, enthusiasm, curiosity or boredom, and attitudes, and their individual perceptions influence this critical communication" (Hardy and Tolhurst 2014, p. 283).

We all have our own memories of the teachers we preferred and those we didn't. The embarrassing attempts at jokes, the meaningful encouragements, the moments of discipline. For the academic year you spent together you united as a group, you enjoyed each other's triumphs and shared in the disappointments, knowing that the person in charge was also living those moments. My early years in school shaped me as a teacher, I loved everything about my primary education and how I was taught, remembering it to be fun, through creative activities but serious when it had to be.

I now work in a large Business School at a post '92 UK University. The cohort sizes are large and culturally diverse and although the students are divided into smaller seminar groups, it is not always easy to develop the same relationships. What does remain constant for me is my attempt at reproducing the comfortable learning environment that I remembered and enjoyed. What I didn't realise then but fully appreciate now, is the effort and planning that clearly underpinned those 'easy going' classes.

S. K. S. Cheung et al. (Eds.): ICBL 2019, LNCS 11546, pp. 3–8, 2019.
https://doi.org/10.1007/978-3-030-21562-0_1

2 Teaching and Learning

For the last 8 years, I have been actively engaged in action research looking at ways that I can change what I do in order to bring about a change in others, primarily encouraging and supporting students through their transition from passive learners to independent and confident young people. During this time, I have reviewed and tried pedagogical structures promoted by others to integrate new technologies and move towards a more student-centred approach. Now, I am moving back towards the school of thought that is firmly in favour of 'instructional teaching' seeing the role of the teacher as pivotal.

2.1 Teaching

Rata (2017) examines two different understandings of knowledge which lead to different approaches to teaching and learning. Referring to and citing the works of Durkheim, Bourdieu, Winch, Popper she explains in each case how knowledge is constructed and how this leads to a different approach to teaching and learning.

One approach described is 'teaching as instruction' and the other is 'teaching as facilitation'. Her purpose for doing this is to contribute to what she acknowledges is a serious challenge to the facilitation approach by discussing and demonstrating how their differences are the result of different understandings of how knowledge is constituted. She argues that the link between the way knowledge is structured and the way it is organised for teaching justifies instructional teaching as the more effective way to develop students' learning. She continues the point that the facilitation approach is considered to be weak because it is primarily a pedagogical approach concerned with motivating students and fails to account for the type of knowledge that constitutes academic subjects. Instructional teaching requires an understanding of the episteme (knowledge-that) and how to connect the abstract concepts to the material world, the process Winch (2013) calls epistemic ascent. The issue for the curriculum and pedagogue is how to demonstrate the connection in the arrangement of conceptual knowledge and its material application so that it is clear to students. Instructional teaching, she concludes, requires an engaging pedagogy which links the epistemically structured ideas to the rules and procedures for their application to real life and that requires 'a knowledge authority' (a teacher) to transmit the knowledge to each succeeding generation.

In their 2016 paper, McPhail and Rata evaluate two distinctive curriculum design types: 21st Century Learning ("21CL") and Powerful Knowledge ("PK"). They argue that the fundamental difference between the two types "lies in what is meant by knowledge (the theory of knowledge), *how* this knowledge is to be organised (i.e. the curriculum design) and *how* it is to be made available (pedagogy)" continuing the importance of understanding how knowledge is structured and organised is foundational to curriculum design.

They clearly state their belief in the PK approach which rests on the logical connections drawn from a theory of knowledge to a curriculum structure which enables conceptual progression leading to student learning, something they consider to be missing from the literature in support of the 21CL.

Rata defines the term ‘Powerful Knowledge’ explaining its importance within a school curriculum and identifying its purpose which is “to assist students to think about the world in abstract or context-independent ways”. Her discussion includes a focus on the relationship between what is taught and how it is taught and the question of ‘how do young people acquire abstract knowledge?’. She acknowledges that to achieve this the “demands on teachers are considerable”. She continues that teachers are required to use a pedagogy of conceptual progression that ensures that the concepts to be taught remain ordered within their systems of meaning, while at the same time recognising students’ differing levels of understanding. Ultimately, she states that “it requires teachers to be knowledgeable about the subject they teach in order to structure concepts from lower-to higher-order complexity” while not accepting that this is simply a case of “adding fact upon fact” in the “stereotype of rote-learning”.

She continues with an explanation citing Vygotsky and Winch that “a pedagogy that can enable epistemic ascent to occur, places conceptual progression at the core of teaching because a teacher can only explain the unknown by linking it to what is already known and building from that foundation in a logical order”, and “that a failure to get the sequencing right, can have adverse pedagogic consequences”.

What is required therefore, is for teachers to have a good understanding of the subject content and the concepts that make up the systems of meaning for that subject. This understanding or familiarity will enable teachers to manage the needs of the subject as well as those of their students.

2.2 Learning

Savin-Baden (1996) seeks to define the concept of problem-based learning (“PBL”). She interprets Barrows, Barrows & Tamblyn, Popper and Knowles as theorists looking to address the “promising solution to many of the difficulties in professional curricula generally” namely, the “over emphasis of memorization and recall of facts”, and “a failure to integrate basic scientific concepts into clinical practice”.

Savin-Baden explains that PBL emerged in the sixties and seventies from the work of Barrows who was looking for a way to help medical students learn how to approach and apply knowledge to a given problem. Working with Tamblyn they define PBL as “the learning which results from the process of working towards the understanding of, or resolution of, a problem”. Popper had previously suggested that “learning takes place through the formulation of problems and through trial and error in solving these problems”, and Knowles argued that teacher centred subject-based learning assumes that the learner’s experience is of less value than the teacher’s. This latter point was in the context of adults as learners.

McCabe & O’Connor in their 2014 paper, explore the concept of student-centred learning in their quest for finding ways of turning students from passive to active learners. Through their own investigation, they evaluate a student-centred approach to learning which they state encourages students to have more responsibility for their learning. They advocate that the process relies heavily on professional confidence to ‘let go’ of traditional teaching responsibilities and their review focuses on the role and responsibility of the lecturer.

Their discussion opens with a core interpretation of SCL namely as a shift in responsibility for learning from lecturer to student, with the latter demonstrating characteristics of autonomous, proactive and constructive engagement. They continue with an acknowledgement from their colleagues that the success of the transition required more than "simply stepping back and letting students take control" instead necessitating lecturers to became "facilitators" in the process. Also citing Knowles, they explain that the effective facilitator is someone who ensures that students are cognisant of what is expected of them and have sufficient capacity to accept ownership of their learning. Translated into their own practice, McCabe & O'Conner's colleagues explained that they tried to guide students, not direct them and without giving away the answer tried to phrase questions so students would realise that the direction they were going in was not the right one. It was a case of finding the appropriate balance, dependent upon a skilful facilitator who could be sensitive and intuitive and then tailor the approach based on the dynamic of each group. Integral to this success also was for "a safe learning environment so that the students felt they had the freedom to make mistakes in a controlled environment".

Tangney (2014) found that student-centred learning is not defined within the pedagogic literature but more generally associated with constructivism or principles associated with a constructivist environment, such as building on prior knowledge, purposeful active learning and sense-making. From her own perspective of a humanist interpretation of SCL, Tangney also argues for the idea of a holistic approach developing ideas of empowerment and emancipation. Citing Brockett, Maslow, Rogers, Rogers & Freiberg she explains that 'humanists are generally concerned with the freedom, dignity and potential of humans' seeing learning as akin to personal growth and self-belief. Summarising these authors, Tangney supports their collective views that SCL is "an individualised approach facilitated by a positive trusting relationship with teaching staff which fosters empowerment".

Learning this way however, requires student buy-in and as McCabe and O'Connor observe: "students are not a homogeneous group" and try as we might, no "one-size-fits-all" strategy is going to work and nor is it necessarily appropriate. Vermunt and Donche (2017) in their review of research and theory development on student learning patterns in higher education and beyond, acknowledge that four qualitative learning patterns have been repeatedly identified, namely, reproduction-directed learning; meaning-directed learning; application-directed learning and undirected learning. While McCabe and O'Connor observe that the first year of higher education is a good opportunity to introduce a new way of learning as students are generally open to and are expecting something "new", Vermunt and Donche's explanation of the "undirected learning" should act as a point of consideration for pedagogues and curriculum designers. Acknowledging that there are many and varied factors as to why students adopt certain learning patterns, this learning pattern can often be seen with students who are in transition from one form of schooling to another such as secondary to higher education. Students who are currently displaying characteristics of the "undirected learner" are not going to find it easy to adapt to a new learning environment, instead attaching great value to fellow students and teachers to provide direction and structure.

3 Blended Learning

Blended Learning ("BL") is widely defined as the combination of traditional face-to-face teaching methods with authentic online learning activities (Davis and Fill 2007).

Adopting technology for the enhancement of learning is not new, there has always been a strong relationship between education and technology (Laurillard 2012). Within the teaching profession there will always be early adopters, innovators keen to make the best use of the latest technology to enhance what they are doing. Developments have shown a standard online pedagogy provides a mix of presentations, automated assessment, peer-assessed assignments and peer discussions.

Laurillard (2012) introduces the concept of teaching as a design science, and particularly the "Conversational Framework" ("CF") as a way of challenging the use of new technologies in learning. Laurillard explains that the aim of the CF is to provide a way of representing the different kinds of roles played by teachers and learners in terms of the requirements derived from different learning concepts. By capturing the pedagogy that the teacher has found to be effective and mapping this against the corresponding principles for designing teaching and learning activities, including how technology can be used, can show the beneficial role of technology.

SCL and PBL are widely used in the context of BL with the 'theory' elements being disseminated via the technology. It is worth noting, that both rely on the pedagogue for structure and guidance, neither able to completely handover the learning process.

4 Conclusion

The plethora of research into E and BL advises that learning with technology needs to be driven by pedagogical principles. Researchers advise that teachers should have ownership of the way the overall design is developed, and particularly when it comes to identifying where in the curriculum the e-learning element will be best placed. The design of an online tool must also be carefully considered as part of the learning process and be easily accessible and user friendly.

Key decisions as to which technologies to incorporate may already have been made by the institution itself which then makes the design process one of best fit. Academics may not have the skills necessary to exploit the technology, or perceive the iterative task of designing, testing, implementing, amending new technological designs too labour intensive to be of much benefit. I would advocate that none of the above must be a barrier for any teacher or lecturer. Instead the design process should become a collaborative learning process between colleagues within an organisation willing to share ideas and examples.

Learner collaboration, however, is more difficult and is typically achieved offline. This part of the pedagogy has to be carefully designed and although there are a variety of tools, wikis, discussion boards etc. they may not be appropriate for all kinds of collaborative learning. Our role may be changing but Pedagogues will always be pivotal when it comes to curriculum design.

References

Davis, H.C., Fill, K.: Embedding blended learning in a university's teaching culture: experiences and reflections. Br. J. Educ. Technol. **38**(5), 817–828 (2007)

Hardy, C., Tolhurst, D.: Epistemological beliefs and cultural diversity matters in management education and learning: a critical review and future directions. Acad. Manag. Learn. Educ. **13** (2), 265–289 (2014)

Laurillard, D.: Building Pedagogical Patterns for Learning and Teaching. Routledge, Oxfordshire (2012)

McCabe, A., O'Connor, U.: Student-centred learning: the role and responsibility of the lecturer. Teach. High. Educ. **19**(4), 350–359 (2014)

McPhail, G., Rata, E.: Comparing curriculum types: 'powerful knowledge' and '21st century learning'. NZ J. Educ. Stud. **53**, 53–68 (2016)

Rata, E.: Knowledge and teaching. Br. Educ. Res. J. **43**(5), 1003–1017 (2017)

Savin-Baden, M.: Problem-based learning: a catalyst for enabling and disabling disjunction prompting transitions in learner stances? Ph.D. thesis, University of London Institute of Education (1996)

Tangney, S.: Student-centred learning: a humanist perspective. Teach. High. Educ. **19**(3), 266–275 (2014)

Vermunt, J.D., Donche, V.: A learning patterns perspective on student learning in higher education: state of the art and moving forward. Educ. Psychol. Rev. **29**, 269–299 (2017)

Winch, C.: Curriculum design and epistemic ascent. J. Philos. Educ. **47**(1), 128–146 (2013)

Understanding Undergraduates' Adoption of Flipped Learning: Integrating UTAUT and Social Presence

Jin Cai[1,2], Harrison Hao Yang[1,3(✉)], and Di Gong[1]

[1] Central China Normal University, Wuhan 430079, China
harrison.yang@oswego.edu
[2] Hubei University of Education, Wuhan 430205, China
[3] State University of New York at Oswego, New York 13126, USA

Abstract. The adoption of modern instructional techniques, such as the flipped learning, are relied upon to improve students' performance in higher education. Despite many clear advantages and positive aspects of flipped learning, user adoption is still slow or in its early phases in many developing countries. Furthermore, very little is known about undergraduates' perception and behavior toward acceptance and use of the flipped learning method. Therefore, this study explores the relationships between five key factors from a social presence-integrated UTAUT model and students' adoption of flipped learning. Structural equation modeling was employed to examine the data of 416 Chinese college freshmen. The results show that facilitating conditions, social presence, and effort expectancy are a significant positive influence on students' adoption. Moreover, facilitating conditions and social influence positively influence students' adoption, mediating by social presence. This study indicates that higher education institutions may achieve an increase in students' adoption of the flipped learning method by emphasizing the attributes explored in our research model.

Keywords: Flipped learning · UTAUT · Social presence · Higher education · SEM

1 Introduction

The flipped learning method (reversed learning or inverted learning) refers to an educational process which swaps events that traditionally took place inside the classroom with the events that traditionally took place outside of the classroom [1]. This learning method describes interactive group learning activities in the classroom, which are supported by individual computer-based instruction outside the classroom [2]. The flipped learning method is important because it overcomes the limitations of physical space and the fixed time frame of traditional teaching, which enables a more personalized learning experience [3]. Additionally, flipped learning provides a more autonomous and cooperative experience [4, 5], increasing the interaction between students' and their instructor [6], and utilizing a student-centered approach to educational delivery [7].

S. K. S. Cheung et al. (Eds.): ICBL 2019, LNCS 11546, pp. 9–21, 2019.
https://doi.org/10.1007/978-3-030-21562-0_2

Although many studies have examined flipped learning and, in general, described the instructional model positively, few studies had investigated the acceptance of flipped learning in higher education. With the widespread implementation of this instructional model, it is important for researchers, practitioners, and administrators to be provided with a comprehensive understanding of flipped learning. Specifically, information should be available to describe the two different stakeholder perspectives: instructors and students.

So far, our previous studies have begun to address this research demand from the instructors' perspective of flipped learning acceptance [8]. However, less knowledge is available to comprehensively describe the issue from the college students' perspective [9]. The current study was designed to propose a social presence-integrated UTAUT model that examines college students' acceptance of flipped learning. The research questions guiding this study are (1) which factors mainly influence Chinese college students' adoption of flipped learning? and (2) What are the relationships between these factors?

2 Theoretical Framework

2.1 Flipped Learning

Lage et al. [1] were among the early pioneers documenting the flipped learning method in higher education. More recently, the Flipped Learning Network (FLN) defined flipped learning as, "a pedagogical approach in which direct instruction moves from the group learning space to the individual learning space, and the resulting group space is transformed into a dynamic, interactive learning environment where the educator guides students as they apply concepts and engage creatively in the subject matter" [10]. It is important to note that this definition distinguishes a flipped classroom from the notion of flipped learning. Researchers have highlighted that flipping a class does not necessarily lead to flipped learning [34]. To further articulate the difference between a flipped classroom and flipped learning, the FLN identified four characteristics of flipped learning as a (1) flexible environment, (2) learning culture, (3) intentional content, and (4) professional educator.

The flipped learning method involves teaching and learning in both the face-to-face classroom, as well as the out-of-class learning management system or related virtual learning environment. So far, we have preliminarily examined students' acceptance of flipped classrooms within cloud classrooms [9]. However, less is known about the holistic picture of flipped learning, particularly from the vantage of students' social presence in such contexts.

2.2 Unified Theory of Acceptance and Use of Technology

In order to improve understanding of user adoption behavior, a series of theories and theoretical models have been developed in recent decades [11–19]. Currently, the Unified Theory of Acceptance and Use of Technology (UTAUT) is the most accurate and prominently cited model for evaluating user acceptance. UTAUT is based upon the integration of eight theories [11–19] is capable of explaining as much as 70% of the variance. UTAUT consists of four major factors: performance expectancy, effort expectancy, social influence, and facilitating conditions.

Performance Expectancy means the degree to which the students believe that using flipped learning approach will help them to attain achievements. Effort Expectancy means how easy it is to use the flipped learning method, including the technologies and cloud classrooms used in flipped learning. Social Influence refers to the degree to which someone perceives that important people believe they should adopt the flipped learning approach. People who are important to college students include college administrators, their course teachers, counselors, roommates, and influential peers, not their parents, because they are seldom involved in the process of their children's college study. Facilitating Conditions refers to the degree to which individuals perceive an effective organization and technical infrastructure that can support the system used in flipped learning.

2.3 Social Presence

Social presence refers to the degree to which a person is perceived as a "real person" in mediated communication [20]. This term was introduced by Short et al. in the 1970s and has been regarded as critical because education relies on efficient communication, and communication may change under the influence of technology mediation [21]. For example, electronic communication often increases the psychological distance between communicators, and tends to be more task-oriented, which makes it less personal [22–25].

Social presence is important because it has been shown to affect users' acceptance of technology [26]. Additionally, the UTAUT factors of social influence [27] and facilitating conditions [21, 23, 28] have been shown to influence social presence. These studies indicate that social presence may be an important factor influencing college students' acceptance of flipped learning. Given that a wide variety of technological phenomena are re-shaping the landscape of education (e.g., E-learning, M-learning, big data, cloud technology, artificial intelligence) the social context of online learning is becoming more complex than ever before. Since the flipped learning model partly requires students to learn online, the influence of social presence becomes a critical variable to understand. Therefore, the proposed research model integrated social presence into our research model for evaluating college students' acceptance of flipped learning.

2.4 Research Model and Hypotheses

Based on our review of the literature, we have proposed a research model that integrates social presence with UTAUT. As shown in Fig. 1, the following hypotheses were proposed:

Hypothesis 1 (H1): The level of Effort Expectancy is positively related to Performance Expectancy.

Hypothesis 2 (H2): The level of Facilitating Conditions is positively related to Social Presence.
Hypothesis 3 (H3): The level of Social Influence is positively related to Social Presence.
Hypothesis 5 (H5): The level of Facilitating Conditions is positively related to User Adoption.
Hypothesis 4 (H4): The level of Effort Expectancy is positively related to User Adoption.
Hypothesis 6 (H6): The level of Performance Expectancy is positively related to User Adoption.
Hypothesis 7 (H7): The level of Social Influence is positively related to User Adoption.
Hypothesis 8 (H8): The level of Social Presence is positively related to User Adoption.

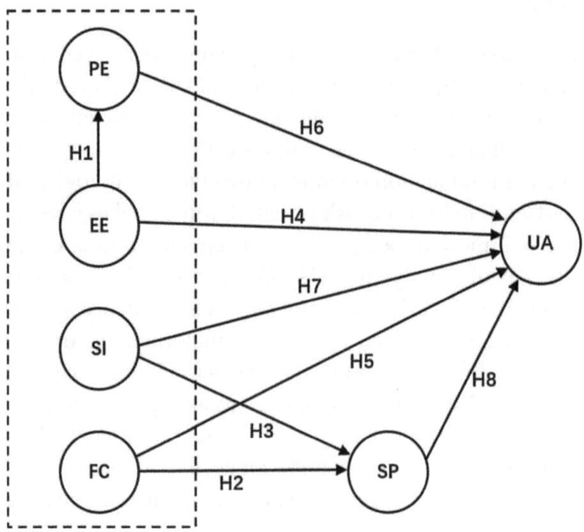

Fig. 1. Research model and hypotheses. Note: EE = effort expectancy; FC = facilitating conditions; PE = performance expectancy; SI = social influence; SP = social presence; UA = user adoption.

3 Methodology

3.1 Participants

A total of 416 first-year college students (freshmen) who came from a local normal university in Central China were the participants of this research. The term "normal university" refers to a higher education institution that is focused on teacher preparation and training. Before individuals started to learn *Computer Basics and Applications,* a compulsory course for all college freshmen in their first semester, they didn't have any experience with flipped learning. The participants consisted of 343 females and 73 males. This gender composition was consistent with the overall gender ratio for the institution, and typical for normal universities in China. The age range of the sample was between 17 to 20.

3.2 Procedure

This study and the course of *Computer Basics and Applications* was carried out over a 12-week period during the fall of 2018. At first, the researchers designed and produced the resources for flipped learning of this course and placed it in the cloud classroom, including instructional video clips, exercises, quizzes, homework assignments, etc., and placed it in a cloud classroom. Then, one of the researchers, who was also an instructor, assisted two other instructors to offer this course to all the participants with an approach of flipped learning. Participants met with their instructor twice a week for a 90-min class, one of which might be lectures, presentations, discussions or other activities in the classroom, and another to practice in a computer lab. With their mobile phones, participants could log in the cloud classroom to learn the online resources flexibly during their extracurricular time. In addition, teachers and students could also use the mobile app to develop some real-time interactive activities in the classroom, such as making attendance, question and answers, and conducting a survey or quiz. In the last week before the end of this course, all the participants were asked to fill out a questionnaire of the study.

3.3 Instrumentation

The UTAUT scale used in this study was adopted from our previous research [9], which was a Chinese translation derived from the Venkatesh et al.'s [13] original UTAUT instrument. The researchers modified this scale slightly to make it suitable for the survey in the context of flipped learning. Finally, the UTAUT scale adopted in this study consisted of five dimensions, a total of 20 items. To be specific, it included performance expectancy (4 items), effort expectancy (4 items), social influence (4 items), facilitating conditions (4 items), and flipped learning acceptance (4 items). One representative item has been included for each dimension: "In my opinion, the adoption of flipped learning may improve my academic performance." (performance expectancy), "I think it is easy to use proficiently an online learning system or platform." (effort expectancy), "The college encouraged me to adopt the flipped learning method." (social influence), "I have the knowledge necessary to adopt the flipped learning method." (facilitating conditions), and "I often use learning resources in the cloud classroom for flipped learning." (flipped learning acceptance). All UTAUT items were measured on a five-point Likert scale ranging from (1) strongly disagree to (5) strongly agree.

A Social Presence Scale was adopted from Gunawardena and Zittle's [20] instrument. It consisted of a single dimension with fourteen items which were measured on a five-point Likert scale ranging from (1) strongly disagree to (5) strongly agree. In order to conduct the survey in the participants' native language, all items were parallel translated from English to Chinese by the researchers firstly. Finally, the survey translation was bilingually reviewed and revised by an educational technology expert with over 20 years of teaching experience in the US and China. Two representative items of this scale are "I felt comfortable interacting with other participants in the cloud classroom for flipped learning." and "I felt that my point of view was acknowledged by other participants in the cloud classroom for flipped learning."

3.4 Data Collection and Analysis Procedure

The questionnaire was directly sent to the class who have just experienced 12-week long flipped learning in Computer Basics and Applications during the period of December 24, 2018 to January 7, 2019. A total of 416 valid responses were received voluntarily and anonymously. The survey data were entered into the computer and saved as.cvs format required by the statistical analysis software.

Structural Equation Modeling (SEM) method was used to verify the research model proposed in this study, and SmartPLS 3.2.6 was employed. The Partial Least Squares (PLS) method is one of the statistical methods that used to search for latent patterns in the data without or with little prior knowledge on how the variables are related [29]. Without any missing values, invalid observations or outliers, the data was preliminarily analyzed with Smart PLS v.3.2.6. As there were as many as 14 indicators to measure the latent variable SP, one of the indicators of SP, of which loading value was 0.626 and slightly below the standard value of 0.7, was trimmed.

4 Results and Discussion

4.1 Overview of the Survey

Table 1 provides an overview of the participants' minimum, maximum, mean scores and standard deviations on the flipped learning acceptance survey. The results showed that responses to all variables were similar. The minimum and maximum ranged from 2 to 5, and the mean scores ranged from 3.61 to 3.70. Social presence (M = 3.61, SD = .57) was shown to have the lowest mean score examined, while user adoption (M = 3.70, SD = .61) was shown to have the highest mean score of the survey.

Table 1. Descriptive statistics

Latent Variables	Min	Max	Mean	SD
Effort expectancy	2	5	3.67	.63
Facilitating conditions	2	5	3.62	.59
Performance expectancy	2	5	3.66	.63
Social influence	2	5	3.69	.62
Social presence	2.07	5	3.61	.57
User adoption	2	5	3.70	.61

Note: n = 416.

4.2 Confirming the Measurement Model

Like all other social science studies, the establishment of reliability and validity of potential variables is a necessary condition for completing structural model testing. The reliability of the measurement model includes indicator reliability and internal consistency reliability, while the validity includes convergent validity and discriminant validity [29, 30]. Therefore, the outer loadings, composite reliability, AVE (Average Variance Extracted) and its square root should be examined and reported [30].

As shown in Table 2, these results were all greater than the ideal criterion presented in the previous literature [31, 32], and indicated that this survey has satisfactory reliability and convergent validity. All the outer loadings were between 0.708 and 0.911. The Cronbach's Alpha coefficients and composite reliability (CR) coefficients showed a range of 0.822–0.934, 0.883–0.945 respectively. Such values were shown to be larger than 0.7, so high levels of internal consistency reliability have been demonstrated among all six reflective latent variables.

Table 2. Results of the measurement model

	Reliability of measures			Convergent validity	Discriminant validity					
	# of Items	Cronbach's Alpha	CR	AVE	EE	FC	PE	SI	SP	UA
EE	4	.907	.935	.783	**.885**					
FC	4	.822	.883	.655	.772	**.809**				
PE	4	.920	.943	.806	.830	.775	**.898**			
SI	4	.910	.937	.787	.806	.795	.791	**.887**		
SP	13	.934	.945	.631	.786	.739	.759	.727	**.794**	
UA	4	.858	.904	.701	.770	.819	.736	.760	.724	**.837**
Ideal criteria	Loadings > 0.7	>0.7	>0.7	>0.5						

To support discriminant validity, square roots of AVEs are reported in bold; EE – effort expectancy; FC = facilitating conditions; PE = performance expectancy; SI = social influence; SP = social presence; UA = user adoption.

As shown in Table 2, it was found that all of the AVE values showed a range of 0.631–0.806 are greater than the acceptable threshold of 0.5, so convergent validity was confirmed. What's more, to evaluate the discriminant validity, the square roots of AVE were compared to correlations among latent variables [31], which were larger than the respective correlation coefficients. Accordingly, the measurement model in this study had good reliability and validity, which had laid a reasonable foundation for the following research.

4.3 Structural Equation Modeling Analysis

This structural model was checked its structural path coefficient sizes and significance by using path coefficients, R^2 value in Bootstrapping. Using a two-tailed t-test with a significance level of 5%, the path coefficient will be significant if the T-statistics is larger than 1.96 [30].

Explanation of Target Endogenous Variable Variance. Shown as Table 3, the coefficient of determination, R^2, is 0.729 for the user adoption endogenous latent variable. It means that the five latent variables (effort expectancy, facilitating conditions, performance expectancy, social influence, and social presence) explain 72.9% of the variance in user adoption. Moreover, facilitating conditions and social influence together explain 59.9% of the variance of Social presence. And effort expectancy explains 68.8% of the variance of performance expectancy.

Table 3. Structural model test

Hypothesis	Independent Variable	Dependent Variable	Path Coefficient	*T*-Statistics	*p*	Result	R^2
H1	EE	PE	.832	37.778**	.000	Supported	.688
H2	FC	SP	.437	7.598**	.000	Supported	.599
H3	SI	SP	.381	6.373**	.000	Supported	
H4	EE	UA	.203	2.554*	.011	Supported	.729
H5	FC	UA	.452	6.710**	.000	Supported	
H6	PE	UA	.025	.342	.732	Rejected	
H7	SI	UA	.129	1.792	.074	Rejected	
H8	SP	UA	.117	2.341*	.020	Supported	

R^2 coefficient of determinations. R^2 of 0.75 is substantial, 0.50 is moderate, and 0.25 is weak.
** $p < 0.05$, ** < 0.001*

Structural Model Path Coefficient Sizes and Significance. Except for H6 (t = 0.342) and H7 (t = 1.792), all other path coefficients in the structural model were statistically significant. The PLS path modeling estimation for this study is shown in Fig. 2. The structural model suggested that facilitating conditions had the strongest effect on user adoption (0.452), followed by effort expectancy (0.203), social influence (0.129), social presence (0.117), and performance expectancy (0.025). The hypothesized path relationship of H5 (Facilitating conditions → Social presence), H4 (Effort expectancy → User adoption), and H8 (Social presence → User adoption) were statistically significant.

Furthermore, facilitating conditions also had the strongest effect on the social presence (0.437), followed by social influence (0.381), as well as effort expectancy had a strong effect on performance expectancy (0.832). H2, H3, and H1 were statistically significant too.

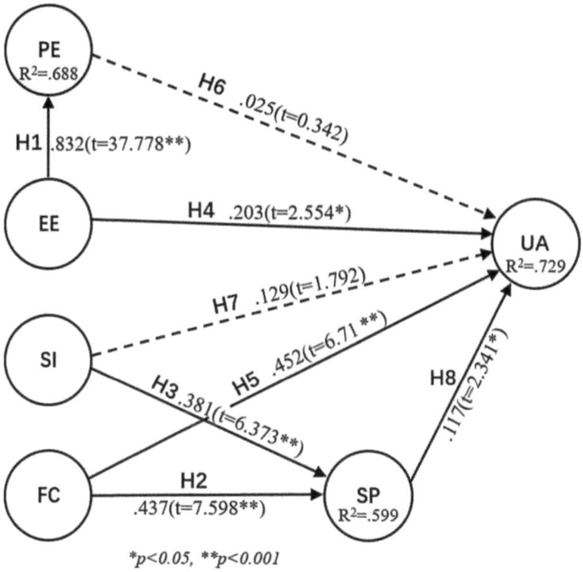

Fig. 2. Structural model results.

4.4 Discussion

By using survey data to validate the research model, we found that part of the UTAUT relationships were confirmed, but some were contradicted in this study.

Firstly, facilitating conditions, effort expectancy which were consistent with the viewpoints of Venkatesh et al. [13]. The college students in this study carried out flipped learning with the online resources of *Computer Basics and Applications* course. Considering that the freshmen have not yet purchased or carried a computer to the campus, a mobile phone app with easy access and the friendly interface was recommended for them. Since the students are very proficient in operating their smartphones, a technology used in flipped learning no longer acts as a barrier to students. In this way, they were more likely to accept flipped learning as technology-supported learning.

Secondly, the UTAUT model use performance expectancy and effort expectancy, which incorporate the determinants of perceived usefulness and ease of use in the original TAM model [13]. Therefore, it was not difficult to understand that effort expectancy put a significant effect on performance expectancy in the results.

Thirdly, social presence was identified as one of the factors with the greatest predictive value for user adoption. Furthermore, it was also an important mediating variable for social influence and facilitating conditions to exert influence on user adoption, because both of them had a significant influence on social presence. Good communication facilities and network environment make individual to communicate with others without obstacles, or even easier, which confirmed that the level of social presence could be cultured and enhanced mentioned in the previous paper [27].

However, there were two factors that had no significant effect on user adoption: performance expectancy and social influence. To be exact, each of them had a positive impact, but not strong. The result that performance expectancy or perceive of usefulness did not reflect the predictability of users' behavioral intention, not only appeared in this study, but also in a few of previous studies [8, 9, 33, 34]. This may be due to the characteristics of the samples. Thomas, Singh and Gaffar suggested that culture and country level differenced moderate the UTAUT effects [35]. The sample of this study was the first-year students of a local normal university. They had little perception and experience of flipped learning, so they did not have a strong sense of the usefulness of flipped learning. This can be understood from the scores of four measuring items of performance expectation. The average scores of the four items were 3.73, 3.64, 3.65 and 3.62, respectively. They distributed between "uncertainty" and "agree", which indicated that students' perceived usefulness of flipped learning was not strong. Even so, things may be going as some researcher mentioned that "even though a technology may be perceived as being advanced, if it does not fit users' task requirements, they may not adopt it" [36]. Perhaps we should give more understanding to students' internal psychological processes, such as how to stimulate students' learning motivation and self-discipline, which have been mentioned by literature on online teaching.

Similar performance expectancy does not agree with the prediction in UTAUT model, nor does social influence. The social influence of an individual comes from the opinions of the people who are important for him. Friedkin and Johnsen mentioned in their research, a person was difficult to maintain one's own opinion on an issue when the other members of his group had relatively uniform opinions on the issue [37]. However, Venkatesh et al. found that social influence seemed to be important only in the early stages of personal use of the technology, which gradually diminished over time and eventually becomes less significant with sustained usage [13].

The influential people for the participants in this study were their classmates and teachers. Assuming that their teachers had less interaction with them, the companion did not seem to have any influence on him. It is recommended that universities and teachers should take the initiative to communicate with students about the knowledge, experience, usage and usefulness of flipped learning, if they want to achieve better teaching results in flipped learning.

5 Conclusion

The purpose of this study is to explore how Chinese college students accept the flipped learning method by understanding the relationships among UTAUT variables and social presence. Through the exploration of survey data gathered from 416 freshmen who just experienced a course taught with the flipped learning method, the variables of facilitating conditions, effort expectancy, and social presence were identified as the key factors that lead to user adoption for flipped learning. SEM analysis also identified social influence as a key factor affecting students' acceptance mediated by social presence.

While flipped learning is becoming a common phenomenon in higher education in developing countries and throughout the world, the results of this study give instructors information to make reasonable design and teaching plans at the beginning of their implementation of flipped teaching. Additionally, the implications of the relationship between UTAUT and social presence observed in this study enrich existing knowledge in ways that can improve the acceptance of computer-mediated learning in higher education and provide a basis for further research on flipped learning. Some suggestions that can be gleaned from this study are as follows: (1) universities and instructors should fully consider the accessibility and conditions of flipped learning, to ensure that they are very easy to participate with; (2) provide students with appropriate technical training to reduce or eliminate barriers to using technology; and (3) build an active community network into the curricular objectives in order to encourage students' interaction with each other.

It should be mentioned that the data was collected within a specific context and participant demographics. Therefore, additional research should explore the topic with varying samples in a variety of academic settings (e.g., different university backgrounds, different class sizes, different specialized courses) to expand understanding and strengthen the generalizability of findings.

Acknowledgments. This work was support by the National Key Research and Development Program of China (2018YFB1004504). The authors also wish to thank Dr. Jason MacLeod for his assistance in editing the research report.

References

1. Lage, M.J., Platt, G.J., Treglia, M.: Inverting the classroom: a gateway to creating an inclusive learning environment. J. Econ. Educ. **31**(1), 30–43 (2000)
2. Bishop, J.L., Verleger, M.A.: The flipped classroom: a survey of the research. In: ASEE National Conference Proceedings, Atlanta, GA, June, vol. 30, no. 9, pp. 1–18 (2013)
3. Bergmann, J., Sams, A.: Flip Your Classroom: Reach Every Student in Every Class Every Day. International Society for Technology in education, Arlington (2012)
4. Larsen, A.J.: Experiencing a flipped mathematics class (2013). Doctoral Dissertation. http://summit.sfu.ca/system/files/iritems1/13608/etd8016_AJLarsen.pdf
5. Boyraz, S., Ocak, G.: Implementation of flipped education into Turkish EFL teaching context. J. Lang. Linguist. Stud. **13**(2), 426–439 (2017)
6. Seaman, G., Gaines, N.: Leveraging digital learning systems to flip classroom instruction. J. Modern Teacher Q. **1**, 25–27 (2013)
7. Aşıksoy, G., Özdamlı, F.: Flipped classroom adapted to the ARCS Model of motivation and applied to a physics course. Eurasia J. Math. Sci. Technol. Educ. **12**(6), 1589–1603 (2016)
8. Cai, J., Yang, H.H., Gong, D., MacLeod, J., Zhu, S.: Understanding the continued use of flipped classroom instruction: a personal beliefs model in Chinese higher education. J. Comput. High. Educ. **31**(1), 137–155 (2019)
9. Yang, H.H., Feng, L., MacLeod, J.: Understanding college students' acceptance of cloud classrooms in flipped instruction: integrating UTAUT and connected classroom climate. J. Educ. Comput. Res. **56**(8), 1258–1276 (2019)

10. Flipped Learning Network (FLN): The four pillars of F-L-I-P (2014). http://classes.mst.edu/edtech/TLT2014/BCH120/Abkemeier–FLIP_handout_FNL_Web.pdf
11. Davis, F.D.: Perceived usefulness, perceived ease of use, and user acceptance of information technology. MIS Q. **13**(3), 319–340 (1989)
12. Davis, F.D., Bagozzi, R.P., Warshaw, P.R.: User acceptance of computer technology: a comparison of two theoretical models. Manag. Sci. **35**(8), 982–1003 (1989)
13. Venkatesh, V., Morris, M.G., Davis, G.B., Davis, F.D.: User acceptance of information technology: toward a unified view. MIS Q. **27**(3), 425–478 (2003)
14. Taylor, S., Todd, P.A.: Understanding information technology usage: a test of competing models. Inf. Syst. Res. **6**(4), 144–176 (1995)
15. Triandis, H.C.: Interpersonal Behavior. Brooks/Cole Publishing Co, Pacific Grove (1977)
16. Rogers, E.M.: Diffusion of Innovations. The Free Press, New York (1995)
17. Fishbein, M., Ajzen, I.: Belief, Attitude, Intention, and Behavior: An Introduction to Theory and Research. Addison-Wesley, Boston (1975)
18. Bandura, A.: Social Foundations of Thought and Action: A Social Cognitive Theory. Prentice Hall, Englewood Cliffs (1986)
19. Ajzen, I.: From intentions to actions: a theory of planned behavior. In: Kuhl, J., Beckmann, J. (eds.) Action Control: From Cognition to Behavior, pp. 11–39. Springer, Berlin (1985). https://doi.org/10.1007/978-3-642-69746-3_2
20. Gunawardena, C.N., Zittle, F.J.: Social presence as a predictor of satisfaction within a computer-mediated conferencing environment. Am. J. Distance Educ. **11**(3), 8–26 (1997)
21. Short, J., Williams, E., Christie, B.: The Social Psychology of Telecommunications. Wiley, London (1976)
22. Gunawardena, C.N.: Social presence theory and implications for interaction and collaborative learning in computer conferences. Int. J. Educ. Telecommun. **1**(2), 147–166 (1995)
23. Kemp, N.J., Rutter, D.R.: Cuelessness and the content and style of conversation. Br. J. Soc. Psychol. **21**(1), 43–49 (1982)
24. Walther, J.B.: Interpersonal effects in computer-mediated interaction: a relational perspective. Commun. Res. **19**(1), 52–90 (1992)
25. Walther, J.B.: Computer-mediated communication: impersonal, interpersonal, and hyperpersonal interaction. Commun. Res. **23**(1), 3–43 (1996)
26. Cheung, C.M.K., Chiu, P.-Y., Lee, M.K.O.: Online social networks: why do students use facebook? Comput. Hum. Behav. **27**(4), 1337–1343 (2011)
27. Tu, C.H., McIsaac, M.: The relationship of social presence and interaction in online classes. Am. J. Distance Educ. **16**(3), 131–150 (2002)
28. Daft, R.L., Lengel, R.H.: Organizational information requirements, media richness and structural design. Manag. Sci. **32**(5), 554–571 (1986)
29. Hair, J.F., Hult, G.T.M., Ringle, C., Sarstedt, M.: A Primer on Partial Least Squares Structural Equation Modeling (PLS-SEM). Sage Publications, Thousand Oaks (2016)
30. Wong, K.K.K.: Partial least squares structural equation modeling (PLS-SEM) techniques using SmartPLS. Mark. Bull. **24**(1), 1–32 (2013)
31. Fornell, C., Larcker, D.F.: Evaluating structural equation models with unobservable variables and measurement error. J. Mark. Res. **18**(1), 39–50 (1981)
32. Chin, W.W.: The partial least squares approach to structural equation modeling. Mod. Methods Bus. Res. **295**(2), 295–336 (1998)
33. Attuquayefio, S., Addo, H.: Using the UTAUT model to analyze students' ICT adoption. Int. J. Educ. Dev. ICT **10**(3), 75–86 (2014)

34. Marchewka, J.T., Kostiwa, K.: An application of the UTAUT model for understanding student perceptions using course management software. Commun. IIMA **7**(2), 10 (2007)
35. Thomas, T., Singh, L., Gaffar, K.: The utility of the UTAUT model in explaining mobile learning adoption in higher education in Guyana. Int. J. Educ. Dev. ICT **9**(3), 71–85 (2013)
36. Zhou, T., Lu, Y., Wang, B.: Integrating TTF and UTAUT to explain mobile banking user adoption. Comput. Hum. Behav. **26**(4), 760–767 (2010)
37. Friedkin, N.E., Johnsen, E.C.: Social influence and opinions. J. Math. Sociol. **15**(3–4), 193–206 (1990)

Double Helix Deep Learning Model Based on Learning Cell

Shengquan Yu[1(✉)], Jinju Duan[2], and Jingjing Cui[1]

[1] Advanced Innovation Center for Future Education, Beijing Normal University, Beijing 100875, China
yusq@bnu.edu.cn
[2] School of Computer and Information Science, Southwest University, Chongqing, China

Abstract. The significance of deep learning lies not only in the construction of knowledge, but also in utilizing collective wisdom embedded in social networks to form a rich social knowledge network. The learning cell platform, which integrates comprehensive information such as interpersonal networks, knowledge networks and learning activities, can provide good support for online deep learning. The double helix deep learning model based on learning cells reflects a deep learning theory of social interaction, collaborative knowledge building and sharing, as well as cognitive development step by step. In this model, knowledge network and social network are two basic frameworks, developing a social knowledge network through the convergence of learning activities. The social knowledge network takes knowledge content as the core node and establishes relationships between two knowledge nodes, knowledge node and human node, as well as two human nodes. In this model, learners and teachers are equal and can exchange their roles. In the initial stage of learning, learners first construct a knowledge network and an interpersonal network through reception learning; with the gradual deepening of participatory learning, collaborative construction based on knowledge interaction promotes the development of knowledge networks; the generation of network nodes based on interpersonal interaction widens interpersonal networks, and personal learning network forms dynamically and develops spirally; in the advanced stage of learning, learners can actively connect with the networks, and construct the social knowledge space of communities through creative learning activities and activity-based knowledge contribution and creation, in order to achieve effective deep learning.

Keywords: Online learning · Deep learning · Learning cell · Double helix learning model · Social knowledge network

1 Introduction

With the continuous development of network and multimedia technology, the network environment that supports teachers and students has been greatly improved, but qualified hardware environment does not really promote the occurrence of deep learning. At present, the main teaching method in online learning is coping the traditional class, namely recording traditional classroom videos with hand-writing on blackboard for

S. K. S. Cheung et al. (Eds.): ICBL 2019, LNCS 11546, pp. 22–45, 2019.
https://doi.org/10.1007/978-3-030-21562-0_3

students to watch and learn, etc. [1]. Such kind of learning is superficial: although it can enable learners to acquire specific knowledge, the acquired knowledge is shallow and superficial, which is not enough for learners to understand a problem as a whole and cannot promote learners to reflect effectively or to transfer and apply knowledge meaningfully. Moreover, the learning process lacks effective reflection mechanisms, and the learners are learning in a predominantly passive state. For the most part, students just remembered the contents mechanically and do not have in-depth discussion of problems. This is currently a common issue in online learning, which results in low-efficiency and low-effect learning, making online learning seem powerless in leading innovative instructional design, and eventually causing great waste of resources. Reflecting on the current educational phenomenon, we find some problems can be summarized as follows:

First, there is so much fragmented knowledge that is difficult for learners to identify useful ones. The fragmented knowledge requires learners to be able to conduct self-directed learning, organize their own knowledge systems and personal knowledge networks. Thus, higher learning goals lead to lower achievements.

Second, online learning tends to make learners feel lonely and frustrated easily. Since most online learning behaviors are passively accepted, and learners lack interaction with peers and learning experts. As a result, the lack of interpersonal communication leads to poor learning performance.

Third, the online learning behavior is relatively simple. In the process of learning, learners passively accept knowledge, do not carry out learning by doing, and cannot apply what they have learned to solve practical problems. At the same time, there are not enough effective supervision for learners or learning activity design and learning behavior planning to support deep participation in the online classrooms, which results in a shallow learning.

In summary, based on the Learning Cell Knowledge Community (LCKC), this paper attempts to propose a knowledge-based learning navigation, construct a double helix learning model which assists group consultation and interaction in interpersonal networks, and construction of multi-dimensional learning behaviors with activities as the main line, and explore how to promote deep learning through online learning designs.

2 Deep Learning Support System Based on Learning Cell

Learning Cell Knowledge Community (LCKC) is an open learning platform based on the new concepts of 'generation', 'evolution', 'adaptation' and 'social cognition', with learning cells as the smallest resource organization unit [2]. The platform consists of six major parts: learning cell, knowledge group, knowledge cloud, learning tool, personal space and learning community.

The deep learning behavior support system is based on the learning cell, which includes four sub-modules: Online Behavior Interactive Module, Knowledge Evolution Module based on Collaborative Wisdom, Visualization and Aggregation Module for Multi-Connected Behavior, Evaluation Module for Motivating Deep Learning.

2.1 Online Behavior Interactive Module

The core functions of Online Behavior Interactive Module are as follows: creation of learning cell knowledge content, collaborative edition of knowledge content, comparison about the evolutionary versions of knowledge content, full-text annotation, paragraph micro-annotation, resource evaluation, resource review, semantic information management, resource semantics associations, learning activities, learning tools, personal space, friends management, knowledge ontology construction, knowledge networks, interpersonal networks, social knowledge networks, semantic tag annotation, semantic searching, community learning and interaction, tools for aggregating resources, etc.

The main goal of the development of online deep learning behavior interactive support module is to realize the interactive support of nine different kinds of deep learning behaviors, and to design corresponding functions according to these nine learning behaviors.

2.2 Knowledge Evolution Module Based on Collaborative Wisdom

The core functions of Knowledge Evolution Module based on Collaborative Wisdom contain: crowdsourcing technology of converging group intelligence, collaborative content editing and version controlling technology, semantic resources modeling technology, dynamic semantic resources aggregating technology, orderly resources evolutionary controlling technology, and visualization path-displaying technology for resource evolution. The group crowdsourcing technology mainly focuses on how to gather the wisdom of groups and to realize orderly coordination. The collaborative content editing and version controlling technology makes adaptive improvement based on existing Wiki technology, so that ordinary users can edit content of the same learning resource synergistically, and also ensure the security of the resource through flexible version controlling technology. The semantic resources modeling technology mainly uses popular semantic web technology, constructs an open learning resource ontology, and provides quick semantic annotation and reasoning of resources; the dynamic semantic resources aggregating technology that aims to realize automatic aggregation between similar resources based on the semantic resource modeling, forming a resource circle within the same theme; orderly resources evolution controlling technology controls the directions of resource evolution through knowledge ontology, content review and other technologies, to avoid purposeless developments; the visualization path-displaying technology for resource evolution is to visualize the evolution process of resources and contribution of various users in different growth processes, enabling learners not only to understand the current knowledge, but also to understand overall how knowledge is developed step by step.

2.3 Visualization and Aggregation Module for Multi-Connected Behavior

The core functions of Visualization and Aggregation Module for Multi-Connected Behavior are as follows: learning path visualization, knowledge network visualization, interpersonal network visualization, social knowledge network visualization, and label clustering, etc. The learning path visualization module visualizes temporal changes in deep learning behavior. The knowledge network visualization module realizes the dynamic demonstration of semantic knowledge relations. The interpersonal network visualization module demonstrates the interpersonal relationship network topology behind the learning behaviors, and the network change pattern, and supports the analysis of interpersonal relationships of learning behaviors. The social knowledge network visualization module displays the knowledge connections and interpersonal relationships behind learning behaviors, integrates material resources with interpersonal resources, and showcases knowledge and interpersonal connections behind the multi-connected deep learning behaviors. The tag clustering module can perform cluster analysis on learning behaviors to realize knowledge discovery of learning behavior data.

2.4 Evaluation Module for Motivating Deep Learning

The core functions of Evaluation Module for Motivating Deep Learning include: learning evaluation plan setting, learning interaction data collection and analysis, multi-dimensional evaluation result display, and diagnostic standard setting, etc.

LCKC provides evaluation services based on procedural information. The service provides evaluation plan design tools for course developers. Developers can set a certain evaluation plan for their courses. According to the plan, the system evaluates the learning process and the overall learning state of the learners with the learning process information of different learners in the course, and gives the results and feedback to the curriculum developers and learners. During the learning process, learners can view their evaluation information at any time, to understand their own learning situation, and to appropriately adjust their learning strategies, realizing process-based visualization assessment (Fig. 1).

In this visualized personal knowledge map below, the core node represents the current user, the dots represent the knowledge points, and the arrows between the knowledge points represent the relationships between them. Different colors of the dots indicate different states. Red indicates that the current user has not fully grasped the theme or knowledge point, blue means that the knowledge point has been created by the current user, and green means that the current user has mastered the knowledge point [3].

The generation of personal knowledge depends on various data in learning interaction. The system automatically collects interaction data of learning behaviors. After analysis and computing, it can be visualized as a personal knowledge map. Through the personal knowledge map, the learner can clearly understand his or her own effort and progress, and eventually can motivate deep learning behaviors.

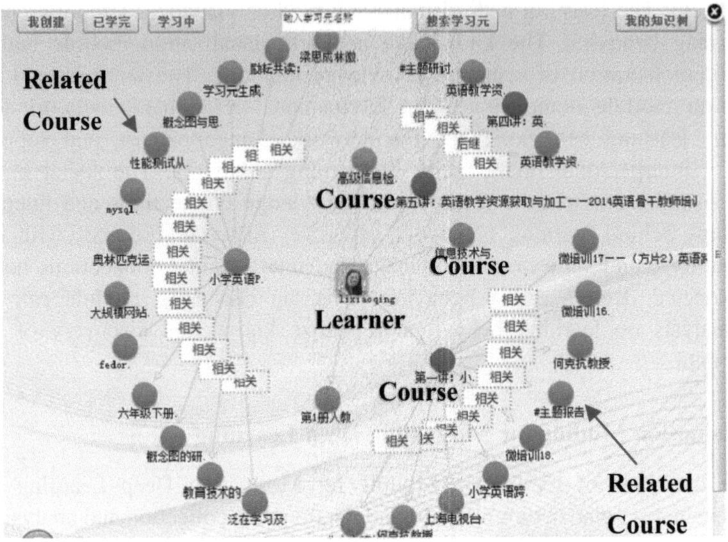

Fig. 1. Visualization evaluation of learner's knowledge map

3 Double Helix Deep Learning Model

Generally speaking, the term *deep learning* is very different from *shallow learning*. Shallow learning is traditionally rote learning. Learners often take shallow learning behaviors such as browsing without thinking, downloading and retrieving information. Such learning behavior does not require too much thinking or cognitive processing, just passively receiving information. The acquired knowledge are isolated, so the knowledge memorization is generally good, but the knowledge transfer and application is unsatisfied.

Deep learning, on the contrary, emphasizes meaningful learning, substantial knowledge building, and adopts learning behaviors that require more cognitive input, such as editing, reconstructing, comparing, and mapping concepts, etc. It involves complex interactions with the learning objects, and often combine and array a variety of simple learning behaviors, such as inquiry, collaboration and so on. Deep learning can critically acquire new ideas and facts based on the in-depth understanding of learning objects, and to incorporate them into the original cognitive construction, to transfer existing knowledge to new situations, to make decisions and solve problems, and to reflect the learning process and comprehension. It forms a constructive, active learning, and the level of knowledge retention and transfer is relatively high [4]. The cognitive psychology theory of deep learning is that knowledge acquired by human beings is stored in the form of networks in the mind. Therefore, the knowledge acquired through learning must be linked with previous knowledge, so that it can be incorporated into a new knowledge system and establish lasting and meaningful connections [5].

Based on the core concept of deep learning, according to the dimensions, levels and relationships of online learning behaviors, this study preliminarily constructs the double helix learning behavior model (Fig. 2) by drawing on the viewpoints of Acquisition Metaphor, Participation Metaphor and Knowledge Creation Metaphor [6], in order to promote the effective occurrence of deep online learning.

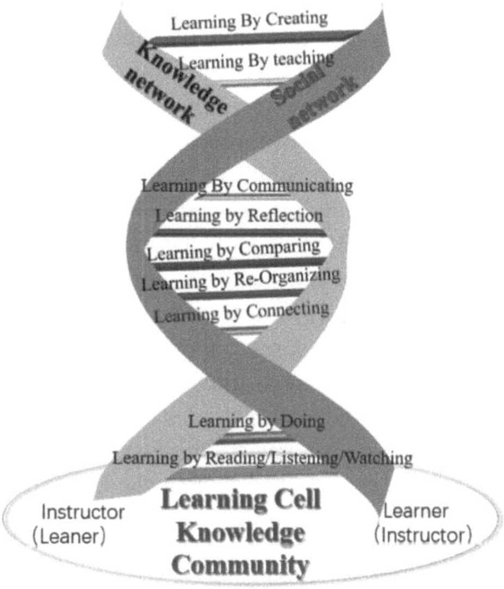

Fig. 2. Double helix deep learning model based on the LCKC

The model is based on LCKC integrating 'learning content + learning activities + learning evaluation + social knowledge network'. In this model, learners and instructors are equal and can exchange their roles. During the specific implementation process, through the design of learner-centered interaction activities, users can be guided to expand the knowledge network and interpersonal network from the bottom up dynamically. And through the spiral development of knowledge network and social network, each learner can go through different levels of learning behaviors and related learning activities. In the initial stage, learners learn passively through the integration of learning resources and activities, and then start constructing knowledge networks and social networks. With the continuous deepening of participatory learning, collaborative construction based on knowledge interaction promotes the development of knowledge networks, and network node generation based on interpersonal interaction widens the existing interpersonal networks. As a result, the interpersonal learning network is being dynamically formed and spirally developed. In advanced stage of learning, learners actively connect to the network, shape network nodes through creative learning activities, build social knowledge space through activity-based knowledge contribution and creation, dynamically construct a social knowledge network learning environment based on interactive connections in real time, and achieve deep learning thoroughly.

3.1 Achieving the Cognitive Development of Higher-Order Ability

This model pursues the deep-level cognitive input in the learning process. In terms of cognitive development, it emphasizes the cultivation of application, analysis, evaluation and creativity, rather than just superficial knowing and understanding in the traditional sense. Remembering, understanding, and application belong to lower competency goals, which can be achieved through solving a series of well-structured problems. Its main role is to enable students to store, consolidate, and simply apply what they have learned. In this process, students only carry out shallow cognitive processing, which is mainly reflected in the acquisition of knowledge. Analysis, evaluation and creation belong to higher-level thinking abilities of development goals [7]. In the process of teaching, a series of more complex learning activities are needed to stimulate students to carry out deep cognitive processing, and to train students to do more difficult or comprehensive thinking exercises, which is mainly embodied in the participation, contribution and creation of knowledge.

This model emphasizes that it is not just to provide students with some simplified questions or basic skills exercises, but to design deep interactive learning activities so that they can learn how to deal with some complex and ill-structured problems in a complicated learning environment, so as to improve deep cognitive processing ability. Based on Bloom's taxonomy of educational goals and the progressive relationship between cognitive goals and cognitive levels, the corresponding sequence of learning activities is designed in an orderly manner, so that the corresponding cognitive goals can be achieved through the design of learning activities at the cognitive level (Fig. 3).

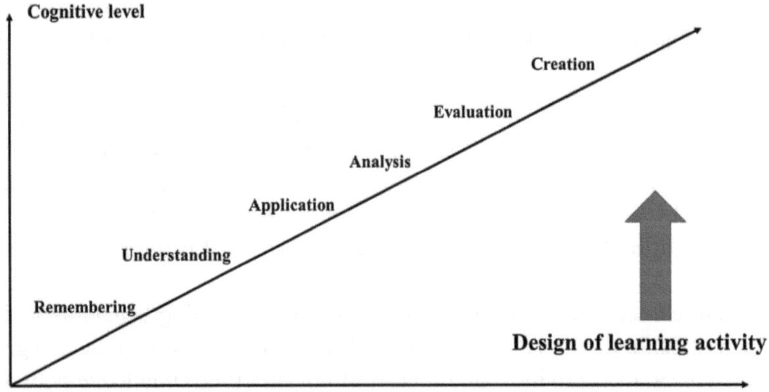

Fig. 3. Design of learning activities to achieve cognitive goals for the promotion of the development of higher-order thinking abilities

In online learning, learning activities and their sequential designs are the bridges and ladders to promote the development of higher-order thinking ability. The learning platform should not only be used as a tool for content storage and management, but also as a tool for students' autonomous learning, collaboration, teaching assessment, knowledge processing, knowledge creation, research and development, and situation exploration. It should be able to present dynamic teaching processes by means of information technology. Besides, as a carrier of content, combined with learning activities, it should achieve in-depth interaction between teachers and their students.

The teaching platform provides various support tools for teachers to organize different levels and types of learning activities, including embedded interactive activities based on learning content, and learning activities based on units, courses, or curricula. In designing some activities, the platform supports teachers to create, set, and adapt activity sequences, and allows teachers to flexibly select and design learning activities based on teaching pedagogies according to their own teaching content, requirements and etc. In learning process, students can complete tasks by participating in relevant activities. Teachers can transfer and operate the corresponding sequence of learning activities according to the condition of the students' learning, and can monitor the operation of the learning activity sequence.

Bloom and Anderson's classification of cognitive goals provides reference for the design of learning activities. Different cognitive levels have different external behavior requirements, which can be realized through the design of different online learning activities. LCKC has designed learning activities for different cognitive levels to support deep cognitive input in the learning (Table 1).

Table 1. Cognitive level of learning behaviours based on LCKC

Cognitive level	Behavioral verb	Typical online learning activities
Remembering	Recognizing, recalling	Browse, download, label, collect, subscribe, take notes, rate
Understanding	Interpreting, exemplifying, classifying, summarizing, inferring, comparing, explaining	Homework, labeling, brief comments, concept maps, Wayne diagrams, six thinking hats, comments, discussions
Applying	Executing, implementing	Online editing, online debate, item design, content rewriting, blogging, production
Analyzing	Differentiating, organizing, attributing	Case analysis, report writing, online speech, investigation design, structure drawing, SWOT analysis
Evaluating	Checking, critiquing	Analytical comments, logical reasoning, complex debates, problem analysis
Creating	Generating, planning, producing	Content creation, planning, problem solving, projects design, exhibition plan

3.2 Multi-Level Learning Behaviors Promoting Cognitive Input

In terms of behavioral activities, Learning Cell emphasizes on all participation and active construction, such as continuous and focused learning and communication, to fully and actively engage in multiple interactions, such as medium interaction, interpersonal interaction and self-interaction, to promote cognition from lower level and state to higher ones, thus achieving cognitive balance.

In addition, Learning Cell also emphasizes on the cultivation of high-order thinking ability through complex interactive activities of deep cognitive input. It is well known that multi-learning behaviors at different cognitive levels are foundation for deep interaction between learners and content. Learning Cell not only contains learning content, but also includes learning activities and behaviors related to the learning content. Through multi-dimensional learning behaviors, learners interact deeply with the learning content. In online classrooms based on Learning Cell, learning behaviors can be clustered into nine types which correspond to nine varying learning activities (Table 2).

According to the metaphor of learning, nine kinds of learning behaviors can be divided into three different types: learning by reading/listening/watching, learning by doing and learning by creating. Among these three types, learning by reading/listening/watching is an individual learning behavior, while learning by doing and learning by creating are cooperative learning and high-level cognitive behaviors. In specific learning processes, such higher level of learning behaviors requires higher-order thinking abilities and the support of knowledge networks and social networks.

Compared with traditional learning management system (LMS), learning cell and its supporting environment can provide learners with a richer learning experience and a more flexible way of knowledge construction and resource sharing, supporting multi-dimensional learning behaviors and intelligent tracking of multiple learning methods and behaviors. Based on the three metaphors of learning and the basic interaction behaviors of the online classroom, we classify learning behaviors of the online classroom into three levels (Table 2), which are the elementary learning stage of individual construction, the intermediate learning stage of group construction and the advanced learning stage of group creation.

Table 2. Analysis of learning behaviour based on LCKC

Learning behavior	Learning activities	Explanation
Learning by reading/learning by listening/learning by watching	Watching video	Teachers build knowledge groups and learning cells to provide students with rich learning materials. Students browse learning material and obtain valuable information
Learning by doing/acting	Download resources, upload resources for exercises and tests	The learning environment realizes the integration of content and activities and resources seamlessly, and realizes internalization of knowledge by completing learning tasks
Learning by connecting	Establish connections between different knowledge units	Through the semantic association and visual navigation of knowledge, we can grasp the knowledge structure as a whole in the interrelation of knowledge, examine and ponder from various angles, deepen the understanding of knowledge, and help stimulate inspiration and promote innovation

(continued)

Table 2. (*continued*)

Learning behavior	Learning activities	Explanation
Learning by re-constructing	Build a personalized learning schedule	With the resource aggregation tools, learners can freely combine and manage multiple small units of knowledge, construct their own knowledge systems, upgrade knowledge management, and form personalized learning courses
Learning by communicating	Group negotiation, communication	Learners acquire knowledge not only through learning materials, but also through communication with experts, partners and learners linked with the learning objects, to build a social knowledge network closely related to the learning content, and to fully absorb the wisdom of others through communication
Learning by collaborating	Collaborative editing	Through collaborative editing and annotation, knowledge can be co-constructed and shared
Learning by comparing	One project or class with different structures	By comparing with each other based on the same topic or task, learners can draw on others' strengths and find their own shortcomings. Besides, learners can build a new understanding of the current content from multiple perspectives, to gain deeper learning experiences
Learning by reflecting	Rethink the evolutionary versions and trajectories of different learning units	Learners can not only learn the current content, but also know the historical process of the growth and construction of a knowledge unit. In the context of this process, they can reflect on the internal logic of knowledge evolution. At the same time, the learning environment should include detailed learning records of the learners, which migrates seamlessly throughout the ubiquitous network and provides exercises and evaluations based on content and activities to facilitate learners' reflection on their learning during the whole process

(*continued*)

Table 2. *(continued)*

Learning behavior	Learning activities	Explanation
Learning by creating	Artifacts	Learners do not only passively accept knowledge, but also form structured expressions based on synthesis, re-construction, reflection, and communication, and therefore actively contribute wisdom, and create new knowledge content
Learning by teaching	Teaching	Learners switch the roles between "teaching" and "learning" and realize learning by teaching through creating their own new learning cells

It can be seen that the multi-dimensional learning behavior based on the LCKC is a combination of 'learning content + learning activities + learning evaluation + social cognitive network' (Fig. 4).

The simplest learning activities are downloading, browsing, watching videos and so on. Learners can learn by reading, watching and listening.

Throughout the learning process, learners participate in and complete the interactive learning activities integrated in the learning content, complete the activities designed by teachers, and learn in interacting. For example, learners can perform learning by doing in tests, exercises and tasks.

For the entire knowledge units, LCKC provides a knowledge network based on semantic association, which is convenient for learners to organize knowledge structure,

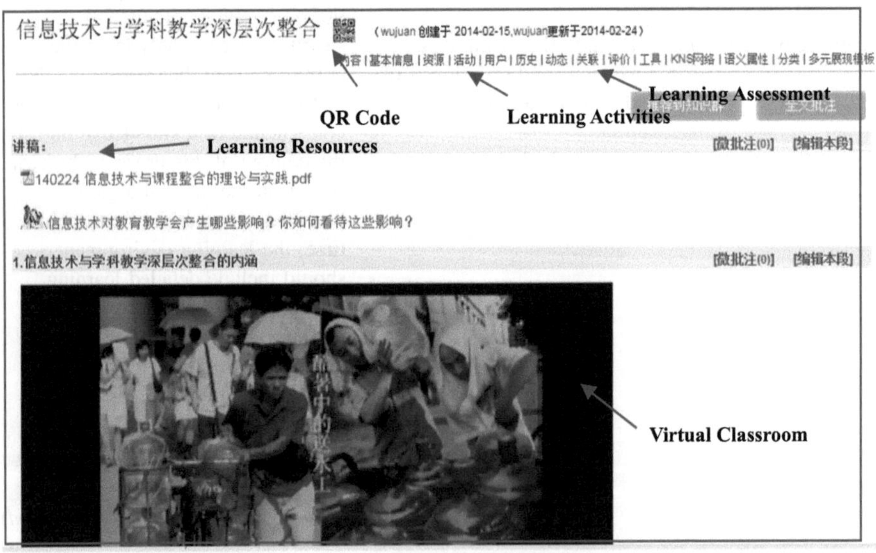

Fig. 4. Online classroom interaction behavior based on learning cells

recall previously memorized knowledge, construct an overall understanding of the entire knowledge system, and achieve learning by doing.

As learning proceeds, learners get a general understanding of the current relevant knowledge content. In order to promote the further development of self-directed learning, they can choose knowledge units that are most interesting to them and establish relations among knowledge units, then realize learning by creating a personalized learning schedule.

In the whole learning process, learners use the KNS network, interpersonal network provided by the platform to communicate with experts and other learners, so that they can obtain relevant information through communication, expand the source of information, and consult and construct meaning in group through comments and discussions, so as to realize learning by communicating.

In the process of learning, learners can also collaborate through annotations and editing of full text. The content editing function provided by the LCKC allows anyone to modify and improve the course content at any time, combined with semi-intelligent content review mechanism, that is, when the edited content is closely related to the original content or after review by the original creator, the system will automatically generate a new course version [3], such as presenting various versions of the designed plans. The content editing function allows the continuous updating and polishing of the course by utilizing group wisdom, avoids waste of resources, and realizes learning by comparing through the visualized comparison of the course versions.

In addition, through the visualized comparison of versions, learners can view the development of knowledge, the associated resources and users (Fig. 5). By viewing the historical track of the growth and construction of a knowledge unit, learners can know the internal logic of the evolution of knowledge in the progress, effectively reflect on their own learning, and thus conduct learning by reflection.

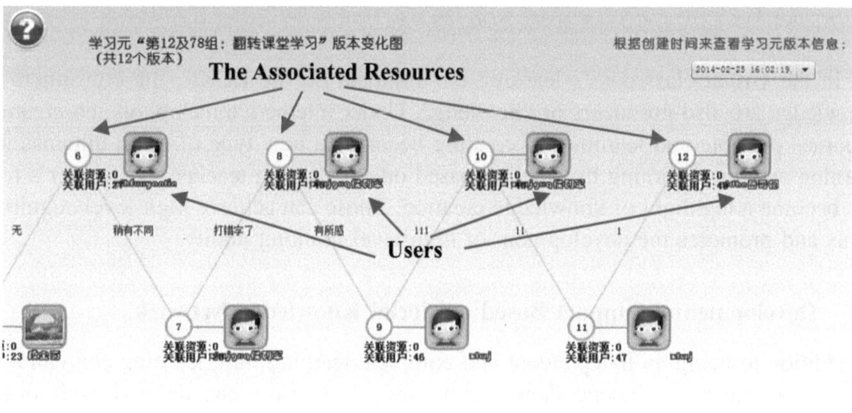

Fig. 5. Learning by reflecting is based on learning trajectories and associated users and resources

Learners not only passively accept knowledge, but also construct a structured expression after synthesis, re-construction, reflection and communication, and actively contribute their own wisdom. They can actively contribute, create new knowledge contents, and realize learning by creation through digital products.

On the LCKC, while 'teaching', it is often able to deepen the remembering and understanding of the content taught by the instructor, and the learners can regularly switch the roles of 'teaching' and 'learning' in the process of communication and collaborative editing. On the basis of constructing new knowledge groups and releasing new learning cells, learners can also realize learning by teaching through publishing teaching and other forms, so that teaching and learning can benefit each other (Fig. 6).

Fig. 6. Learning by teaching is based on content creation and publishing

In the virtual classroom's learning environment on the LCKC, the consumers of knowledge are also producers of knowledge. Under interactive metaphors, co-creation becomes possible and learning by creating becomes a new type of multi-dimensional learning activity. Learning by creating based on exchanging teacher and learner's role has become a highlight of knowledge creation. Those can achieve high-level cognitive goals and promotes the development of high-level thinking ability.

3.3 Developmental Support Based on Social Knowledge Network

In addition to being an independent and complete learning unit, learning cell can also serve as an intact and independent learning unit. It is also a channel and medium for learners' cognitive network connectivity. Through interaction with learning content, the learner forms a knowledge network, and the relevant learning groups can constitute a social network. The superposition of multi-dimensional interaction behaviors of 'human-knowledge-human' and 'knowledge-human-knowledge' promotes the formation of a social knowledge network. Therefore, in this model, the knowledge network and the social network are two supporting pillars. Social knowledge networks are formed by connecting learning activities. It is not only a support to promote deep learning, but also a goal to enable effective deep learning.

Knowledge Network

Relevant contents are connected by internal connections and logic, and then a knowledge network forms. The knowledge network pays attention to knowledge possessed by a learning community and focuses on knowledge association, which embodies the concept of knowledge distributed storage.

Semantic-based technology is used to construct knowledge networks for learning cell, so that same or similar content can be aggregated into a thematic knowledge network. Thus, learners can better learn through network navigation. With the continuous enrichment and evolution of learning content, units of the same or similar topics gradually converge into a knowledge network, and learners can better plan their learning goals and paths.

A knowledge network includes not only individual learners, but also other people and communities. A knowledge network focuses on thematic aggregation. Under the thematic aggregation, it generates, connects, refines and deepens views, and focuses on the reorganization and acquisition of relevant viewpoints and topics (knowledge). This makes topic-based learning become one of the most important learning models in knowledge networks. In this model, knowledge network learning focuses on learners' knowledge acquisition, learners' interconnection, contribution and creation of knowledge networks, while topic-based learner aggregation is the most typical online interaction model, which makes group collaboration and group knowledge construction relatively easy.

Social Network

In online learning, learners learn from not only resources but also the social network built about a certain knowledge point, which are an important part of the learning process [8]. A social network emphasizes the relationships and interactions among them. Learners can express their views, ideas, comments and so on in the social network, which links them to other people interested in the same or similar topics, and therefore gain further knowledge through the expansion of relationships.

A visualized social network organizes learners with common interests and hobbies together, or separates members with different interests and topics into different knowledge-based themes to build new communities, which will enhance members' interests and enthusiasm in exploring common topics and interests, and promote the deeper development of knowledge construction of individuals and groups (Fig. 7).

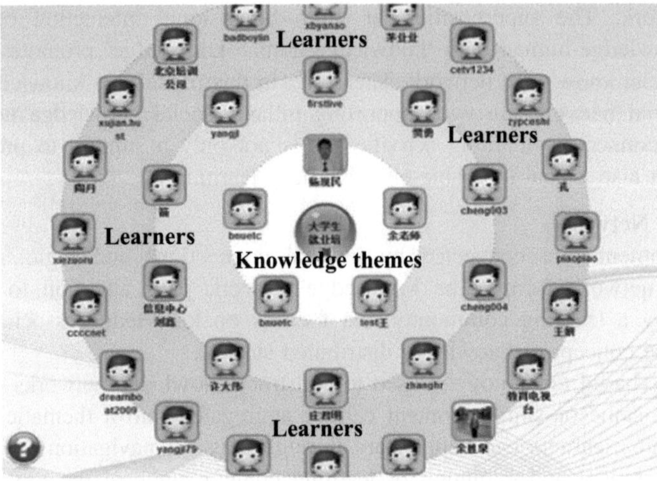

Fig. 7. Knowledge-centered social network based on learning cell

In the open knowledge community of learning cell, the initial content will become the learning basis of knowledge community. Each learner can construct, share and create community knowledge by participating in corresponding learning activities and carrying out corresponding social interaction, thus complement and upgrade the learning content. As learning goes on, personal knowledge is gradually externalized into community knowledge. The scattered and disordered knowledge of individual learners is gradually condensed into a collective and orderly knowledge network. Through the continuous social interaction within groups, the knowledge network evolves and develops spirally, and finally promotes learning through top-down knowledge absorption and internalization. It can be observed that in the learning process based on social knowledge networks, knowledge is constructed and shared together. The content at the initial stage is the foundation of the knowledge development, and activities are the carrier of knowledge diffusion and creation. Learning based on social knowledge network promotes the ecological development of knowledge (content) networks through the integration of curricula, resources and activities.

Social Knowledge Network

With learners constantly interacting with each other, a cognitive network with the same learning interests, hobbies and frequent interactions takes shape, namely the social knowledge network (Fig. 8). Each learner is an entity in the cognitive network space, representing as a node, and can establish connections with different learners' nodes through learning resources or other individual learners. The strength of connections between or among nodes is represented by a multi-factor cognitive model. With the continuous learning and interaction of learners, the state and connection of nodes in the learning community network is getting updated continuously [3].

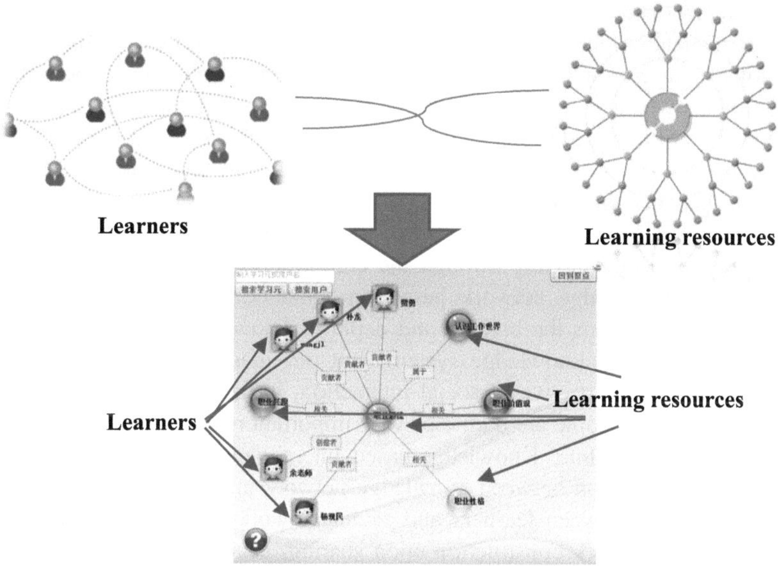

Fig. 8. Social knowledge network

Learning cell combine the evolvable material resource with human resource to form a KNS (Knowledge Network Social Service) that can dynamically evolve and self-develop [8], which reflects the connection between material resources and human resources, builds network aggregation to a certain scale and depth, and will have social intelligence. Different from the general communication network defined by social networks, a social knowledge network is a network composed of knowledge and people. It is constructed in the process of deep interaction between people and knowledge. With a social cognitive network, learners can not only obtain the required material resources, but also find the corresponding human resources. For example, through certain learning content, the learner is able to quickly locate the most authoritative experts or suitable learning partners in this content field. We can see that, as a resource to promote deep learning, the human networking has become more and more significant. If learners can participate in resource-related interpersonal networking while obtaining material resources, they can thus gain knowledge and wisdom from other learners.

Deep Learning Based on Social Knowledge Network

A social knowledge network integrates knowledge network and social network; it is an effective scaffolding to promote deep learning interaction, and an important bridge to promote effective occurrence of multi-level interaction. Learning based on a social knowledge network is a kind of connected and creative learning. This integrated learning method connects learners and content, and promotes better collaborative and creative learning activities as well as deep learning.

The interaction between learners and knowledge networks focuses on the acquisition, reorganization and creation of knowledge structures. The visualization of the navigation, organization and cognitive processes can effectively support the construction of knowledge, such as learning by reading/listening/watching. The structure and association of knowledge can be understood by searching for knowledge through a network. Typical types of activities are such as learning by reorganizing, establishing connections between knowledge systems (networks) and reorganizing or reconstructing learners' knowledge structures. As a part of the knowledge ecology, learners can also keep the ecosystem developing through the contribution and creation of knowledge. The visualized knowledge network based on semantic association is a multi-path cognition, which expands the breadth and depth of knowledge construction, builds a scaffolding to structure knowledge system, and provides new possibilities for deep learning. From the perspective of social interaction, in the learning process based on knowledge network, people are a kind of very important resources, playing the role of both medium and pipeline. Knowledge-based interpersonal interaction requires collaboration and interaction between knowledge network and social network.

The interaction between learners and social networks is about promoting group participation and network construction upon sharing, negotiating and communication to study 'who knows whom', and to let learners access more content through connection. Therefore, discussion and communication have become important learning methods [9]. A social network focuses on the sharing and communication of interpersonal knowledge, and focuses on group cognition and group knowledge construction. 'People' can learn from each other and can be a source of knowledge. In social networks, people are an important part of building this 'pipeline'. In addition to being an independent and complete learning unit, it can also serve as a mediator for learners to recognize network inter-connectivity. In other words, people who learn the same or similar subject content can also realize the collaborative interaction between a knowledge network and a social network through learning resources.

In a social knowledge network, knowledge network and social network are synergistic and interactive, and they are mutually permeated and transformed. The dynamic development provides the possibility of dynamic connection and transformation between the individual internal cognitive network and the external cognitive network, which guarantees a sustainable development of deep learning. With a knowledge network, learners can establish dynamic connections between learners and teachers, share the interpersonal network and social knowledge network in the learning process, and meet the needs of socialized learning. With social networks, knowledge nodes gain continuous knowledge diffusion, knowledge dissemination and knowledge creation through the group's cognition and cooperation. Knowledge is in a dynamic and changing development process. As long as learners keep in touch with current medium (contents or learners), they can grasp the ecological nature of the personal learning network at any time (Fig. 9).

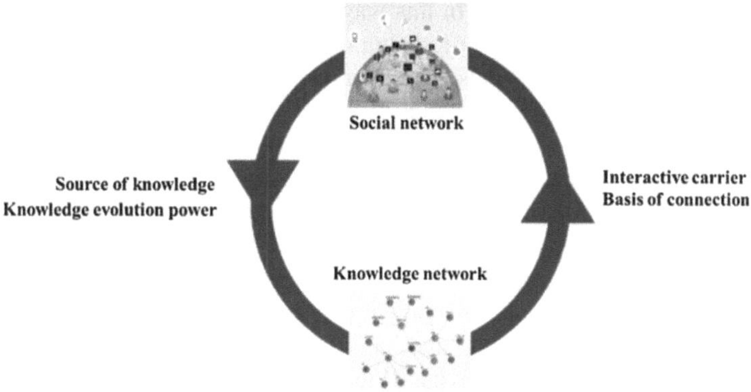

Fig. 9. Penetration and transformation of the knowledge network and social network

In the social knowledge network, the learning channel has changed from focusing 'human' to both 'human' and 'knowledge', thus promoting a new way of learning, namely connective learning. The paradigm of learning moves from traditional constructive learning to connective learning in the new social learning era. During the construction of learning network, its nodes can be either human or knowledge. The process of connecting and constructing a personal social knowledge network through connection facilitates the depth and breadth of individual socialized learning, as well as promotes the process of connecting and transforming individual internal and external cognitive networks. In this process of interaction, learners improve their own personal cognitive networks, and also form part of the social network, sharing and constructing social cognitive network (Fig. 10).

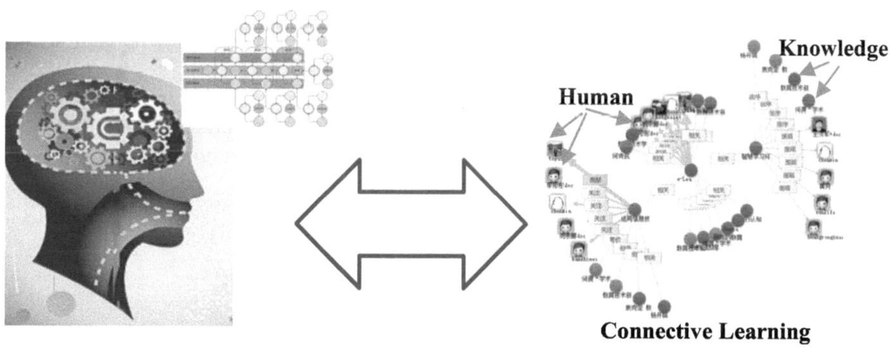

Fig. 10. Learning is the process of sharing and constructing individual and social cognitive networks

Social knowledge network unloads part of knowledge processing and interpretation to the nodes of learning network, and learners can establish various interpersonal network nodes according to the learning subjects, so that each node can store and provide the knowledge they need. In this way, part of the individual learning work is unloaded onto the network, in order to better develop higher-order thinking ability and achieve higher-level cognitive goals, better conduct group development and knowledge creation, and better achieve deep learning.

From the perspective of knowledge construction and community knowledge creation, the social knowledge network provides an open learning environment with ecological attributes. Through knowledge contribution and creation, learners constantly promote the evolution of knowledge nodes, and keep the knowledge nodes updated in real time through the learners' distributed cognition, and the way they learn in relationships. With the continuous development of learning, knowledge in the knowledge community is gradually increasing, and has been continuously evolving through collective wisdom [10]. On the other hand, the connection and interaction of learners enables individual-level knowledge to spread to collective-level and become public knowledge. Knowledge is transformed and distributed in human resource, namely the social network. In the network, people become the carrier of knowledge and related services, thus the sociality of knowledge has been constantly evolving.

Learning environment based on social knowledge network is a complex and distributed learning, which is based on social knowledge sharing, dissemination and creation. In the interaction between individuals and the environment, the nodes of the network are 'people' and 'knowledge', and the pipeline and medium carrying the distributed knowledge base may be a knowledge network or a social network related to the relevant knowledge node. Therefore, in this learning environment, knowledge nodes provide continuous knowledge diffusion, dissemination and creation through group cognition and collaboration. Knowledge is a dynamic process of development. As long as learners keep in touch with the current medium (contents or learners), they can obtain the ecology of the individual learning network at any time.

The connectivism learning theory puts learning context into the social network structure, and believes that learning is the reconstruction and establishment of nodes and relationships in knowledge network structures, "learning is the process of connection of network nodes" [11]. It can be said that learning based on social knowledge networks fully reflects connectivism. It is considered that learning is 'network connection and network creation'. It is a kind of deep learning that connects user nodes and knowledge nodes in learning network and promotes knowledge contribution and creation to shape new network nodes.

4 Open Course Design Practice of Deep Learning

Teachers participating in the 'National Training Program for Prominent Teachers in Primary and Secondary Schools' mainly come from the 'Basic Education Innovation Exploration and Experiment' project, which is organized and implemented by the School of Educational Technology of Beijing Normal University. There are more than 30 pilot areas with more than 400 primary and secondary schools joining in the project. In order to better promote teachers' professional development and cultivate research-oriented teachers, the project team organizes'National Training Program for Prominent Teachers in Primary and Secondary Schools' once a year. The trainees are qualified teachers and leaders selected from each experimental area. By virtue of the LCKC and its supporting environment, the training takes activities as its main line and the social knowledge network as the interactive and collaborative approach, and covers multi-dimensional learning behaviors to promote deep learning.

Knowledge Acquisition Stage

In order to enable teachers to think, gain and practice while learning, the project team independently designed and developed training courses, and submitted their contents, such as learning resources, lecturer notes, learning activities and evaluation plans to the 'National Training Program for Prominent Teachers in Primary and Secondary Schools' before the start of the training. Teachers watch the lectures and download the learning resources to complete the process of knowledge acquisition.

At the same time, the teachers participating in the training program need to decide topics and upload an instructional design plan on the LCKC. All instructors and teachers trained can watch, collaboratively edit, micro-annotate or comment to promote the teachers' learning by doing. Once all the teachers have submitted their instructional design plans, the instructors of the training program group the participating teachers according to similarity of instructional themes and the difference of geographical location of the teachers, in order to facilitate deeper communication in group and to promote the transformation and output of the content in order to test training performance.

Interactive Learning Stage

The one-week intensive training is an important phase to realize deep learning in online classrooms and a great opportunity to establish a social knowledge network and create a learning community of teachers.

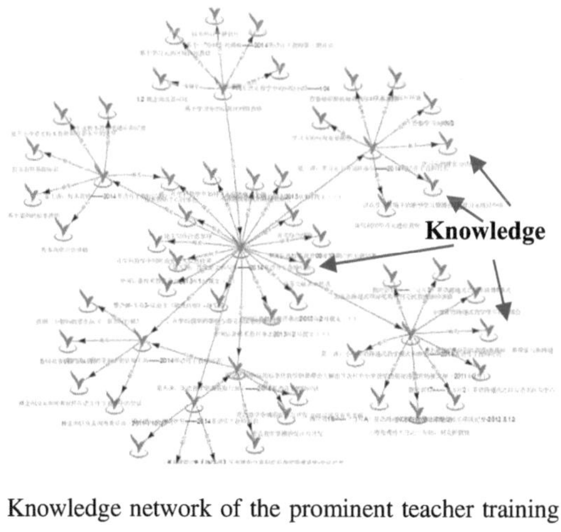

Fig. 11. Knowledge network of the prominent teacher training program

The design of the course content is coherent, covering from theoretical research, technical operation to teaching practice, and establishes the connection between knowledge through semantic association and visual navigation (Fig. 11) to help teachers understand the relationship between topics, deepen the overall understanding of the course and realize learning by connecting.

The teaching content of each topic contains learning activities, which instructs the teachers to communicate, share, negotiate, cooperate, and apply. For example, in the learning process of 'Lecture 8 - Regional Teacher Training Based on Learning Cell Knowledge Community, the trainer had designed learning activities for teachers to combine theory with practice and apply the theories they had learned previously into teaching.

In order to ensure the in-depth construction of a social knowledge network and realize deeper understanding of the course, the training takes the instructional design plans submitted by teachers in the preliminary preparation as the carrier, guides teachers to share with each other, and then chooses an instructional design plan in the group for collaborative exchange and consultation to discuss, modify and improve jointly. Based on the experience and consensus, trainees and trainers collectively modify the instructional design plan of other members in the group. At the same time, trainers from the project can interact with interested experts and peers, share their own experiences and views, learn from professionals or peers' expertise, or consult with them on certain problems (Fig. 12), to absorb others' wisdom in communication, to build and share in a cooperative manner, and to improve self-learning by comparing.

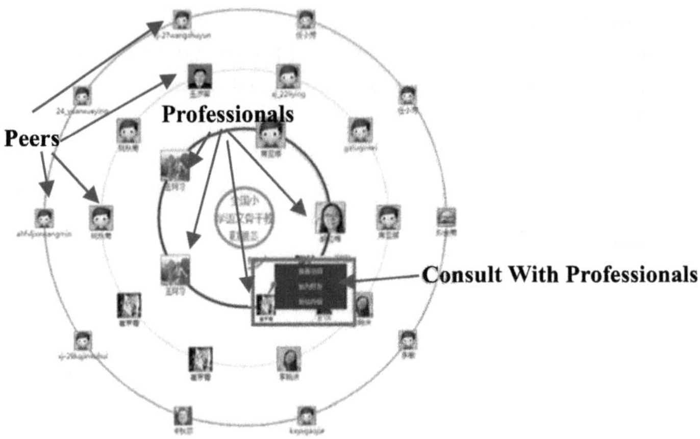

Fig. 12. Look for experts or peers in interpersonal network on LCKC

Content Creation Stage

During the one-week face-to-face training, prominent teachers are encouraged to reflect his or her individual knowledge construction and collaborative knowledge construction based on the online learning trajectory of their training, and to enrich the social cognitive network by guiding the individual teachers to interact with other individuals through learning evaluation program designed by the curriculum designer (Fig. 13).

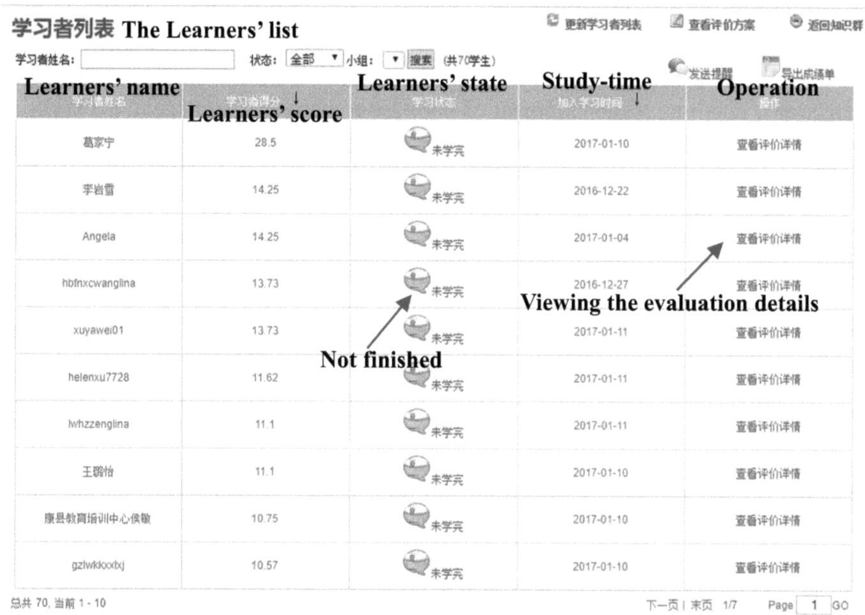

Fig. 13. Teachers' participation in course study

In the meantime, this training also includes remote tracking of the training effect for one semester after face-to-face training. The trainees need to complete five practical tasks in the following semester, consisting of a technical work, a public class, a topic discussion, a live or distance training, and a research paper. The five practical tasks follow the course design ideas of group training, which not only helps teachers to transform the content of the training into products for teaching or research, but also guides teachers to carry out all-round practical exercises around a teaching or research theme to realize the combination of theory and practice, and to promote thusly the output of deep learning results.

The training is oriented towards practical application, which promotes teachers' self-reflection, enhances teachers' sense of innovation and the value of the training results in large scale. Thus it continuously promotes the ability structure of individual teachers and their groups, and cultivate real research-oriented teachers.

5 Summary

LCKC integrates comprehensive information such as interpersonal network, knowledge network and learning activities, which offers support to solve shallow learning problems in current online education.

The construction of social knowledge networks is an effective way of deep learning on the LCKC. The system can easily form a closely integrated cognitive network between knowledge and knowledge, knowledge and people, and people and people by establishing semantic relations between different learning cells, learning cell and people, and different peoples. From this aggregated cognitive network, it is possible to quickly and accurately find learning cell sets and interpersonal resource sets with certain semantic associations. With multi-dimensional learning behaviors and activity interactions, continuous development of knowledge networks and social networks has laid the foundation for the construction of learners' groups, learning behaviors and knowledge networks, and interpersonal networks, which enhance the effective occurrence of deep learning.

The double helix deep learning model of the LCKC reflects this kind of deep learning concept, which is a model of deep learning with group construction and sharing. During the process of learning, from the initial stage of learning by reading to the final stage of learning by creating and learning by teaching, change is reflected in learning participation, that is, the transition from passive learning to active learning, the transformation from individual learning to group collaboration, from knowledge acceptance to knowledge creation, from being a learner to a teacher.

The social knowledge network is established based on the corresponding learning behaviors, so the knowledge network not only reflects the connection between knowledge and knowledge, but also the connection between people and knowledge, people and resources. In these connections, the emphasis on human-oriented knowledge flow is to achieve the transfer, sharing, creating and applying knowledge among participants in the network. The significance of deep learning lies not only in the construction of knowledge content, but also in the use of collective wisdom contained in social networks to form a rich social knowledge network. Individuals can enrich and improve the network's content in collaborative learning, not only to acquire existing knowledge, but also to grasp the methods of learning and the ways to obtain extra knowledge, and to form a network of knowledge with people interacting and intertwined, through which learners can acquire required knowledge continuously. Different from the interpersonal relationship established by the general social network, the social knowledge network takes the knowledge content as the core node, and establishes a relationship between knowledge and knowledge, knowledge and people through knowledge content. The connection between learners and knowledge enables the original knowledge content to gain more development. The cognitive wisdom of all learners is gathered through the learning materials, and thus a social knowledge network, which can evolve dynamically and develop by itself, is formed with material resources and human resources.

References

1. Yu, S.: The development of learning resources construction (part 2) [学习资源建设发展大趋势(下)]. J. China Educ. Info. (01), 3–7 (2014, In chinese)
2. Yu, S., Yang, X., Chen, G.: Learning resource designing and sharing in ubiquitous learning environment: the concept and architecture of learning cell. [泛在学习环境中的学习资源设计与共享—"学习元"的理念与结构]. J. Open Educ. Res., 47–53 (2009, In chinese)
3. Yu, S., Chen, M.: Design of micro-lecture based on learning cell system [基于学习元平台的微课设计]. J. Open Educ. Res. (01), 100–110 (2014, In chinese)
4. Sawyer, R.K.: The Cambridge Handbook of the Learning Sciences, pp. 1–661. Cambridge Press, Cambridge (2005)

5. Duan, J., Yu, S.: Overview of study on deep learning with e-learning based on learning science [学习科学视域下的e- Learning 深度学习研究]. J. Distance Educ. **4**(08), 43–51 (2013, In chinese)
6. Hakkarainen, K.P., Palonen, T., Paavola, S., Lehtinen, E.: Communities of Networked Expertise: Professional and Educational Perspectives. Emerald Group Publishing, Bingley (2004)
7. Anderson, L.W., et al.: A Taxonomy for Learning, Teaching, and Assessing: A Revision of Bloom's Taxonomy of Educational Objectives, abridged edition, pp. 25–28. Longman, White Plains (2001)
8. Yu, S., Chen, M.: The characteristics and the trend of ubiquitous learning resources construction: exemplified by the "Learning Cell Resource Model" [泛在学习资源建设的特征与趋势——以学习元资源模型为例]. J. Mod. Distance Educ. Res. (06), 14–22 (2011, In chinese)
9. Duan, J., Yu, S.: Construction of learning model based on social knowledge network [基于社会性知识网络的学习模型构建]. J. Mod. Distance Educ. Res. (04), 91–102 (2016, In chinese)
10. Yang, X., Chen, G., Yu, S.: Design of learning cell system and analysis of its application scenarios [学习元平台的设计及其应用场景分析]. J. E-education Res., 55–61 (2013, In chinese)
11. Siemens, G.: Connectivism: a learning theory for the digital age. J. Instr. Technol. Distance Learn. **2**(1), 3–10 (2005)
12. Bransford, J.D., Brown, A.L., Cocking, R. (eds.): How People Learn; Brain, Mind, Experience, and School. National Academy Press, Washington (2000)

Johann Amos Comenius and His Legacy at the Information Age

Miloslava Černá[(✉)]

Faculty of Informatics and Management, University of Hradec Kralove, Rokitanskeho 62, Hradec Kralove, Czech Republic
miloslava.cerna@uhk.cz

Abstract. The main idea of this paper is to illustrate validity and functionality of educational principles, which were stated by Comenius already in the 17th century in the dark time of religious, power, consequently social, scientific and cultural changes in Europe but which are incredibly eternal, vivid and efficient up to now in the so-called information society. These principles are shown in the eLearning environment. This presentation encompasses two main areas which inherently blend together: didactic area which represents the theoretical level and the practical level with examples of applied Comenius principles in the current educational situation in teaching/learning languages at the Faculty of Informatics and Management, University of Hradec Králové. Modern approaches to learning languages mingle with the medieval approach to the process of education. This paper begins with introducing the theologian and philosopher Johann Amos Comenius who was born in the Czech kingdom under the rule of Habsburg dynasty at the very end of the 16th century. His importance and contribution as a reformer of the educational system is briefly outlined so that the readers could get acquainted with his ideas born and developed at the outbreak of a new epoch. This is followed by an illustration of selected timeless didactic principles formulated by J.A. Comenius applied in the current concept of teaching/learning languages with focus on the design of accompanying e-course.

Keywords: Philosophy · Pedagogy · Didactics · Blended learning · Nature · Knowledge

1 Introduction

Johann Amos Comenius was ranked among 50 influential thinkers in the area of education from the time of Confucius to the 19th century [1].

One of main missions, maybe the most important one, was to make the world better that intertwines through his works. Comenius' work has so many forms, but above all, it represents a unique and original synthesis directed by its reformative program into the future. His efforts for harmonious humanity have exceeded the horizon of his time. According to Jan Kumpera [2] this idea is most explicitly formulated in Comenius magnus opus from 1644 De rerum humanarum emendatione consultatio catholica - General consultation on reform of Human Affairs [3]. Comenius' educational

S. K. S. Cheung et al. (Eds.): ICBL 2019, LNCS 11546, pp. 46–56, 2019.
https://doi.org/10.1007/978-3-030-21562-0_4

philosophy is clear - only education can develop human qualities. Only this path leads to the gates of wisdom, only this way it is possible to improve the individual, the nation, the humanity. Comenius described the educational activity and the 'light of knowledge' as the 'wisest weapon' that can fight the ignorance [4].

Can you see the parallel with astonishing saying of Howard Earl Gardner?

> *"I want my children to understand the world, but not just because the world is fascinating and the human mind is curious. I want them to understand it so that they will be positioned to make it a better place. Knowledge is not the same as morality, but we need to understand if we are to avoid past mistakes and move in productive directions. An important part of that understanding is knowing who we are and what we can do... Ultimately, we must synthesize our understandings for ourselves. The performance of understanding that try matters are the ones we carry out as human beings in an imperfect world which we can affect for good or for ill." (Howard Gardner 1999).* [5]

2 Comenius Significance in His Time and Now

Comenius made his name as a scholar - reformist during his lifetime. He lived in the time of vital changes when old medieval structures based on given privileges were giving way to new social and economic horizons, in the time of chaos when old was leaving and new was being created. European science was undergoing complex changes. Enlightenment, philosophical movement with rationalistic thinking, which highlights possibilities of human reason and science came on the world stage.

2.1 Comprehensive Consideration

In Comenius' work Renaissance and humanism as well as enthusiasm to new scientific trends are reflected as they influenced his work. At the beginning in his internal exile in East Bohemia, his creative activity aimed at local issue of reforming the Czech situation in Catholic Habsburg Empire. Soon since the 1630' since the time when he, as well as, other people who didn't want to convert to Catholicism had to emigrate his work was given a wider scope. He could see that the Czech question should be resolved within the wider framework of a new pan-European arrangement. Therefore, Comenius used more and more Latin, the international language of European scholars.

A modern Latin textbook *Janua linguarum reserata* - The Gate of Languages Unlocked which was published in 1631 brought him European fame [6]. This textbook provided students with basic encyclopaedic knowledge. The idea of connection between the knowledge and language is of key importance. However, pedagogy and didactics weren't a goal, but a means to know the world Practical part of the paper stems from this work.

Comenius fully concentrated on the pansophia, or the omniscience, of a comprehensive and well-arranged system of knowledge, through which the Czech reformer wanted to bring education out of the labyrinth of chaos and confusion [2]. Comenius' proposals received considerable acclaim throughout Europe, particularly in England. Comenius was invited by a group of reform politicians and scholars to start working on establishing Collegium lucis 'The College of Light' in London which was supposed to be a kind of international academy. Due to the outbreak of the English revolution his plans failed but the program Via lucis has survived and is published up to present days [7].

The death of Comenius, the last Bishop of Bohemia Brethren, seems to symbolically close the development of the Czech Reformation. With the onset of the utilitarian Enlightenment, the influence of Comenius' work began to fade rapidly. In spite of the fact that the Enlightenment objected Comenius ideas, his scientific ideas led to establishment of scientific societies and academies [4].

Until the 19th century, Comenius was nearly forgotten. German classical philosophy rejecting unilateral enlightenment rationalism rediscovered Czech reformer Comenius. It is worth mentioning German writers Johann Wolfgang Goethe and Johann Gottfried Herder who were able to appreciate this scholar. J. W. Goethe liked his textbook with pictures Orbis Sensualium Pictus (Visible World in Pictures) [8], which was published in many European languages but first in Latin and German. Theologian and philosopher J. G. Herder appreciated Comenius' ideas of peace, better organization of mankind, and the careful care of mankind [9].

Comenius' work became widely translated and published in the 20th century not only in Europe but also in the United States or Japan.

In our country there were and are outstanding comeniologists who have worked out Comenius legacy and brought it to the professional and public audience. Comenius work is approached and predominantly researched from pedagogical, linguistic, ethical, anthropological and theological perspectives, e.g. [2, 10–13].

2.2 Democracy and Psychology in Comenius Legacy

Comenius developed and promoted a new concept of education that radically diverged from what was known in his epoch. At that time, the society was hierarchically divided and he sought to ensure that all people, men and women, receive the same education, regardless of race, nationality and social status which bears a strong democratic feature, the right to education for all [14]. Czech reformation followed the idea that all people are equal because they are God's creatures, so they have the same right to education. He later called the concept pansophic, and determined his achievement of life wisdom as his specific goal [15].

Dagmar Capkova interprets Comenius' well-known *didactic motto omnes, omnia, omneno*, as the foundations of his democratism, for omnes stands for all people, who ought to learn and be taught omnia, that is, everything necessary, in all possible ways (omneno), in order to live in harmony. Moreover, Capkova sees the roots of Comenius democratism already existing in the Hussite and Brethren traditions: [16].

As the founder of modern pedagogy, he also took psychological considerations into account. Hence the *emphasis on didactic methods to be natural, non-violent and consistent with gradual mental development*. "Omnia sponte fluant, absit violentia rebus" - Let it flow freely, without a violent solution. Piaget highlighted psychological value of Comenius principles:

- dependence between cognitive functions and activity
- the principle of positive and affective motivation,

- the principle of consecutive development,
- the aspects of facilitation/inhibition of the educational process,
- the principle of teacher-learner cooperation [17].

2.3 Two Influential Thinkers and Their Approach to Nature

The nature of Comenius work draws, follows and develops thoughts of a wide scale of thinkers from Antic time via strong influence of humanist and renaissance epoch to his contemporaries.

Privilege position has Francis Bacon with his *materialism, scientific approach to nature*, see more in Comenius and Bacon: Two Early Modern Paths to Restoring Knowledge by Čížek [18] or Patočka [19].

Comenius approach to nature was not knowledge-based, but educational – based [20].

Another influential philosopher was theologian Thomasso Campanella and his perception of nature and sensualistic attitude to knowledge, see *Philosophia sensibus demonstrata* ("Philosophy demonstrated by the senses") [21]. Campanella was a vigorous critic of the traditional Aristotelian approach to knowledge and strove for a fundamental reform. His project of a unified system of all the sources of knowledge included *experience, reason, and faith*. These, he hoped, would penetrate all branches of knowledge and would lead toward goals of emendation in the society [22]. Idealistic utopian ideas formulated in The City of Sun can be found in Comenius work as well, see more Comenius and Campanella by Patocka [23].

3 Didactics and Selected Principles

The term Didactics as the art of teaching, learning and pedagogical skills was introduced by German pedagogue and reformist Wolfgang Ratke. Young Comenius met with Ratke´s reformist educational concept in Hebron where he studied [24].

This article stems predominantly from Comenius masterpieces Didactica Magna [25] and Janua linguarum reserata (The Gate of Languages Unlocked) [6]. Latin textbook Janua linguarum reserata emphasized what later became an increasingly popular inductive approach instead of the common grammar-translation approach to language education. Capkova states in her paper School and Formation of Humanity that the idea of didactics, played the vital role in the process of restoration and that Comenius himself considered didactics as an 'art of arts' [20].

The core of his Didactics consists of 29 didactic rules or fundamentals according to Comenius ranked into three chapters: *How to make education certain, How to make education easy, How to make education thorough.* Patocka selected the following principles to show their eternity: the principle of realism; *the principle of things before words; words as auxiliary tools; the principle of object teaching; the principle of learning with understanding; the principle of progress from the particular to the abstract, but also from the whole to the parts, from the simple to the complex, from the easy to the difficult; the principle of fundamental periodicity,* etc. [26].

'Principle of graduality' was selected as the first principle because it is considered a main construction element. This principle relates not only to the way study material should be worked out and presented to students but it also relates to the whole concept of education which is designed on this principle based on four phases human beings go through like four seasons in the nature. Lukas and Munjiza bring in their study a simplified pattern of this concept:

1. School of infancy where *external senses should be exercised*;
2. Maternal school (general school) where *internal senses should be encouraged* like *imagination and memory*;
3. Latin school (grammar school) where *understanding and reasoning* should be developed and finally
4. *Academy should raise the will to study* [24].

At that time at the Comenius time 'Life-long education' expression was not established, however now Comenius' concept of education is commonly considered as a life-long process, see more [16] or above mentioned Lukas and Munjiza study [24].

Lukas nad Munjiza highlighted their study the following principles: *visuality, systematicity, democraticism, appropriateness*. Fundamental principle to which everything relates is *naturalness*.

In the practical part of the paper, university environment is discussed. The university environment corresponds to the Comenius fourth level of the educational concept, to the level called Academy. We will not focus only on the motivational factor characterizing this Comenius level Academy - 'to encourage students to aspire to education' *but to the whole scale encompassing senses, imagination and memory, understanding and reasoning and willingness to study*. Don´t these terms like memory, understanding, reasoning remind us Bloom´s taxonomy little bit? That might be an issue into the discussion. In some way, these cognitive processes are imbedded in the thoughtfully formulated targets of individual lessons in e-courses according to Bloom´s taxonomy.

Simonova discussed Comenius principles in engineering education. She pointed out how these principles are interconnected [27]. On the following examples we will try to illustrate, how selected principles work, how they are applied sometimes in language subjects as a whole as well as in individual activities.

The Principle of Purposefulness. Teaching is a purposive activity, which requires stating *strategic and partial objectives*, explaining them to students and thus motivating them to reach objectives defined at the beginning of the process. These objectives or targets are formulated at individual levels of teaching/learning the subject. Firstly, they are formulated as general targets in the syllabus and then target(s) in individual lessons, which are narrowly tailored to fit the discussed topic. Here can be seen the great advantage of virtual environment in which students can approach study material and organizational information anytime and from anywhere. Proper formulating targets is mastery but the effort pays. Because clearly formulated targets enable students realize complex of activities which they are required to do and at the same time they learn what knowledge to gain and practice thinking. Bloom taxonomy is widely utilized when targets of learning are formulated to explicitly state what level of competences will be aimed at. Figure 1 illustrates targets of the subject formulated in the syllabus, which is openly accessed in the university study system Stag.

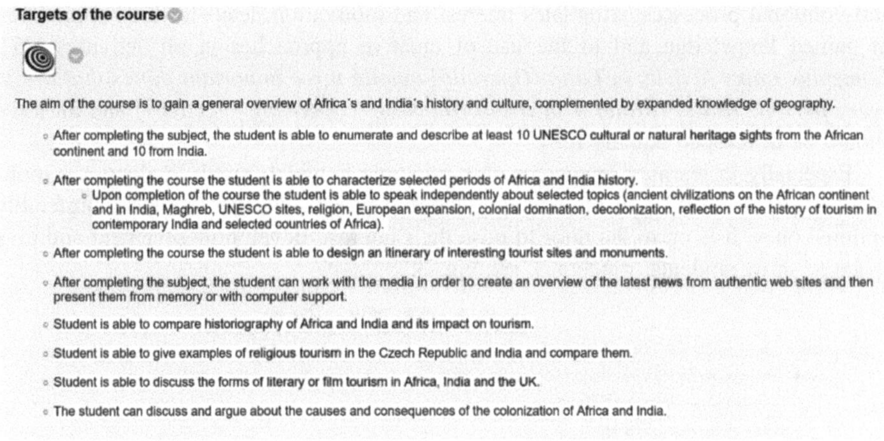

Fig. 1. Structure of the lesson with defined objectives

The same targets are then placed in the e-course accompanying the subject. The target of the lesson is shown in the Fig. 2. Examples were taken from the compulsory subject 'On culture and Literature of Africa and India' within the Management of Tourism bachelor study program.

Fig. 2. Structure of the e-course and an entry into the lesson with its targets

There are two sections in Fig. 2. Beside the main window of the e-course Content section there can be seen the structure of the course corresponding to the desired faculty design. There is a faculty policy that the e-courses should have the same structure consisting of selected basic tools offered by the LMS Blackboard: Study Guide, Content, Tasks and Tests. This requirement corresponds to the following J.A. Comenius principle, which is *Systematicness*.

The principle of steady and systematic approach is a commonly accepted principle where nobody would believe that it was formulated nearly 400 years ago. The principle of systematic approach has been discussed in the previous paragraph. It was applied in the design of the e-course as a whole utilizing defined set of tools which are used in all other e-courses regardless the study field.

Principle of activeness was also completely breakthrough in Comenius time. The principle comes from individual activity of a single student, arises cognitive, emotional and volitional processes, stimulates interest and motivation, leads towards application of gained knowledge and to the use of creative approaches in all activities [27]. *Comenius ranks Activity in Latin 'Operatio' among three important things that are in every person: ratio – oratio – operatio (thinking – speaking – activity)* and all three should be developed equally [28].

Especially in learning languages, this principle is widely used. Students are motivated to get involved into the teaching/learning process via various tasks preferably optional ones. It is up to the tutor to raise their interest, develop involvement and give space to show students′ outcomes, see Fig. 3.

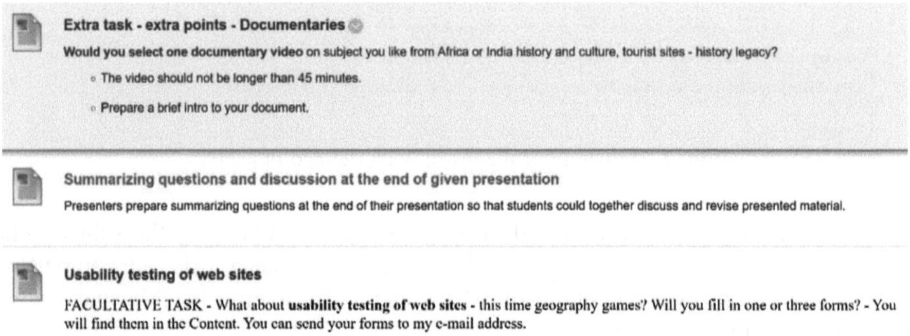

Fig. 3. Tasks - encouraging activity

Beside *principle of activeness* at least two more principles can be shown in this Fig. 4.: *principle of engaging senses* into the learning and *principle of fun.*

Comenius describes school as the 'workshop of humanity' where everything should be taught through the medium of senses. Information technologies enlarged possibilities in using senses in teaching/learning. In the Fig. 3 students are asked to work with video: to select an appropriate video fitting the studied topic and prepare a brief introduction to the video in the written form which will be placed into the e-course. Then they present the introduction with the outline of the video content to the audience where they also justify their choice and recommend the website with the video, it means *ratio – oratio – operatio.* This task is on voluntary base, so there is a willing, psychological moving moment, which is essential to work with during learning/teaching process – now we speak about the psychocognitive approach [29].

Principle of fun means that learning must be done in a pleasant form. According to Comenius, *the principles to be adopted in education should be easy and pleasant* [28]. *Comenius developed the idea to Schola ludus* as another didactic invention (School as Play), which he introduced as a scholar in his stay in Hungary. Visualisation plays important role. The idea of so-called Homo Ludens is based on the idea that person develops his skills and possibilities through games, he/she discovers their skills and develop themselves through them. Learner′s playfulness is at liberty of decision-making and action and he/she assumes own thinking – all based on the fundamental triad *ratio – oratio – operatio (thinking – speaking – activity).* Person develops on the experiences that connect to those that he/she already own. Schola ludus representing dramatized selected subjects is designed to animate the traditionally passive education by a theatre performance. In our example, students are given optional task to play geography games, see Fig. 4 the bottom section. Students′ task is to do website analysis of selected websites offering geography games. Within working on the analysis students also play geography games as a part of the whole task [30]. This way of exploring websites is used in subjects of Professional English as well as subjects on Culture and Geography of English speaking countries. In this example, we can see how principles mingle, e.g.: principle of systematic approach, because the task is based on a standard method of web analysis, principle of activeness – it is a facultative task, willingness to study, principle of graduality – because students can select the level of difficulty in games and of course, principle of fun.

The principle of clearness also works with senses which have to be activated. This enables students to research the real life as direct opinion, form ideas on their own experience as indirect opinion and thus continually and simultaneously develop the whole personality. As gnoseology shows the process of cognition begins with sensory perception and leads to general thinking and verification of conclusions. In practice this principle is applied in visual aids, explanatory examples, motoric training, using symbols and schemas, watching films and last but not least in a clear way of teacher's explanations. At present the ICT provide teachers with wide range of technologies suitable for the purpose [27]. In teaching learning languages the necessity of connection with reality is magnified, students are motivated and led to use language for real-life purposes, many of them participate in Erasmus study programmes abroad, use language in their work, etc. Students should be able to work with authentic material; the power of authentic material is that it can help to create the desired atmosphere to start the lesson, it is 'piece of reality' which can shift students concentration, activate them, make formulate their opinion and respond to other opinions and ideas. Figure 4 shows instruction in the Discussion section in the e-course for part-time students, where they are made to work with authentic material, select news, place them into the Forum and during face-to-face present the news and run conversation.

Latest news *(work with* ***authentic*** *material - don't translate from Czech to English)*

Will you place here your latest news. Make your contribution interesting - try to raise your friends′ interest to respond to it. Good luck in collecting extra-points :-)

Will you prepare at least **3** pieces of **news per semester** (12 sentences at least)?.

You can talk on **world, national or local news**, you can choose information from **newspaper, TV or website** - everything is up to you. Just get ready to talk:-)

Optional task: you can place your news into this section - raise attention, interest, provoke so as some of your classmates could feel like making comment on your contribution.

Fig. 4. Students' work with authentic material

Up to now, description of Comenius' principles was predominantly done from the tutor′s perspective. Students' language needs analysis is a valuable source of information for teachers. We have run a longitudinal survey on utilization of social applications, language educational portals and current possibilities of virtual learning space in teaching/learning languages in the university setting for a decade. Needs analysis is a research tool the survey is based on. Findings from the needs analysis map students experience with online sources and their perception and potential benefits in mastering the language. Findings always get reflected in the follow-up step in a slight adaptation of study material on the virtual platform. Students also formulate their requirements on educational language sources. On some requirements, Comenius principles can be seen. Firstly, students highlight the essence of fun – principle of fun, study material should be presented in a pleasant way, utilizing e.g. games for practising vocabulary and grammar. Students offered some app, which would make them study without feeling that they are studying. Currently habit trackers are popular – so it might be one of solutions. Secondly, students appreciate when study materials in the language portals, are divided into competence levels – principles of systematicity, appropriateness and graduality. Thirdly, more than half of students required possibility of testing with a variety of tests and feedback which corresponds to the Comenius principle of practising memory 'Repetition is an antidote to forgetting' [28]. Surprisingly, students demanded properly worked out grammar with examples in the language portals, Comenius placed vocabulary before grammar in teaching languages. The parallel with Comenius is in students' requirement that vocabulary from everyday life be practiced. Comenius idea about learning languages was based a bilingual approach. Czech portal *'Help for English'* is the most favorite language educational portal used by our students in last 5 years. They find it easy explanations are in Czech language. The second reason of its popularity is the fact that students used it at the secondary school. Popularity of applications is increasing, students gave tips which might be roughly divided tips fitting 'vocabulary' development: *gartic.io, seduo, agendaweb.com, cinema lingua, or application Memrise*, and tips fitting practising 'grammar': *english grammar in use, grammarly.com* and Czech portal *umimeanglicky.cz. examenglish.com.*

4 Conclusion

This article tries not to be a systematic study on any of the many facets of Comenius' massive production. It is just a modest reflection of the Comenius legacy in philosophy, humanism and pedagogy. We pay tribute to the Comenius, and special thanks go to the comeniologists who, with tireless vigor, try to bring Comenius legacy closer to the present world.

Information and communication technologies have become a natural part of our lives. Learning languages with the support of information and communication technologies is at this information age natural. *Comenius concept of education with its fundaments is still 'alive', applicable and used at our age.* All the fundaments are based on the same principle of natural analogy and embody three common characteristics (*triad*): (1) Consistency of correlation of things and their names – senses (as many as possible) must be involved in the process of learning; things themselves must be learned together with their names. (2) Appropriateness of phasing and progression of teaching. (3) Suitability and pleasantness of the teaching method, which is determined not only by the proper choice of the learning matter, but also by the proper (nonviolent) methodological treatment of the matter. All that fits current age.

Final paragraph is devoted to Comenius and technologies. Comenius was keenly interested in scientific development, although he wasn´t able to accept many of inventions. He was neither an exact scientist nor indigenous mathematician - yet today we value his ability to warn against abuse of science and its dehumanization [2].

Professor of Palacký University in Olomouc and comeniologist Pavel Floss was asked in the interview how would Comenius manage todays rush development of technology, computers and the Internet. His response follows: "*Comenius lived in the beginning of the era of inventions, he was open to the novelties, and was proud that his century was the century of technology development. But his (Comenius') sentence is remarkable: We can gain a lot, but if we expect salvation from science and technology, we will be like squirrels closed in a cage of our own folly* [14].

Acknowledgement. The paper is supported by the project SPEV 2019 at the Faculty of Informatics and Management of the University of Hradec Kralove, Czech Republic. In addition, the authors thank Anna Borkovcova for her help with the project.

References

1. Palmer-Cooper, J., Bresler, L., Cooper, E.: Fifty Major Thinkers on Education: From Confucius to Dewey. Routledge, London, New York (2001)
2. Kumpera, J.: Poselství J.A. Komenského pro vzdělanost a humanitu dneška. (J.A. Komenský's Message for Today's Education and Humanity). A paper presented on 15 November 1999, on the anniversary of Comenius' death, at the General Meeting 1999 - A Hundred Years in the Middle of Europe, organized by the Pangea Foundation in Prague (1999). http://www.vialucis.cz/Komensky.htm. Acccsscd 15 Fcb 2019
3. Comenius. J.A.: De rerum humanarum emendatione consultatio catholica. Academia, Praha (1966)
4. Kumpera, J.: Jan Amos Komenský: poutník na rozhraní věků (Jan Amos Comenius: a pilgrim on the edge of ages). Amosium, Ostrava (1992)
5. Smith, M.K.: Howard Gardner and multiple intelligences. The encyclopedia of informal education (2002/2008). http://www.infed.org/mobi/howard-gardner-multiple-intelligences-and-education. Accessed 16 Mar 2019
6. Comenius, J.A.: The gate of languages unlocked, or, a seed-plot of all arts and tongues: containing a ready way to learn the Latine and English Tongue. Printed by T.R. and N.T. for the Company of Stationers, London (1673)
7. Comenius, J.A.: Via Lucis. SPN, Praha (1961)
8. Comenius, J.A.: The Orbis Pictus of John Amos Comenius. Singing Tree, Detroit (1968)
9. Adler, H.: Johann Gottfried Herder's Concept of Humanity. Stud. Eighteenth-Century Culture **23**, 55–74 (1994). https://muse.jhu.edu/. Accessed 3 April 2019
10. Sokol, J.: Filosofická antropologie, Člověk jako osoba (Philosophical Anthropology, The Human Being as a Person), Portál, pp. 15–16 (2002)
11. Patocka, J.: Philosophical Basis for Comenian Pedagogy. In: Ceskoslovenska Akademie ved, Pedagogica, no. 2, pp. 137–177 (1957)

12. Hábl, J.: Lessons in Humanity From the Life and Work of Jan Amos Komenský. Verlag für Kultur und Wissenschaft Culture and Science Publ. Dr. Thomas Schirrmacher Bonn (2011)
13. Kišš, I.: The concept of paradise as the theological starting point for Comenius' pedagogy. In: Chocholová, S. (ed.) Johannes Amos Comenius: The Legacy to the Culture of Education, pp. 104–111. Academia, Prague (2009)
14. Perknerová, K.: Stále aktuální Komenský. (Komensky is still topical). Newspaper Denik.cz. VLTAVA LABE MEDIA (2012). www.denik.cz/z_domova/stale-aktualni-komensky-20120327.html. Accessed 3 April 2019
15. Small, M.L.: The Pansophism of John Amos Comenius (1592–1670) as the Foundation of Educational Technology and the Source of Constructive Standards for the Evaluation of Computerized Instruction and Tests. In: International Conference on Technology and Education, March 1990, pp. 1–11. ERIC. ED325079, microfiche (1990)
16. Čapková, D.: Pojetí vzdělání jako celoživotního procesu v díle Komenského. The Concept of Education as a Lifelong Process in the Work of Komensky (Contribution to Discussion) J. A. Komenský Pedagogical Institute, Czechoslovak Academy of Sciences (1970). http://pages.pedf.cuni.cz/pedagogika/?attachment_id=8897&edmc=8897
17. Piaget, J.: Jan Amos Comenius, por Jean Piaget. https://www.ufrgs.br/psicoeduc/piaget/jan-amos-comenius-por-jean-piaget/. Accessed 3 April 2019
18. Čížek, J.: Komenský a Bacon: Dvě raně novověké cesty k obnově vědění (Comenius and Bacon: Two Early Modern Paths to Restoring Knowledge). Pavel Mervart, Cerveny Kostelec (2017). https://doi.org/10.5817/pf18-1-1766
19. Patocka, J.: Komenský a Bacon (Comenius and Bacon). In: Schifferova, V. (ed.) ID., Komeniologické studie III, Praha, pp. 557–570 (2003)
20. Čapková, D.: Škola a utváření lidství v pojetí J.A. Komenského, (School and Formation of Humanity in the Notion of J.A. Komenský). In: Pedagogica XLI, 5–6, p. 557 (1991)
21. Campanella, T.: Philosophia sensibus demonstrata, trans. ed. L. De Franco. Vivarium, Naples (1992)
22. Campanella, T.: The City of the Sun. Merchant Brook, USA (2010). ISBN10 1603862889
23. Patocka, J.: 3.64. Campanella a Komenský. In: Jan Patočka - repository. Dostupné z (1983). http://archiv.janpatocka.cz/items/show/1017. Accessed 3 April 2019
24. Lukas, M., Munjiza, E.: Education system of John Amos Comenius and its implications in modern didactics. Zivot i skola **31**(1), 32–44 (2014)
25. Comenius, J.A.: The Great Didactic [Didactica Magna]. Translated into English and edited with biographical, historical and critical introductions by M.W. Keatinge. Russell & Russell, New York (1967)
26. Patočka, J.: Náčrt pedagogického univerzalismu J.A. Komenského (A Sketch of the Pedagogical Universalism of J.A. Komenský) in Komeniologické studie III (Comeniological Studies, vol. III), p. 199. Oikoymenh, Praha (2003)
27. Simonova, I.: Technical Education versus Jan Ámos Komenský. In: Engineering Education, Book of Abstracts, 18–21 September 2006, p. 110. Tallin State University (2006). ISBN 9985-59-646-3
28. Comenius, J. A.: Selections from his works. SPN, Praha (1964)
29. Cerna, M.: Psychodidactic approach in the development of language competences in university students within blended learning. Open Learn. **33**(2), 142–154 (2018)
30. Černá, M.: Website analysis in the context of practicing geography: from first impression to recommendation - case study. In: Huang, T.C., Lau, R., Huang, Y.M., Spaniol, M., Yuen, C.H. (eds.) Emerging Technologies for Education. Lecture Notes in Computer Science, vol. 10676, pp. 304–313. Springer, Cham (2018). https://doi.org/10.1007/978-3-319-71084-6_34

Personalized and Adaptive Learning

An Adaptive Blended Learning Health Education Model for Families of a Parent with Serious Medical Problems

Jayshiro Tashiro[1,2](✉) and Anders Hebeler[3]

[1] Associate Graduate Faculty in the School of Graduate and Postdoctoral Studies, University of Ontario Institute of Technology, Oshawa, ON, Canada
jay.tashiro@uoit.ca
[2] Adjunct Faculty in Biology, Pima Community College, Tucson, AZ, USA
[3] Trumbull High School, Trumbull, CT, USA

Abstract. We propose a blended learning model that will provide evidence-based medical education and psychological support for families in which a parent has a serious medical condition. The twelve leading causes of death in the United States include diseases and injuries with pathophysiological and psychological facets most adults and the vast majority of children do not understand. An intriguing problem in blended learning emerged as we studied how to create a blended learning environment that could provide families with evidence-based support for dealing with medical problems. The model we developed is based on deep knowledge adaptive learning engines to assess both parents' and children's prior knowledge and accuracy of such knowledge as well as each learner's readiness to engage in learning, and then to create teaching-learning-assessment environments tailored to the needs and prior knowledge of each family member.

Keywords: Patient education · Blended learning · Evidence-based instruction · Educational technology · Courseware · Adaptive learning engines

1 Introduction

1.1 The Promise and Reality of Blended Learning

Previous impact analyses of healthcare technologies on care planning and delivery revealed important relationships between the transformation of healthcare and the transformation of evidence-based practices in patient education [1, 2]. However, a broad literature and website review convinced us two clusters of factors inhibit development of educational environments that "really work" to improve patient education and, in particular, education of family members in which a parent has a serious medical condition. The first cluster of factors is a set of knowledge gaps about what really works in most educational settings, including face-to-face, blended learning, or totally online learning [1]. Earlier studies revealed at least 10 critical gaps in our knowledge about how educational environments and materials "really work" to change

S. K. S. Cheung et al. (Eds.): ICBL 2019, LNCS 11546, pp. 59–71, 2019.
https://doi.org/10.1007/978-3-030-21562-0_5

an individual's learning outcomes and willingness as well as ability to engage in and sustain healthy behaviors based on what has been learned [1, 3].

Described more completely by Tashiro and colleagues [1], these gaps include our incomplete knowledge of the following: (1) how educational environments improve disposition to learn; (2) relationships of learning outcomes to the level of realism and relevance in an educational environment; (3) how to determine thresholds of learning experiences that lead to measurable outcomes; (4) how to assess learning to determine authentic learning outcomes; (5) delineation of cognitive processes and domains being instantiated and the stability of knowledge retained; (6) what processes improve disposition to act on knowledge gained; (7) what processes influence accurate knowledge transfer; (8) how learning outcomes are developed during the learning process (e.g., conceptual and performance competencies); (9) how misconceptions are developed during and sustained after working within an educational environment; and (10) how do educator-learner and learner-learner social networks or e-communities impact learning. These 10 gaps have not been bridged, in part because truly inclusive and adaptive educational environments have been hard to build and evaluate.

The second cluster of factors are related to availability of patient educational materials. Studies of healthcare systems in many different countries reveal the economic burden of increased incidence of chronic diseases. Yet, many unhealthy behaviors can be changed, including health risk behaviors that cause a high percentage of illness, suffering, and early death from chronic disease. Experts have argued healthcare costs can be lowered substantially if educational outreach reduced health risk behaviors [1].

However, other complexities evolve when an adult in a family with children has a serious medical condition. Tan and colleagues argued that models of blended learning coupled to patient monitoring could be a critical pathway for helping individuals manage chronic disease or reduce the potential for developing chronic conditions [1, 2]. Patient education, especially if coupled to family education (broadly defined), would have to integrate ongoing education with remote patient monitoring, but also bridge the 10 knowledge gaps. Many of the problems faced by inclusive family education about medical issues can be gleaned from a review of studies on the patient portals now becoming popular in the United States and other countries [4–6]. The impact of disease on family members also has been studied [7–9].

Yet, the majority of patient portals and websites for healthcare education have neither adaptive capacities for interactive patient monitoring nor provide sensible linkages to a healthcare provider who may have recommended a portal for patient education. We found no adaptive learning sites that provided articulated parent and child health education. While many health-related websites provide information to help parents with their own medical conditions, none also provide integrated learning environments for both parents and children. There are some websites that provide general strategies an ill-injured parent could use to help their children understand an adult's medical issues, but these often are not illness-injury specific [10, 11]. We concluded that the literature on patient portals and health information sites we have reviewed cannot address either the barriers presented by the 10 knowledge gaps or the need for improved parent-child interactions and learning during periods of illness or injury that impact an entire family.

1.2 Adaptive Learning for Family Outreach to Improve Health and Maintain Family Stability

An adaptive teaching-learning-assessment environment could be designed to bridge the 10 knowledge gaps and also engage a patient, significant other, and their children in learning activities appropriate to their respective needs, prior knowledge, and developmental stage [1–3]. Such environments would have to engage ill or injured adults and their families in learning activities appropriate to their respective needs. Three barriers are immediately obvious. First, an ill or injured adult and family members would need access to devices (computers, cell phones) and internet connections that allow affordable, easy, and on-demand access to an online educational program [1, 3–6]. Second, the majority of adult patients would require a blended learning experience involving face-to-face time with a skilled healthcare educator who could coach each adult parent and other family members to find and use the online support, to provide ongoing support with educational materials, and to provide referral to a technical support group [2].

Third, and especially in the context of limited time for healthcare providers to engage ill-injured adult patients let alone other family members, the educational environments must sensibly provide and integrate six levels of adaptive capacities: (1) analysis of the end-users internet and device capacities; (2) assessment of the ill or injured adult's and adult significant other's prior knowledge, with subsequent capacities for using such assessments to create educational environments specific to each individual adult; (3) teaching modules for adults about evidence-based ways to help their children understand health and wellness, with special foci on the facets of the ill or injured adult in the family; (4) assessment of the each child's prior knowledge and development stage, with subsequent capacities for using such assessments to create educational environments specific to each individual child; (5) a continuously updated data analysis engine that creates a record of learning for of both the ill or injured adult and other family members, with algorithms coupled to provide two feedback systems: (a) evidence-based input to adults and children, and (b) clinical flags that would alert healthcare providers of physiological or psychological problems emerging within the family; and finally, (6) linkages between an ill or injured parent's health status and a regional or national database of adults, but also linkages from data analyses of children's understanding of disease and injury to a regional or national database of children that could be disaggregated by age, gender, ethnicity, and prior knowledge for different disease-injury conditions of parents (such databases allow ongoing research and evidence-based system updates).

Tashiro and colleagues [1] concluded that effective patient education should be re-conceptualized as a type of blended learning. Based on a taxonomy for blended learning [12], patient education could include a low face-to-face component and a high online component. However, ongoing monitoring of the patient could be built into an adaptive teaching-learning-assessment environment that sent a clinical flag to the patient's care manager if the patient deviated from a care plan or suffered an exacerbation of a chronic illness or an injury. In such cases, the patient would be contacted by a healthcare provider who could provide support through face-to-face synchronous online chats, with or without video to help the patient find care for an exacerbation or re-engage with the care plan. To make the next step for parent-child support, we conducted a case study to understand critical issues related to parent-child health education in a family with an ill or injured adult.

2 A Case Study of Factors Shaping Adaptive Blended Learning Environments for Ill or Injured Adults and Their Children

The senior author (Tashiro) had been studying models for patient education for the past decade. Previous studies conducted by other researchers revealed the impact of a parent's illness or injury on members of the family [7–9]. In July 2017, an unusual opportunity emerged. Tashiro's third child, a daughter then 46 years old, had experienced a suite of medical issues, which appeared to be endocrinological in nature. However, she (hereafter referred to as Rose) was diagnosed with a benign brain tumor —in technical terms a right sphenoid wing-cavernous sinus meningioma. Tashiro, a doctoral-trained nurse, provided ongoing educational support, mostly in the form of explaining what the physicians were telling Rose and working with her to explore evidence-based websites that described her condition, its diagnosis, treatment, and prognosis. Some of the discussion between father and daughter explored how to explain her condition to her three children, the oldest a young man aged 15 and twin daughters aged 10 at the time of diagnosis. In brief, Tashiro's daughter, son-in-law, and grandchildren were caught in the upheaval faced by many families: a parent has a medical problem and she as well as her significant others—including children—may not understand the pathophysiology or psychological stressors of an illness or injury.

Over the course of 18 months, Tashiro closely followed Rose's progress and eventual intra-cranial surgery to reduce the size of the meningioma, which had begun to impinge on the right optic nerve. Anders Hebeler, the junior author and Tashiro's grandson, experienced his mother's condition first-hand within the family dynamic of an adult with a serious medical condition. We decided to study the family experience.

Methodology. We developed the research from an interview model that is qualitative and conducted as a reflective ethnographic study of a what a parent and child understood about the mother's benign brain tumor—a meningioma—and what her son understood about his mother's condition, including diagnosis, treatment, prognosis, and recovery from surgery to reduce the meningioma. This type of ethnographic research was derived from new models of ethnographic research [9, 13–16], but also shaped by the methods of filmed interviews collected from diverse people, some of whom had experienced trauma, for example: (1) the National Public Radio Story Corp; (2) The Japanese American National Museum's interviews of people of Japanese ancestry (most of whom were American citizens) interned in American relocation centers during World War II; and (3) videotaped interviews of Holocaust victims in the United States Memorial Holocaust Museum.

The research model is reflective and ethnographic because Tashiro suggested this study only after his daughter had fully recovered from intra-cranial surgery and received a good prognosis. Furthermore, as a nurse and healthcare educator, Tashiro provided pre- and post-surgical patient education for support of his adult daughter and her spouse, but not their children. Below, we describe the careful attention to parent-child interactions and also the method of videotaping. Again, we emphasize that the patient Rose is the child of the senior author Tashiro and mother of the junior author Hebeler. Hebeler filmed his mother's responses to eleven questions:

1. How was your meningioma diagnosed?
2. How would you describe a meningioma?
3. What was your experience with physicians and other health care providers during the early period of diagnoses?
4. What treatment options were described for you?
5. What prognosis was projected for you?
6. How did you help you children learn about your condition?
7. When you found out surgery was recommended for your meningioma, what did you decide to tell your children?
8. As a parent preparing to have your surgery, what did you tell your children?
9. How did you prepare your children for their first visit to the ICU after your surgery?
10. How did you prepare your children for post-operative recovery at home?
11. If you had to start over, what would you have done the same and what would you have done differently for yourself and for your children?

These 11 questions were developed by the authors based on earlier research studies [7–9], were based on research related to parent-child interactions during health crises, and also reflected what Hebeler wanted to know about his mother's medical condition. The authors set the order of the questions because they knew the unfolding of Rose's condition from diagnosis to recovery from surgery. The interviewer (Hebeler) asked Rose each of the 11 questions—which we refer to as the "Main Questions." For each Main Question, the interviewer allowed Rose to respond, but never prompted or led Rose in her answers. Once a Main Question had been answered, the interviewer posed three Follow-up Questions related to the respective Main Question. As with each Main Question, the interviewer did not offer prompts of any kind, allowing Rose to speak until she indicated she had answered the respective follow-up question.

Follow-up questions were structured within a KWL Rubric created by the National Education Association [17]: The **K** stands for "Know"—<u>What Did You **K**now</u>? The **W** stands for "Want"—<u>What Did You **W**ant to Know</u>? The **L** stands for "Learned"—<u>What Have You **L**earned</u>. These interviews were filmed, with separate videos for each of the eleven main questions and their respective three Follow-up Questions. The 11 videos were each 10–15 min in length, and each video included responses to a Main Question as well as responses to the three respective Follow-up Questions.

As an example, consider Question 1: How was your meningioma diagnosed? After Rose responded, the interviewer asked the three follow-up questions for Question 1 in the sequence of the KWL Rubric: (1) What did you <u>know</u> about meningioma diagnosis? (2) What did you <u>want to know</u> about meningioma diagnosis? And (3) What have you learned about meningioma diagnosis? Both authors analyzed the videos using a data table to take notes on Rose's responses in the videos. Each table provided data collection cells for the Main Question and its Follow-up Questions. Notes on the response to Main Question were recorded in a separate table cell. Then data for each Follow-up Question were recorded in one of three columns, using the K-W-L rubric: Column 1—What Did You Know, Column 2—What Did You Want to Know, and Column 3—What Have You Learned [17]. As mentioned above, the research model also was derived from research on qualitative interviews and connective ethnography [9, 15, 16].

During December 2018–January 2019, the video-taped responses of the patient were analyzed for thematic threads. By "thematic" we mean clusters of related commentary entered by the researchers in the three KWL columns. The cluster analysis involved identifying themes within each Main Question and its respective Follow-up Questions, but also across Main Questions and their Follow-up Questions. This approach allowed generalization of themes across Rose's retrospective of her lived experiences from diagnosis through surgery and into post-surgical recovery in the hospital and at home. This approach is similar to content analysis of text.

Results of Phase 1 Research. While the KWL model has many values, analysis of themes can be confounded across what a person knows, what that person wants to know, and what the same person has learned. We discovered eleven distinct themes within the patient's responses. These themes are presented in Table 1, and for each we added interpretive analysis. In subsequent discussion of the themes, we will use the shorthand convention of K1–K3 for the three themes under "What Do I Know," W1–W5 for the five themes under "What Do I Want to Know, and L1–L3 for the themes under "What Have I Learned."

3 SIGNAL PATCH—A New Framework for Patient Education SIGNAL—Serial Integration of Guiding Nodes for Adaptive Learning

Prior research by Tashiro and colleagues resulted in a research platform called **SIGNAL**—Serial Integration of Guiding Nodes for Adaptive Learning (see references 36–42 in [1] for technical details). This platform allowed creation of a space-time mapping of each individual's conceptual and performance competencies to their decisions during engagement in educational and knowledge transfer activities [1, 3]. An assessment system identified misconceptions of each individual as they explored learning activities within an online or computer-based system. Each misconception identified could then be mapped to Learning Activities in which an individual engaged. For the research reported herein, we used the 11 themes of Rose's responses as a framework for a *Gedanken* experiment based on the question, "How can **SIGNAL** be modified to provide support for adults with illness of injury who want to help their children and significant others understand the medical issues and possible disruptions of family routines?"

Starting with the design and programming of **SIGNAL** [1, 3], we knew the adaptive teaching-learning-assessment system could bridge the 10 knowledge gaps described earlier. Our *Gedanken* experiment explored each subsystem of **SIGNAL** and studied how each subsystem could be re-designed to address the patient-child educational themes in Table 1. Since we had already built **SIGNAL**, the "thinking experiment" involved deciding what modification of each **SIGNAL** subsystem would be required to accommodate a blended learning environment used by a healthcare educator, an ill or injured adult, and that adult's significant others—including children. Through several redesigns and modifying **SIGNAL** subsystem capacities, we were able to create **SIGNAL-PATCH**—**S**erial **I**ntegration of **G**uiding **N**odes of **A**daptive **L**earning for **P**arents' and **T**heir **C**hildren's **H**ealth.

Previous research examined impacts of illnesses and injuries on family quality of life [7–11]. Golics and colleagues [8] identified 10 themes across 26 medical specialty areas that impact quality of life: emotional, daily activities, family relationships, sleep and health, holidays, support and medical care, work and study, financial concerns, social life, and activity planning. Golics provides a type of "breadth" analysis, while the approach taken in our research provides a type of "depth" analysis. In comparison to the survey methods used by Golic, the videotaping of Rose probed more deeply into individual experiences and the 11 themes we identified provide key details essential to developing an adaptive educational and support system. Combining thematic analyses like Golics [8) with our deeper probe was essential for our *Gedanken* experiment to study how to build adaptive teaching-learning-assessment environments for patient education that is inclusive of the patient but also of other family members.

Figure 1 shows a diagrammatic representation of **PATCH** as refined from the earlier **SIGNAL** system (for technical details see references 36–42 in [1]). The result is a set of interconnected software engines that monitor educational activities of an ill or injured adult and a child learner. Below, we describe the components of **SIGNAL-PATCH** evolving from our reflective ethnographic study of a parent with a serious medical issue and her child. For each **PATCH** subsystem, we note which of the 10 the knowledge gaps can be bridged by the knowledge engines within the respective subsystem. Also note that for every subsystem we have listed the themes from Table 1 each subsystem can cover and so provide adaptive support for educational activities of an ill-injured parent and their significant others in the family—including children.

Subsystems of **PATCH** shown within Fig. 1:

(1) A parent and child, together or individually, access a Web-based Inclusive-Adaptive Interface to learn about healthcare issues—for example, a parent's medical problems that the child may not understand. Gaps Bridged: 1. Themes Covered: K1–K3

(2) The Inclusive-Adaptive Interface (IAI) collects data on the learner's needs and preferences, creating a Leaner Profile (LP) database that becomes part of an Electronic Learning Record (ELR). The IAI, LP, and ELR create learning opportunities to improve both parent's and child's disposition to engage in learning and creating a record of learning activities. Gaps Bridged: 1–10. Themes Covered: W1–W5.

Table 1. Extracted themes from structured interviews of a patient with a meningioma.

What Did I Know (K)
K1: Inadequate Knowledge—How to deal with knowing little about a medical condition, its diagnosis, treatment, and prognosis, but also about how to communicate with the family.
K2: Difficulty Contextualizing Medical Information—How to contextualize pathophysiological information and also information about psychology of living with an illness or disease?
K3: Anxiety and Fear of Death—How do patients deal with anxieties when healthcare providers provide too little counseling or referral to psychotherapists to help patients understand medical contexts and provide psychological support.
What Did I Want to Know (W)
W1: Explanation and Contextualization—How to help a patient (and family) understand medical terminology and procedures?
W2: Support of Healthcare Coach—How can contact with patients who had gone through the same diagnosis and treatment provide important insights?
W3: Experience and Training of Health Teams—From the early stages of diagnosis through surgery and recovery, how does a patient evaluate and work with members of the health team?
W4: Explanation of Dangers and Outcomes—The idiosyncratic nature of some illnesses and injuries creates difficulties in specifying exact pathways of treatment and recovery, so how could a healthcare educator provide specific support for an individual patient?
W5: Sharing Information with Family Members—A parent's illness or injury has complex impacts on a spouse and children, but how does the patient communicate to family members in ways that do not add increased psychological stress to family members?
What Did I Learn (L)
L1: Building a Partnership with Health Team Members—How does a patient and family build trust in and partnerships with diverse healthcare providers?
L2: Knowledge Gaps—How can educational support reduce patients' gaps in knowledge and reduce differences in what the patient perceived and what family members perceived during the various periods of diagnosis, treatment, visitation in the hospital, and recovery at home?
L3: Truth Telling and Authenticity—Patients may want to help their children understand a medical condition and its treatment, but do not want them to become as fearful as the patient may have been during the stages of diagnosis, treatment, and recovery for a medical condition. How can a patient be authentic with their family and communicate essential information to family members without causing them undue psychological stress.

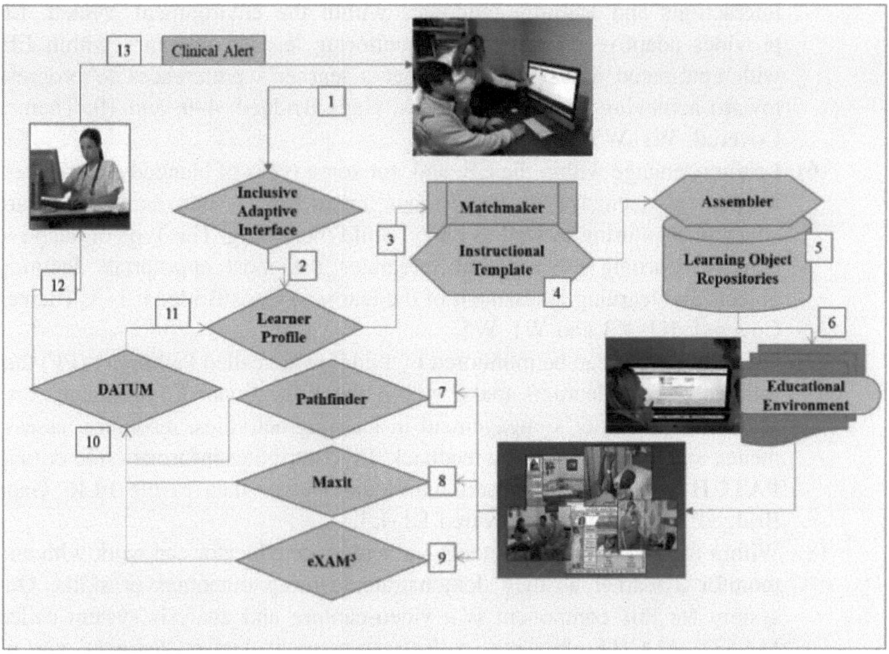

Fig. 1. Diagrammatic representation of the SIGNAL-PATCH environment

(3) The LP data stream to a MatchMaker (MM) system that selects an Instructional Design Template (IDT) based on a theory of cognition and behavioral change chosen by a healthcare education expert and consistent with the medical issues of the parent but informed by each learner's needs and preferences. These needs and preferences include the learner's prior knowledge, their developmental stages (e.g., psychological readiness but also capabilities for concrete and formal operational reasoning, disposition to engage in learning, and expectations for as well as value placed on learning). MM and IDT work together in ways that can improve disposition to engage in learning as well as disposition to act on knowledge gained. Gaps Bridged: 1, 2, 3, 6. Themes Covered: K1–K3 and W1–W3.
(4) The MatchMaker engine then reads the metadata from the IDT.
(5) The Assembler Engine (AE) reads the IDT and metadata brought to it by MM, searches Learning Object Repositories (LOR) to find and collate learning activities, resources, educational scaffolding, learning assessments, psychological assessments, and feedback personalized for the learner, and then organizes the assemblage to create a Web-based personalized teaching-learning-assessment-diagnostic Educational Environment (EE). AE, IDT, MM, LOR, and EE work in concert to create teaching-learning-assessment environments that are responses to data about the individual learner's

interactions and learning outcomes within the environment created. EE provides adaptive capacities for monitoring learner outcomes within EE, with automated adjustments to meet a learner's preferences to progress toward achieving learning outcomes. Gaps Bridged: 4–9, and 10. Themes Covered: W1–W5 and L1–L3.

(6) Learners engage within the EE, and, for some types of blended experiences, learners also engage in face-to-face interactions—such as a healthcare educator mentoring as well as parent-child mentoring. This type of adaptive blended learning environment integrates the most appropriate learning objects and learning assessment of the learners. Gaps Bridged: 1–3. Themes Covered: K1–K3 and W1–W5.

(7) Parent and child can be monitored by middleware called Pathfinder (PF) that follows choices learners make within the Educational Environments and also times a learner's engagement in learning activities, resources, assessments, and use of diagnostic feedback. PF contributes information to critical **PATCH** subsystems that add individual learner data to the ELR. Gaps Bridged: 1–10. Themes Covered L1–L3.

(8) Within the face-to-face moments—a healthcare educator can work with and monitor a learner as they demonstrate learning outcomes or skills. Our system for this component is a video-capture and analysis system called MAXIT. MAXIT efficiently collects assessment data on learners' performance competencies. Gaps Bridged: 4–5 and 7–9. Themes Covered: W1–W5 and L1–L3.

(9) Prior to, simultaneously with, or after learning-demonstration activities, learners enter an assessment engine called $eXAM^3$, which assesses their learning outcomes within a cognitive taxonomy selected by a healthcare team member (e.g., Bloom's Revised Taxonomy or a skills-based rubric or a clinical expert panel rubric for a knowledge or skills domain). $eXAM^3$ evolved as an assessment engine with diagnostic feedback capacities, including assessments of both cognitive and psychological profiles. Gaps Bridged: 7–9. Themes Covered: L1–L3.

(10) PathFinder, MAXIT, and $eXAM^3$ stream a learner's data to a data analysis and knowledge system called DATUMM, which can analyze accuracy of learners' knowledge but also assess emotional-psychological profiles.

(11) DATUMM analyzes the data, creates new information about the learner, and sends information back to the Learner Profile but also to a healthcare educator assigned to a family. These new data sets integrate into and update the Learner Profile and healthcare educator databases, with revised data and information facilitating adaptive changes: (1) to the flow beginning with the MatchMaker and ending in new configurations of the Educational Environment; but also (2) to a clinical flag system to alert the healthcare educator assigned to the family. Data from the Learner Profile also streams into a subcomponent—the Electronic Learning Record, through time creating a longitudinal record of a learner's progress. DATUMM is most similar to the analytics engines now used widely in a number of applications. Gaps Bridged: 1–10. Themes Covered: K1–K3, W1–W5, and L1–L3.

(12) & (13) DATUMM sends clinical alerts to a healthcare team member if a patient or family members are not using the educational system or if results of use suggest errors in patient and family members understanding of critical medical and psychological issues. Gaps Bridged: 1–10. Themes Covered: K1–K3, W1–W5, and L1–L3.

3.1 Limitations of the Current Research and Future Work

Our reflective ethnographic study of a family is limited and can be criticized for possible intrafamilial biases in theme interpretation. However, the data collection did allow a reasonable start for a *Gedanken* experiment. We recognize the need to examine many different families to develop the **PATCH** system more completely as well as to validate how and why such a system bridges the 10 knowledge gaps we identified as well as improving patient-family outcomes in the situation of an ill or injured adult parent who has children. Future research with **PATCH** will focus on the psychology of parent-child interactions during situations when a parent is ill or injured.

4 Conclusions and Recommendations

The research literature provides many theories of cognition and learning as well as theories of behavioral change [1–3]. We argue that **PATCH** could be used to test theoretical frameworks that have been proposed for cognition and learning, for example contrasting health-related learning outcomes for theories such as Adaptive Character of Thought, Cognitive Load, Cognitive Flexibility, and Situated Learning theories [1]. Adaptive Character of Thought and Cognitive Load theories cluster into the more individualistic structured theories of learning. Cognitive Flexibility and Situated Learning theories fit within what many educators call a constructivist framework [1]. However, theories of learning must be coupled to theories of behavioral change to understand how individuals learn and then act on what they have learned as evidenced by intention or direct action to reduce their health and psychological risks [1–3].

Sincc **PATCH** has been designed as an adaptive learning environment that will provide support for parents and children when a parent has an illness or injury, we need to develop large-scale research that examines which theories of learning and cognition coupled to which theories of behavioral change will provide the most satisfactory framework for parent-child support during medical crises for a parent. As we studied patients, especially when children become involved in learning about a parent's illness or injury a single theory of learning and cognition may not work for all parent-child educational settings. Such a possibility has encouraged us to think about creating new types of educational environments with administrative dashboards designed to allow healthcare educators to select a grounded theory most appropriate to a type of adult medical problem and another more suited to the developmental stage of the children in the family. Such a dashboard could be used to set **PATCH**'s Assembler engine to particular grounded theories, which automatically would configure learning activities, learning objects, and authentic assessments consistent with the selected theory as well as with the learner's prior knowledge and cognitive developmental stage.

As a closing note, consider that American healthcare insurers often contract with patient management companies that work directly with insured individuals to improve their health outcomes and so reduce healthcare costs. Tashiro and colleagues [1] noted the enormous costs in American healthcare, most of which has been spent on care related to relatively few chronic illnesses. One model used by these patient management companies has been to provide more active support of insured individuals in order to reduce or modify health risk behaviors by improving healthcare education for all family members. Systems like **PATCH** could play important roles in direct blended learning outreach to insured individuals and their families, providing educational support for parents and children in ways that reduce risks for chronic illness but also provide evidence-based support to reduce stressors on an injured or ill parent and significant others—including children.

References

1. Tashiro, J., Hung, Patrick C.K., Martin, M.V.: Can an evidence-based blended learning model serve healthcare patients and adult education students? In: Cheung, S.K.S., Kwok, L.-f., Kubota, K., Lee, L.-K., Tokito, J. (eds.) ICBL 2018. LNCS, vol. 10949, pp. 17–42. Springer, Cham (2018). https://doi.org/10.1007/978-3-319-94505-7_2
2. Tan, J., Hung, P., Dohan, M., Trojer, T., Farwick, M., Tashiro, J.: Gateway to quality living for the elderly: charting an innovative approach to evidence-based e-health technologies for serving the chronically ill. In: Proceedings of the 13th IEEE International Conference on Computational Science and Engineering, CSE-2010, 11–13 December, Hong Kong (2010)
3. Tashiro, J., Hung, P., Vargas Martin, M., Hurst, F., Brown, A.: Personalized-adaptive learning—an operational framework for developing competency-based curricula in computer information technology. Int. J. Innov. Learn. **19**(4), 412–430 (2016)
4. Alpert, J., Krist, A., Aycock, R., Kreps, G.: Applying multiple methods to comprehensively evaluate a patient portal's effectiveness to convey information to patients. J. Med. Internet Res. **18**(5), e112 (2016)
5. Irizarry, T., DeVito Dabbs, A., Curran, C.: Patient portals and patient engagement: a state of the science review. J. Med. Internet Res. **17**(6), e148 (2015)
6. Ammonwerth, E., Schnell-Inderst, P., Hoerbst, A.: The impact of electronic patient portals on patient care: a systematic review of controlled trials. J. Med. Internet Res. **14**(6), e162 (2015)
7. Golics, C., Basra, M., Finlay, A., Salek, M.S.: The impact of disease on family members: a critical aspect of medical care. J. R. Soc. Med. **106**(10), 399–407 (2013). https://doi.org/10.1177/0141076812472616
8. Golics, C., Basra, M., Salek, M.S., Finlay, A.: The impact of patients' chronic disease on family quality of life: an experience across 26 specialties. Int. J. Gen. Med. **6**, 787–798 (2013). https://doi.org/10.2417/ijgm.s45156
9. Wittenberg, E., Saada, A., Prosser, L.: How illness affects family members: a qualitative interview survey. Patient **6**(4), 257–268 (2013). https://doi.org/10.1007/s40271-013-0030-3
10. Healthcare Toolbox: Basics of trauma-informed care. http://healtcaretoolbox.org/for-parents-and-children.html. Accessed 25 Jan 2019
11. American Family Physician: Talking with children about a parent's serious illness. Am. Fam. Physician, **68**(9) (2013). www.aafp.org/afp. Accessed 25 Jan 2019

12. Tashiro, J., Hung, P.C.K., Martin, M.V.: Evidence-based educational practices and a theoretical framework for hybrid learning. In: Kwan, R., Fong, J., Kwok, L.-f., Lam, J. (eds.) ICHL 2011. LNCS, vol. 6837, pp. 51–72. Springer, Heidelberg (2011). https://doi.org/10.1007/978-3-642-22763-9_6
13. Wald, H., Dube, C., Anthony, D.: Untangling the web—the impact of internet use on health care and physician-patient relationship. Patient Educ. Couns. **68**, 218–224 (2007)
14. Tashiro, J., Hung, P.C.K., Martin, M.V., Tashiro, R.R.: What really works in hybrid learning: a cognitive perspective. In: Cheung, S.K.S., Kwok, L.-f., Yang, H., Fong, J., Kwan, R. (eds.) ICHL 2015. LNCS, vol. 9167, pp. 15–35. Springer, Cham (2015). https://doi.org/10.1007/978-3-319-20621-9_2
15. Kendall, L.: The conduct of qualitative interviews – research questions, methodological issues, and researching online. In: Coiro, J., Knobel, M., Lankshear, C., Leu, D.J. (eds.) Handbook of Research on New Literacies, pp. 133–149. Lawrence Erlbaum Associates, New York (2008)
16. Leander, K.A.: Toward a connective ethnography of online/offline literacy networks. In: Coiro, J., Knobel, M., Lankshear, C., Leu, D.J. (eds.) Handbook of Research on New Literacies, pp. 33–65. Lawrence Erlbaum Associates, New York (2008)
17. National Education Association—Know, Want to Know, Learned. Accessed 20 Dec 2017. http://www.nea.org/tools/k-w-l-know-want-to-know-learned.html

How Learning Has Been Personalised: A Review of Literature from 2009 to 2018

Kam Cheong Li and Billy Tak-Ming Wong(✉)

The Open University of Hong Kong, Hong Kong, China
{kcli, tamiwong}@ouhk.edu.hk

Abstract. This paper presents a comprehensive study of the literature related to personalised learning in the past decade, summarising how, and in what aspects, learning has been personalised. The study covers a total of 179 relevant articles collected from the Web-of-Science and Scopus databases. The results show that, between 2009–13 and 2014–18, there was a clear upward trend—a 120% increase in the number of relevant publications over the years. The research and practice have become more diversified in terms of the target learners, research issues, and objectives. The means to achieve personalised learning mainly involve educational technologies, where emerging technologies such as learning analytics, massive open online courses and augmented/virtual reality have been increasingly used. The results reveal the areas for further investigation, such as the challenges arising from the adoption of emerging technology, the aspects of learning receiving little attention, and the changing role of teachers in the move to student-centred personalised learning.

Keywords: Personalised learning · Differentiated learning · Technology-assisted learning · Student-centred

1 Introduction

Personalisation has become emphasised in contemporary education. It is understood as an umbrella term covering various concepts, such as individualisation, student-centredness, student agency, learner profiles, and a flexible learning environment [1]. Patrick et al. [2] define personalised learning as "tailoring learning for each student's strengths, needs and interests—including enabling students' voices and choices in what, how, when and where they learn—to provide flexibility and supports to ensure mastery of the highest standards possible" (p. 4). This contrasts with the conventional "one-size-fits-all" education where students receive identical types of instruction, assignments and assessments without considering their individual differences and needs.

The past decade has witnessed numerous ways of personalising learning at all levels of education. Examples range from new teaching and learning approaches, such as adaptive programmes and flipped classrooms, to various forms of e-learning, such as massive open online courses (MOOCs) and mobile learning, as well as the use of learning analytics and educational big data [3, 4]. These approaches give greater flexibility for learners whose learning activities are tailored for them, regardless of time

S. K. S. Cheung et al. (Eds.): ICBL 2019, LNCS 11546, pp. 72–81, 2019.
https://doi.org/10.1007/978-3-030-21562-0_6

and place. The benefits of personalised learning have been widely reported. For instance, in a personalised learning programme for K-12 schools in the USA, Education Elements [5] showed that the students achieved an average increase of 130% in reading and 122% in maths in their examination results. Also, the USA's National Association of State Boards of Education [6] summarised various findings on student problems, showing that many of the difficulties in schools—such as student alienation and high dropout rates—were the consequences of not attending to students' individual needs, and inflexible teaching and learning methods. Personalising the learning experience of each student is then proposed as one of the goals for policy reform in education.

Despite the wide range of studies in this area, the relevant literature reviews have only addressed specific aspects of personalised learning. For example, Scott et al. [7] focused on the use of 3D technologies for creating an adaptive virtual learning environment. Berge [8] reviewed the cases on mobile learning for enabling learners to choose what, how, and where to learn. O'Donnell et al. [9] addressed only the issues and problems in assessing students' prior knowledge for tailoring learning contents for them. Also, Gabarre et al. [10] conducted a critical review on personalised language learning with mobile devices and social media. The lack of a comprehensive review in this area poses difficulties in understanding how personalised learning can be achieved in various forms.

This paper aims to provide a comprehensive review of studies related to personalised learning, and summarises the aspects of learning which have been personalised and the means for achieving them. The following sections first review relevant studies on this topic, and then describe the methodology and results for the review. Their implications and potential directions for future studies are also discussed.

2 Literature Review

Relevant studies on personalised learning have addressed a wide range of issues in this area. Early work, such as Clarke [11], already advocates the need for personalised learning, stating that school systems which provide undifferentiated education would undermine the overall performances of students because it neglects the fact that different students learn differently. Chen and Macredie [12] summarised the individual differences of learners into prior knowledge, cognitive style and gender, for which appropriate learning methods should be devised.

Personalised learning can be achieved through various means, which commonly involve technologies. For example, Jewitt et al. [13] proposed a learning platform for English learning in schools, which allowed students to access a broader range of learning resources and so enhanced their learning experiences. Kim et al. [14] presented another e-learning system which implemented real-time interactive video contents and provided learners with useful statistics about their learning progress, in order to help them to accomplish the learning objectives. Kong and Song [15] reported an initiative to encourage in-service teachers to bring their own devices as a 'personalised learning hub' for supporting the reflective engagement in a teacher professional development programme.

In relation to the effects of personalised learning, Campbell et al. [16] summarised its benefits as (1) enabling students to set their own targets, (2) allowing them to understand their progress better via continuous self-assessment for learning, (3) offering chances to have learning flexibility in terms of time and place, and (4) promoting students' self-motivation and self-regulation. In particular, Inayat et al. [17] delivered vocational training courses in a personalised e-learning environment, which was found to enhance learners' experience and learning outcomes. Hopkins et al. [18] showed that personalised learning could help to maintain connectedness to learning for children with health conditions during their time in hospital, and thus achieve inclusiveness in education. Besides the advantages, O'Donnell et al. [19] state that there are also issues, controversies and problems related to designing personalised learning activities, such as the limited technological literacy of students or teachers, the privacy issues in making use of learners' information, and the difficulties and cost for authoring diverse materials for personalised learning practices.

The literature on personalised learning reveals the diversity of development in this area. However, there is a lack of a comprehensive review which summarises the related work, resulting in difficulty in getting an overview of its current status in research and practice, as well as trends in publications.

3 Methodology

This study aims to review the publications related to personalised learning. It focuses on finding out (1) what aspects of learning have been personalised; (2) how learning has been personalised; and (3) the objectives of personalised learning. Relevant articles were collected from the Web-of-Science and Scopus for the period 2009–2018, using the keyword "personalised/personalized learning" for searching. A total of 406 results were initially found. Articles were excluded if they (1) were not written in English; (2) were not accessible in full paper form; and (3) did not involve personalised learning practices. Finally, a total of 179 studies were identified as relevant and were selected for the review.

The details of the selected articles were then coded and categorised, covering (a) year of publication; (b) level of education; (c) research issue; (d) means to achieve personalised learning; (e) aspects of learning being personalised; and (f) the objective of personalised learning. The information between 2009–13 and 2014–2018 was also compared in order to identify the trends in personalised learning.

4 Results

4.1 Year of Publication

Figure 1 shows the number of publications related to personalised learning through the years. There was a general upward trend—a 120% increase in the number of publications from 2009–13 to 2014–18. Since all the articles collected involved the practice of personalised learning, this result indicates that personalised learning has become an increasingly prevalent topic in research and practice.

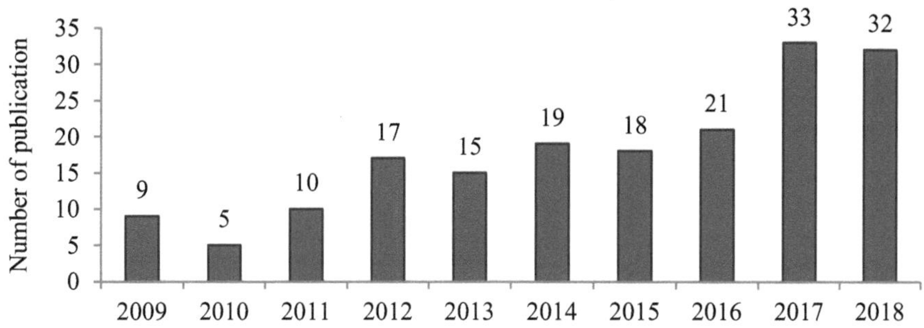

Fig. 1. Year of publication

4.2 Level of Education

Figure 2 presents the educational levels of the target learners in the studies collected. In the 2009–13 period, over half of the target participants were from higher education (56%), followed by primary (31%) and secondary (9%) education. In the 2014–18 period, higher education remained the largest target group, but with a lower proportion (46%). There was also a drop in the proportion of studies on primary education by 16%, but an increase of 10% in secondary education, as well as a higher proportion in preschool education, online learning and vocational training. The results indicate that studies on personalised learning have become more widespread among different educational levels.

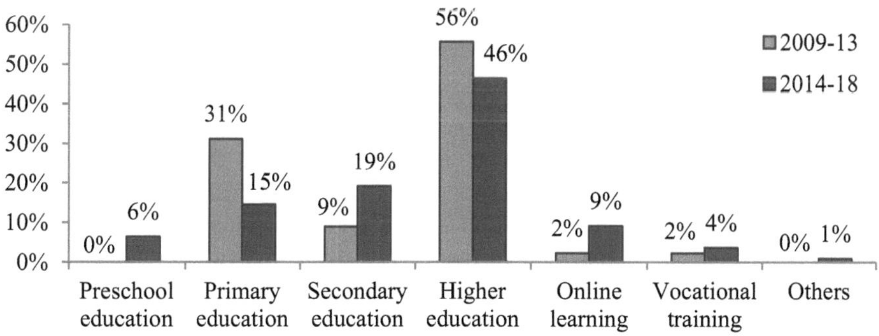

Fig. 2. Educational levels of target learners

4.3 Research Issues

Figure 3 shows the research issues related to personalised learning for the two periods. In 2009–13, above half (57%) of the articles addressed the effectiveness issues, followed by the satisfaction of learners (29%) and feasibility (12%) (i.e. whether personalised learning is compatible with conventional learning approaches). In 2014–18, effectiveness (50%) and satisfaction (19%) remained the two major research issues, but feasibility (2%) was not a focus any more. Instead, a greater variety of research issues were found in the second periods, including engagement, acceptance, learning outcomes, adaptability, challenges, and motivation for learners. This reflects that a greater range of research issues in personalised learning was being investigated.

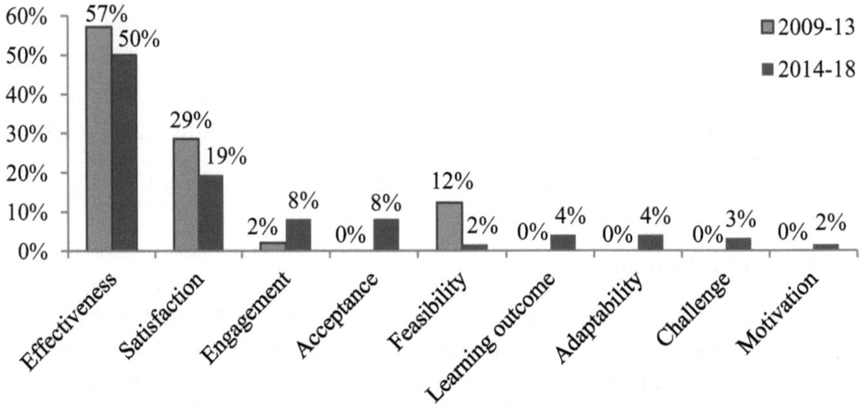

Note: A study may cover more than one issue.

Fig. 3. Research issues for the studies

4.4 Means to Achieve Personalised Learning

Figure 4 presents the means to achieve personalised learning in the studies. In the first period, a higher proportion of studies (32%) involved the development of intelligent learning systems for experimenting with new technologies (e.g. semantic web) and coping with learners' individual characteristics (e.g. cognitive abilities). This was followed by the use of mobile learning (e.g. supporting context-aware ubiquitous learning), intelligent tutoring systems (e.g. providing personalised recommendations), and learning management systems (e.g. integrating adaptive features) (15% for all three). In the second period, a broader range of means were found—and those which had emerged or become more popular in this period included learning analytics, MOOC, a flexible curriculum and instructional design, individual education plans, flipped classrooms and augmented/virtual reality. There were also other initiatives (4%), including the provision of academic advisory services, and the use of digital storytelling, geospatial technology, and speech recognition technology.

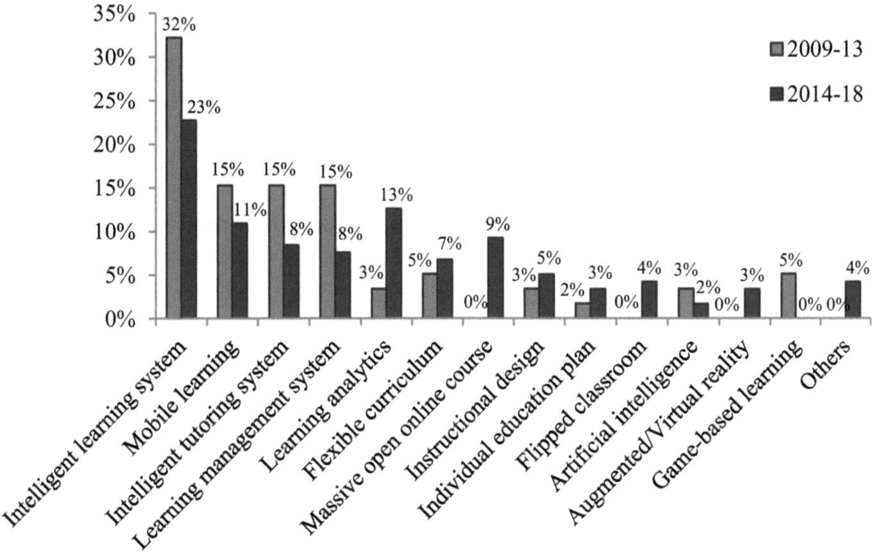

Note: A study may cover more than one means.

Fig. 4. Means to achieve personalised learning

4.5 Aspects of Personalised Learning

Figure 5 illustrates the aspects of learning which were personalised in the studies. The results for the two periods were similar. Learning methods were most frequently addressed, accounting for about half of the studies in each period. This was followed by learning materials, including the provision of materials catering for learners' needs and allowing learners to have flexibility in accessing their preferred materials. The time and places for learning, as well as teaching methods, were also the foci in some studies, with time for learning more frequently addressed in the second period. In addition, there were other aspects of personalisation, such as assessment methods and academic support for learners.

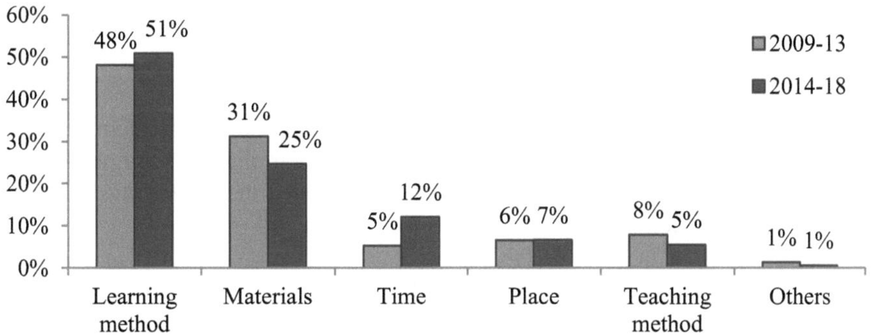

Note: A study may cover more than one aspect.

Fig. 5. Aspects of learning being personalised

4.6 Objectives of Personalised Learning

Figure 6 depicts the objectives of personalised learning as shown in the studies. For both periods, the largest proportion of studies (23% and 31%, respectively) were concerned with whether personalised learning could increase learning effectiveness, which is normally represented by a learner's academic performance. This was followed by the objectives of providing learners with a personalised learning path, and enhancing their learning motivation, learning outcomes, learning experience, and learning satisfaction. In the second period, there were also some studies with objectives from the teachers' perspective, such as predicting learners' learning outcomes as well as improving instructional practice and teaching performance.

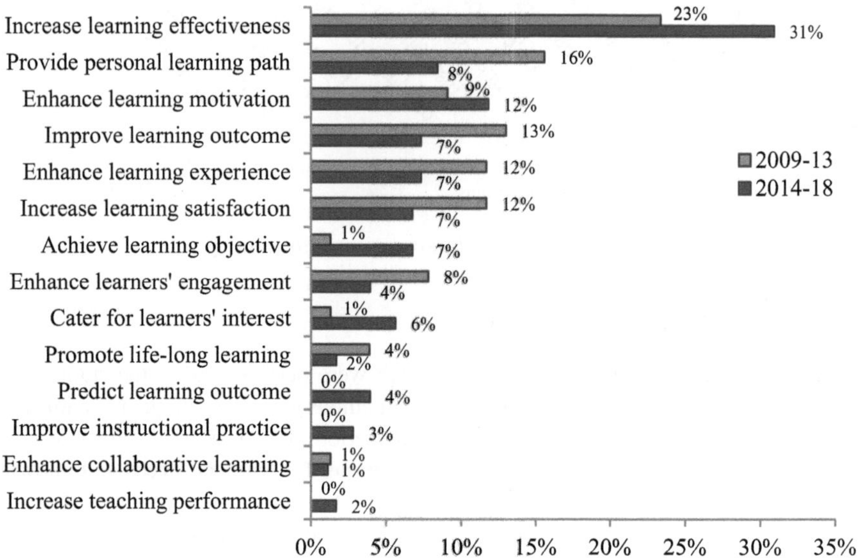

Note: A study may cover more than one objective.

Fig. 6. Objectives of personalised learning

5 Discussion

The findings of this study provide a comprehensive overview of the literature related to personalised learning in the past decade, showing how learning has been personalised in various studies. As a general trend, the studies revealed that personalised learning had become more widespread in terms of both research and practice.

Despite the fact that most of the studies reviewed were conducted in the higher education sector, there was a trend for other education sectors—ranging from preschool to secondary education, as well as online learning and vocational training—to be receiving increasing attention. Patrick et al. [2] interpret this as being due to the common efforts by the sectors to facilitate learners' success through addressing their individual differences and needs, and to capitalise on the latest technological advances for achieving this goal. Following the prevalence of personalised learning in research and practice, the focus of the literature has shifted from mainly examining the effectiveness of various ways to achieve personalised learning and learners' satisfaction with them to a wider range of issues related to their implementation, such as learners' acceptance, adaptability and challenges.

The various means for achieving personalised learning indicate that the conceptualisation of personalised learning—as an umbrella term overlapping with other education concepts, such as differentiated instruction and learning analytics—can be played out in a myriad of ways [1]. The means are not limited to technologies, but also cover flexibility in curriculum and instructional design, as well as individual goal-setting for learners. The recent studies further demonstrate the potential of emerging technologies for personalising learning, as shown by the increasing use of learning analytics, MOOCs and augmented/virtual reality. However, while recent work has started to address the research issues related to the challenges for personalised learning, the difficulties related to the use of emerging technologies in personalised learning practices have yet to be widely examined [20–22]. For example, Gašević et al. [23] point out the critical challenges for learning analytics to make a long-term impact on the practice of learning and teaching—such as the data limitations and lack of a data-informed decision-making culture, which may also hinder its effective use for personalised learning. Future studies should address this gap so that the potential of the latest technologies can be fully exploited for achieving personalised learning.

The aspects of learning being personalised in previous studies focus mainly on learning methods and materials. The relevant learning methods have commonly involved the application of personalisation strategies in a conventional classroom setting, student-centred activities, and the use of technology for planning, instruction, assessment and record-keeping [24]. The aspect of learning materials was related to their provision, recommendation and access for individual students based on their profiles [25]. However, other aspects, such as the time and place for learning, have been studied less, and the diverse needs of learners on these aspects might have been neglected [26]. The results suggest that, for a more balanced development, future studies should pay more attention to the aspects of learning which have received less consideration to date.

The wide range of objectives of personalised learning shown in the previous studies suggest different ways for attaining its benefits for learners and teachers. Other than increasing learning effectiveness, as a major objective found in the studies, most of the other objectives were usually related to learners, such as learning motivation, experience, satisfaction, engagement, and interest. Those related to teachers, such as improving instructional practice and teaching performance, have been covered only in a few studies in recent years. In particular, while personalised learning emphasises student-centredness to respond to students' individual needs and interests, and gives them more control over their own learning, the roles of educators and students in the learning and teaching process are also reshaped [2]. How educators have transformed themselves for offering personalised support for students should receive more consideration in future studies.

6 Conclusion

This paper has presented a comprehensive review of studies related to personalised learning in the past decade. The results highlight a growing interest in this area from the field, as well as a broadening focus on its research and practice in terms of the range of educational levels, research issues, and objectives. They also show how, and in what aspects, personalised learning has been achieved. Most of the means for achieving personalised learning involve the use of technology, including particularly the latest technologies, such as learning analytics, MOOCs and augmented/virtual reality which have emerged in recent years.

The results contribute to revealing the latest development in personalised learning and the research directions which are worth further investigation. First, the increasing adoption of emerging technologies, besides allowing more possibilities for personalising learning, also leads to the challenges arising from the technologies themselves that need to be tackled. Second, the aspects of learning other than learning methods and materials, such as the time and place for learning, should receive more attention. Finally, the perspective of teachers, in particular their changing role in the trend to student-centred personalised learning, has yet to be adequately addressed. Future work on these research directions will help to realise the potential of personalised learning in diverse educational contexts.

References

1. Groff, J.: Personalized learning: The state of the field & future directions. Center for Curriculum Redesign (2017)
2. Patrick, S., Kennedy, K., Powell, A.: Mean what you say: defining and integrating personalized, blended and competency education. International Association for K-12 Online Learning (iNACOL), Vienna (2013)
3. Li, K.C., Wong, B.T.M.: Advancing teaching with massive open online courses: a review of case studies. Int. J. Innov. Learn. **25**(2), 141–155 (2019)
4. Li, K.C., Wong, B.T.M., Choi, S.P.M.: Trends in learning analytics practices: a review of higher education institutions. Interact. Technol. Smart Educ. **15**(2), 132–154 (2018)
5. Education Elements: 2016–2017 impact reprot: Building capacity for personalized learning and more. Education Elements (2017)
6. National Association of State Boards of Education: Most likely to succeed: Policy making in support of a restructured high school. NASBE, Alexandria (2002)
7. Scott, E., Soria, A., Campo, M.: Adaptive 3D virtual learning environments – a review of the literature. IEEE Trans. Learn. Technol. **10**(3), 262–276 (2017)
8. Berge, Z.L.: If you think socialisation in mLearning is difficult, try personalisation. Int. J. Mob. Learn. Organ. **5**(3/4), 231–238 (2011)
9. O'Donnell, E., Sharp, M., Wade, V., O'Donnell, L.: Personalised e-learning: the assessment of students' prior knowledge in higher education. In: Wang, V.X. (eds) Handbook of Research on Education and Technology in a Changing Society, pp. 744–755. IGI Global (2014)
10. Gabarre, S., Gabarre, C., Din, R.: Personalizing learning: a critical review of language learning with mobile phones and social networking sites. J. Adv. Res. Dyn. Control. Syst. **10**(2), 1782–1786 (2018)

11. Clarke, J.: Changing systems to personalize learning: Introduction to the personalization workshops. Brown University (2003)
12. Chen, S.Y., Macredie, R.: Web-based interaction: a review of three important human factors. Int. J. Inf. Manag. **30**(5), 379–387 (2010)
13. Jewitt, C., Clark, W., Hadjithoma-Garstka, C.: The use of learning platforms to organise learning in English primary and secondary schools. Learn. Media Technol. **36**(4), 335–348 (2011)
14. Kim, J., Hwang, D., Park, S.I., Lee, H., Hong, C., Kim, W.: Personalized interactive e-learning system using expanded SCORM. Appl. Math. Inf. Sci. **8**(1L), 133–139 (2014)
15. Kong, S.C., Song, Y.: An experience of personalized learning hub initiative embedding BYOD for reflective engagement in higher education. Comput. Educ. **88**, 227–240 (2015)
16. Campbell, R.J., Robinson, W., Neelands, J., Hewston, R., Mazzoli, L.: Personalised learning: ambiguities in theory and practice. Br. J. Educ. Stud. **55**(2), 135–154 (2007)
17. Inayat, I., ul Amin, R., Inayat, Z., Salim, S.S.: Effects of collaborative web based vocational education and training (VET) on learning outcomes. Comput. Educ. **68**, 153–166 (2013)
18. Hopkins, L., Moss, J., Green, J., Strong, G.: Embedding learning in a paediatric hospital: changing practice and keeping connected. Int. J. Incl. Educ. **18**(3), 312–321 (2014)
19. O'Donnell, E., Sharp, M., Wade, V.P., O'Donnell, L.: Challenges encountered in creating personalised learning activities to suit students learning preferences. In: Kats, Y., (ed.) Learning Management Systems and Instructional Design: Best Practices in Online Education, pp. 263–287. IGI Global (2013)
20. Wong, B.T.M.: Learning analytics in higher education: an analysis of case studies. Asian Assoc. Open Univ. J. **12**(1), 21–40 (2017)
21. Wong, B.T.M.: Factors leading to effective teaching of MOOCs. Asian Assoc. Open Univ. J. **11**(1), 105–118 (2016)
22. Li, K.C., Lee, L.Y.-K., Wong, S.-L., Yau, I.S-Y., Wong, B.T.-M.: Evaluation of the use of mobile devices for clinical practicum in nursing education. In: Cheung, S.K.S., Kwok, L.-f., Kubota, K., Lee, L.-K., Tokito, J. (eds.) ICBL 2018. LNCS, vol. 10949, pp. 215–226. Springer, Cham (2018). https://doi.org/10.1007/978-3-319-94505-7_17
23. Gašević, D., Dawson, S., Pardo, A.: How do we start? State and directions of learning analytics adoption. International Council for Open and Distance Education (2016)
24. Lee, D., Huh, Y., Lin, C.Y., Reigeluth, C.M.: Technology functions for personalized learning in learner-centered schools. Educ. Technol. Res. Dev. **66**(5), 1269–1302 (2018)
25. Yao, C.B.: Constructing a user-friendly and smart ubiquitous personalized learning environment by using a context-aware mechanism. IEEE Trans. Learn. Technol. **10**(1), 104–114 (2017)
26. Li, K.C., Wong, B.T.M., Wong, B.Y.Y.: Catering for diverse needs for student support: differences between face-to-face and distance-learning students. In: the 29th Annual Conference of the Asian Association of Open Universities, Kuala Lumpur, Malaysia (2015)

A Personalized Task Recommendation System for Vocabulary Learning Based on Readability and Diversity

Haoran Xie[1], Minhong Wang[2], Di Zou[1(✉)], and Fu Lee Wang[3]

[1] The Education University of Hong Kong, Tai Po, New Territories, Hong Kong SAR, China
dzou@eduhk.hk
[2] The University of Hong Kong, Pokfulam, Hong Kong Island, Hong Kong SAR, China
[3] The Open University of Hong Kong, Ho Man Tin, Kowloon, Hong Kong SAR, China

Abstract. Vocabulary learning is the foundation of language acquisition for second language learners. To assist language learners' vocabulary learning, this research investigated a personalized task recommendation system based on readability and diversity. A word learning theory, the involvement load hypothesis, has also been applied as the theoretical framework of the system to facilitate task recommendation. Ten Chinese learners of English were invited to participate in the research and used the system for vocabulary learning for around two weeks. These students were all intermediate learners. The participants' learning experience, outcomes, motivation and attitude were measured respectively using questionnaires, pretests, posttests, and interviews. The results showed that the participants were very satisfied with the learning experience, and positive learning outcomes and attitudes were observed. Many students stated that they would love to keep using the proposed recommendation system for future language learning. It is also suggested that the wide use of this system will benefit many self-access language learners.

Keywords: Personalized learning · Word learning · Recommendation system · Diversity · Readability

1 Introduction

The rapid growth of Web resources in recent years has provided new learning methods and opportunities (e.g., learning applications for mobile phones, massive open online courses [MOOCs] and augmented reality or virtual reality) for language learners. Self-access learners can acquire desired knowledge and skills at their own pace using the extensive collection of learning resources on the Web. However, learners are easily distracted due to information overload in the era of big data (Bawden and Robinson 2009). For example, high drop-out rates are always observed in MOOC platforms for self-paced learners (Perna et al. 2014). According to Nielson (2011), only 7 out of 176 participants used their developed computer-assisted language-learning system named

S. K. S. Cheung et al. (Eds.): ICBL 2019, LNCS 11546, pp. 82–92, 2019.
https://doi.org/10.1007/978-3-030-21562-0_7

Auralog for more than 25 h. To address this problem, computational personalized models have been proposed and widely adopted in e-learning systems (Chen 2008; Chen and Chung 2008; Hwang et al. 2010; Hwang et al. 2012; Zou et al. 2014; Brusilovsky et al. 2016; Xie et al. 2016a, b and 2017a, b). Computational personalized models can cater to individual learning needs and only provide necessary learning resources according to personalized learning objectives.

This research aims to integrate personalized techniques in the field of computer science to a set of developed learning tasks in the field of vocabulary learning in a recommendation system. Rather than focusing on offering different learning sequences of target words to learners in extant studies related to computer-assisted vocabulary learning (Chen and Chung 2008; Chen and Li 2010; Huang et al. 2012; Golonka et al. 2014; Huang and Chiu 2015; Tsai et al. 2016), the research focused on personalized vocabulary learning and were guided by a linguistic learning theory called "involvement load hypothesis (hereafter, ILH)" (Laufer and Hulstijn 2001).

Specifically, two personalized strategies, diversity and readability which are corresponded to the cognitive dimension and motivational dimension of the ILH, were integrated into the proposed vocabulary learning systems. Diversity refers to suggest more diverse learning tasks to the learner. The purpose of diversity is to train various aspects of word usage by recommending various types of learning tasks according to the cognitive load distributions of learners. For example, a learner who has taken too many cloze-exercises recently will be suggested to take other types like inferencing so that the learner will be trained in both "search" and "evaluation" components of word usage according to involvement load hypothesis (Laufer and Hulstijn 2001; Zou 2017). The readability refers to provide more readable contexts to a specific learner. The objective of readability is to support self-paced vocabulary learning and increase the motivational loads by offering learning tasks with readable contexts. For example, a learner who is familiar with computer science articles according to his/her learning history will be recommended to take the task contexts related to computer science. In this way, the self-paced vocabulary learning will be supported with task containing preferred topics, which may further increase the motivational loads (i.e., from moderate to strong in the need component) according to the involvement load hypothesis (Laufer and Hulstijn 2001; Lee and Pulido 2017).

Furthermore, there have been several studies to support and verify the effectiveness of employment of diversity and readability in learning. Readability and diversity have been found by numerous studies on both e-learning and vocabulary acquisitions to be effective personalized strategies in facilitating vocabulary learning. Specifically, Lee and Pulido (2017) found that tasks with familiar contexts or interesting topics to learners will facilitate vocabulary learning. Kim and Tracy-Ventura (2013) argued that the repetition of the same type of learning tasks will reduce learning interest and fail to assist learners in processing a word in a new context. Furthermore, the integration of readability and diversity into a personalized learning system can improve word-learning retention rate and increase learning motivation, as shown in our earlier study (Zou et al. 2014; Xie et al. 2016a, b). This is innovative research on personalized language learning as it was guided by the linguistic theory, ILH, for task recommendations.

2 Literature Review

2.1 Personalized Techniques

Personalized techniques are crucial tools to address information overload in the era of big data. Jeh and Widom (2003) presented graph-theoretical results, and proposed a technique based on these results, that encodes personalized views as partial vectors which enable search engines to add bias importance scores according to a user-specified set of initially interesting pages. Speretta and Gauch (2005) explored the use of a less-invasive means of gathering user information for personalized search by building user profiles based on activities at the search site itself and studying the use of these profiles to provide personalized search results. Dou et al. (2007) presented a large-scale evaluation framework for personalized search based on query logs, and then evaluated five personalized search strategies (including two click-based and three profile-based ones) using a 12-day MSN query log.

Xie et al. (2012) introduced the concept of user communities in social media platforms and presented a personalized view for the resources to accurately access information. Kumar and Sharan (2014) proposed a framework for constructing an enhanced user profile by using user's browsing history and enriching it using domain knowledge which can be used to improve the performance of personalized Web search. Wang et al. (2016) proposed a preference recommendation scheme to complement a user's concept map to improve the accuracy of the personalized search.

Aside from the aforementioned computational models, personalized e-learning systems have also been developed. For example, Chen (2008) assessed a genetic-based personalized e-learning system that can generate appropriate learning paths according to the incorrect testing responses of an individual learner in a pre-test. The idea has been adopted in a mobile vocabulary learning system for personalization based on item–response theory (Chen and Chung 2008). Chen and Li (2010) proposed a personalized vocabulary learning system to be used in the school setting. Huang et al. (2010) developed a ubiquitous English vocabulary-learning system to assist students in experiencing a systematic vocabulary learning process in which ubiquitous technology is used to develop the system, and video clips are used as the material. Golonka et al. (2014) reviewed various technology-enhanced language-learning systems developed in recent years. In our previous studies (Zou et al. 2014, 2017; Xie et al. 2016a, b), several personalized strategies, including readability and diversity, are compared with non-personalized vocabulary-learning systems and were found to be effective.

2.2 Vocabulary Acquisition

Research on vocabulary acquisition mainly covers two areas: word knowledge and vocabulary learning. Topics in word knowledge involve numerous issues related to words, such as what different types of knowledge word knowledge entail and how one's word knowledge can be measured, whereas topics in vocabulary learning emphasize on questions, such as how various aspects of word knowledge can be effectively acquired, what aspects are generally easier to acquire and why.

Word Knowledge. Researchers in vocabulary acquisition generally agree that word. Knowledge is a continuum of one unique system composed of receptive and productive knowledge (Crow 1986; Webb 2005). For the measurement of word knowledge, researchers argued that distinction should be made between the breadth and depth of word knowledge (Read and Chapelle 2004; Nassaji 2006). The breadth dimension, also referred to as vocabulary size, refers to the number of words that learners know at a particular level of language proficiency (Horwitz 1988). A typical method for measuring breadth is the vocabulary-level test (Read 2007). The depth dimension, on the other hand, represents the quality of words known by a learner (Schmitt 2008). Some evaluation methods have been devised to measure the depth of word knowledge, such as word association test (Bahar and Hansell 2000) and lexical frequency profile (Laufer and Nation 1995).

Vocabulary Learning. Vocabulary learning is a cumulative process with an incremental nature (Fraser 1999). Two main kinds of taxonomies are used to classify different types of vocabulary learning: implicit and explicit, incidental and intentional (Laufer and Hulstijn 2001; Schmitt 2008). According to Laufer and Hulstijn (2001), the recognition and production of vocabulary learning mainly involve implicit learning, while mediation and meaning involve an explicit process. However, finding a situation in which only one type of learning is engaged is challenging (Reber 1989). Another theory demarcates vocabulary learning with the intention to ensure that a distinction is made between incidental learning and intentional learning. Intentional learning is primarily intended to deliberately commit word knowledge in mind, while incidental learning is intended to place the attention in another place and learn them indirectly. A typical example of an incidental vocabulary learning activity is that students read and negotiate the meaning of a word (Newton 2001). These theories and findings are critical to developing vocabulary-learning systems for language learners.

3 Method

3.1 Personalized Framework Construction

The personalized framework was adopted from our previous study on a personalized vocabulary-learning system (Zou et al. 2014). Generally, the personalized framework was developed based on the relationships among learners, tasks and words. As shown in Fig. 1, the relationships of these three parties were essentially in a hierarchical structure. Each learner had learned several learning tasks, and each task contained many target words within a task. Furthermore, one target word may be included in multiple learning tasks. The core of the personalized framework was the learner model, which consisted of three categories of data:

Historical Learning Tasks. The category of data was the set of all tasks that had been learned by the user. The timestamp and post-test results of each historical task had been recorded. The data were kept for the understanding of the workload and knowledge of all target words of each learner.

Task Type Preferences. The task type preferences estimated the degree of preferences for a learner to a specific task type. The preference degrees based on the assumption that learners were preferable to the task types that had not been encountered in his/her recent learning.

Word-Knowledge Degrees. Word-knowledge degrees were the data on the degrees of word knowledge which were measured by the involvement load hypothesis and learning performance.

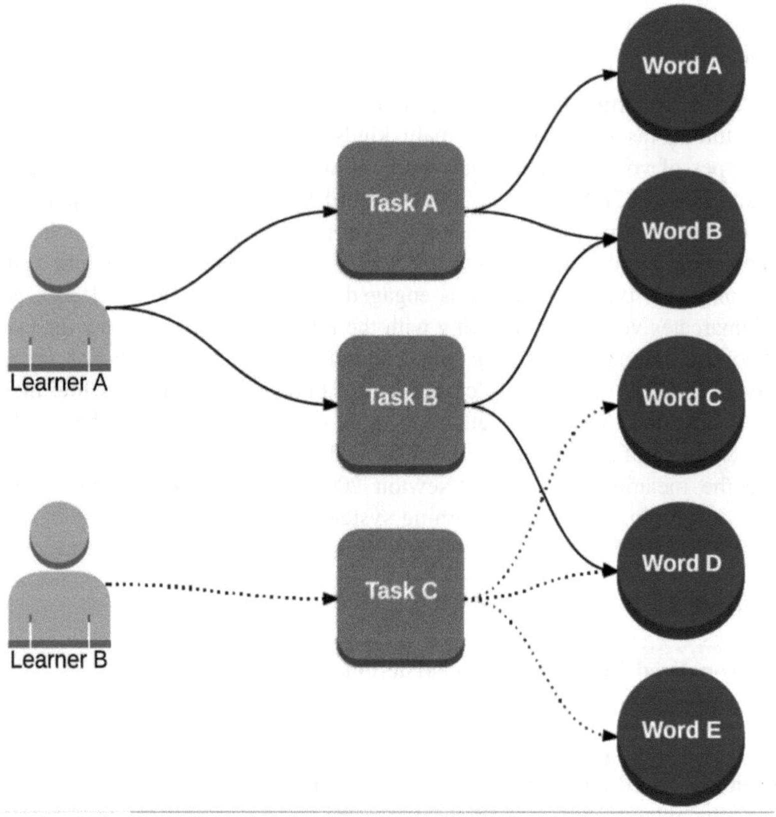

Fig. 1. The relationships among learners, tasks and words (Zou et al. 2014)

3.2 Learning Task Development

Two principles were adopted for the development of learning tasks. Firstly, the workload of each learning task ought to be relatively small to ensure that the learner can complete the task within 10 min. Secondly, the learning tasks ought to have different working loads distributed in all three components (i.e., search, evaluation and need) of the involvement load hypothesis. Specifically, the following tasks were developed for the project:

Cloze Exercises. The learner is given an excerpt of an article and must identify the correct word choice to fill the blank in the article.

Sentence Writing. The learner is to use the target word to create an original context surrounding the word.

Reading Comprehension and Dictionary Consultation. The learner is provided with a short paragraph of an article and required to consult the e-dictionary for target words.

Reading Comprehension and Inferencing. The learner is provided with the same excerpt of an article and required to write the semantic meaning of target words.

In the personalized learning process, the learners were recommended to do some learning tasks. As mentioned, personalized learning followed two strategies: (i) readability (e.g., a learner who was familiar with computer science articles according to his/her learning history would be recommended to take on computer science-related tasks) and (ii) diversity (e.g., a learner who had recently taken too many cloze exercises would be advised to take other types of tests, such as inferencing exercises).

Table 1. Dimensions, components and degrees in ILH (Zou et al. 2014)

	Search	Evaluation	Need
None	√	√	√
Moderate	√	√	√
Strong	–	√	√
No. of levels	2	3	3

Furthermore, these tasks had been investigated in our previous studies (Zou 2016, 2017) and found to be effective in covering different components in the involvement load hypothesis, as shown in Table 1.

3.3 Recommendations Based on Readability and Diversity

The main objective of recommendation in the vocabulary learning system was to suggest learning tasks to learners to facilitate their self-paced vocabulary learning. To increase the learning motivation, two factors, namely, readability and diversity, were considered.

Diversity. Diversity refers to suggest more diverse learning tasks to the learner. The purpose of diversity was to train various aspects of word usage by recommending various types of learning tasks according to the cognitive load distributions of learners.

For example, a learner who had taken too many cloze-exercises recently would be suggested to take other types like inferencing so that the learner can be trained in both "search" and "evaluation" components of word usage according to the ILH. In other words, the task type should be different from recent learning tasks taken by the learner (Xie et al., 2016a, b). This strategy has been theoretically supported by a linguistic study (Kim and Tracy-Ventura 2013) which argued that the repetition of the same type of learning tasks would reduce the learning interest and fail to assist learners in processing a word in a new context. Formally, diversity can be interpreted as selecting tasks which had the maximal overall dissimilarity with the learner's recent learning tasks.

$$t'' = arg\ \max_{t \in T}\left(\sum\nolimits_{t_i \in T_i} dis(t, t_i)\right) \tag{1}$$

In Eq. (2), t and T are defined as above, t_i is a recent learning task, T_i is a set of recent learning tasks in the learner's profile as defined in Eq. (2) and $dis(t,t_i)$ is the degree of the task type dissimilarity between two tasks. The aim of argmax function is to select the task t'' with the maximal overall dissimilarity.

Readability. Readability refers to provide more readable contexts to a specific learner. The objective of readability was to support self-paced vocabulary learning and increase the motivational loads by offering learning tasks with readable contexts. For example, a learner who was familiar with computer science articles according to his/her learning history would be recommended to take the task contexts related to computer science. In this way, the self-paced vocabulary learning would be supported with tasks containing preferred topics, which may further increase the motivational loads (i.e., from moderate to strong in the need component) according to the ILH (Laufer and Hulstijn 2001; Lee and Pulido 2017). The assumption is that learning motivation would be increased if the learner has extensively read the learning context (Xie et al. 2016a, b). This assumption has been supported by a recent linguistic study (Lee & Pulido) which investigated the effect of readability. Formally, readability is expressed by the following mathematical measurement:

$$read(C, L) = \frac{C \cdot L}{||C|| \times ||L||} \tag{2}$$

In this equation, C is a word vector of context, and L is the word-knowledge vector of a learner. A high value of reading indicates high readability. The recommendation algorithm would select tasks with high readability.

The recommendation algorithm was a content-based approach which aimed to identify the most similar/nearest items based on the learner personalized model. The content-based approach, which only required a short period of user interaction with systems, would be more robust to the data sparsity problem than collaborative filtering recommendations. Table 2 presents the detailed steps of the recommendation algorithm. The core idea was to recommend a learning task to optimize both readability and diversity based on the learning logs of the learner.

Table 2. Learning task recommendation algorithm

```
Data: learner profile l_j; the set of learnt tasks T_j and words W_j in l_j;
Result: The recommended learning task Tk_g
for each t_x ∈ T do
    Compute dis(t_x, T_j) for each t_x by Equation (1);
    for each type(Tk_a) == t_x do
        Compute read(c_a, W_j) for each c_x by Equation (2);
        Compute overall = dis() × read();
    end
end
Choose Tk_* with the max overall value;
Tk_g ← Tk_*;
```

3.4 Experimental Verification

The task was to design experimental processes to verify the effectiveness of the proposed system for vocabulary learning. The evaluation processes involved two stages.

Preliminary Stage. The preliminary stage had two steps. Firstly, the invited subjects (university graduates) took traditional instructions in an online English course to ensure that the learner could review skills and basic knowledge of vocabulary learning. Secondly, an online training workshop was organized to demonstrate how the system was used. This stage aimed to verify whether all participants had common knowledge of vocabulary learning skills and system usage.

Learning Stage. The learning stage can be divided into three steps: (a) pre-tests and pre-questionnaires, (b) vocabulary learning via the system, and (c) post-tests and post-questionnaires. The first step aimed to examine the proficiency of the participants. The duration of this step was approximately two weeks. The final step was to conduct a post-test and post-questionnaire. The word knowledge and retention rate were examined to verify the proposed system.

3.5 Participant Recruitment and Assignment

10 Chinese learners of English were invited to participate in the experiments of this project.

- Language proficiency. The participants were all intermediate English learners.
- Disciplines. The participants were from different disciplines (e.g., science, arts, engineering, social science).
- Demographic features. The participants aged between 18 and 21. The numbers of male and female learners were equal.

4 Results and Conclusion

The results showed that the students had a very positive attitude toward this word learning system and considered it "motivative and effective". All participants reported that their learning experience was very satisfactory, and they were interested in the recommended tasks. Concerning the learning outcomes of the learners, the posttest scores indicated that most learners benefited much from the learning experience. Many participants felt excited that the system could recommend tasks that they tended to enjoy learning based on their learning history and personal preferences. One student commented in the post-interview that "I'm surprised about how smart the system is". Around 90% of the participants agreed that it was effective to learn target words through doing different word learning tasks, as diverse tasks focus on different aspects of word knowledge, and doing various tasks assisted them in learning various knowledge aspects. Participants also felt the interface user-friendly and the system easy-to-use.

Generally, 9 out of 10 participants stated that they would love to keep learning with this system, as they believed that the system could help them improve their English language proficiency. One student reported that "this system is very useful for self-access learners who cannot seek help from teachers anytime; if the system can be widely applied, a large number of students would be able to successfully improve their language learning effectiveness and efficiency".

This research investigated a personalized word learning system which recommended vocabulary learning tasks under the guidance of the ILH. The results showed that the participants were very satisfied with the learning experience, and positive learning outcomes and attitudes were observed. This research is limited in that only a small number of students participated in the research, and future studies may involve a larger sample size so that the research findings can be better generalized.

Acknowledgement. The research in this paper was supported by the Innovation and Technology Fund (Project No. GHP/022/17GD) from the Innovation and Technology Commission of the Government of the Hong Kong Special Administrative Region, the Standing Committee on Language Education and Research (EDB(LE)/P&R/EL/175/2), the Government of the Hong Kong Special Administrative Region and the Funding Support to ECS Proposal Rated 3.5 (RG16/2018-2019R), The Education University of Hong Kong.

References

Bahar, M., Hansell, M.H.: The relationship between some psychological factors and their effect on the performance of grid questions and word association tests. Educ. Psychol. **20**(3), 349–364 (2000)

Bawden, D., Robinson, L.: The dark side of information: overload, anxiety and other paradoxes and pathologies. J. Inf. Sci. **35**(2), 180–191 (2009)

Brusilovsky, P., Somyürek, S., Guerra, J., Hosseini, R., Zadorozhny, V., Durlach, P.J.: Open social student modeling for personalized learning. IEEE Trans. Emerg. Top. Comput. **4**(3), 450–461 (2016)

Chen, C.M.: Intelligent web-based learning system with personalized learning path guidance. Comput. Educ. **51**(2), 787–814 (2008)

Chen, C.M., Chung, C.J.: Personalized mobile English vocabulary learning system based on item response theory and learning memory cycle. Comput. Educ. **51**(2), 624–645 (2008)
Chen, C.M., Li, Y.L.: Personalised context-aware ubiquitous learning system for supporting effective English vocabulary learning. Interact. Learn. Environ. **18**(4), 341–364 (2010)
Crow, J.T.: Receptive vocabulary acquisition for reading comprehension. Mod. Lang. J. **70**(3), 242–250 (1986)
Dou, Z., Song, R., Wen, J.R.: A large-scale evaluation and analysis of personalized search strategies. In: Proceedings of the 16th International Conference on World Wide Web, pp. 581–590. ACM (2007)
Fraser, C.A.: Lexical processing strategy use and vocabulary learning through reading. Stud. Second. Lang. Acquis. **21**(02), 225–241 (1999)
Golonka, E.M., Bowles, A.R., Frank, V.M., Richardson, D.L., Freynik, S.: Technologies for foreign language learning: a review of technology types and their effectiveness. Comput. Assist. Lang. Learn. **27**(1), 70–105 (2014)
Horwitz, E.K.: The beliefs about language learning of beginning university foreign language students. Mod. Lang. J. **72**(3), 283–294 (1988)
Huang, Y.M., Huang, Y.M., Huang, S.H., Lin, Y.T.: A ubiquitous English vocabulary learning system: evidence of active/passive attitudes vs usefulness/ease-of-use. Comput. Educ. **58**(1), 273–282 (2012)
Huang, Y.M., Chiu, P.S.: The effectiveness of a meaningful learning-based evaluation model for context-aware mobile learning. Br. J. Educ. Technol. **46**(2), 437–447 (2015)
Hwang, G.J., Kuo, F.R., Yin, P.Y., Chuang, K.H.: A heuristic algorithm for planning personalized learning paths for context-aware ubiquitous learning. Comput. Educ. **54**(2), 404–415 (2010)
Hwang, G.J., Sung, H.Y., Hung, C.M., Huang, I., Tsai, C.C.: Development of a personalized educational computer game based on students' learning styles. Educ. Technol. Res. Dev. **60** (4), 623–638 (2012)
Jeh, G., Widom, J.: Scaling personalized web search. In: Proceedings of the 12th International Conference on World Wide Web, pp. 271–279. ACM (2003)
Kim, Y., Tracy-Ventura, N.: The role of task repetition in L2 performance development: what needs to be repeated during task-based interaction? System **41**(3), 829–840 (2013)
Kumar, R., Sharan, A.: Personalized web search using browsing history and domain knowledge. In: Proceedings of the International Conference on Issues and Challenges in Intelligent Computing Techniques (ICICT), pp. 493–497. IEEE (2014)
Laufer, B., Hulstijn, J.: Incidental vocabulary acquisition in a second language: the construct of task-induced involvement. Appl. Linguist. **22**(1), 1–26 (2001)
Laufer, B., Nation, P.: Vocabulary size and use: lexical richness in L2 written production. Appl. Linguist. **16**(3), 307–322 (1995)
Lee, S., Pulido, D.: The impact of topic interest, L2 proficiency, and gender on EFL incidental vocabulary acquisition through reading. Lang. Teach. Res. **21**(1), 118–135 (2017)
Nassaji, H.: The relationship between depth of vocabulary knowledge and L2 learners' lexical inferencing strategy use and success. Mod. Lang. J. **90**(3), 387–401 (2006)
Newton, J.: Options for vocabulary learning through communication tasks. ELT J. **55**(1), 30–37 (2001)
Nielson, K.B.: Self-study with language learning software in the workplace: What happens. Lang. Learn. Technol. **15**(3), 110–129 (2011)
Perna, L.W., Ruby, A., Boruch, R.F., Wang, N., Scull, J., Ahmad, S., Evans, C.: Moving through MOOCs: understanding the progression of users in massive open online courses. Educ. Res. **43**(9), 421–432 (2014)

Read, J., Chapelle, C.A.: A framework for second language vocabulary assessment. Lang. Test. **18**(1), 1–32 (2001)

Read, J.: Teaching and learning vocabulary: bringing research into practice. Stud. Second. Lang. Acquis. **29**(1), 128–129 (2007)

Reber, A.S.: Implicit learning and tacit knowledge. J. Exp. Psychol. Gen. **118**(3), 219 (1989)

Schmitt, N.: Review article: instructed second language vocabulary learning. Lang. Teach. Res. **12**(3), 329–363 (2008)

Speretta, M., Gauch, S.: Personalized search based on user search histories. In Proceedings of the 2005 IEEE/WIC/ACM International Conference on Web Intelligence, pp. 622–628. IEEE (2005)

Tsai, P.S., Tsai, C.C., Hwang, G.H.: The effects of instructional methods on students' learning outcomes requiring different cognitive abilities: context-aware ubiquitous learning versus traditional instruction. Interact. Learn. Environ. **24**(7), 1497–1510 (2016)

UBS: Do I earn enough for the life I want? The Report on Prices and earnings, pp. 1–42 (2015)

Wang, H., Shao, S., Zhou, X., Wan, C., Bouguettaya, A.: Preference recommendation for personalized search. Knowl.-Based Syst. **100**, 124–136 (2016)

Webb, S.: Receptive and productive vocabulary learning: the effects of reading and writing on word knowledge. Stud. Second Lang. Acquis. **27**(01), 33–52 (2005)

Xie, H., Li, Q., Cai, Y.: Community-aware resource profiling for personalized search in folksonomy. J. Comput. Sci. Technol. **27**(3), 599–610 (2012)

Xie, H., Li, Q., Mao, X., Li, X., Cai, Y., Rao, Y.: Community-aware user profile enrichment in folksonomy. Neural Netw. **58**, 111–121 (2014)

Xie, H., et al.: Incorporating sentiment into tag-based user profiles and resource profiles for personalized search in folksonomy. Inf. Process. Manag. **52**(1), 61–72 (2016a)

Xie, H., Zou, D., Wang, F.L., Wong, T.L., Rao, Y., Wang, S.H.: Discover learning path for group users: a profile-based approach. Neurocomputing, **254**, 59–70 (2017a)

Xie, H., Zou, D., Lau, R.Y., Wang, F.L., Wong, T.L.: Generating incidental word-learning tasks via topic-based and load-based profiles. IEEE Multimedia, **23**(1), 60–70 (2016b)

Xie, H., Zou, D., Wang, F.L., Wong, T.-L.: A review on recent development of the involvement load hypothesis. In: Cheung, S.K.S., Kwok, L., Ma, W.W.K., Lee, L.-K., Yang, H. (eds.) ICBL 2017. LNCS, vol. 10309, pp. 447–452. Springer, Cham (2017b). https://doi.org/10.1007/978-3-319-59360-9_39

Zou, D., Xie, H., Li, Q., Wang, F.L., Chen, W.: The load-based learner profile for incidental word learning task generation. In: Popescu, E., Lau, R.W.H., Pata, K., Leung, H., Laanpere, M. (eds.) ICWL 2014. LNCS, vol. 8613, pp. 190–200. Springer, Cham (2014). https://doi.org/10.1007/978-3-319-09635-3_21

Zou, D., Xie, H., Wang, F.L., Wong, T.-L., Wu, Q.: Investigating the effectiveness of the uses of electronic and paper-based dictionaries in promoting incidental word learning. In: Cheung, S.K.S., Kwok, L., Yang, H., Fong, J., Kwan, R. (eds.) ICHL 2015. LNCS, vol. 9167, pp. 59–69. Springer, Cham (2015). https://doi.org/10.1007/978-3-319-20621-9_5

Zou, D., Xie, H., Rao, Y., Wong, T.L., Wang, F.L., Wu, Q.: A comparative study on various vocabulary knowledge scales for predicting vocabulary pre-knowledge. Int. J. Distance Educ. Technol. **15**(1), 69–81 (2017)

Zou, D.: Comparing dictionary-induced vocabulary learning and inferencing in the context of reading. Lexikos **26**(1), 372–390 (2016)

Zou, D.: Vocabulary acquisition through cloze exercises, sentence-writing and composition-writing: extending the evaluation component of the involvement load hypothesis. Lang. Teach. Res. **21**(1), 54–75 (2017)

A Design Framework of Virtual Reality Enabled Experiential Learning for Children with Autism Spectrum Disorder

Chen Li(✉), Horace Ho Shing Ip, and Po Ke Ma

Centre for Innovative Applications of Multimedia and Internet Technologies, City University of Hong Kong, Kowloon, Hong Kong
{richard.li,horace.ip,pokema}@cityu.edu.hk

Abstract. Experiential learning is one of the most widely applied learning theories for virtual reality enabled learning, because virtual reality environment, especially immersive virtual reality environment, allows learners to actively experiment and reflectively observe in a safe and authentic environment. Our previous studies have shown that experiential learning could also be applied within a virtual reality learning environment for children with autism spectrum disorder (ASD) in various learning domains. However, there is a lack of in-depth discussion on how to systematically design, engineer and evaluate virtual reality enabled experiential learning activities for children with ASD and other complications (e.g., anxiety disorder, attention deficit hyperactivity disorder (ADHD), etc.). In this paper, we share our experience on applying experiential learning theory on the design of social competence learning in the immersive virtual reality environment for the children ASD, in order to address two fundamental questions. First, how different immersive virtual reality environments, such as the CAVE and head-mounted displays, affect the design of the virtual reality learning scenarios. Second, how the virtual reality learning contents can be designed to facilitate experiential learning in an immersive virtual reality environment for the ASD population. Our small-scale study shows that children with ASD often need facilitation during experiential learning in the immersive virtual reality environment and our design of providing in-VR facilitation can meet their learning needs.

Keywords: Experiential learning · Virtual reality · Autism spectrum disorder

1 Introduction

Kolb's experiential learning model (ELM) is typically represented as an iterative four-step learning cycle [1]. The four steps are concrete experience, reflective observation, abstract conceptualization, and active experimentation. The basic idea of ELM is to provide a learning environment in which learners can actively experiment and test hypothesis which is usually conceptualized from the learners' previous experiences, resulting new experiences and knowledge for new situations. Interactive media technologies, such as immersive virtual reality environments, can provide a safe and authentic environment for experiential learning [2]. Previous studies show that ELM is

S. K. S. Cheung et al. (Eds.): ICBL 2019, LNCS 11546, pp. 93–102, 2019.
https://doi.org/10.1007/978-3-030-21562-0_8

one of the most important theories guiding technology enabled learning activities in various fields, ranging from mainstream education to professional/vocational training [3, 4]. Moreover, our previous studies have also shown that experiential learning in immersive virtual reality environments, such as the Cave Automatic Virtual Environment (CAVE), could improve social competences of children with autism spectrum disorder [5, 6]. However, there is a lack of in-depth discussion on how to systematically design and engineer virtual reality enabled experiential learning for children with ASD and other complications (e.g., anxiety disorder, attention deficit hyperactivity disorder (ADHD), etc.). In this paper, we will address two fundamental questions regarding the use of virtual reality technologies to help learning for children with ASD. First, how different immersive virtual reality environments, such as the CAVE and head-mounted displays, affect the design of the virtual reality learning scenarios. Second, how the virtual reality learning contents can be designed to facilitate experiential learning in the immersive virtual reality environment for the ASD population. Our small-scale trial shows that children with ASD often need facilitation during experiential learning in the immersive virtual reality environment and our design of providing in-VR facilitation can meet their learning needs. This paper is organized as follow. In Sect. 2, we review the related studies covering the experiential learning theories, virtual reality enabled learning and the empirical studies on virtual reality enabled learning which adopted the experiential learning theories. In Sect. 3, we propose our design of the virtual reality enabled experiential learning for children with ASD and why the virtual reality learning scenarios are designed in the proposed way. We also compare how different immersive virtual reality environments affect the design of the learning scenarios. Section 4 will present the case study findings of the small-scale trial. The paper is concluded in Sect. 5, with our plan for future works.

2 Related Work

2.1 Experiential Learning

The concept of experiential learning, as proposed by Kolb, is formed around the iterative learning cycle consisting four steps, namely concrete experience, reflective observation, abstract conceptualization, and active experimentation [1, 7]. The cycle begins with concrete experience, which is usually yield from actively experiencing and thinking of learners in the given situation. Following concrete experience, reflective observation emphases the analysis and discussion of the observed outcomes of the experiencing. In the third step, abstract conceptualization, the learners are expected to understand the situations and propose the hypothesis. Finally, learners are expected to test the hypothesis by actively experimenting in new situations, resulting the articulation of new knowledge and the development of new skills. Although there are criticisms of the Kolb's model claiming that learning may not necessarily take place in a sequential fashion [8], we see more and more studies that apply the model in a broad range of fields and settings ever since Svinicki and Dixon recommended the model as a framework for designing classroom activities [9]. Specifically, experiential learning enabled by interactive media technologies such as games and immersive virtual reality environments, is becoming increasingly popular as the technologies develop. For example, Jarmon et al. used the Second Life multi-user virtual world and designed the learning activities by applying experiential learning theories to teach graduate students interdisciplinary communication [10]. The results demonstrated the effectiveness of using multi-user virtual world as a platform for the delivery of project-based experiential learning. Le, Pedro and Park designed an online social virtual reality system as a platform for the construction safety education by applying experiential learning theories [11]. The study indicated that the social virtual reality system is useful in improving safety experiential learning of the workers' identification of safety risks and general risk awareness. Sung et al. applied Kolb's model on the design of an experiential game-based learning approach [12]. Results showed that the proposed approach is effective in terms of enhancing the students' learning motivation, deep learning strategy and acceptance of the technology. All these studies share the same advantage of interactive media technologies, which is the ability of creating authentic and safe environments where learners are allowed to actively experiment, observe and receive real-time feedbacks.

2.2 Immersive Virtual Reality Environment

There are various immersive virtual reality environments for delivering virtual reality learning contents. Modern immersive virtual reality environments can be categories as the projection-based installations, such as the Cave Automatic Virtual Environment (CAVE) [13], and the head-mounted displays (HMDs). Projection-based installations, as the name suggests, usually have a number of projection walls arranged in a way to form an immersive environment. For most of such installations, motion trackers are used to track the viewer's head and or body gestures, enabling real-time perspective simulation and interactions. The advantage of using projection-based installations is that they allow multiple users to share the same physical environment. This is particularly interesting for the delivery of virtual reality learning contents since it allows educators to provide facilitation when needed while keeping the learners engaged in the immersive virtual reality environment. The major drawbacks of projection-based immersive virtual reality environments are the technical complexity and the very specified and demanding venue requirements, making the use of such installations for educational purposes on a large-scale infeasible [14]. On the other hand, the new generation of the head-mounted displays, especially the commercially available models such as the Oculus Rift and HTC VIVE, can provide an even more immersive experience while keeping the technical complexity transparent to the end users. Moreover, HMDs are more portable and require much less space to set up, making the use of HMDs for educational purposes on a large-scale much more feasible than the use of projection-based immersive virtual reality environments. However, when wearing the HMDs, the viewers' vision is totally isolated from the real surroundings, raising concerns on the use of HMDs on the ASD population [15]. More recent studies show that when wearing the HMDs, people with ASD can comprehend the virtual reality contents well and are able to interact with the virtual objects, avatars and scenes in the designated ways [16]. Li, Yuan and Ip also conducted a research study that focuses on the use of the off-the-shelf HMDs, Oculus Rift headset with the Oculus Touch controllers in this case, for delivering learning contents for young children with ASD [17]. The results were encouraging, but it was also pointed out that the learning contents needed to be further adapted for the HMD immersive virtual reality environment not only in the ways of interacting with the learning content, but also the pedagogical design. In a short conclusion, the use of HMDs on the ASD population for educational purposes seems to be feasible and more practical when being compared with the use of projection-based immersive virtual reality environments such as the CAVE, however, the virtual reality contents need to be adapted appropriately which is yet to be explored.

2.3 Virtual Reality Enabled Learning for ASD Population

Previous studies show that virtual reality is believed to be an effective tool for various domains of learning on the ASD population. Among all these domains, social competence training is one of the mostly addressed domains [5, 6, 18, 19], due to the fact that social competence training is extremely crucial to help children with ASD better participate in the community [20]. Previous studies have found that by employing virtual reality technologies, the highly interactive and vivid virtual scenes delivered in an immersive virtual reality environment (e.g., the CAVE), can provide an authentic place where the children can practice their social skills without worrying about potential hazard and or unnecessary embarrassment in the real world [3]. The employment of virtual reality technologies on the ASD population can be traced back to the 1990s. Strickland et al. conducted an exploratory study in 1996 regarding the use of virtual reality technologies as a tool for children with ASD [15]. Despite of the poor ergonomics of the early generation of the HMDs, the two participants could accept the device with little assistance; and more importantly, they were able to comprehend the virtual reality scenes presented to them. Followings this study, we see a great number of empirical studies that use various types of immersive virtual reality environments to deliver learning contents for the children with ASD. Among these studies, the study conducted by Ip et al. adopting the randomized two group experiment design is the largest, in terms of the number of subjects [6]. A total number of 94 children with clinical diagnosis of ASD participated the study. As demonstrated by the standardized test results, the 14-week training, covering 6 different virtual reality learning scenarios delivered in the CAVE immersive virtual reality environment, enhanced the children's emotion expression and regulation, and social interactions. As the development of virtual reality and relevant technologies, the latest generation off-the-shelf HMDs have much better ergonomics and a personal computer even a laptop is now powerful enough to drive these HMDs and render high resolution virtual scenes at high refresh rate, making it possible to deliver virtual reality learning contents to the children with ASD on large scale. We have seen a few piloting studies on this [16, 17]. However, the effectiveness of the content design as well as the pedagogical design are yet to be systematically study and evaluated.

3 Method

3.1 Design Framework and Virtual Reality Learning Scenarios

The objective of the proposed design framework (see Fig. 1), which is based on Kolb's experiential learning model (ELM), is to provide necessary facilitation inside the immersive virtual reality environment to the children with ASD during learning so that the learning could take place smoothly and the intended learning outcomes could be achieved effectively. Specifically, two types of learning contents were designed to help achieve the designated objective, namely interactive social stories and social incident experiencing. An interactive social story usually consists of a group of illustrations telling a social story and/or teaching social norms; the children were expected to understand the situation and respond in a socially appropriate way in-VR by tapping the rating buttons (see Fig. 2). The social incident experiencing takes place in virtual reality learning scenarios, which were adapted from our previous studies using the CAVE immersive virtual reality environment [5, 6]; the children would experience pre-plotted social incidents from a first-person perspective in the immersive virtual reality environment.

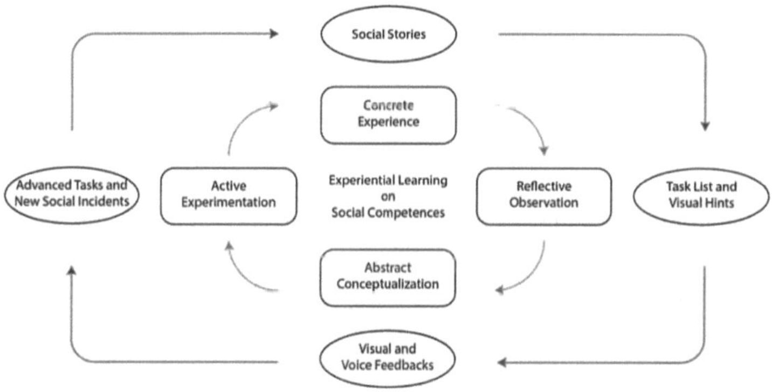

Fig. 1. The design framework based on Kolb's experiential learning model.

Fig. 2. Screen capture of the interactive social stories in VR where the children are expected to rate whether it is socially appropriate based on their own understanding of the social situation.

As we know that during the virtual reality enabled experiential learning, children with ASD tend to need a certain degree of facilitation and using the HMD as the immersive virtual reality environment will most likely confine the children in the virtual reality learning scenarios, the adaption also involved adding in-VR facilitations throughout the four stages of the Kolb's model. Specifically, task list and visual hints were added to help the children understand the social scenarios and/or the emotions of others; the design aligns with the objectives of social competence training as well as the concrete experience and the reflective observation steps of Kolb's experiential learning model. The visual and voice feedbacks were added to help the children abstractly conceptualize what they had just experience in the interactive social stories, before they started to experience the pre-plotted social incidents, where the children were expected to try out their newly gained knowledge and coping skills, so that they could achieve the active experimentation stage of Kolb's model. During the active experimentation stage, if the children encountered problems and facilitations were needed, the visual hints, visual and voice feedbacks, which they referred to in the previous stages, will again provide in-VR real-time facilitations.

Moreover, we still believe in the prominent facilitation from the educators. Thus, the experiential learning will always end with the debriefing session during which the educators could provide facilitations which could not be provided inside the virtual reality learning scenarios.

3.2 The Immersive Virtual Reality Environment

The immersive virtual reality environment we used for this study is the off-the-shelf HMD named Oculus Rift, with the Oculus Rift Touch controllers. Both the HMD and the controllers support 6 degree-of-freedom tracking in a 3-meter-by-3-meter space. However, due to the constrains of the length of the cable connecting the HMD and the computer, the actual immersive virtual reality environment is confined in a 2-meter-by-2-meter space for safety considerations. This area is marked in the virtual scenes so even when the learners are wearing the HMDs, they are still able to see where the boundaries are. The virtual reality learning contents were running on a Lenovo Legion Y720 15.6-inch laptop computer with Intel i7-7700HQ processor, 16 GB of RAM, NVIDIA GeForce GTX 1060 graphics card and 256 GB solid state drive. We choose this setup since it allows us to scale up the studies in the future and help more beneficiaries. The virtual reality contents were optimized to reach 90 frames per second rendering on this setup to minimize any uncomfortableness caused by the rendering lag.

3.3 Participants and Evaluation

A total number of 3 children with clinical diagnosis of ASD were invited to join the piloting study. Demographics of the participants are reported in Table 1. Consents were obtained from their parents and schools before we started. No personal identifiable information would be disclosed, and names used in this paper were made-up for referencing purpose only. The children were invited to join the 32-session virtual reality enabled experiential learning in their schools lead by a trained psychologist. The psychologist observed and facilitated the children's exposure to the virtual reality learning scenarios. The whole session was videotaped, and the research team evaluated and wrote case reports based on the psychologist's on-site observation and the video clips.

The evaluation was conducted on two axes, the content axis and the facilitation axis (see Fig. 3). Reports were written by the facilitators based on how the participants utilize the facilitations and how they achieve the intended objectives by going through the contents. Specifically, the children were reported on their comprehension and responds to the task list and visual hints during the interactive social stories challenge. The team also observe whether they could adapt what they have learned from the interactive social stories to the first-person social incident learning. The learning effectiveness was assessed based on the children's comprehension and responds to the feedbacks during the experiencing and their exhibited behaviors after the virtual reality enabled learning. Moreover, the children's acceptance of the immersive virtual reality technology (i.e., the HMD) was also observed and noted in this study. Several case studies are reported in the next section.

Table 1. Demographics of the participants.

Name	Gender	Age (years)	Grade
Jason	Male	8	P2
Edward	Male	10	P4
Lewis	Male	8	P3

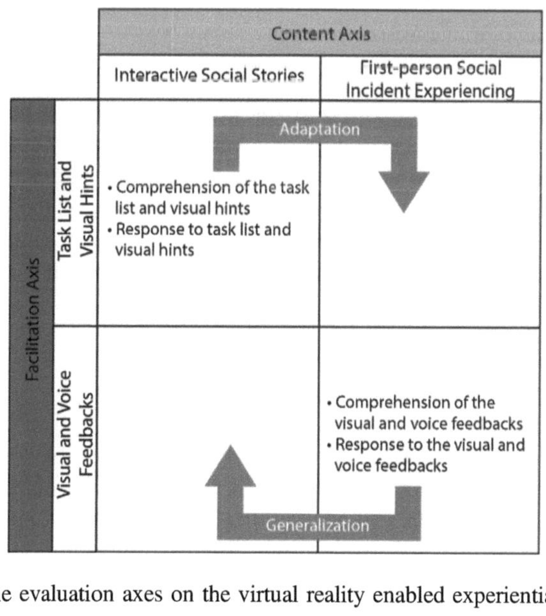

Fig. 3. The evaluation axes on the virtual reality enabled experiential learning.

4 Case Study Results

Case Report - Jason

Jason refused to wear the HMD for his first trial. He kept shaking his head and stated that he was scared. The educator let him know he would receive supports through the scenario and tapped on his shoulder. He then tried to wear the HMD by narrowing his eyes, but soon he wanted to take the HMD off. As the sessions progressed, Jason was able to wear HMD and he became eager to start the session. He gradually learned to refer to the task list and with support from both the visual hints and the educator, he quickly learned to follow the task list. However, he sometimes missed the feedbacks during the incident experiencing. The educator needed to rephrase the voice feedbacks. We believe this may partially due to his attention deficits and he exhibited the needs of longer-than-usual time to process voice instructions. During the first-person social incident experiencing, he found it challenging due to his rigid thinking. But when the virtual reality contents promote him with visual hints and feedbacks he had experienced before, Jason's thinking became more flexible. Moreover, with more practicing, he learned to generalize social norms to new situations without the need of explicit visual hints.

Case Report - Edward

Edward was willing to wear the HMD at the very first trial. He always wanted to check if the educator was with him when he was exposed to the virtual reality learning contents. He also reported he felt a bit dizzy after took off the HMD, but he had no issue following the task list and visual hints and was able to complete the first-person social incident experiencing in a very consistent and socially appropriate manner. Edward also exhibited his ability of generalizing what he had experienced in the immersive virtual reality environment to real life scenarios, especially when he was with his peer students in classroom settings.

Case Report - Lewis

Lewis was willing to wear the HMD at the very first trial and he reported that he enjoyed the virtual reality exposure a lot. He was able to quickly comprehend the task list and the visual hints and exhibited great consistency and independency when responding to the interactive social stories. The adaptation of the coping skills and social norms was also quite good; he could control his emotion quite well in the first-person social incident experiencing. After the virtual reality enabled learning, he had no problem in recalling the follow of the social stories.

5 Conclusion and Future Work

Besides to share our experiences in the use of virtual reality enabled approaches for the learning of children with ASD, this paper aims to address two fundamental questions regarding the adoption of Kolb's ELM in immersive virtual reality environments on the ASD population. The first question is how different immersive virtual reality environments, such as the CAVE and HMDs, affect the design of the virtual reality learning scenarios; and second, how the virtual reality learning contents can be designed to facilitate experiential learning in the immersive virtual reality environment for the ASD population. Based on our experience, we found that the delivery of experiential learning in HMDs requires more in-VR facilitations. This is due to the special learning needs of the ASD population and the uniqueness of HMDs, which is the complete isolation of the user from the surroundings during VR exposure. More importantly, our approach of enabling in-VR task list, hints and real-time feedbacks is an effective way of providing in-VR facilitation, no matter in which type of immersive virtual reality environments the learning contents were designed to be delivered. However, during our piloting study using the HMDs, we found that two of the three participants exhibited the feeling of "insecure" when wearing the HMDs and being exposed to the virtual scenarios for the very first times. Our planned future works include (1) to expand the scale of the experiment in terms of the number of participants, and (2) to use standardized assessment tools to further investigate the effectiveness of the virtual reality enabled experiential learning on social competences for children with ASD.

Acknowledgement. This work was partially supported by the Quality Education Fund of the HKSAR.

References

1. Kolb, D.A.: Experiential learning: Experience as the source of learning and development. FT Press, Upper Saddle River (2014)
2. Kalyuga, S.: Enhancing instructional efficiency of interactive e-learning environments: a cognitive load perspective. Educ. Psychol. Rev. **19**(3), 387–399 (2007)
3. Fernández-Herrero, J., Lorenzo, G., Lledó Carreres, A.: A Bibliometric Study on the Use of Virtual Reality (VR) as an Educational Tool for High-Functioning Autism Spectrum Disorder (ASD) Children (2018)
4. Smith, M.J., et al.: Brief report: vocational outcomes for young adults with autism spectrum disorders at six months after virtual reality job interview training. J. Autism Dev. Disord. **45** (10), 3364–3369 (2015)
5. Ip, H.H., et al.: Virtual reality enabled training for social adaptation in inclusive education settings for school-aged children with autism spectrum disorder (ASD). In: Cheung, Simon K.S., Kwok, L.-f., Shang, J., Wang, A., Kwan, R. (eds.) ICBL 2016. LNCS, vol. 9757, pp. 94–102. Springer, Cham (2016). https://doi.org/10.1007/978-3-319-41165-1_9
6. Ip, H.H., et al.: Enhance emotional and social adaptation skills for children with autism spectrum disorder: a virtual reality enabled approach. Comput. Educ. **117**, 1–15 (2018)
7. Kolb, D.A.: Experiential learning theory and the learning style inventory: a reply to Freedman and Stumpf. Acad. Manag. Rev. **6**(2), 289–296 (1981)
8. Beard, C.M., Wilson, J.P.: Experiential Learning: A Best Practice Handbook for Educators and Trainers. Kogan Page Publishers, London (2006)
9. Svinicki, M.D., Dixon, N.M.: The Kolb model modified for classroom activities. Coll. Teach. **35**(4), 141–146 (1987)
10. Jarmon, L., Traphagan, T., Mayrath, M., Trivedi, A.: Virtual world teaching, experiential learning, and assessment: an interdisciplinary communication course in second life. Comput. Educ. **53**(1), 169–182 (2009)

11. Le, Q.T., Pedro, A., Park, C.S.: A social virtual reality based construction safety education system for experiential learning. J. Intell. Robot. Syst. **79**(3–4), 487–506 (2015)
12. Sung, H.Y., Hwang, G.J., Lin, C.J., Hong, T.W.: Experiencing the analects of confucius: an experiential game-based learning approach to promoting students' motivation and conception of learning. Comput. Educ. **110**, 143–153 (2017)
13. Cruz-Neira, C., Sandin, D. J., DeFanti, T.A.: Surround-screen projection-based virtual reality: the design and implementation of the CAVE. In: Proceedings of the 20th Annual Conference on Computer Graphics and Interactive Techniques, pp. 135–142. ACM (1993)
14. Ip, H.H.S., Li, C.: Virtual reality-based learning environments: recent developments and ongoing challenges. In: Cheung, S.K.S., Kwok, L.-f., Yang, H., Fong, J., Kwan, R. (eds.) ICHL 2015. LNCS, vol. 9167, pp. 3–14. Springer, Cham (2015). https://doi.org/10.1007/978-3-319-20621-9_1
15. Strickland, D., Marcus, L.M., Mesibov, G.B., Hogan, K.: Brief report: two case studies using virtual reality as a learning tool for autistic children. J. Autism Dev. Disord. **26**(6), 651–659 (1996)
16. Newbutt, N., Sung, C., Kuo, H.J., Leahy, M.J., Lin, C.C., Tong, B.: Brief report: a pilot study of the use of a virtual reality headset in autism populations. J. Autism Dev. Disord. **46** (9), 3166–3176 (2016)
17. Li, C., Yuan, S.N.V., Ip, H.H.: A Case Study on Delivering Virtual Reality Learning for Children with Autism Spectrum Disorder Using Virtual Reality Headsets, pp. 728–734 (2018). https://doi.org/10.21125/edulearn.2018.0267
18. Kandalaft, M.R., Didehbani, N., Krawczyk, D.C., Allen, T.T., Chapman, S.B.: Virtual reality social cognition training for young adults with high-functioning autism. J. Autism Dev. Disord. **43**(1), 34–44 (2013)
19. Matsentidou, S., Poullis, C.: Immersive visualizations in a VR cave environment for the training and enhancement of social skills for children with autism. In: 2014 International Conference on Computer Vision Theory and Applications (VISAPP), vol. 3, pp. 230–236. IEEE (2014)
20. Chasson, G., Jarosiewicz, S.R.: Social competence impairments in autism spectrum disorders. In: Patel, V., Preedy, V., Martin, C. (eds.) Comprehensive Guide to Autism, pp. 1099–1118. Springer, New York (2014). https://doi.org/10.1007/978-1-4614-4788-7_60

Content Development for Blended Learning

The Preference of Electronic, or Printed Materials Revisited

Ivana Simonova(✉)

Jan Evangelista Purkyne University, 40096 Usti nad Labem, Czech Republic
ivana.simonova@ujep.cz

Abstract. The paper presents results of the research dealing with students′ preferences of electronic, or printed materials in 2019 at two intentionally selected higher education institutions in the Czech Republic: Faculty of Education (FE), University of Jan Evangelista Purkyne, Usti nad Labem, and Faculty of Informatics and Management (FIM), University of Hradec Kralove. Data were collected from 185 participants who were to fulfil the task within English for Specific Purposes – they searched for sentences containing selected grammar phenomena. Totally 8,140 sentences were collected and structured under ten types of electronic and printed sources (professional book, fiction long, fiction short, article, other source. Data were processed by Fisher's exact test. The hypothesis expecting association between the type of institution and type of source was verified. FE students preferred printed books of long fiction (novels) but also used e-books, both of long fiction and on professional content, whereas FIM students exploited two types of sources only: e-articles and printed books relating to their profession and/or field of study.

Keywords: Electronic · e- · Printed · Study materials · Sources · English grammar · ESP · English for specific purposes · Higher education

1 Introduction

Generation Y, also called Gen Y, or Millennials, are mostly defined as the group of people born from early 1980s to early 2000s. Although their characteristics slightly differ depending on various factors, the increased use and familiarity with e-technologies are widely accepted features [1]. At the end of the second decade of the second millennium (i.e. in 2019), the youngest members of this group are at the age of university students, whilst the oldest ones are going to reach the age of 40. The term of millennials was first used in 1987, around the time, when the children were entering the pre-school education, and the media were first identifying their prospective link to the new millennium as the year of secondary school graduation [2]. These students see themselves as digital natives [3], i.e. the first generation which grew up surrounded by information and communication technologies (ICT); however, they were exceptionally used at schools before 2000. The ICT implementation was reflected in educational documents, curricula and methodological materials published by both the European Commission [4–6] and national bodies [7]. Many of them have still been working, the others target to the future [8].

S. K. S. Cheung et al. (Eds.): ICBL 2019, LNCS 11546, pp. 105–116, 2019.
https://doi.org/10.1007/978-3-030-21562-0_9

As widely known, the first reflection of ICT enhancing the process of instruction from the learners′view was highly positive, been mostly influenced by the newness of this didactic means, which strengthened learners′motivation towards learning, e.g. [9, 10]. However, decades are passing quickly, and ICT have become standard within the process of instruction. Currently, all learners – either millennials and younger ones, or adults and senior adults, consider both the devices and their exploitation part of common life. This fact removes ICT from the position of a new, strongly motivating didactic means. Then, the question appears, what the current position of ICT in education really is. Therefore, *the main objective of this paper is to analyze and discuss results of the research comparing the exploitation of electronic and printed sources for educational purposes by millennials at two higher education institutions.*

2 Theoretical Background

A decade ago (2009), the first law was passed in the U.S. which required all university textbooks to be available in electronic form by 2020. Another one (passed in 2011), demanded public schools to convert their textbooks to digital versions. Within the Czech higher education system, as required by the Czech National Accreditation Office, electronic (e-) support for each subject is required, which mostly means designing and running the online course in the learning management system (LMS). Following this e-trend, we might expect that students' familiarity with ICT and their preference to other types of study materials will definitely result in better learning results, as learners also state. However, this expectation is not necessarily true. First, the positive features of ICT – accessibility and portability, which are highly appreciated by the users – do not automatically mean students learn more just because of the personal preference. Second, there exist differences between reading the printed and electronic materials. For example, as discussed by Alexander and Singer [11], students had expressed their preference to everything electronic (e-sources in general, e-study materials, e-tests, e-communication, various types of mobile devices etc.) by stating they learned more, easily, faster; but this did not prove in their real performance. Already in 1992, Alexander and Singer [11] found out that students were able to better comprehend printed information from texts longer than one page, which seemed to relate to the disruptive effect of scrolling on the comprehension. The findings proved students′opinions neither in testing different levels of comprehension, nor in the time needed for reading printed and electronic texts. To sum up, the results discovered that

- reading was faster from e-texts than from printed materials;
- students considered their comprehension higher from e-materials despite the fact test results showed overall higher scores in reading from printed sources;
- the type of text did not matter in understanding the main idea; however, in answering specific questions the comprehension was significantly better from printed texts [11].

As reported by Nielsen company in 2018 [12], the printed form of study materials would always have a place in education. Their research discovered students preferred printed to electronic materials – 39% of students bought new printed materials, 13%

borrowed them from libraries and 17% bought used printed study materials; only 31% of students purchased e-materials. The difference in reading comprehension when words are displayed on a screen, or on the paper, was also researched by Kottke [13]. She particularly focused on the question to what extent the processing of information affected. All these questions were already answered in 1980s. However, the situation has changed substantially since thanks to the technological development. When researching current students´opinions, their answers are identical in identifying slower, less attentive and less comprehensive reading from e-texts. Other studies indicate that people process data more shallowly from e-sources than they do when studying from printed ones, e.g. Liu [14]. Morineau et al. [15] and Ackerman and Goldsmith [16] addressed these questions by comparing learning from texts on screen (e-sources) to learning the same texts from paper (printed sources), and took the metacognitive processes into account. They discovered that those students reading from screens performed worse and were overconfident about their success. They conclude that irrespective immense technological advances learners still prefer studying from printed materials rather than from computer screens. The results suggest that the primary differences between the two possibilities are not cognitive but rather metacognitive, particularly the prediction of performance is less accurate. More generally, this study highlights the contribution of metacognitive regulatory processes to learning.

To sum up, a decade ago people tended to prefer reading texts in depth from printed sources rather than from electronic materials, including e-books, as numerous scientists proved, e.g. Jamali, Nicholas, and Rowlands [17], Woody, Daniel, and Baker [18], Olsen, Kleivset, and Langseth [19]. Thus a question arises whether the observed screen inferiority depends on the reluctance of the participants regarding studying texts on screen. Indeed, the results of Ackerman and Goldsmith [16] were collected from students who strongly prefer printed versions to e-sources. However, Ackerman and Lauterman [20] detected similar results among engineering students who were under mild time pressure. Importantly, these students were used to reading from screen and have only a moderate preference for print. Other studies found out that part of the difference between the way people absorbed information from e-books versus paper might be due to approaching e-books differently – generations of e-book readers evolve, and people become more accustomed to the idea of sitting down with a digital textbook [21].

In the Czech Republic, researches were also conducted focusing on the use of electronic and printed study materials with higher education students. At the Faculty of Informatics and Management (FIM), University of Hradec Kralove (UHK), strong preference for e-sources was detected already in 2009 [22]. The result was understood in relation to the main interest of the students, i.e. in information technologies, which naturally resulted in their preference to e-sources. Even before 2009, the IT equipment and access to the Internet at FIM were above standard [23: 64, 65, 91, 92] and analysis of financial expenses [23: 70] gave preference to ICT-enhanced instruction, particularly to the use of e-sources in all subjects, including English language. At the Faculty of Education, University of Jan Evangelista Purkyne, Usti nad Labem, where pre-service teachers were educated, strong preference was given to the direct method of teaching English language and ICT were marginal in this process. Therefore, data were neither collected, nor published at that early period.

3 Methodology

The above mentioned higher education institutions serve as sample ones in our research: FIM as the leader in the field of e-learning implementation in the Czech Republic; FE as a faculty preparing pre-service teachers, where no special attention was paid to the ICT implementation. Within the research, students of both institutions were given the identical task – to learn and practise selected phenomena of English grammar through collecting sentences when reading texts relating to their field of study, i.e. IT with FIM students and English literature, linguistics and educational science with FE students. Types of sources students exploited to fulfil the task were monitored and analyzed. So that this learning objective to be reached, blended approach was applied combining face-to-face lessons and autonomous work in LMS, as described in detail below where

- first, the process of teaching/learning English at both institutions is introduced;
- second, the process of fulfilling the task is described;
- third, research design is presented.

3.1 Teaching/Learning English at FE and FIM

As students of different levels of knowledge attend English courses at both institutions, blended learning approach is applied to practising English grammar. The starting level of the first-year students of the bachelor study programme of English language and literature at FE is B2 (upper intermediate level) according to Common European Framework of Reference for Languages (CEFR) [24], and B1 (intermediate level) for bachelor students of Applied Informatics and Information Management at FIM. CEFR defines learning outcomes within General English; however, English for Specific Purposes (ESP) is taught to these students, focusing on linguistics and literature with FE students and IT field with FIM students.

At FE, students develop their knowledge of English grammar in six courses of Practical Language (i.e. 90 min per week each) during the bachelor study programme. In the subjects, all four language skills are under the focus, and also grammar and professional vocabulary from the field of linguistics and literature. Moreover, all other subjects are taught in English, half-and-half by qualified native speakers and Czech teachers of English. It means students are exposed to the English speaking environment during the whole study, which results in having high level of practical knowledge of English. Online courses in the Learning Management System (LMS) Moodle can be designed and used by the teachers. On the other side, not much attention is paid to the system and theory of grammar, which should not be omitted at this level of foreign language learning.

At FIM, students attend one face-to-face lesson of ESP per week (i.e. 90 min, or four three-hour blocks per semester) where mostly direct communication activities are conducted, and they also have additional materials for reading, practising and testing their knowledge available in the LMS Blackboard [25].

3.2 Process of Fulfilling the Task

The research process consisted of three phases.

In Phase 1, the pre-test detecting students′starting knowledge was conducted on the first face-to-face lesson in FE and FIM groups, i.e. before the process of learning started. Each student was given a sheet of paper where titles of 44 grammar phenomena were listed in the left column. Students were to write a simple sentence containing the phenomenon in appropriate context to the right column. For the purpose of the research, the phenomena were structured into two groups following the CEFR: A2 level (Basic user – elementary level; G1-20) and B1 level (Independent user – intermediate level; G21-44). The time period for completing the list was 70 min. After the lesson, each sentence was assessed by the teacher (one point per correct sentence).

In Phase 2, autonomous out-of-school work was conducted for six weeks. Students′ task was to read texts (fiction and professional texts relating to their field of study and/or work, i.e. novels, stories, but not poetry, professional books, articles in journals, web pages etc.), and fill in the same list of 44 grammar phenomena with sentences found in the texts they read. Citations were strongly required. When finished, the list was submitted to the teacher and feedback was provided to each student stating whether sentences are correct, or other ones need to be found, and why.

In Phase 3, student′s final knowledge was tested at the end of semester in the form of face-to-face credit test. Identically to previous phases, students were to fill in the same list of 44 grammar phenomena with their own sentences which they considered appropriate to each phenomenon. This task was rather difficult because not only the knowledge of grammar phenomena, but also the context and professional vocabulary were required [25].

3.3 Research Design

For the purpose of this research, sentences collected in phase 2 were used, particularly the citations were crucial. They enabled us to distinguish what type of source students read to find the appropriate sentence.

Research Question, Objective and Hypothesis

Reflecting the theoretical background, the question appears what influences students′ choice of the type of sources they study from – are there personal features, previous work and/or study experience, interests? Are their preferences connected to the field (study programme, institution) they study? Do the students prefer e-sources to printed ones, or vice versa? What were the preferences of each group? These questions led us to the question whether FIM students use e-sources more frequently, whilst FE students prefer printed sources. Consequently, the research objective was to discover what type (s) of sources students exploit and whether their choice/preference depends on the type of institution they attend.

Therefore, the null and alternative hypotheses were stated as follows:

H0: The type of source cited does not depend on the type of institution.
Ha: The type of source cited depends on the type of institution.

Research Sample
Totally, 185 students of two universities participated in the research:

- Faculty of Education (FE): N = 91; (M = 32; F = 62);
- Faculty of Informatics and Management (FIM): N = 94; (M = 71; F = 20).

The age interval of the research sample is from 20 to 41 years; i.e. all of them can be considered Gen Y members. They all participated in three phases of the research, particularly Phase 2 and cited all the sources of collected sentences properly.

Research Methods and Tools
Types of sources students read and collected the appropriate sentences from, were structured into ten types:

- Type 1: Electronic book dealing with the professional topic reflecting student´s field of education, or work.
- Type 2: Electronic book – fiction, long, e.g. novels.
- Type 3: Electronic book – fiction, short, e.g. stories.
- Type 4: Electronic article dealing with the professional topic reflecting student´s field of education, or work.
- Type 5: Electronic sources not listed above.
- Type 6: Printed book dealing with the professional topic reflecting student´s field of education, or work.
- Type 7: Printed book – fiction, long, e.g. novels.
- Type 8: Printed book – fiction, short, e.g. stories.
- Type 9: Printed article dealing with the professional topic reflecting student´s field of education, or work.
- Type 10 Printed sources not listed above.

Totally, 8,140 sentences were collected (4,136 by FE students; 4,004 by FIM students). The occurrence of cited sources was monitored and presented in the form of 2 x 2 contingency table considering the institution (FE, or FIM), type of source used (e-sources: types 1-5; printed sources: types 6-10), and the group of grammar phenomena (G1-44; G1-20; G21-44). If the student used more than 50% of e-sources out of total amount of 44, 20 and 24 grammar phenomena, they were included in the group of e-source users; if the student used more than 50% of printed sources, they were classified in this group of printed source users. The occurrences were processed by Fisher´s exact test.

4 Research Results

Research results are displayed and considered from various views. Following the methodology, first, results of testing the alternative hypothesis are presented; then, additional detailed data enhancing the result are displayed.

4.1 Testing the Hypothesis

The alternative hypothesis Ha stating that *the type of source cited depends on the type of institution* was verified.

The result of Fisher's exact test showed that two-tailed P value is less than 0.0001, which means the association between rows (institution) and columns (outcomes, i.e. type of source) is considered to be extremely statistically significant. Occurrences were considered in three groups: all grammar phenomena (G1-44), grammar phenomena required for the B1 level of CEFR (G1-20), grammar phenomena required for the B2 level of CEFR (G21-44).

From the above listed ten types of sources, no occurrences of types 5 and 10 were detected. Therefore, these types are omitted in following tables and figures. In Table 1, we can see that within all grammar phenomena (G1-44), 34 students of FE exploited more than 50% of e-sources compared to 60 students working with printed sources, whilst 67 students of FIM exploited more than 50% of e-sources compared to 24 students working with printed sources. Identical occurrences were discovered within the group G1-20. In the group G21-44, the occurrences differed slightly (FE: e-sources 38, printed sources 56; FIM: e-sources 63, printed sources 28). The data clearly show there was no/hardly any difference between the three groups of grammar phenomena (G1-44; G1-20; G21-44); therefore, further on, results in the G1-44 group are presented.

Table 1. Distribution of students using e-sources and printed sources in FE and FIM in three groups (total amount).

Grammar phenomena	Institution	Students using e-sources (N)	Students using printed sources (N)
G1-44	FE (N = 94)	34	60
	FIM (N = 91)	67	24
G1-20	FE	34	60
	FIM	67	24
G21-44	FE	38	56
	FIM	63	28

N: total amount

As the amount of students in groups was not identical (FE: N = 94; FIM: N = 91), the distribution of students using e-sources and printed sources is also displayed in per cent in Fig. 1.

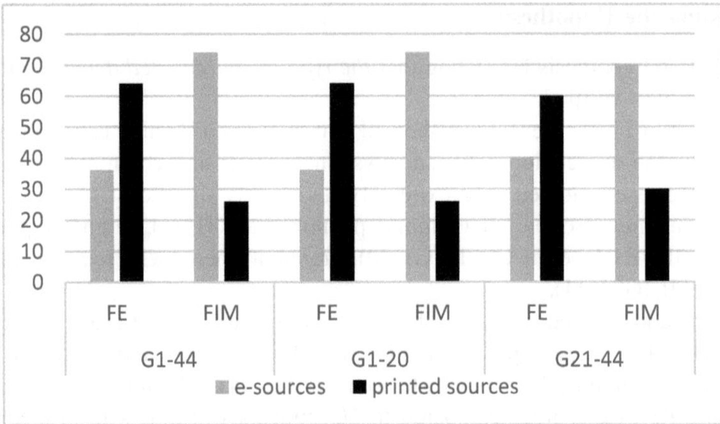

Fig. 1. Distribution of students using e-sources and printed sources in FE and FIM in three groups (per cent).

4.2 Detailed Occurrences of Types of E-Sources and Printed Sources Used by FE and FIM Students

The collected sentences (8,140) were structured under eight of ten types of sources (because of zero occurrence, types 5 and 10 are omitted). Results are displayed in Table 2 (total amounts) and Fig. 2 (per cent). The results show that eight types of sources (four e-sources and four printed sources) were exploited by FE students when searching for sentences with appropriate grammar phenomena, and type 7 (printed book – fiction, long, e.g. novels) was most frequently used. FIM students exploited two types of sources only: type 4 (electronic article dealing with the professional topic reflecting student´s field of education, or work) which was the most frequently exploited e-source, and type 6 (printed book dealing with the professional topic reflecting student´s field of education, or work) was the only exploited printed type of source.

Table 2. Types of e-sources and printed sources in FIM and FE groups (total amounts, G1-44).

	Type 1	Type 2	Type 3	Type 4	Type 6	Type 7	Type 8	Type 9
FE	316	850	16	442	256	2,178	58	12
FIM				2,988	1,016			

The predominance of type 4 (e-source, article dealing with the professional topic reflecting student´s field of education, or work) with FIM students and type 7 (printed book – fiction, long, e.g. novels) with FE students are distinctly visible in Fig. 2.

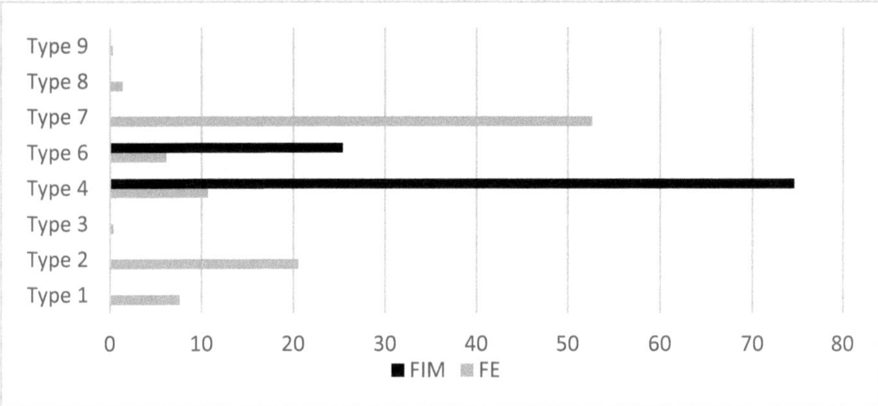

Fig. 2. Types of e-sources and printed sources in FIM and FE groups (per cent, G1-44).

In Fig. 3, amounts of students (in per cent) are compared who exploited a single type of source when searching for sentences (i.e. not one source, but one *type* of source, e.g. e-articles from several web pages, manuals, or e-journals were employed). Aside from types 4 and 7, type 1 (electronic book dealing with the professional topic reflecting student´s field of education, or work) and type 2 (electronic book – fiction, long, e.g. novels) were used as single types of sources.

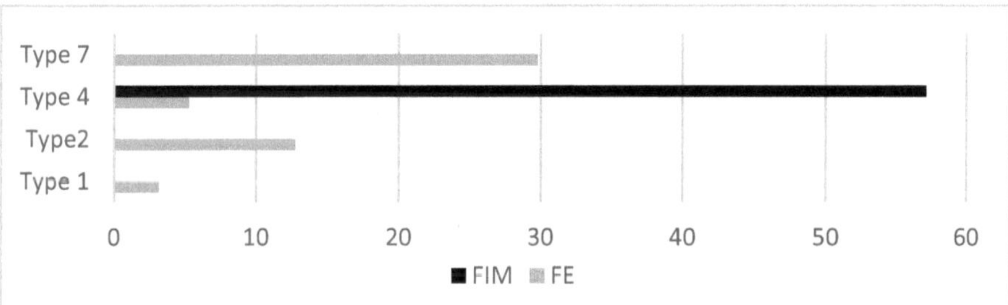

Fig. 3. Types of e-sources and printed sources exploited as a single source when searching for sentences in FIM and FE groups (per cent, G1-44).

5 Discussions and Conclusions

Our results clearly proved that the type of source cited depended on the type of institution the user attended. The data were collected within teaching/learning selected grammar phenomena in English for Specific Purposes. Another question is whether the results would be identical or different in other subjects, and at other institutions. This could be the topic for future research. However, we do not expect to get different results from several reasons, e.g. FIM students, who are engaged in information technologies, consider the exploitation of e-sources to be a logical approach. Therefore, e-articles were the most frequently used type of source, which was probably caused by the immediate availability on the Internet. The same reason could be applied to reading e-books which were used by FE student, even though neither as the most frequently used type of source, nor as a single source. A decade ago, e-books were believed to become a new and strong medium. The amounts of electronic versions of books traditionally available in printed format were growing, been supported by the popularity of note-books, tablet and advanced mobile devices and technologies in general. In the U.S., sales increased by 117% in 2011 [26] and were still rising all over the world later on. In the Czech Republic, the e-book sale was also increasing. In 2018, more than one million of e-books were sold, which is 4% increase compared to 2017. However, these numbers include both the fiction and professional books. Audio-books (fiction only) are the most popular of all; the sales increased of 37 per cent compared to 2017. On the contrary, the production of printed higher education textbooks is decreasing – fewer titles were published last year, which could have been caused by the state economic situation, and also by lower demand from students´side – some of them (as minimum) have got used to exploiting e-sources, mostly available free of charge [27]. This result could be applied to the FIM students, as our results proved. The most popular printed textbooks are available also in electronic format; however, there are hardly any text-books published in e-format only.

According to Ng, Schweitzer and Lyons in 2010 [28], those who were most likely to use electronic textbooks were primarily students of the Gen Y age group, who were constantly connected through technology. Even though Gen Y is comfortable with the use of technology and they are very well known for their technological savviness, they have not grown up with using ICT at school [29]. Perhaps as a result of this lack of technology usage for education, today – as university students – some of them (except IT students) have become hesitant to adopt e-textbooks [30–32], despite the fact that the e-textbooks have a number of advantages over traditional printed textbooks. Based upon Gen Y's professed familiarity with technology, they were expected this generation to embrace e-textbook technology but previous research proved this not to be true.

Moreover, several researches focused on the use of e-textbooks in libraries for out-of-school learning, e.g. [33, 34]. The findings discovered various ways in which users' acceptance of e-books may be encouraged. The availability of the source, both electronic and printed, is the feature that influences the preference.

The likely forecast is that students will continue to use printed sources for some purposes and e-sources for other purposes. The digital revolution came here to stay, and for more than a decade, some scientists and authorities were trying to shift education solely to e-books and e-forms.

However, the appropriateness of the didactic means used should always be the main criterion. We state this as long-year supporters of e-learning and ICT-implementation in education. Reflecting the discovered findings, we propose following: let´s keep both the printed and e-sources and exploit one or both depending on the educational environment, learning objective, content, and other conditions. Thus the Comenius motto ´Let everything flow freely in the absence of violence´ (Omnia sponte fluant, absit violentia rebus) will be fully applied [35].

Acknowledgements. The paper is supported by IGA2019 project.

References

1. Horovitz, B.: After Gen X, Millennials, what should next generation be? USA Today (2012). http://usatoday30.usatoday.com/money/advertising/story/2012-05-03/naming-the-next-generation/54737518/1. Accessed 30 Dec 2018
2. Strauss, W., Howe, N.: Millennials Rising: The Next Great Generation. Vintage Original, New York (2000)
3. Prensky, M.: Digital natives, digital immigrants. On Horiz. **9**(5), 1–6 (2001)
4. European Commission: White Paper on Growth, competitiveness, and employment. The challenges and ways forward into the 21st century. European Commission, Brussels (1993)
5. European Commission: White Paper on Education and Training - Teaching and Learning - Towards the Learning Society. European Commission, Brussel (1995)
6. International Commission on Education for the Twenty-first Century (Delors, Jacques, chairman): Learning: the treasure within. Report to UNESCO of the International Commission on Education for the Twenty-first Century (highlights) (1996)
7. Framework Educational Programmes (2007). http://www.msmt.cz/vzdelavani/skolstvi-v-cr/skolskareforma/ramcove-vzdelavaci-programy. Accessed 30 Dec 2018
8. EU priorities on education and training post 2020 – towards a European right to training for all (2018). https://www.etuc.org/en/document/eu-priorities-education-and-training-post-2020-towards-european-right-training-all. Accessed 30 Dec 2018
9. InfoDev: Impact of ICTs on Learning & Achievement. A Knowledge Map on Information & Communication Technologies in Education. http://www.infodev.org/articles/impact-icts-learning-achievement. Accessed 12 Dec 2018
10. What the research says about ICT and motivation. http://39lu337z51l1zjr1i1ntpio4.wpengine.netdna cdn.com/wp-content/uploads/2016/04/wtrs 05 motivation.pdf. Accessed 12 Dec 2018
11. Alexander, P.A., Singer, L.M.: The Conversation, Oct. 15, 2017, 9:31 PM. A new study shows that students learn way more effectively from print textbooks than screens. https://www.businessinsider.com/students-learning-education-print-textbooks-screens-study-2017-10. Accessed 22 Jan 2019
12. Nielsen company: Textbook trends: How U.S. college students source course materials. Accessed 22 Jan 2019
13. Kottke, I.: Is there a difference in reading comprehension? (2014). https://springfieldprinting.com/is-there-a-difference-in-reading-comprehension/. Accessed 22 Jan 2019
14. Liu, Z.: Reading behavior in the digital environment. J. Doc. **61**(6), 700–712 (2005)
15. Morineau, T., Blanche, C., Tobin, L., Guéguen, N.: The emergence of the contextual role of the ebook in cognitive processes through an ecological and functional analysis. Int. J. Hum.-Comput. Stud. **62**(3), 329–348 (2005)
16. Ackerman, R., Goldsmith, M.: Metacognitive regulation of text learning: On screen versus on paper. J. Exp. Psychol.: Appl. **17**(1), 18–32 (2011)
17. Jamali, H.R., Nicholas, D., Rowlands, I.: Scholarly e-books: the views of 16,000 academics: results from the JISC national e-book observatory. In: Aslib Proceedings: New Information Perspectives, vol. 61, pp. 33–47 (2009)
18. Olsen, A.N., Kleivet, B., Langseth, H.: E-book readers in higher education. student reading preferences and other data from surveys at the University of Agder. Sage Open, **3**(2) (2013)
19. Woody, W.D., Daniel, D.B., Baker, C.A.: Ebooks or textbooks: students prefer textbooks. Comput. Educ. **55**(3), 945–948 (2010)
20. Ackerman, R., Lauterman, T.: Taking reading comprehension exams on screen or on paper? A metacognitive analysis of learning texts under time pressure. Comput. Hum. Behav. **28**, 1816–1828 (2012)

21. Ferro, S.: Five reasons why physical books might be better than e-books. http://mentalfloss.com/article/69380/5-reasons-physical-books-might-be-better-e-books. Accessed 22 Jan 2019
22. Simonova, I.: The effective e-learning applied in foreign language instruction. In: Pokrivcakova, S., et al. (eds.) Cudzie jazyky a kultúry v modernej škole, pp. 198–227. Masaryk University, Brno (2009)
23. Simonova, I., Poulova, P., Sabatova, M.: On Contribution of Modern Technologies Towards Developing Key Competences. M. Vognar, Hradec Kralove (2009)
24. Common European Framework of Reference for Languages (CEFR). https://en.wikipedia.org/wiki/Common_European_Framework_of_Reference_for_Languages. Accessed 22 Jan 2019
25. Simonova, I.: Enhancing learning success through blended approach to learning and practising English grammar: research results. In: Cheung, S.K.S., Kwok, L.-f., Kubota, K., Lee, L.-K., Tokito, J. (eds.) ICBL 2018. LNCS, vol. 10949, pp. 69–80. Springer, Cham (2018). https://doi.org/10.1007/978-3-319-94505-7_5
26. Millar, M., Schrier, T.: Digital or printed textbooks: which do students prefer and why? J. Teach. Travel. Tour. **15**(2), 166–185 (2015)
27. Hospodarske noviny. https://byznys.ihned.cz/c1-65962830-za-knihy-loni-utratili-cesi-temer-osm-miliard-roste-prodej-e-knih-naopak-klesa-produkce-vysokoskolskych-ucebnic. Accessed 26 Jan 2019
28. Ng, E., Schweitzer, L., Lyons, S.: New generation, great expectations: a field study of the millennial generation. J. Bus. Psychol. **25**, 285–292 (2010)
29. Shin, W., Allen, M.: Working with Generation-D: adopting and adapting to cultural learning and change. Libr. Manag. **28**(1/2), 89–100 (2007)
30. Knutson, R., Fowler, G.: Book smarts? E-texts receive mixed reviews from students. Wall Street J. D1 (2009)
31. Sadon, R.: The state of the e-textbook. PC World (2010). http://www.pcworld.com/article/203001/the_state_of_the_etextbook.html. Accessed 24 Jan 2019
32. Yu, R.: Technology, costs, lack of appeal slow e-textbook adoption. USA Today (2012). http://www.usatoday.com/tech/news/story/2012-01-16/ebook-textbook-sales/52603526/1. Accessed 24 Jan 2019
33. Rowland, I., Nicholas, D., Jamali, H.R., Huntington, P.: What do faculty and students really think about e-books? In: Aslib Proceedings, vol. 59, no. 6, pp. 489–511 (2007)
34. Nicholas, D., Rowlands, I., Jamali, H.: E-textbook use, information seeking behavior and its impact: case study business and management. J. Inf. Sci. **36**(2), 263–280 (2010)
35. Hromadka, J.L., Molnar, A. (eds. and transl.): J. A. Comenius – A perfect reformation. Praha, Comenius Faculty of Theology (1957)

Summarization Exercises and Interpreting Performance in Blended Interpreting Training

Yinghui Li[1] and Hengbin Yan[2(✉)]

[1] School of English and Education/Bilingual Cognition and Development Lab, Center for Linguisitics and Applied Linguistics, Guangdong University of Foreign Studies, Guangzhou, China
liyinghui@gdufs.edu.cn

[2] Faculty of English Language and Culture, Guangdong University of Foreign Studies, #2 North Baiyun Avenue, Baiyun District, Guangzhou 510420, China
yhb@gdufs.edu.cn

Abstract. Nineteen student interpreters who were unbalanced Chinese-English bilinguals were recruited. Their performance in a Chinese-to-English (C-E) consecutive interpreting (CI) task, performance in an English-to-Chinese (E-C) CI task, and performance in two summarization tasks respectively following the two CI tasks were examined. Results showed that (1) no significant difference was found in students' overall interpreting performance between C-E and E-C CI, but their performance in target language grammaticality and appropriateness was found significantly better in E-C than in C-E CI; (2) students achieved significantly better performance in the summarization following C-E CI than they did in the summarization following E-C CI; (3) in E-C CI (but not in C-E CI), summarization performance was significantly correlated with interpreting performance (both overall performance and performance in target language grammaticality and appropriateness); besides, summarization performance had significant and positive predictive power on interpreting performance in E-C CI. Pedagogical implications are discussed.

Keywords: Blended learning · Interpreting training · Student interpreter · Summarization · Interpreting performance

1 Introduction

In the trend of globalization, the need for qualified interpreters increases quickly, calling for more efficient and on-demand interpreting training. As interpreting activities are characterized by input ephemerality and output immediacy (i.e., during interpreting interpreters are usually exposed to the source language only once and required to produce a first-and-final translation of the source language information) [9, 18, 21], student interpreters who are intended to become professional interpreters and to produce high-quality interpreting performance need intensive training and extensive practice until they succeed in circumventing their language constraints, psychological-cognitive constraints, and physical constraints [15]. The traditional interpreting training, which is mainly classroom-based, is limited in reach and the time or opportunity

S. K. S. Cheung et al. (Eds.): ICBL 2019, LNCS 11546, pp. 117–127, 2019.
https://doi.org/10.1007/978-3-030-21562-0_10

for instruction/practice, and it thus no longer meets the aforementioned needs from the interpreting market and from interpreting training.

Owing to emerging computer-assisted interpreting training (CAIT) technologies, interpreting training is now updated and revolutionized into a blended mode, which enables interpreting training to meet the growing need for proficient interpreters in a more efficient and effective way. Based on the idea of blended learning (i.e., that the traditional face-to-face and the technology-mediated instruction are converged without the presence of instructors and learners in the same physical environment required [7]), we can see in blended interpreting training that (1) interpreting training takes place in a digital interpreting laboratory equipped with state-of-the-art technology, where either teacher-led instruction or decentralized self-regulated learning can be implemented; (2) learning management systems such as *Moodle* are applied in interpreting training; (3) student interpreters independently make use of online terminology management systems (which can be established and maintained both by their interpreting instructors and by themselves) to prepare for in-class and after-class interpreting tasks assigned to them; (4) in a self-paced and collaborative virtual training environment, student interpreters accomplish interpreting tasks with feedback from peers/human instructors/e-instructors provided via the Internet (e.g., chat systems, discussion forums) shortly after the answer/interpreting output is submitted; (5) student interpreters, who become more self-regulated, autonomously look for and finish online exercises that are devised on the basis of real-life interpreting corpora (which offer access to transcribed input and output texts aligned with audio-visual recordings), and then they share and discuss their answers/interpreting output in class with peers and interpreting instructors [5, 6, 11, 13, 16].

Among exercises commonly adopted in blended interpreting training, summarization is the one frequently used (see a review on interpreting exercises in [8]). A popular type of summarization exercises is summarizing source language (SL) input immediately after interpreting (named "post-interpreting summarization" henceforth). According to previous studies on the benefit of summarization as an interpreting exercise [14, 17], post-interpreting summarization, which is usually introduced and assigned to student interpreters *before* interpreting, helps promote student interpreters' interpreting proficiency in three main ways, including (1) keeping student interpreters attentive to SL information during interpreting, (2) encouraging students to adopt a global approach when they listen to the SL, which can in turn assist them in comprehending SL details (especially the underlying SL logic), and (3) requiring student interpreters to weigh the importance of each SL message, which to some extent can avoid verbosity and redundancy in target language (TL) reformulation.

These potential benefits of post-interpreting summarization, however, are not yet examined empirically but are mainly speculations based on personal experience. So far we do not have sufficient empirical evidence showing how performance in post-interpreting summarization relates to interpreting performance, in particular how performance in this interpreting exercise may explain or help improve interpreting performance. The present study is intended to address these issues empirically. Post-interpreting summarization is widely used in training programmes of consecutive interpreting (CI), since this interpreting mode requires efficient summarization and recall of (SL) information just as summarization exercises demand. The present study thus focuses on CI rather than other interpreting modes.

2 Research Background

Though summarization is widely used as an exercise in translating and interpreting training [8, 17], empirical research is scarce on how interpreting performance is related to summarization performance. A previous study [4] compared the performance of short-story recalling and the performance of digit recalling between two groups of student interpreters at the advanced level (Group A and B). Group A was asked to articulate in their L1 (Italian) and Group B in L2 (English). Both groups recalled short stories under two recalling conditions, including recalling after listening to the story and recalling after doing simultaneous interpreting (SI) in which the story was delivered as SL input, with Group A interpreting from L1 to L2 and Group B in the opposite direction. When recalling digits, the two groups recalled under four conditions, including listening to digits, shadowing digits (i.e., repeating them out loud immediately after listening to them), listening to digits accompanied by articulatory suppression (i.e., listening to digits when uttering irrelevant syllables at the same time), and simultaneously translating digits.

After comparing the performance in recalling stories and the performance in recalling digits from three dimensions (Dimension 1: within group and across different recalling conditions; Dimension 2: between groups and under the same recalling condition; Dimension 3: between groups, with data of different recalling conditions collapsed together), the study found that the performance in short-story recalling after simultaneous interpreting (SI) was not so good as the performance after listening to the story. Besides, the digit recalling performance of the students who finished SI (before recalling) was found not as good as the performance of those who recalled under the other three conditions. These findings seemed to indicate a negative relation between interpreting experience and the efficiency of recalling SL input (short stories/digits), but due to the lack of related previous empirical research, further examination of this relationship is warranted. Besides, given that summarization as an exercise is widely used in CI training in both directions of each language pair (among which the most common pairs are L1–L2, L1–L3, and L2–L3), investigation is also needed on how the relationship between summarization and interpreting performance may potentially differ between CI of two opposite interpreting directions.

3 Research Design

To fill in these research gaps, the present study invites student interpreters of intermediate-high level of interpreting proficiency as participants, investigating and comparing their performance in L1-to-L2 (Chinese-to-English in this case, C-E for short henceforth) CI and their performance in L2-to-L1 (English-to-Chinese in this case, E-C for short hereafter) CI. Besides, the current study will also examine their performance in post-interpreting summarization concerning the two CI tasks. To avoid potential weaknesses caused by a small sample size of participants, the present study is to collect data from more than 15 participants [3]; and to avoid potential intervening effect due to any heterogeneity between groups, this study adopts a *within*-group design. The present research aims at answering two questions:

(1) How do interpreting performance and post-interpreting summarization differ between C-E CI and E-C CI?
(2) How does student interpreters' interpreting performance relate to their post-interpreting summarization respectively in C-E CI and in E-C CI?

3.1 Participants

Altogether 19 postgraduate students enrolled in an intensive interpreting programme in a national key foreign studies university were recruited as participants on a voluntary basis. When the data in the current study was collected, all the participants had field experience in interpreting and had been trained in interpreting for 300 h on average. All the student interpreters, who had spent at least ten years in learning English as a foreign language in China before they were enrolled in the aforementioned interpreting training programme were in general unbalanced Chinese-English bilinguals.

3.2 Materials and Procedure

Materials in CI Tests. The C-E CI test used in the current study was adapted from an eight-minute speech concerning a promotion of laptops for kids. The E-C CI test given by another male speechmaker, which was also converted from an eight-minute speech, was a general introduction of the 2007–2008 financial crisis. The original speech for C-E CI was delivered by a male speechmaker at an average rate of 249 words per minute and the original speech for E-C CI was given by another male speechmaker at a mean rate of 143 words per minute. Given that the participants were unbalanced Chinese-English bilinguals, the current study divided each speech into segments that comprised two to three sentences. The two CI tests were considered homogeneous with difficulty levels appropriate for the current participants based on three pieces of evidence, including (1) results in a pilot study participated in by five student interpreters from the same population as the 19 participants in the main study, (2) judgments on the difficulty level of the C-E CI task and the E-C CI task from five experienced interpreting instructors that were working at the identical university as the participants, and (3) a questionnaire about material appropriateness following the two CI tests in the main study. The E-C CI task was the same as used in [1], where more details about the task and the procedure can be found.

Procedure of CI Tests. Participants took the CI tests in a digital interpreting laboratory for blended interpreting training. During each CI test, they heard one segment at a time. When each segment ends, they were cued to begin interpreting. In accordance with the pilot study, the duration for rendering every segment was 1.5 times the duration of the segment. At the end of the interpreting time, participants would hear a signal followed by a short interval. Afterwards, participants heard a new segment and continued to interpret. Taking notes and referring to the notes were both allowed during the test. The order of the two CI tests was counterbalanced within group.

Procedure of Post-Interpreting Summarization. Immediately after each CI test, participants independently wrote a summary (about 150 to 200 words) of SL input in their L1 (i.e., Chinese). The time limit in this data collection session was 15 min, which, according to the pilot study, was proven sufficient for the participants to finish the task.

Scoring of Interpreting Performance. Two interpreting instructors (also working as professional interpreters with five years of field experience on average) listened to the recordings of all the participants' interpreting output and independently graded their CI performance based on identical scoring criteria. According to the criteria, which are generally accepted in CI training programmes, a participant's total score (100%) was composed of two proportions: (1) information accuracy and completeness ("Information" henceforth), which took up 67%, and (2) TL grammaticality and appropriateness ("TL expressions" henceforth), which occupied 33%. Each participant's final score in either CI test was equal to the mean of the scores given by the two raters (inter-rater coefficient $r = .95$)

Scoring of Post-Interpreting Summarization. The scoring of post-interpreting summarization centered on two issues: (1) how accurately and completely students can summarize the critical SL messages; (2) how logical the summarized messages were. In each CI test, there were in total nine pieces of critical SL information, and thus nine points was the full mark in summarization. Two university English teachers rated all the participants' summaries independently and when there was disagreement in rating, these two raters discussed until they reached a consensus. Each student interpreter's final score of each summary was the average of the scores given by the two raters (inter-rater coefficient $r = .93$).

4 Results

Data from the 19 participants were analyzed with the software R [19], specifically *psych* package [20], *rcompanion* package [12], and *MASS* package [22]. The effect size (Cohen's *d*) was equal to the difference between two means divided by the pooled standard deviation of the data. Cohen's *d* can be as small as .01 and as large as 2.00, with .20 being the threshold for a small effect, .50 for a moderate effect, and .80 for a large effect [2].

4.1 Summarization and Interpreting Performance

As shown in Table 1, our participants' performance in C-E CI was rated 81.21 (SD = 6.84) on average, which was not significantly different from their performance in E-C CI (Mean = 82.00, SD = 5.16), $t(18) = -.47$, $p = .646$). The results confirmed the general homogeneity in the two CI tests. Table 1 also demonstrated that the participants did not differ significantly in the sub-score of *Information* between C-E and

E-C CI ($t(18) = 1.57$, $p = .14$), while they achieved higher sub-scores in *TL expressions* in E-C CI (Mean = 29.18, SD = 2.34) than they did in C-E CI (Mean = 26.53, SD = 3.61, $t(18) = -3.15$, $p = .006 < .01$), showing that our student interpreters, who were unbalanced Chinese-English bilinguals, performed better in TL grammaticality and appropriateness when they were asked to interpret into their L1 than into L2.

Table 1. Interpreting performance and summarization at two stages (N = 19)

		C-E		E-C		*t*	Effect size
		Mean	SD	Mean	SD		
Interpreting performance	*Information*	*54.68*	*3.59*	*53.16*	*2.85*	*1.57*	*.46*
	TL expressions	*26.53*	*3.61*	*29.18*	*2.34*	*−3.15***	*.81*
	overall	81.21	6.84	82.00	5.16	−.47	.13
Summarization		5.47	1.46	2.29	.92	10.48**	1.58

Note. **: $p < .01$.

In terms of post-interpreting summarization, significant difference was found between the two interpreting directions, with the summarization after C-E CI (Mean = 5.47, SD = 1.46) better than the summarization after E-C CI (Mean = 2.29, SD = .92, $t(18) = 10.48$, $p = .000 < .01$). As summarization of SL information is closely related to SL comprehension, the results suggest that our participants, who were student interpreters and unbalanced Chinese-English bilinguals, probably comprehended SL input more efficiently when they interpreted from L1 than from L2.

4.2 Relationship Between Summarization and Interpreting Performance

Correlation. As presented in Table 2, the correlation between summarization and the overall performance in C-E CI was not found significant ($r = .25$, $p = .293$). Neither was significant correlation found between summarization and either sub-score of interpreting performance (see Table 2 for details). By contrast, a significant and positive correlation was found between summarization and the overall performance in E-C CI ($r = .48$, $p = .040 < .05$), particularly between summarization and *TL expressions* in this CI test ($r = .53$, $p = .019 < .05$). These results indicate that in E-C CI, the student interpreters who comprehended and recalled SL information more cost-effectively would probably interpret better (either in terms of the overall performance or specifically in terms of *TL expressions*), and vice versa.

Table 2. Correlation (r) between summarization and interpreting performance (N = 19)

	Overall interpreting score		Information		TL expressions	
	C-E	E-C	C-E	E-C	C-E	E-C
Summarization	.25	.48*	.14	.39	.31	.53*

Note. *: $.01 \leq p < .05$.

Predictive Power of Summarization on Interpreting Performance. As significant correlations were reported between the student interpreters' summarization performance and performance in E-C CI, a question was raised whether the performance in such a typical exercise frequently used in blended interpreting training can predict student interpreters' interpreting performance. To answer this question, the present study conducted two linear regressions, with the performance (both overall score and *TL expressions*) in E-C CI as the dependent variable in each regression and their summarization score in the corresponding CI test as the independent variable (see Table 3). Results show that summarization scores significantly explained 23% variance in the overall interpreting score ($R^2 = .23 = 23\%$, $F = 4.95$, $p = .040 < .05$) and 29% variance in *TL expressions* ($R^2 = .29 = 29\%$, $F = 6.78$, $p = .019 < .05$). As the β values were above zero in both regressions, the predictive power of summarization scores on interpreting performance was positive, indicating that student interpreters' efficiency in post-interpreting summarization probably had a positive moderating effect on their performance in E-C CI.

Table 3. Predictive power of summarization on interpreting performance (N = 19)

Regression	Dependent variable(s)	Independent variable	R^2	F	β
1	Overall score	Summarization	.23	4.95*	2.67
2	*TL expressions*		.29	6.78*	1.36

Note. *: $.01 \leq p < .05$.

5 Discussion

The present within-group study scrutinized and compared 19 intermediate-high-level student interpreters' performance in CI of two directions between Chinese and English. Moreover, the current study examined these student interpreters' performance in two summarization tasks respectively following the two CI tasks. With a series of quantitative analyses, three major findings were attained. First, no significant difference was found in CI performance between the two interpreting directions (Chinese-to-English or English-to-Chinese), whereas the results showed that our student interpreters achieved better performance in TL grammaticality and appropriateness in E-C CI than in C-E CI (see Table 1). These results suggest that first, the two CI tests were homogenous in general. Second, the results indicate that student interpreters probably enjoy greater advantage in the delivery of TL output when the TL is L1 than when it is L2. These results are consistent with our intuition, given that student interpreters, who are mostly unbalanced bilinguals, usually have a higher proficiency level (in particular of speaking) in their L1 than in L2. On the other hand, the results suggest that L2-speaking drills are still imperative in the blended interpreting training programme for intermediate-high or postgraduate student interpreters.

The present study also found that student interpreters achieved better scores in the summarization after C-E CI than they did after E-C CI (see Table 1), indicating that they were more efficient in comprehending and retrieving SL information when the SL was their L1. As SL comprehension and recall is of vital importance in CI, the results also suggest that English (i.e., L2) listening comprehension should be highlighted, and thus sufficient related exercises should be provided even in the interpreting training programme for postgraduate student interpreters, if these students would like to achieve a summarization performance in E-C CI as efficient as in C-E CI. Exercises of L2 listening are especially necessary given that the majority of these students are intended to take interpreting as their professional career. In fact, student interpreters need to be competent particularly in L2-to-L1 CI (also referred to as into-A CI), since CI of this direction is the most popular CI mode in the interpreting market (especially in West Europe).

In terms of the relationship between post-interpreting summarization and interpreting performance, no significant correlation between the two variables was found in C-E CI (see Table 2). This result suggests that in CI from L1 to L2, the student interpreters' interpreting performance may not be so closely related to their efficiency in SL comprehension and in SL information recall as it was in CI from L2 to L1. Notwithstanding the importance of SL proficiency in interpreting, student interpreters can be homogeneous in their SL comprehension when the SL was their L1, and their interpreting performance was therefore more influenced by their TL proficiency (their L2 speaking in this case), which probably resulted in the aforementioned absence of significant correlation between summarization and interpreting performance in C-E CI.

Meanwhile, the current study found that student interpreters' post-interpreting summarization was significantly correlated with their interpreting performance (both overall score and the sub-score of *TL expressions*) in E-C CI (see Table 2). Besides, their summarization performance significantly explained/predicted more than 20% variance in their interpreting performance (see Table 3). These results first confirmed our intuition that interpreters' comprehension and recall of SL information plays a crucial role in their interpreting output. Second, the results suggest that at the intermediate-high or postgraduate stage of interpreting training, student interpreters who are more efficient in comprehension and recall of SL messages are more likely to perform better in interpreting, especially in TL grammaticality and appropriateness.

Pedagogically speaking, our findings indicate to interpreting instructors and curriculum developers that to student interpreters, improvement in post-interpreting summarization can to some extent promote interpreting performance. In a learner- or learning-centered blended interpreting training, it is thus suggested that (1) student interpreters should enjoy sufficient and easy access to online and offline interpreting materials (especially in their self-paced training session) based on which they take a more active role in practising post-interpreting summarization whenever and wherever they want; (2) either in classroom-based instruction or via online chatting systems/discussion forums, interpreting instructors introduce to student interpreters (or student interpreters share with each other) useful summarization strategies/tactics that students can deploy into their autonomous summarization practice; interpreting instructors can also design for students a proper number of memory exercises such as the "retrieval exercise", which is found to be helpful in improving trainees' summarizing ability [10, 23], and make the exercise available for students in an online interpreting exercise repository; (3) after student interpreters have achieved a certain training goal with summarization exercises, interpreting instructors can provide personalized suggestion (better via the Internet and after class) to each individual student about follow-up exercises, preparing students for skill transition from summarization exercises to interpreting activities.

6 Conclusion

In blended interpreting training, post-interpreting summarization is an exercise widely used. The present study, which invited 19 student interpreters who were at the intermediate-high/postgraduate stage of interpreting training, investigated the students' performance in CI of two directions between Chinese and English as well as their performance in post-interpreting summarization. The results showed that student interpreters did not differ in their overall interpreting performance between the two CI directions (C-E and E-C), but they achieved better performance in TL grammaticality and appropriateness in E-C CI than in C-E CI. The results also showed that the participants achieved better performance in post-interpreting summarization in C-E CI than in E-C CI. The current study also found that in E-C CI, interpreting performance was closely related to summarization performance, with the latter significantly and positively predicting the former.

From a pedagogical perspective, these findings suggest that summarization as an interpreting exercise has a potential positive effect in promoting interpreting performance, and thus more finely-designed summarization exercises and related quiz/test items could be introduced into our future interpreting training programmes. To apply summarization exercises more efficiently in blended interpreting training, interpreting instructors and curriculum developers can make full use of the latest information technologies to capture the most updated interpreting materials online when developing summarization exercises. To augment its promoting effect on interpreting performance (particularly in self-paced interpreting training), online summarization exercise repositories/systems can cater to each student interpreter's individual needs of training by offering (1) accurate and efficient assessment of current summarizing ability, (2) tasks of an appropriate difficulty gradient, (3) tasks of rich topic variety, (4) concise and timely assessment of the summaries handed in by students, and (5) a portfolio automatically built for each individual student, recording the history of their practice in summarization and facilitating their self-reflection on the practice. Empowered by CAIT and latest technologies like Big Data and artificial intelligence, interpreting instructors (either human instructors or e-instructors) can provide to students opportune and personalized feedback on their summaries (including but not limited to comments, advice, strategies) along with proper follow-up exercises (including but not limited to L2-learning drills, summarization exercises, and memory practice), encouraging student interpreters to take a more autonomous and spontaneous role in practicing summarization and to transfer the skills they acquire in summarization exercises to the more challenging task, interpreting.

Acknowledgements. The authors are grateful to Prof. Yanping Dong from Bilingual Cognition and Development Lab, Guangdong University of Foreign Studies (GDUFS) for her supervision to the current research. The authors also thank members from Bilingual Cognition and

Development Lab, GDUFS for their assistance in data collection. The research was supported by a grant (BCD201702) from Bilingual Cognition and Development Lab, GDUFS, a grant (290-XGS17023) directly from GDUFS, and a grant (GD18YWW02) from Guangdong Planning Office of Philosophy and Social Science.

References

1. Cai, R., Dong, Y., Zhao, N., Lin, J.: Factors contributing to individual differences in the development of consecutive interpreting competence for beginner student interpreters. Interpret. Translat. Train. **9**(1), 104–120 (2015). https://doi.org/10.1080/1750399X.2015.1016279
2. Cohen, J.: Statistical Power Analysis for the Behavioral Sciences, 2nd edn. Lawrence Erlbaum Associates, Mahwah (1988)
3. Creswell, J.W.: Educational Research: Planning, Conducting, and Evaluating Quantitative and Qualitative Research, 4th edn. Pearson, Boston (2015)
4. Darò, V., Fabbro, F.: Verbal memory during simultaneous interpretation: effects of phonological interference. Appl. Linguist. **15**(4), 365–381 (1994). https://doi.org/10.1093/applin/15.4.365
5. Fantinuoli, C.: Computer-assisted preparation in conference interpreting. Translat. Interpret. **9**(2), 24–37 (2017). https://doi.org/10.12807/ti.109202.2017.a02
6. Fantinuoli, C.: Computer-assisted interpreting: challenges and future perspectives. In: Pastor, C., Durán-Muñoz, I. (eds.) Trends in E-Tools and Resources for Translators and Interpreters, pp. 153–174. Brill | Rodopi, Leiden (2018). https://doi.org/10.1163/9789004351790_009
7. Graham, C., Dziuban, C.: Blended learning environments. In: Spector, M. (ed.) Handbook of Research on Educational Communication and Technology (3rd Edition), pp. 269–276. Erlbaum, New York (2008)
8. Jones, R.: Conference Interpreting Explained. Routledge, New York, NY (2014)
9. Kao, P.C., Craigie, P.: Evaluating student interpreters' stress and coping strategies. Soc. Behav. Pers. Int. J. **41**(6), 1035–1043 (2013). https://doi.org/10.2224/sbp.2013.41.6.1035
10. Karpicke, J.D., Roediger, H.L.: The critical importance of retrieval for learning. Science **319** (5865), 966–968 (2008). https://doi.org/10.1126/science.1152408
11. Ko, L., Chen, S.: Online-interpreting in synchronous cyber classrooms. Babel **57**(2), 123–143 (2011). https://doi.org/10.1075/babel.57.2.01ko
12. Mangiafico, S.: An R Companion for the Handbook of Biological Statistics, version 1.3.2 (2015). http://rcompanion.org/rcompanion/
13. Mayor, B., Ivars, J.: E-learning for interpreting. Babel **53**(4), 292–302 (2007). https://doi.org/10.1075/babel.53.4.01may
14. Meyer, I.: A translation-specific writing program: Justification and description. In: Krawutschke, W. (ed.) Translator and Interpreter Training and Foreign Language Pedagogy, pp. 119–131. John Benjamins, Amsterdam (1989)
15. Moser-Mercer, B.: Skill acquisition in interpreting. Interpret. Translat. Train. **2**(1), 1–28 (2008). https://doi.org/10.1080/1750399X.2008.10798764
16. Motta, M.: A blended learning environment based on the principles of deliberate practice for the acquisition of interpreting skills. Interpret. Translat. Train. **10**(1), 133–149 (2016). https://doi.org/10.1080/1750399X.2016.1154347
17. Niedzielski, H., Kummer, M.: Learning translating and interpreting through interlanguage. In: Krawutschke, W. (ed.) Translator and Interpreter Training and Foreign Language Pedagogy, pp. 132–146. State University of New York at Binghamton, New York, NY. (1989)

18. Pöchhacker, F.: Introducing Interpreting Studies. Routledge, London (2004)
19. R Core Team: R: A Language and Environment for Statistical Computing (2018). https://www.R-project.org/
20. Revelle, W.: Psych: Procedures for Personality and Psychological Research (2018). https://CRAN.R-project.org/package=psych
21. Setton, R.: Meaning assembly in simultaneous interpretation. In: Pöchhacker, F., Shlesinger, M. (eds.) The Interpreting Studies Reader, pp. 178–202. Routledge, London (2002)
22. Venables, W.N., Ripley, B.D.: Modern Applied Statistics with S, 4th edn. Springer, New York (2002). http://www.bagualu.net/wordpress/wp-content/uploads/2015/10/Modern_Applied_Statistics_With_S.pdf
23. Zhou, A., Ma, X., Li, J., Cui, D.: The advantage effect of retrieval practice on memory retention and transfer: based on explanation of cognitive load theory. Acta Psychol. Sin. **45**(8), 849–859 (2013). https://doi.org/10.3724/SP.J.1041.2013.00849

Hotel Process Simulator

Petra Poulova[1(✉)], Miloslava Cerna[1], Jana Hamtilova[1], Filip Malý[1], Tomáš Kozel[1], Pavel Kriz[1], Jan Han[2], and Zdenek Ulrych[3]

[1] Faculty of Informatics and Management, University of Hradec Kralove, Rokitanskeho 62, Hradec Kralove 500 03, Czech Republic
{petra.poulova,miloslava.cerna,jana.hamtilova, filip.maly,tomas.kozel,pavel.kriz}@uhk.cz

[2] Institute of Hospitality Management in Prague, Svídnická 506, Prague 181 00, Czech Republic
han@vsh.cz

[3] University of West Bohemia, Univerzitni 8, Pilsen 306 14, Czech Republic
ulrychz@kpv.zcu.cz

Abstract. The computer simulation of the world are predominantly perceptual stimuli that allow the user to manipulate the elements of the model world and create a sense of realism. Modeling and simulation serves primarily to illustrate and describe individual processes, their structure and, above all, their behavior. Using simulation experiments, the entire model is examined under different conditions and in different states that represent different variants of these systems. Simulation as a method is used not only for innovation and for optimization of business processes, but has proven itself in education and human resource development. Currently, there are some schools and educational institutions around the world providing the opportunity to attend part of the training courses using simulation games.

Keywords: Application · E-learning · Game · Process · Simulation · Smart device

1 Introduction

Nowadays, we are experiencing increasing interactions between individuals and smart environments, whether it is the interaction of smart devices during ordinary activities such as smart homes, washing machines, refrigerators, air conditioning, toothbrushes connected to a mobile phone or teaching/learning and bringing certain elements of reality through virtual 3D world.

There is growing emphasis on teachers in passing their knowledge and experience to students to get students more engaged because students expect more interaction and communication in the online world. [1] The virtual world is the type of online community, which is primarily a form of computer-simulated environment that users can use, create, and interconnect certain objects [2].

The computer simulation of the world are predominantly perceptual stimuli that allow the user to manipulate the elements of the model world and create a sense of

S. K. S. Cheung et al. (Eds.): ICBL 2019, LNCS 11546, pp. 128–136, 2019.
https://doi.org/10.1007/978-3-030-21562-0_11

realism. These simulations are now used in many industries, whether it's the business sector or the activities of different organizations [3].

Simulators and their possibilities will be described in this work together with examples of utilization of virtual reality for educational purposes.

2 Process Management

At the turn of the 80s and 90s of the last century it became clear that the old way of managing companies is inadequate under the new conditions. The company can no longer be organized on the basis of firmly defined organizational structure, where each employee has a predetermined place, defined responsibilities and relevant authority. Such management presupposes firmly defined structure, activities and follow up events and connections; it is the idea of precisely defined and unchanging particular sequence of activities [4].

Economic and other subjects have to adapt quickly to competitive pressures, they often have to leave outdated usual work practices and organizational structures.

Today's organizations are in a situation where they have to have a particularly good understanding of themselves and their position in the competitive world. This self-centered approach raises emphasis on monitoring the processes in the organization and their optimization for the final recipient [5].

The so-called the business process management is starting to be applied as an approach allowing the organization to react flexibly to the changed external and internal conditions of its operation. So today's organizations face a challenging task - a change in the nature of their functioning.

The basis of a new type of organization is the concept of business processes as a set of activities that requires one or more inputs and forms an output that represents a value for the customer [6].

The advent of process management is closely tied to the massive development of information technology over the last few decades, allowing management of activities to the level of business processes. The existing management methods and hierarchical organizational structure of enterprises in the new information age began to seem inadequate. Process management allows monitoring of the organization from multiple perspectives than it can be in the case of functional management. Process management can describe it through implemented activities, can measure, evaluate, change and adapt them if necessary. Compared to previously used functional management in an organization, process management makes the workflow more transparent. The described processes allow for measurement of their performance and scheduling of resources required to produce a given amount of output. It is possible to monitor reality and compare it with the plan defined in the description of the process. Customers become part of the production process and their different requirements can be met more easily. Workers build a more direct relationship with the customer and their goal is not to fulfill the command, but to satisfy customer needs. This is also the main priority of the participants in the process. In addition, the process management presupposes teamwork and therefore the chance of better use of workers.

In order to convert elements from the real world into virtual ones, we need to know these elements thoroughly and consequently we have to be able to reproduce what works and what is needed for it to work. In connection with an enterprise, this process is called process management.

Process management describes all activity in an enterprise that is then integrated into processes that are more sophisticated. Via these processes, the company optimizes its entire organization in order to be efficient completely not only in partial processes.

A prerequisite for an efficient process management is above all a sufficient level of knowledge of the organization's partial processes and setting out the objectives of the whole enterprise and the system. Only when we know the individual processes in detail can we see their shortcomings. There are a lot of ways to identify the behavior of individual processes, but we will focus on modeling and simulation [7].

3 Modeling and Simulation of Hotel Processes

Modeling and simulation serves primarily to illustrate and describe individual processes, their structure and, above all, their behavior. All modeling follows specific methodologies, such as the BPMN methodology. These tools can help to realize deficiencies in the business. Based on models and simulations, business processes can be upgraded and optimized at much lower costs than in the real world [7].

Using simulation experiments, the entire model is examined under different conditions and in different states that represent different variants of these systems. These experiments provided sufficient answers to questions like 'What would happen if…?' or 'How will the model change, if…?' [3].

During the simulation, it is possible to monitor other things such as:

- Time requirements for individual processes and their activities
- The number of units served or unserved
- Lengths of queues
- The level of use of individual resources and devices [8].

There are a number of modeling tools that help to display business processes easily.

One of the tools is the ARIS Express software application, Free Modeling Software, which is designed for casual users and beginners. It is focused on the creation and design of business models, but can also be used in educational systems. The user interface is intuitive and looks professional [9].

Jan Han of the University Hotel in Prague has already dealt with modeling of hotel processes. His model contained a description of the hotel reception process of the hotel reception, see Fig. 1.

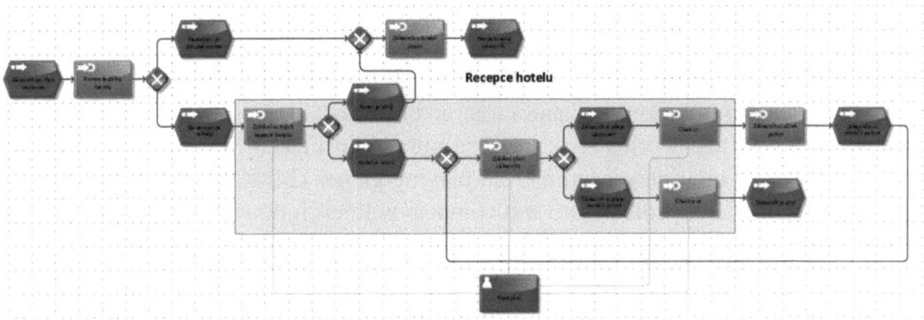

Fig. 1. Hotel processes [3]

The simulation experiment on behavior of selected processes in a hotel reception was worked by the Institute of Hospitality Management in Prague with the help of Simulation System Arena, see Fig. 2.

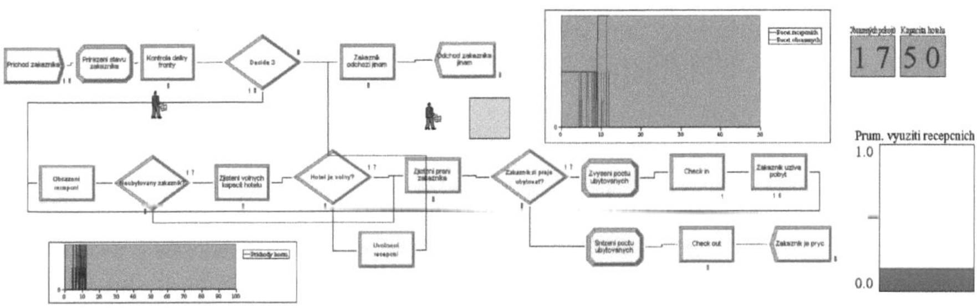

Fig. 2. Simulation of hotel processes [3]

According to Han, the level of similarity of created process models with reality is decisive for the validity of the results of individual simulation experiments. Business systems, and therefore models of hotels and restaurants are stochastic systems, since many states occur with a certain probability and cannot be 100% determined in advance [3].

Modeling and simulation in some business sectors are commonplace; unfortunately, hotels and gastronomy are still in their infancy despite the fact that these models prove to be one of the effective ways to improve the quality and efficiency of service delivery.

3.1 Social Virtual Worlds

This subchapter brings description of simulators that are currently available. There is also brief historical look back at the development of computer games that simulate the construction of hotels, virtual worlds and so on.

Koster, an experienced developer of virtual worlds in the 1990s, defines the virtual world as "a spatial representation of a permanent virtual environment that can be experienced by many participants at the same time who are represented in avatars." [10].

However, today's social virtual worlds are a bit different, they begin to reflect Stephenson's metaverse vision, which is defined as a future massive network of interconnected digital worlds. Several million people already use this type of environment for communication, collaboration, or business [11].

Since then, virtual worlds have evolved into sophisticated 3D interactive systems such as massively multiplayer online role-playing games (MMORPGs) through which millions of people chat, collaborate and compete with each other through their avatars.

Second Life

One of the best examples of the development of Stephenson′s metaverse concept is Second Life (www.secondlife.com). Second Life experts have enabled users to build and personalize their avatars, private virtual premises (land) and objects (houses and clothing) through a powerful and easy-to-use interface.

Second Life's population grew from 64 acres in 2003 to 65,000 acres today and from 2 million in 2006 to more than 9 million today. This world can be virtual, but money is real. There are companies and banks that advertise and sell real products and services, by creating virtual stores or by entering a link inside.

Second Life has its traditional web sites. Similarly, it is also true for some universities and teachers where they mediate their lectures and courses in Second Life virtual environments. [12] (Figs. 3, 4 and 5).

Fig. 3. Second Life

Hotel Simulators - Computer Games

There are plenty of online and offline hotel simulators. Their main task is the creation of a dream hotel, according to the idea of an individual. These are the simulators, which are intended mainly for the entertainment and leisure than to have a certain amount of value added.

The most popular game is Hotel Habbo. This game was founded in 2000 and has grown every month so that every month is housed five million unique visitors in a total of 32 portals country-specific. Hotel Habbo therefore remains one of the most popular SVWs for young people. According to Sulake, a Finnish platform provider, 90% of its users are between 13 and 18 years of age [13].

The fundamental difference from Second Life is its environment. Running on a web browser, its environment "resembles a huge contemporary western interior, which is presented in three-dimensional graphics of isometric 'retro style' and surrounds block avatars, each of which controlled by a user" [14].

In other words, Habbo avatars do not resemble human beings, but they look more like cartoon characters. Habbo Hotel aims to provide young users with a safe and friendly environment; therefore, activities that are located in Second Life, such as cyber-violence, gambling or sex, are forbidden. Additionally, users remain anonymous in Habbo; disclosure of identity or contact information within the platform is prohibited; it is mediated by the operator [13].

Fig. 4. Habbo Hotel

4 Virtual Environment and Education

Simulation as a method is used not only for innovation and for optimization of business processes, but has proven itself in education and human resource development. Currently, there are some schools and educational institutions around the world providing the opportunity to attend part of the training courses using simulation games, or adoption of business process optimization through simulation experiments [3].

Virtual museum can be example. Current technologies allow external presentation of objects such as museums or other outdoor sites and attractions. Their tour can be conveyed remotely, for example from another state.

Many of the world's museums are performing interactive trends; their internet presentations provide a virtual interactive presentation of exhibits and electronic communication, beside up-to-date information enticing visitors on their activities.

In this context, we can mention, for example, the Virtual Egyptian Antiquity Museum (The Virtual Egyptian Antiquity Museum – accessible from http://www.touregypt.net/museum) or a virtual tour of the Lascaux Cave in France (http://archeologie.culture.fr/lascaux/fr#/en/00.xm).

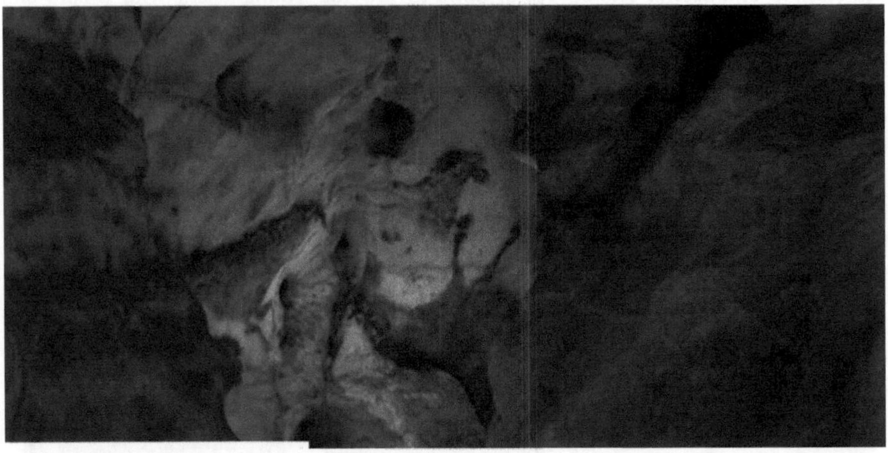

Fig. 5. Cave Lascaux

Another example can be Investment games.

We use some example of such a game in the teaching of economics at our faculty. Students have no experience with investing on the stock exchange and over the counter markets and they would like to get improved in this area.

The actual evaluation of individual investment competitions was conducted via decision support system, specifically in the program Criterium Decision Plus version 3.0. [15] As one of the criteria for evaluation it is also possible to use SMART technology, which is being used by investors when monitoring the development of the financial market and making trades [16].

5 Conclusion

Virtual Reality is a technology that enables a user to interact with a simulated environment. Virtual reality technologies create the illusion of the real world (e.g., combat training, piloting, learning or the fictional world of computer games).

It is a visual, auditory, tactile or other experience creating a subjective impression of reality using computer imaging equipment, special audiovisual helmets, glasses, etc. motion sensing, and stimulating touch or other techniques evoking perception and sensation.

Sooraj et al. researched differences in ability to acquire skills through tablets and virtual reality in their study [17]. It was researched whether students had learned and memorized more components using a tablet or virtual reality. After completing the "lesson", everything was tested on a real motorcycle. The results were unambiguous; the participants who learned through the virtual reality achieved much better results than the students who watched the teaching material on tablets only.

Our team now prepare Virtual Hotel Process Simulator which combines computer games and virtual reality. The simulator is trying to show the operation of the hotel from the employee perspective; the user passes as manager, receptionist, etc., so there is possibility to look and map the whole situation.

Acknowledgments. This study is supported by the TACR project TL01000191 and SPEV project 2019, run at the Faculty of Informatics and Management, University of Hradec Kralove, Czech Republic.

References

1. Oblinger, D.: Boomers, Gen-Xers a millennials: understanding the new students. EDUCAUSE Rev. **38**(4), 37–47 (2003)
2. Bishop, J.: Enhancing the understanding of genres of web-based communities: the role of the ecological cognition framework. Int. J. Web-Based Communities **5**(1), 4–17 (2009)
3. Hán, J.: Modelování a simulace procesů v hotelnictví a gastronomii [online]. COT (2017). https://www.icot.cz/modelovani-a-simulace-procesu-v-hotelnictvi-a-gastronomii. Accessed 09 Nov 2018
4. Řepa, V.: Podnikové procesy. Procesní řízení a modelování. Grada Publishing, Praha (2007)
5. Pekárková, L.: Techniky modelování a optimalizace podnikových procesů. Thesis. Masarykova univerzita, Brno (2007)
6. Hammer, M., Champy, J.: Reengineering the Corporation: A Manifesto for Business Revolution. Nicholas Brealey Publishing, London (1993)
7. SANKOT, J.: Využití software Adonis pro popis podnikových procesů. Thesis, Bankovní institut vysoká škola, Praha (2011)
8. Hán, J., Beránek, M., Belešová, S., Mrkos, D., Studnička, P., Sochůrková, M.: Vybrané kapitoly z hotelnictví a gastronomie. Ubytovací služby. Wolters Kluwer, Praha (2016)
9. Shyshkina, H.: Nástroje pro modelování a optimalizaci podnikových procesů. Masarykova univerzita, Brno (2016)
10. Koster, R.: A virtual world by any other name? (2004). http://terranova.blogs.com/terra_nova/2004/06/a_virtual_world.html. Accessed 01 Nov 2018
11. Hendaoui, A., Limayem, M., Thompson, C.W.: 3D social virtual worlds: research issues and challenges. IEEE Internet Comput. **12**(1), 88–92 (2008)
12. Kaplan, A.M., Haenlein, M.: The fairyland of second life: virtual social worlds and how to use them. Bus. Horiz. **52**(6), 563–572 (2009)
13. Mäntymäki, M., Riemer, K.: Digital natives in social virtual worlds: a multi-method study of gratifications and social influences in Habbo Hotel. Int. J. Inf. Manage. **34**(2), 210–220 (2014)
14. Lehdonvirta, V., Wilska, T., Johnson, M.: Virtual consumerism: case Habbo Hotel. Inf. Commun. Soc. **12**(7), 1059–1079 (2009)

15. Svobodova, L., Cerna, M.: Investment competitions on the current local scene from students' perspective – case study. In: Uskov, V.L., Howlett, R.J., Jain, L.C. (eds.) Smart Education and Smart e-Learning. SIST, vol. 41, pp. 417–427. Springer, Cham (2015). https://doi.org/10.1007/978-3-319-19875-0_37
16. Černá, M., Svobodová, L.: Development of financial and language competences via on-line games and tests. In: European conference on e-Learning, ECEL 2015. Reading: Academic publishing (2015)
17. Sooraj, K., Unnikrishnan, R., Bhavani, R.R.: Virtual reality learning environments for vocational education: a comparison study with conventional instructional media on knowledge retention. In: IEEE 18th International Conference on Advanced Learning Technologies (2018)

Adaptive Content Development for Blended Learning in Microscopic of Herbal Medicines

Bunyapa Wangwattana(✉) and Verayuth Lertnattee(✉)

Faculty of Pharmacy, Silpakorn University, Nakhon Pathom 73000, Thailand
{wangwattana_b, lertnattee_v}@su.ac.th

Abstract. In the academic year of 2017, the fourth year pharmacy students were assigned to gather herbal microscopic information of 6 unknown herbs using the developed web-based tool on the Plant Histology and Identification of Plant-powdered Drugs. Microscopic photos were uploaded into the system and used as reference pictures for identifying the powdered medicines. The content was created and adapted by students, teachers and a voting mechanism of the system. Information of microscopic images could be accessed by students. This blended learning gave students the opportunity to select the learning methods that best suited their own preferences, traditional method, a new method or both. Furthermore, we analyzed the students' satisfaction and opinions of the tool. The results showed the students were satisfied with the content development and thought the tool was useful for microscopic learning. With this system, the content will be dynamically developed by students, teachers and the system.

Keywords: Microscopic herbal powdered drugs · Herb identification · Adaptive content

1 Introduction

Pharmacognosy is one of the subjects for pharmacy students. The subject is linking crude drugs of natural origin, such as plants, animals, or minerals, and their chemical compounds which contain pharmacological activities. The subject includes authentication and quality control of herbal drugs, from raw materials of plants until herbal finished products [1]. The contents of quality controls of herbal drugs are followed by the methods in pharmacopoeias [2–4]. To authenticate herbal drugs, macroscopic and microscopic examinations of herbal drugs are necessary. In Thailand, sometimes herbal drugs are sold on the market in their powdered form. The microscopic examination is a crucial method to identify the herbal powdered drugs [4].

To identify the herbal powdered drugs using the microscopic method, the pharmacy students need to learn the theory of histology and need to practice in the laboratory classes. In the Faculty of Pharmacy, Silpakorn University, the microscopic examination was set in the Pharmacognosy laboratory on the topic of Plant Histology and Identification of Plant-powdered Drugs. The traditional way to learn this topic is for students to be assigned to identify the unknown powdered drugs using the black and white drawing pictures from textbooks as the references [4, 5]. The problem is that the

S. K. S. Cheung et al. (Eds.): ICBL 2019, LNCS 11546, pp. 137–148, 2019.
https://doi.org/10.1007/978-3-030-21562-0_12

black and white drawings could not show the real characteristics of the cells or tissues, and the unclear drawings made the students misunderstand.

The information technology (IT) has a key role in all fields including education. In pharmacy school, the technology was implemented to support the students learning [6]. A mix of traditional classroom-based learning and information technology tools are often found and is called blended learning. One of the more effective IT tools is designed in a web-based format. Students can access the website from wherever and whenever they want. This makes the web-based format a good platform for blended learning. Also the websites could apply to support collaborative learning, it depends on the teachers' objectives and learning plans. Creating content for blended learning involves several components: once content is developed, it must be managed, delivered, and standardized. In this paper, we present the process to develop content for blended learning of the microscopic method in herbal powdered drugs. The content we developed in this work is adaptive content created by students, teachers and the voting mechanism of the system. The content was delivered to the students using a web-based tool. The blended learning classroom of the microscopic method in herbal powdered drugs was implemented and was able to solve the problems we found in the traditional way of study.

2 Learning About Herbal Medicines in Pharmacy Curriculum

In the Faculty of Pharmacy, Silpakorn University, the subjects involved in herbal medicines were designed for the second year, third year and fourth year pharmacy students. The second year students have to learn about the macroscopic examination of herbal drugs, both the whole fresh plants and crude drugs. They were expected to identify some herbal medicines that are widely used in Thailand. The phytochemistry related to pharmacological activities were set to the third year pharmacy students. During the fourth year, the pharmacy students have to learn about quality control for herbal medicines, both qualitative and quantitative methods. Among the qualitative methods, microscopic examination of herbal powdered drugs is one of the crucial methods that is specified in many herbal monographs and pharmacopoeias [2–5]. The fourth year pharmacy students should have the microscopic examination skill to authenticate herbal powdered drugs.

Traditional way of learning microscopic method in Pharmacy Course is only face-to-face classrooms, i.e. lecture classes and laboratory practice classes. The contents of the lecture class for the topic of microscopic examination of herbal medicines consists of the theory of histology, plant tissue and cell types, how to use the microscope, how to stain tissue, and so on. To authenticate the herbal powdered drugs, the students have to know the basics of histology, the cell and tissue types that should be found in each part of the plants. For example, the trichrome, the stomata and guard cells should be found in leaves, and the pollen grains should be found in flowers and also can be used to identify the plant species.

The pharmacy students have to practice to use the microscope for herbal drug identification. The practice classes were divided into 2 laboratories. The first laboratory, the pharmacy students had to practice to use the microscope for examining the known samples. The samples consisted of 4 parts of plants, i.e. Senna (*Cassia angustifolia*) leaves, roots of Rhubarb (*Rheum palmatum*), Pepper (*Piper nigrum*) fruits, and Datura (*Datura metel*) flowers. All samples represented the tissues and cells of leaves, roots, fruits and flowers. In the second laboratory, the 6 unknown samples were randomly identified by students, i.e. cannabis (*Cannabis sativa*) flowers, leaves of tea (*Camellia sinensis*), leaves of *Senna alata*, saffron (*Crocus sativa*), Turmeric (*Curcuma longa*) rhizomes and roots of Rauwolfia (*Rauvolfia serpentina*).

The students did the experiments by comparing the tissues and cells they found under the microscope with the black and white drawing pictures from textbooks and some pharmacopoeias, such as Thai Herbal Pharmacopoeia as references. Figure 1 shows the example of drawing pictures of the *Senna alata* similar to the drawings shown in textbooks. If the students found the related cells as the references, they had to draw the cells they found in the report. However, there are some problems with this learning method, such as the reference drawings may not be able to express all details of the characteristic cells or tissues used for identification. Moreover, the reference pictures were shown in black and white, while the real samples showed their specific color under the microscope. These colors are important information used to authenticate the herbal drugs. Sometimes the colors of tissue and cell showed the thickness of the cell wall, and sometimes the colors indicated the substances in the cells. Furthermore, each herbal powdered sample has its own characteristic cells that all pharmacy students should know. Due to the limitation of time, the students could not have the opportunity to examine all samples. While the teachers expected the students to gain experience with all samples. To solve these problems, the new way of learning in microscopic method in herbal powdered drugs was created.

Fig. 1. The example drawings of *Senna alata* leaves in their powdered drug.

3 Content Development for Blended Learning

Blended learning is a blend of learning techniques to enhance the learning experience. Blended learning courses should contain between 30% and 79% of online content, with the remaining portion of the course content delivered by non web-based methods, such as face-to-face instruction or paper textbooks [7]. Each student requires different learning methods and has their own preferences. Blended learning programs may mix several forms of learning tools, such as real time collaboration software, web-based courses, and traditional instructor-led training. A combination of face-to-face learning and online activities is often used in blended learning programs [8].

Content comprised all instructional material. To develop engaging blended learning content, the teacher should have in-depth understanding about the content and also be able to differentiate between various delivery methods. Content management, such as all the administrative functions, needed to make the content available to learners. A learning-management system, for example, is an internet-based software that facilitates the delivery and tracking of blended learning. The collaboration tools are used to improve the learner engagement [9].

4 Adaptive Content Development Using Blended Learning

From the traditional way of learning microscopic method, only the face-to-face classrooms were used. The students had to compare the cells and tissues they found under the microscope with the reference drawing photos from textbooks. Also the students had to draw the pictures of the characteristic cells on the paper and reported to the teacher. Nowadays digital technology plays an important role in our daily life. The digital camera was combined with the mobile phone and can be used as equipment in education. The digital camera which is attached to the mobile phone gives high quality digital photo files. Instead of drawing the cells or tissues found under the microscope, taking photos is the best way to collect the microscopic information. They can express all details such as the layers of tissue or thickness of the cell wall, also the colors of the cells. The files are easier to copy, edit and share, compared with the hard copy of drawn pictures.

To solve the problems previously explained, we developed the content for blended learning in the microscopic method of herbal powdered drugs. In the second laboratory class, groups of 4–5 students were assigned to authenticate two unknown herbal powdered drugs randomly. Students had to search for the characteristic cells and tissues of assigned samples under the microscope, then the photos of the characteristic cells were taken using digital cameras on their own mobile phones. The digital photos were gathered together in a web-based tool we created, KUIHerbRx2017. We developed the web-based tool for blended learning and also supporting students' collaborative learning in microscopic of herbal powdered drugs based on our available web-based resource, KUIHerb. The KUIHerb or the Knowledge Unifying Initiator for Herbal Information is a web-based tool for knowledge management in herbal information. The KUIHerb's users are the people who had experience in herbs and traditional medicines. However, KUIHerb has some limitation and is not suitable for students' learning. The KUIHerbRx was created and used as a web-based tool for the exchange of herbal information between students and also teachers [10]. The URLs of KUIHerbRx were not opened to public access. Therefore, the KUIHerbRx was created for supporting the pharmacy students' learning of herbal drugs. The tool can be modified to match with the teachers' plan and activities depending on the objectives of learning. The

KUIHerbRx is a useful tool for blended learning and to encourage students' collaborative learning [11, 12]. KUIHerbRx2017 is a modified version of KUIHerbRx which contains special tabs to support the students' learning, such as a products tab and a microscopic tab. In this work, the microscopic tab was taken into account. This microscopic tab was designed to upload the microscopic photos taken by the students in the laboratory class, the keywords and the contributors were also added. The other students could then access the web-based tool to study the microscopic information easily by themselves. The web page of *Curcuma longa* and the microscopic tab in KUIHerbRx2017 was shown in Figs. 2 and 3., respectively.

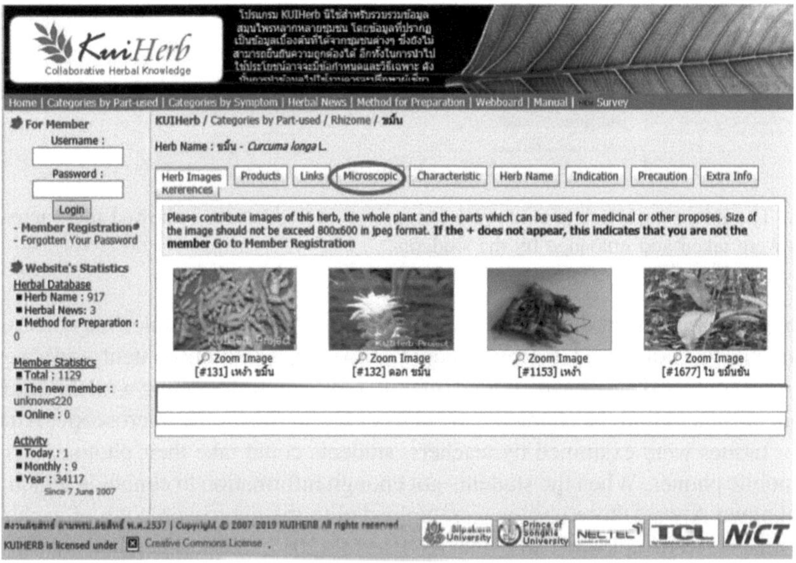

Fig. 2. The web page of *Curcuma longa* in KUIHerbRx2017 showed special tabs; products and microscopic tab.

The tool was also designed to support collaborative learning among the students. Students were encouraged to share the knowledge of their particular sample set with others. The characteristic cells or tissues found under the microscope by the students were then inspected by the teachers, then the photos were taken. The microscopic information of all unknown herbal powdered drugs was examined again by the instructors after uploading to the website as a database contributed by the students as part of the exercise. The students were also assigned to create their report in digital file format, which contained the photos taken by each group of students. The students were expected to integrate the microscopic information they found and summarized which the unknown samples were. The report was then sent to the teacher via email.

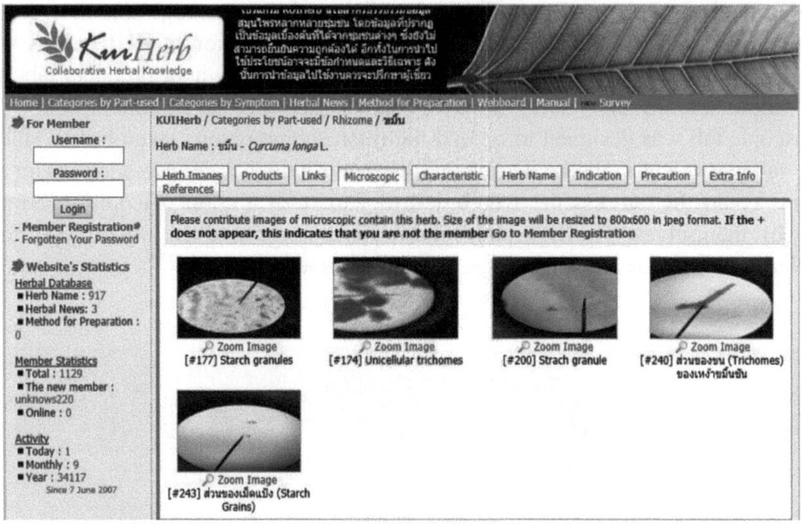

Fig. 3. The microscopic tab of *Curcuma longa* in KUIHerbRX2017 showed the microscopic photos were taken and uploaded by the students.

For adaptive content development, a microscopic content module was constructed. This module was composed of a microscopic tab, a page for editing content, and a page for presenting content. These pages started off with no content. Beginning with the unknown A, students had to find the characteristic cells or tissues under the microscope. After the cells or tissues were examined by teachers, students could take their photographs with their mobile phones. When the students got enough information to conclude which plant the unknown A was, those photos were uploaded to the microscopic tab of each plant. After images were uploaded into the KUIHerbRx2017, the teacher had to check all microscopic information of each plant. Some incorrect information, such as the wrong conclusion, and/or unacceptable images, i.e. unclear/blurry images, including their keywords might be uploaded, these could be deleted from the system. Note that all plants used in an experiment were distributed to all groups as the first set of unknowns (unknown A). When students examined the unknown B, they could compare their photographs with contributed images in the KUIHerbRx2017 from unknown A. With the voting mechanism in the KUIHerbRx2017, popular images would move to the top of the page based on a number of clicks, these are assumed to be sets of high-quality images. It should be easier for students to compare their photographs with high quality microscopic images in the system. The content of microscopic images, keywords and suggestions were dynamically improved. The adaptive content of microscopic information of powdered drugs is useful for supporting the learning of herbal medicine. The comparison of traditional learning and our proposed learning methods is presented in Table 1.

When the content was developed on the web-based tool, the personalized learning could be implemented. The students who needed to improve their skill in microscopic method for herbal drug identification could practice more by themselves. Two factors could be customized, i.e., samples and references. For samples, they could select any kinds of samples, i.e., no sample, known samples or unknown samples. The number of samples they used might be varied. In term of references, the textbooks, the KUIHerbRx2017 or both could be applied. Moreover, a review of the lesson is supported by the KUIHerbRx2017 whenever and wherever. This personalized learning is based on each student's interests, available time, and skills.

Table 1. Comparison of the traditional learning and the proposed method.

Topic	Traditional method	Proposed method
Using blended learning	No	Yes
References	Drawings in textbooks	Uploaded photos by students
Picture characteristics	Black and white drawings	Multi-color photographs taken from a mobile phone
Collaboration and share	Intra-group	Intra- and Inter-groups
Lesson review	Difficult to review	Easy to review, anytime and anywhere
Information of herbs	Only for herb identification with microscopic method	Information of herbs from the KUIHerbRx2017
Content	Static content based on textbooks	Adaptive content based on students' upload pictures and information

5 Setting, Learning Design and Evaluation

The modified KUIHerbRx with the microscopic tab was set up in the academic year 2017. The content development topic was used with 172 of the fourth year pharmacy students, academic year 2017 in the Plant Histology and Identification of Plant-powdered Drugs laboratory class with unknown samples. Groups of students with 4 or 5 students each could access the KUIHerbRx2017 website using the user names and passwords given by the administrator. The 6 kinds of unknown samples, cannabis (*Cannabis sativa*) flowers, leaves of tea (*Camellia sinensis*), leaves of *Senna alata*, saffron (*Crocus sativa*), Turmeric (*Curcuma longa*) rhizomes and roots of Rauwolfia (*Rauvolfia serpentina*), were labeled as 1, 2, 3, 4, 5 and 6 respectively. Each group was assigned 2 samples out of a possible 6 marked as "Unknown A" and "Unknown B". These samples were randomized to each group. Every group of students was assigned to examine the unknown A first. After they uploaded the photos of unknown A to the KUIHerbRx2017, then unknown B could be examined.

To examine the unknown A, the traditional way of learning explained previously was used. The tissues or cells that were found under the microscope were compared to the black and white drawing pictures in textbooks. To examine unknown B, the tissues and cells found under the microscope could be compared with the photos of unknown A uploaded to the tool and/or from the textbooks as references. Each student could customize the sources of reference they wanted to use, the web-based form or textbook form or both, depends on how they learned best. This is a part of personalized learning. At the end of the class, we evaluated the students' satisfaction and opinions about the web-based tool using the questionnaire.

The assigned report of each group of students had to be sent to the teacher within a week after the laboratory class. The photos taken by students in each group were examined. The students had to show their ability to integrate the microscopic information and that they could conclude the knowledge they had studied from this blended classroom.

The process design for content development for blended learning in microscopic examination of herbal powdered drugs was shown in Fig. 4. The available web-based tool, KUIHerb, was modified and used as the platform for blended learning called KUIHerbRx2017. The modified website contained a special module called the microscopic content module which is used for uploading the microscopic information by students. The microscopic content module consists of images, keywords, contributors and suggestions. The microscopic photos were uploaded to the image area. The keyword was the detail of each image, including the magnification power. The contributors showed the ID of the student who uploads the photo. Any comments or suggestions could be added to the suggestion area. The activities were designed for the students to create content on their own, that is the microscopic information. The content obtained from the students had to be screened by the teachers, then added to the system. The uploaded microscopic information was examined again by instructors for quality control. In case there were some mistakes, such as the information was uploaded to the wrong plant, the information was deleted. The students were encouraged to contribute to the assignment of their particular sample set with others. Then the other students could use the content in their learning. Evaluations of students' satisfaction and their opinions were done after the class. The students' learning outcome was assessed through the assignment and the report by the teachers.

6 Results and Discussions

6.1 Evaluation of Students' Satisfaction Using the Questionnaire

The questionnaire was given to the students to evaluate the students' satisfaction and opinions of the tool we used. The questionnaire consisted of 2 sentences with the 5 levels Likert scale. The number 5 to 1 were referred to as "Definitely Agree", "Agree", "Uncertain", "Disagree" and "Definitely Disagree", respectively. The students who answered the questionnaire made up 78.49% of the class. The result of the evaluation was shown in Table 2.

The average scores in all topics were higher than 4, showing the students were satisfied to use the KUIHerbRx2017 for learning microscopic method in herbal powdered drugs and for collaborative learning in this topic. Some students also gave extra opinions that can be concluded:

- The KUIHerbRx2017 is user friendly.
- The tool is useful for students because students can search for other information, not only microscopic photos.
- The information in KUIHerbRx2017 is very useful, and will be more useful if the information could be shared in public.
- The photos should be approved by teachers before uploading to prevent incorrect information.
- Sometimes the uploaded photos were lost.
- The URLs were difficult to access.

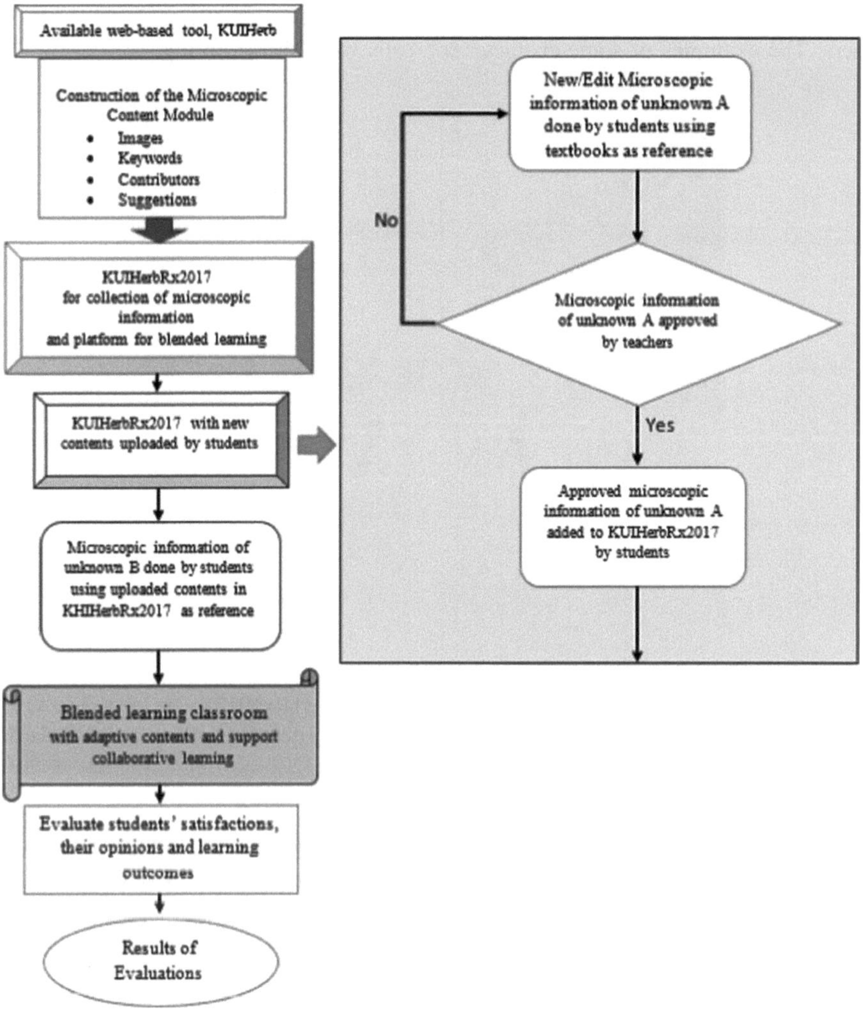

Fig. 4. The process of content development for blended learning in microscopic examination of herbal powdered drugs.

Table 2. The results from questionnaires.

Topics for evaluation	Mean ± SD
Satisfaction of KUIHerbRx2017	4.16 ± 0.08
KUIHerbRx2017 is useful for microscopic learning	4.28 ± 0.18

6.2 Evaluation of Students' Collaboration and Learning Outcomes

The microscopic photos uploaded to KUIHerbRx2017 were evaluated by teachers. The photos uploaded to the KUIHerbRx2017 which show the characteristic cells and tissues are selected for use as references for authenticating the herbal powdered drugs for others. The examples of some characteristic cells were shown in Fig. 5.

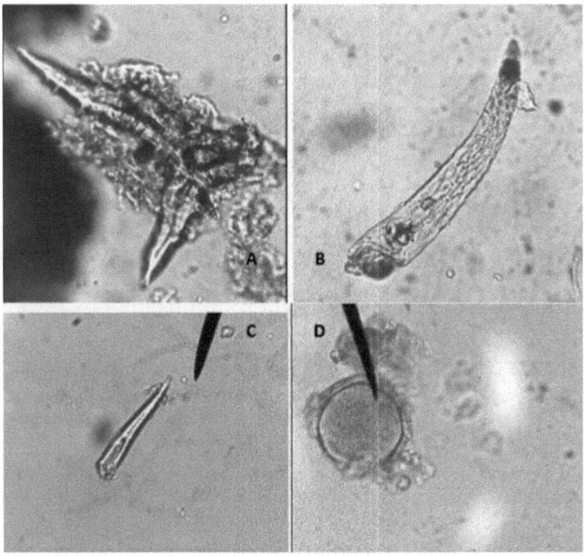

Fig. 5. The microscopic photos were uploaded to the KUIHerbRx2017 by the students; (A) The Idioblast cell from Tea leaves, (B) Cannabis Trichrome, (C) Trichrome of *Senna alata* leave and (D) Pollen grain of Saffron.

The KUIHerbRx2017 was used as a platform for collaborative learning. The students had to find the characteristic cells or tissues for each sample under the microscope. The cells were checked under the microscope by the teachers to prevent students' misunderstanding. The microscopic photos of these cells or tissues were taken and shared with other students by uploading to the microscopic tab on KUIHerbRx2017 website. These were then checked again by teachers for quality control. Once uploaded they were used as the reference photos by other groups. This is the opportunity for students who did not have a chance to examine those unknown samples by themselves to study the other unknown powdered drugs. The number of images contributed to KUIHerbRx2017 was shown in Table 3. The numbers of deleted images were also reported. These images were filtered out due to incorrect, unclear, and incomplete images.

The students had to observe the powdered drugs using the organoleptic methods, such as the color of the powder, characteristic smell, then combined with the characteristic cells and tissues they found under the microscope in each unknown powdered drug. The unknown powdered drugs were identified using the information they found. The students had to conclude which the unknown samples were and reported what they had learned from this class. The report was sent to the teachers via email. The results from the students' report showed that they have the ability to integrate the knowledge from both organoleptic methods and microscopic information of unknown herbal drugs and could summarize the knowledge they had learned from the class.

Table 3. The numbers of images contributed to the KUIHerbRx2017.

Herb	# Presented Images	# Deleted images	# Groups
Rauvolfia serpentina	39	9	9
Curcuma longa	15	2	6
Senna alata	51	11	12
Cannabis sativa	20	5	8
Camellia sinensis	34	6	7
Crocus sativa	39	11	12

7 Conclusion and Future Works

The adaptive content development for blended learning in the microscopic method of herbal drugs was designed to use the web-based tool to be a platform for blended learning. The available web-based tool, KUIHerb, was modified to be used as a blended learning tool called KUIHerbRx2017. The website was modified to contain a special module called the microscopic content module which is used for uploading the microscopic information by students. The microscopic content module consists of images, keywords, contributors and suggestions. The microscopic photos were uploaded to the image area. The keyword was the detail of each image, including the magnification power. The contributors showed the ID of the student who uploads the photo. Any comments or suggestions could be added to the suggestion area. All of the microscopic information was created and adapted dynamically by the teachers and students' collaboration. Also, popular photos, measured by clicking on "Zoom Image", were moved up the ranking to allow easier access. This was done by the voting mechanism in the KUIHerbRx2017.

The adaptive content development supported microscopic learning. The students could use the microscopic information uploaded to KUIHerbRx2017 as the reference to authenticate the unknown herbal powdered drugs instead of black and white drawings from textbooks. However, the students could select the method of learning that is best suited for them. This is a part of personalized learning that allows them to tailor their experience. Moreover, not only in the microscopic photos, but the other herbal information in the KUIHerbRx2017 is also useful for learning about herbal medicine.

From the evaluation results, most students were satisfied to use the KUIHerbRx2017 to support their learning about herbal medicine. There are still some issues with the KUIHerbRx2017, but these will be patched and fixed soon. We plan to use the fixed web-based tool as a reference database for learning microscopic method in academic year 2018. The microscopic database established in KUIHerbRx2017 is very useful information to authenticate the herbal powdered drugs. The database can be developed and used as a public database to identify other herbal powdered drugs in the future.

Acknowledgments. This work was partially supported by Instructional Innovation Development Project, Silpakorn University (2018).

References

1. Sarker, S.: Pharmacognosy in modern pharmacy curricula. Pharmacogn. Mag. **8**(30), 91–92 (2012)
2. British Pharmacopoeia Commission, Great Britain: Medicines Commission, and General Medical Council (Great Britain).: British Pharmacopoeia 2000, vol. 1. Bernan Press (PA), (2000)
3. United States Pharmacopeial Convention: United States Pharmacopeia and National Formulary (USP 41-NF 36). Rockville, MD (2016)
4. Thai Pharmacopoeia Committee: Thai Herbal Pharmacopoeia, vol. 1. Department of Medical Sciences, Ministry of Public Health, Nonthaburi, Thailand (1995)
5. Council of Europe: European Pharmacopoeia, 6th edn. Strasbourg, France (2007)
6. Fox, B., Flynn, A., Fortier, C., Clauson, K.: Knowledge, skills, and resources for pharmacy informatics education. Am. J. Pharm. Educ. **75**(5), 93 (2011)
7. Allen, I.E., Seaman, J., Garrett, R.: Blending in: the extent and promise of blended education in the United States. Sloan Consortium. PO Box 1238, Newburyport, MA 01950, (2007)
8. Singh, H.: Building effective blended learning programs. Educ. Technol.-Saddle Brook Then Englewood Cliffs NJ- **43**(6), 51–54 (2003)
9. Shivam, R., Singh, S.: Implementation of blended learning in classroom: a review paper. Int. J. Sci. Res. Publ. **5**(11), 369–372 (2015)
10. Lertnattee, V., Chomya, S.: Using a learning tool for improving results from a multi-lingual and multi-cultural herbal search engine. In: Advanced Materials Research vol. 1030, pp. 1859–1863. Trans Tech Publications, Switzerland (2014)
11. Lertnattee, V., Wangwattana, B.: Using blended learning for collaborative learning in herbal medicine. In: Cheung, S.K.S., Kwok, L.-F., Ma, W.W.K., Lee, L.-K., Yang, H. (eds.) ICBL 2017. LNCS, vol. 10309, pp. 307–318. Springer, Cham (2017). https://doi.org/10.1007/978-3-319-59360-9_27
12. Wangwattana, B., Lertnattee, V.: Using a collaborative tool for complementing knowledge of aromatic herbs and volatile oils. Adv. Sci. Lett. **24**(11), 8518–8522 (2018)

Experience in Blended Learning

Lecture Recordings at the University – Analysis and Evaluation of Implementation Possibilities

Tobias Hirmer(✉) and Andreas Henrich(✉)

University of Bamberg, An der Weberei 5, 96047 Bamberg, Germany
{tobias.hirmer,andreas.henrich}@uni-bamberg.de

Abstract. Despite constant criticism on lectures as didactic instruments, they remain the most common form of teaching [11]. Due to the rising need for flexibility in the learning process, lecture recordings are seen as a possibility to capture this demand. This paper presents an empirical study conducted at the University of Bamberg, Germany, and a literature review that evaluated main requirements for a lecture recording solution in the specific blended learning scenario at the faculty of Information Systems and Applied Computer Sciences at the University of Bamberg. Additionally, possible recording and distribution solutions have been analyzed. The results have been captured in a summarizing recommendation for the specific case at the University of Bamberg.

Keywords: Blended learning · Lecture recordings · Requirements

1 Motivation and Introduction

Today's society lives in a world of constant change. Within the growing digitization of our lifes, the process of learning happens more and more independent from time and place [3, p. 53]. Therefore, flexible learning scenarios seem to play a major role in today's modern society. This change poses main challenges for universities. Mastering these challenges can be important to match up in a digitized world [20, p. 102]. In contrast, e-learning at universities itself has been in process for over 20 years [20, p. 104]. New media is used for planning and preparing lessons, but lesser for imparting content [7, p. 57f.]. As one option in this direction lecture recordings are frequently used at universities. In relation to the need of flexibility in the learning process, lecture recordings can capture the demand for flexible learning [22, p. 210]. At the faculty of Information Systems and Applied Computer Sciences (IS & ACS) at the University of Bamberg, only a few chairs use this digitized form of teaching. As the chairs have different approaches and settings of their lecture recordings, introducing a standardized solution would facilitate the maintenance for the lecturers and the ease of use for students.

The following paper presents the results of a research study at the Chair of Media Informatics at the University of Bamberg. Main goal of this study was to identify specific requirements for lecture recording systems in a blended learning scenario as well as presenting and analyzing some possible capture and distribution solutions. The

S. K. S. Cheung et al. (Eds.): ICBL 2019, LNCS 11546, pp. 151–163, 2019.
https://doi.org/10.1007/978-3-030-21562-0_13

priority of this paper is to present the main results of the requirements analysis. In the beginning, a short summary of the background and related work is presented. Subsequently a literature review in Sect. 3 and the presentation of an empirical study at the University of Bamberg in Sect. 4 form the requirements analysis. In Sects. 5 and 6 a short summary of the investigated recording and distribution solutions is given. The resulting recommendation for the IS & ACS faculty and the University of Bamberg is presented in Sect. 7.

2 Background and Related Work

In the following, the lecture itself, its recording as well as the advantages and disadvantages of lecture recordings will be described more concretely. Despite constant criticism on lectures as didactic instruments, they remain the most common form of teaching [11].[1] The main reason is the possibility to communicate knowledge efficiently and economically [4, p. 603]. Furthermore, the lecture represents the personality of the lecturer better than a book [10, p. 42]. More concretely, the credibility and the motivation of the lecturer play an important role in the learning process [18, p. 500f.]. With regard to digitization, the lecture is particularly well suited for recording and making it available on the Internet compared to other forms of teaching at the university [12, p. 7].

The term lecture recording can be defined in many ways. Demetriadis and Pombortis [2, p. 147] for example differentiate strictly between e-lectures and live-digitized-lectures, whereas Glowalla [4, p. 606] uses a more open definition. In this paper, lecture recordings are defined as video-recordings of a lecturer's lesson independent from the place of the recording that is provided to the students [19, p. 13]. From a didactic perspective, the idea of lecture recordings is to give the students the possibility to use the video of the lecture to review the lecture and prepare for the exam [6, p. 63]. In a logfile analysis, Zupancic and Horz [24] have found that, especially during the audit period, the number of uses of the recordings rises. Both the revision and the preparation for the exam are good examples for the flexibility that lecture recordings provide. There are a few other reasons why this flexibility is needed. From the lecturer's perspective, lecture recordings can compensate the lecturer's occasional absence during illness or professional travel [15, p. 81]. From the student's perspective, lecture recordings enable him or her to study even in case of illness, long distance to the university, and in life situations that make it difficult to study in a regular way [21, p. 236]. Moreover, lecture recordings can be a solution for universities comprising locations scattered all over a city [21, p. 236].

In general, lecture recordings are seen as a noticeable relief in everyday study life for students and lecturers [21, p. 240] [22, p. 214f.]. This can be confirmed by the desire for a higher supply of lecture recordings [22, p. 214f.]. However, there are some negative aspects in the use of lecture recordings. One of the main critical points is the lack of interaction with the lecturer [15, p. 86]. Students do not see the relevance to ask questions if a lecture is recorded [21, p. 236]. Another common problem is reduced

[1] Already in 1902 Paulsen [16, p.237f.] reported that the lecture was criticized in its role as the dominant form of teaching in higher education.

attendance when recordings are available for a lecture [13, p. 35] [23, p. 200]. This is only one fear that lecturers have about the use of lecture recordings. The handling of new software and hardware can be perceived as a burden, copyright and intellectual property lead to legally unclear situations and comparison with other lecturers is regarded as a concern [1, p. 80]. All these aspects indicate possible hurdles in the establishment of lecture recordings. Since the lecturers can be seen as critical stakeholders for the establishment of lecture recordings at a university due to the worries and the resulting acceptance hurdles, appropriate measures should be taken with this group [6, p. 69].

So far, the key terms as well as the main benefits and disadvantages of lecture recordings were described. Based on this, relevant functions of a system for recording lectures will be presented in the following section.

3 Literature Review

This section summarizes a literature review on important functions of lecture recordings. These requirements will be compared with the results of the conducted empirical study later in this paper.

In principle, a lecture recording should provide the same information as the classroom lecture. This includes, among other things, that the lecturer is both audible and visible [4, p. 605]. A lecture recording should therefore at least ensure the speaker's voice and a recording of the script [13, p. 27]. The addition of a video is controversially discussed in the literature. While the higher (personnel) costs and the restriction of the lecturer's freedom of movement have to be accepted [13, p. 27], the recording of the lecturer offers significant advantages. With a video recording of the lecturer, the majority of students rate their work with the lecture recording as more effective than attending the lecture [4, p. 612]. Similar evidence can be found for the concentration in learning [4, p. 612f.]. A "talking head" also leads to a higher commitment of the students [5, p. 45].

An important feature of lecture recordings is the possibility to take notes. Adding own notes as well as seeing the lecturer's notes are both rated as important features of a lecture recording from the student's perspective [8, p. 45f.]. In addition, students should be able to use keywords to selectively navigate to specific parts of the recording in order to recapitulate selected topics [4, p. 605]. As mentioned in the previous section, lecture recordings are frequently used to prepare for the exam. In this case, the search and navigation with specific keywords is a highly relevant feature. Another function desired by students is the adjustment of the playback speed, to improve the understanding of the content [8, p. 49]. Thus students can independently deal with a lecture at their own learning pace [15, p. 81] [6, p. 73]. As a result, students can take individual breaks in case of attention difficulties without missing any content [6, p. 72].

As mentioned in the previous sections, lecture recordings are criticized because of the missing social aspect. Therefore, forms of social interaction can be relevant for lecture recordings. Possible solutions might be, for example, a feedback channel to the lecturer via e-mail, the exchange between students through discussion forums or a chat function [14, p. 7]. However, lecture recordings are not intended to be a communication or interaction medium, but merely an information instrument [15, p. 86].

In general, central elements regarding the acceptance of a software are its perceived usability and ease of use [6, p. 64]. Therefore, these elements should also be considered in the context of possible lecture recording solutions. Another important factor is the deployment of the lecture recordings. Lampi et al. [13, p. 29] demand a fast availability of the recordings. More specifically, a period between 4 and 24 h can be assumed [21, p. 237]. In addition, the software should support the interactive elements of a lecture as well as enable a simple preparation and integration into the learning management system [13, p. 29]. For optimal video length, Guo et al. [5, p. 44] recommend to divide the video into small parts of less than six minutes, due to the result, that the engagement has decreased with increasing video duration. From a didactic point of view, it would therefore be conceivable to divide the lecture recordings into smaller parts.

4 Empirical Study at the University of Bamberg

Two separate online surveys were conducted to evaluate the main requirements for a lecture recording system from the perspective of the students and the lecturers. The structure of the questionnaire was based on the functions from the literature review as well as on the questionnaires of Rohs and Streule [17] and Höver et al. [9]. 10 lecturers and 143 students from the faculty of IS & ACS participated in the online surveys. Correspondingly, 8.4% of the students at the IS & ACS faculty took part in the online survey. The students were able to participate in the online survey in July 2018 for about three weeks. Regarding the online survey for the lecturers, 16 lecturers received a personal invitation via e-mail. The participation on the online survey was restricted to the professors and their temporary lecturers because these two groups hold the lectures. The lecturers were able to participate in the online survey in July and August 2018 for about four weeks. Following the survey, the lecturers had the possibility to attend a separate interview. Hence, three lecturers were interviewed. The main results of the surveys and interviews will be presented hereafter.

To evaluate the relevance of lecture recordings at the University of Bamberg, students and lecturers were asked to rate the supply and demand of lecture recordings in general. Therefore, both groups were confronted with items (statements) which they had to evaluate on a scale from 1 (do not agree at all) to 5 (fully agree). The students rated the sufficient supply of lecture recordings with a mean of 1.76, a median of 2 and a standard deviation (SD) of 0.878. Half of the lecturers did not see a sufficient supply of lecture recordings (1.0) whereas the other half did not answer this question. A similar result can be seen in the demand for lecture recordings. For the students a scale over four items showed a mean of 4.3, a median of 4.5 and a SD of 0.7. The results of the lecturers are a bit lower. There a scale over three items was rated with a mean of 3.2, a median of 3.33 and a SD of 1.433. These results support the high demand for lecture recordings described in the literature analysis. In the specific case of the IS & ACS faculty of the University of Bamberg the results indicate that there is a major demand and a significant relevance for the use of lecture recordings.

Furthermore, the lecturers were asked about their hopes and fears regarding lecture recordings. Most lecturers have the hope that lecture recordings enable a flexible learning for the students and that they will understand the contents of the lecture better.

The most common fear is that students will be absent due to the recording of the lecture. Three lecturers have also selected data protection problems and legal vulnerability due to errors in content. These fears coincide with the descriptions in Sect. 3. These aspects will be considered in the concluding recommendation at the end of this paper.

The central aim of the empirical study was to evaluate the main requirements of a lecture recording system. The following paragraphs will present the relevant results, beginning with the core functions from students' and lecturers' point of view. Therefore, Table 1 shows the comparison of relevant functions from the users' view between the students and lecturers.

Table 1. Rated features of lecture recordings from the users' perspective (sorted with respect to the student rating; 1 = "not important at all" to 5 = "very important").

Function	Student			Lecturers		
	Mean	Median	SD	Mean	Median	SD
Download option	4.14	5	1.195	3.78	5	1.716
Table of contents with navigation	3.98	4	1.087	4.11	5	1.054
Adjusting the playback speed	3.89	4	1.418	4.29	5	0.951
Video of the lecturer	3.88	4	1.080	4.11	5	1.167
Search option	3.65	4	1.125	4.22	4	0.833
Creating notes	3.05	3	1.435	2.78	2	1.716
Save and export notes	2.98	3	1.395	2.38	2	1.685
Leave questions for lecturers	2.89	3	1.256	2.88	3	1.458
Leave questions for other students	2.37	2	1.186	3.5	3.5	1.309
Subtitle	2.23	2	1.232	3.33	3	1.323
Chat to discuss with other students	2.14	2	1.141	3.0	3	1.414

Interpreting the table, it becomes clear that both lecturers and students rate the same five functions as important or very important. Only the order is different. Some of the evaluated functions were already discussed in the literature review. The table of contents with navigation and the search options are needed to enable the students to navigate to specific parts of a lecture and search for specific content. The adjustment of the playback speed helps the students to learn in their own pace. The video of the lecturer has also been discussed previously. The results indicate that for the realization of lecture recordings at the University of Bamberg, a video recording of the lecturers should be integrated into the recording. Both lecturers and students voted it as important. The SD of these five functions is about 1, except for the adjustment of the playback speed by the students and the download option by the teachers. With the help of this overview, it is also possible to exclude some requirements for the implementation at the University of Bamberg. The creation of notes and a direct possibility for social interaction do not seem to be relevant for students and lecturers. Another question for the students showed, that only one in three students asks questions in a lecture. Students were also asked how often they take notes during a lecture. The majority of students just rarely or sometimes take notes. These results verify the less valued functions in Table 1. However, these aspects have been seen as relevant in the literature review in Sect. 3. The results of this empiric study indicate, that for the specific blended learning scenario at the IS & ACS faculty of the University of Bamberg, these functions might not be relevant. Subtitles seem irrelevant, too. However, the relevance should be discussed. Comparing the answers from students and lecturers, the different opinions regarding subtitles' importance might arise from the structure of this empiric study. The online survey was only available in German. International students therefore probably did not participate in this study. However, a subtitle might be particularly relevant for this group.

Additionally, lecturers were asked about the important functions of a lecture recording system from the producer's point of view. Table 2 shows the results. Like in the previous section, the highest valued functions (with a mean of more than 3.5 and a median of at least 4) were integrated into the list of requirements. Some of these points have also been verified by the interviews discussed later in this paper. Even though the integration of interactive elements is less valued, it will be integrated into the list of requirements because of the results of the interviews. In comparison to the literature review, especially the possibility to directly upload the recorded lectures into the learning management system is rated as important. This result indicates that for the case of the University of Bamberg, there is a need for a possible recording or distribution solution to enable this feature for the used learning management system Moodle. The SD reveals that the lecturers sometimes had very different opinions. The export to common file formats, the automated post-processing and the mentioned direct upload to the learning management system all have a SD of more than 1.3. This fact leads to a less important role of these functions.

Table 2. Rated functions of lecture recordings from the producer's view.

Function	Mean	Median	SD
Simple and time-saving recording function	4.78	5	0.667
Recording system independent from presentation computer	4.63	5	1.061
Export to common file formats (e.g. AVI, MPEG4, MP4)	4.56	5	1.333
Integration of a lecturer video	4.56	5	0.726
Automated post-processing/cutting	4.00	4	1.323
Direct upload to learning management system (e.g. Moodle)	3.89	5	1.537
Recording of multiple screens	3.67	3	1.323
Recording with multiple cameras	3.56	3	0.882
Placement of annotations	3.33	4	1.414
Recording of public questions	2.89	3	1.537
Integration of interactive elements (e.g. Quiz)	2.89	3	1.537

Besides these functions, the survey also evaluated the time of provision, the length of a lecture recording and the used devices from the students' perspective. At the time of provision, the majority of the students have opted for an availability of the lecture recordings within a few days (74 mentions) or hours (49) after the face-to-face lecture. In combination with the knowledge of Sect. 3, this seems to be an appropriate period of time to provide a lecture recording.

The major part of the students prefer a length of 60–90 min for a recording (42.7%) followed by a 31–45 min recording (28%). In contrast to the recommendation of Guo, Kim and Rubin [5, p. 44] to shorten the video, this result implies to remain with the classical lecture length for a recording. Among the used devices, laptops predominate with 93%. Slightly more than half of the students (58.7%) use a desktop PCs to watch recorded lectures. 33.6% of the students use a tablet and 29.4% use their mobile phone to watch a lecture recording. Since about one third of the students uses mobile devices, it becomes clear that a lecture recording should be optimized for these devices, too.

At last, the results of the interviews are presented. For a more structured presentation, the results are differentiated between technical and organizational requirements. The technical requirements are relevant for the list of requirements at the end of this section. The organizational requirements will later be applied when formulating an implementation recommendation for the IS & ACS faculty and the University of Bamberg. The interviews showed partly dissenting opinions regarding the requirements of the lecture recording system. Hence, a wish from one lecturer to establish one lecture recording solution for the whole university seems difficult to realize.

In order to take the different requirements into consideration, previously excluded aspects are also discussed again if necessary. Despite being rated as less important in Table 2, the support of interactive elements will be integrated in the list of requirements. It might be important for those lecturers, who want to organize their lectures more interactively. Therefore, a lecture recording system should support this opportunity. Consequently, the possibility to create simple learning videos independent from a lecture recording should be supported too. Two of the interviewed lecturers emphasized stability and user-friendliness as one of the central requirements for the recording system. In terms of user-friendliness, the focus is not only on a simple recording function but also on a short set-up time. This is also in line with the previous results of the survey. As well, there is a clear trend in the amount of the post-processing. All three lecturers support a solution, which, in the ideal case, would be completely applicable without post-processing. Especially with this time-consuming task, the desire for a central support office at the university becomes obvious. Beyond the technical support, one of the interviewed lecturers sees the need for legal support from the university in order to prevent anxiety among the lecturers. He sees legal uncertainties in the publication of recordings as a central hurdle to making lecture recordings freely available.

Concluding the previously shown results, Table 3 shows the list of requirements for a lecture recording solution in the specific blended-learning context of the IS & ACS faculty at the University of Bamberg. To this end, a separation between functional and non-functional requirements was used.

Table 3. List of important requirements for a lecture recording system.

Functional requirements	Non-functional requirements
Adjusting the playback speed	Fast deployment
Table of contents with navigation	Support of mobile devices
Search option	Simple recording function
Download option	Independence of presentation computer
Video of the lecturer	Independence of operating system
Support for interactive elements	Automated post-processing
Export to common file formats	
Direct upload to learning management system (e.g. Moodle)	
Creation of learning videos	

5 Consideration of Exemplary Recording Systems

Based on the derived list of requirements in Table 3, four lecture-recording solutions were analyzed: OBS-Studio, Camtasia, ActivePresenter and Panopto.[2]

The Open Broadcaster Software (OBS-Studio) is a free and open source software for video recording.[3] OBS-Studio is available for Windows, MacOS and Linux. At the University of Bamberg, the chair of Privacy and Security in Information Systems uses this software. The free and open availability of the source code is one big advantage of OBS-Studio. It is also possible to capture different scenes and switch these within the recording process. Furthermore, OBS-Studio is a simple and clear recording tool that enables lecture recordings independent of the presentation computer. However, it should be noted that this simplicity also means that limited functions have to be accepted.

Camtasia is a screen-capturing tool, which offers extensive editing options for the recorded video clips in addition to the recording function.[4] Camtasia is offered as a single or volume license and is available for Windows and MacOS. At the University of Bamberg the chair of Media Informatics is recording the lectures with Camtasia. With regard to the functional requirements, especially the comprehensive HTML5-Player can be evaluated as positive. However, the rather rigid format and the dependence on the presentation computer has to be criticized. Camtasia's project files are stored in a proprietary format that does not allow easy processing outside of Camtasia. In addition, the recording sources are limited to the screen and one camera. It is therefore not possible to record different scenes and does not allow more than one camera perspective.

[2] Please note that we have evaluated the current versions in 2018 according to our best possibilities. Errors in the evaluation can therefore not be excluded.

[3] https://obsproject.com/ [28.03.2019].

[4] https://www.techsmith.com/video-editor.html [28.03.2019].

ActivePresenter is an e-learning authoring tool that also contains a screen recorder and a video editor.[5] The program is available in three successive variants for Windows and MacOS: a Free Edition, a Standard Edition and a Pro Edition. The extensive functions offered by the program allow different application scenarios. However, the dependency on the presentation computer as well as a proprietary file format can be listed as points of criticism. An advantage of ActivePresenter is the possibility of responsive design. In order to use all relevant advantages of ActivePresenter, the Pro Edition is required.

Panopto is an all-in-one video content management system.[6] The program includes video recording, editing and publishing, as well as an integrated video management system. The Computing Centre of the University of Bamberg currently has a Panopto test system at its disposal. In this section, only the video recording and viewing features will be shortly assessed. The editing, publishing and integrated video management system will follow in the next section. Panopto contains a separate recorder software and an extensive video player. The recorder is available for Windows and MacOS. Lecturers need to install it on their presentation computer and can use it for creating and uploading the lecture recordings. If technically equipped lecture rooms are offered, Panopto also enables a recording independent from the presentation computer. Moreover, the lecturer can control and manage the recording via the browser or the Panopto App. The post-processing is happening online integrated in the Panopto video management system. The Panopto player is also integrated into the video platform. It enables most of the evaluated functional requirements and much more besides. Overall, Panopto is a very powerful and comprehensive all-in-one solution for creating lecture recordings and other video content. The functions allow a wide range of application scenarios.

6 Distribution and Presentation Solutions

In Sect. 5, four software solutions for recording lectures were examined and compared. With the exception of Panopto's all-in-one solution, the reviewed software were primarily recording solutions. An open point is the distribution and presentation of the recordings. Therefore, the following section introduces the compared distribution solutions.

Following on from the previous section, Panopto's video platform will first be considered. The video management system of Panopto enables a wide-range of post-processing options for the recorded lectures. Moreover, interactive content in form of quizzes can be added. The direct integration of recorded lectures into a learning management system is supported too. For the University of Bamberg, Moodle is relevant here. The text editor in Moodle can be used to integrate videos directly from Panopto with the help of a special button. A small disadvantage remains: The embedded player in Moodle supports only a part of the comprehensive functions of the Panopto Player. Furthermore, Panopto offers a wide-ranging analysis of the usage data.

[5] https://atomisystems.com/activepresenter/ [28.03.2019].

[6] https://www.panopto.com/ [28.03.2019].

A free counterpart to Panopto is Opencast. Opencast is an open source system for recording, editing, publishing and managing video content in the academic field.[7] The features of Opencast include all steps involved in creating a recording. Lecture recordings can be scheduled and automatically recorded via capture agents. Alternatively, self-recorded lectures can be uploaded. The videos are distributed via the video management system of Opencast and can be integrated into learning management systems. As an open source solution, Opencast offers many opportunities but also several hurdles. The open source code as well as the large and active community offer the possibility to customize Opencast freely according one's own needs and to benefit from the experiences of the community. However, Opencast is also very complex, since the university has to master the necessary skills for maintenance and operation by itself. With regard to the use for lecture recordings, Opencast is also convincing because it was created by universities for precisely this purpose and is therefore optimized for the academic use.

Beyond Panopto and Opencast, two other solutions were discussed: Lecture2Go and Open edX. Lecture2Go is a platform for the distribution of video recordings developed by the regional computer centre of the University of Hamburg. The portal software is available to other educational institutions as open source. Furthermore, Open edX is a free open source course management system, that is used for the provision of massive open online courses. In addition to the Open edX Studio for the creation of courses, the system also includes its own learning management system. Compared with Opencast and Panopto, Lecture2Go and Open edX have some disadvantages that made them less convincing for the use at the University of Bamberg.

7 Recommendations

Concluding the results of the previous sections, this section will summarize them in a short recommendation for the IS & ACS faculty and the University of Bamberg. This recommendation consists of three areas: general organizational aspects, comparison of the recording system and recommendable distribution and presentation solutions.

Organizational Recommendations. The survey of the lecturers showed that a pure fixation on lecture recordings is not the solution to all problems. More interactive instructional videos are also desired, which should be taken into account in a potential software solution to enable a university-wide recording solution. Furthermore, the demand for technically equipped lecture rooms can be extracted from the interviews. Equipped lecture rooms would offer the potential for individual recording solutions to enable a computer-independent recording, as well as being a simple and timesaving recording option to the lecturer. Both, the statements from the interviews and some of the results of the online survey, indicate that lecturers want more support from the university. In comparison to Sect. 3 this might lead to less restraint of the lecturers in using a lecture recording system. These factors are especially relevant because, as mentioned earlier, the lecturers are a critical part in establishing a lecture recording solution at a university.

[7] https://opencast.org/ [28.03.2019].

Recording Software. In Sect. 5, four possible programs for recording lectures were analyzed. With regard to the IS & ACS faculty in Bamberg, it is difficult to find a solution acceptable to all lecturers due to the diverse requirements. Considering the recording program alone, Camtasia is suitable for many recording purposes and offers a powerful HTML5 player. However, the main drawback is the dependency on the presentation computer. OBS-Studio, is the only one of the three considered pure recording programs that allows remote controlled recording. On the contrary, OBS-Studio is limited with regard to the player functions and the application scenarios and can only be expanded by a great deal of effort. Panopto as a comprehensive solution can score here, as both recording variants are possible, but have certain limitations.

Distribution and Presentation. Compared with Opencast and Panopto, Lecture2Go and Open edX have some disadvantages that made them inappropriate for the use at the University of Bamberg: Lecture2Go offers only a small community and less functions, while Open edX is a competitor of the well-used learning management system Moodle, which indicates that the use at the University of Bamberg might not be advisable. Opencast and Panopto, however, seem to be possible solutions. Panopto as well as Opencast fulfill a large part of the evaluated requirements. Both solutions would therefore be conceivable for the University of Bamberg. Compared to Panopto, Opencast probably offers more flexibility regarding new features because of the freely available source code. However, problems would have to be solved either independently or with the help of the community. Panopto would be the much simpler solution because of the support of the provider. There are two possible ways. The decision for a provider such as Panopto or a recording solution implemented in-house like Opencast should be based on the strategic orientation of the university.

8 Summary and Future Work

This paper showed the relevant requirements for a recording solution in the specific context of a blended-learning scenario at the IS & ACS faculty of the University of Bamberg. Moreover, possible recording and distribution solutions have been discussed and compared. The results of the study as well as the comparison of the recording and distribution solutions have been summarized in a recommendation for the University of Bamberg and the IS & ACS faculty.

The legal discussion regarding lecture recordings as well as financial feasibility of the recommended aspects remain open. For these topics, an independent consideration in the context of further work is recommended.

References

1. Collie, L., Shah, V., Sheridan, D.: An end-user evaluation of a lecture archiving system. In: Plimmer, B. (ed.) Proceedings of the 10th International Conference NZ Chapter of the ACM's Special Interest Group on Human-Computer Interaction, CHINZ 2009, pp. 77–80. ACM Press (2009)

2. Demetriadis, S., Pombortsis, A.: E-lectures for flexible learning: a study on their learning efficiency. J. Educ. Technol. Soc. **10**(2), 147–157 (2007)
3. Dittler, U.: Die 4. Welle des E-Learning: Mobile, smarte und soziale Medien erobern den Alltag und verändern die Lernwelt. In: Dittler, U. (ed.) E-Learning 4.0, pp. 43–67. De Gruyter Oldenbourg (2017)
4. Glowalla, U.: Utility und Usability von E-Learning am Beispiel von Lecture-on-demand Anwendungen. In: Steffens, C. (ed.) Entwerfen und Gestalten, pp. 603–623. No. 18 in ZMMS Spektrum, VDI-Verl (2004)
5. Guo, P.J., Kim, J., Rubin, R.: How video production affects student engagement. In: Sahami, M., Fox, A., Hearst, M.A., Chi, M.T. (eds.) Proceedings of the First ACM Conference on Learning @ Scale Conference - L@S 2014, pp. 41–50. ACM Press (2014)
6. Hamborg, K.C., Ollermann, F., Meyknecht, G., Meier da Fonsecca, V., Rolf, R.: Akzeptanz von Lehrveranstaltungsaufzeichnungen - Befunde aus zwei empirischen Studien. In: Desel, J. (ed.) DeLFI 2012, pp. 63–74. GI-Edition, Ges. für Informatik (2012)
7. Handke, J.: Patient Hochschullehre. Tectum (2014)
8. Hermann, C., Lauer, T., Trahasch, S.: Eine lernerzentrierte Evaluation des Einsatzes von Vorlesungsaufzeichnungen zur Unterstützung der Präsenzlehre. In: Mühlhäuser, M., Rößling, G., Steinmetz, R. (eds.) DeLFI 2006, pp. 39–50. GI-Edition, Ges. für Informatik (2006)
9. Höver, K.M., Rößling, G., Mühlhäuser, M.: Studierende, das Web und Vorlesungsaufzeichnungen. In: Kerres, M. (ed.) DeLFI 2010 - 8. Tagung der Fachgruppe E-Learning der Gesellschaft für Informatik e.V, pp. 121–132. GI-Edition, Ges. für Informatik (2010)
10. Jackstel, R., Jackstel, K.: Die Vorlesung - akademische Lehrform und Rede. Dt. Verl. d. Wissenschaften, Berlin (1985)
11. Kerres, M., Schmidt, A.: Zur Anatomie von Bologna-Studiengängen. Die Hochschule **2**, 173–206 (2011)
12. Ketterl, M., Mertens, R., Schmidt, T., Morisse, K.: Techniken und Einsatzszenarien für Podcasts in der universitären Lehre (2006)
13. Lampi, F., Kopf, S., Effelsberg, W.: Mediale Aufbereitung von Lehrveranstaltungen und ihre automatische Veröffentlichung. In: Mühlhäuser, M., Rößling, G., Steinmetz, R. (eds.) DeLFI 2006, pp. 27–38. GI-Edition, Ges. für Informatik (2006)
14. Merkt, M.: Didaktische Optimierung von Videos in der Hochschule (2015). https://www.e-teaching.org/etresources/pdf/erfahrungsbericht_2015_merkt_didaktische_optimierung_video.pdf
15. Mertens, R., Krüger, A., Vornberger, O.: Einsatz von Vorlesungsaufzeichnungen. In: Hamborg, K.C. (ed.) Good practice: netzbasiertes Lehren und Lernen, pp. 79–92. Osnabrücker Beiträge zum medienbasierten Lernen, Electronic Publ (2004)
16. Paulsen, F.: Die deutschen Universitäten und das Universitätsstudium. A. Asher & Co (1902)
17. Rohs, M., Streule, R.: Untersuchungen zum Einsatz von Electures an Hochschulen - Sichtung eines Forschungsfeldes. In: Schwill, A., Nicolas, A. (eds.) Lernen im digitalen Zeitalter, pp. 189–196. Logos-Verl (2009)
18. Roth, G.: Warum sind Lehren und Lernen so schwierig? Zeitschrift für Pädagogik **50**(4), 496–506 (2004)
19. Schaarschmidt, N., Börner, C.: Videoeinsatz an sächsischen Hochschulen – Anwendungsszenarien. In: Bergert, A., Lehmann, A., Liebscher, M., Schulz, J. (eds.) Videocampus Sachsen - Machbarkeitsuntersuchung, pp. 11–31. Technische Universität Bergakademie Freiberg, 1. Auflage edn. (2018)
20. Scheer, A.W.: Hochschule 4.0. In: Dittler, U. (ed.) E-Learning 4.0, pp. 101–123. De Gruyter Oldenbourg (2017)

21. Tillmann, A., Bremer, C., Krömker, D.: Einsatz von E-Lectures als Ergänzungsangebot zur Präsenzlehre. In: Csanyi, G.S., Reichl, F., Steiner, A. (eds.) Digitale Medien - Werkzeuge für exzellente Forschung und Lehre, pp. 235–249. Medien in der Wissenschaft, Waxmann (2012)
22. Tillmann, A., Niemeyer, J., Krömker, D.: Flexibilisierung des Studienalltags durch eLectures. In: Pongratz, H. (ed.) DeLFI 2015, pp. 209–218. GI-Edition, Ges. für Informatik (2015)
23. Williams, A., Birch, E., Hancock, P.: The impact of online lecture recordings on student performance. Australas. J. Education. Technol. **28**(2), 199–213 (2012)
24. Zupancic, B., Horz, H.: Lecture recording and its use in a traditional university course. In: Caspersen, M.E., Joyce, D., Goelman, D., Utting, I. (eds.) Proceedings of the 7th Annual Conference on Innovation and Technology in Computer Science Education – ITiCSE 2002, pp. 24–28. ACM Press (2002)

ICT in Special Educational Needs Schools from Teachers' Perspective: A Survey

Vojtech Gybas[1(✉)], Katerina Kostolanyova[1], and Ivana Simonova[2]

[1] University of Ostrava, Ostrava, Czech Republic
{vojtech.gybas, katerina.kostolanyova}@osu.cz
[2] University of Jan Evangelista Purkyne, Usti nad Labem, Czech Republic
ivana.simonova@ujep.cz

Abstract. The paper presents results of the research dealing with ICT instruction conducted within all (i.e. 273) schools for learners with special needs (SEN) in the Czech Republic. Totally, 882 respondents (511 teachers, 266 class teachers, 105 teaching assistants) participated in the research. Data were collected via questionnaire consisting of 28 items and requiring open, closed, or combined types of answers. The questionnaire was sent by e-mail in e-form to all headmasters of Czech SEN schools and was also available on the social network Twitter. The questionnaire was anonymous; if double submissions appeared, one of them was included in the sample only. Collected data provide detailed information about the sample group (age, gender, qualification, teaching practice). They are displayed in tables and show results in three fields: (1) ICT equipment and teachers' skills in working with PC, notebook, tablet and interactive board, (2) teachers' view on what teachers' and learners' favourite ICT are, and (3) teachers' feedback on the Framework Educational Programme for SEN schools.

Keywords: Special educational needs · SEN · Information and communication technologies · ICT · Teacher · Equipment · Skills · Framework educational programme

1 Introduction

Either we agree, or not, e-society is here to stay, and information and communication technologies (ICT) have become a common part of life. Current children have got used to having ICT everywhere since the early age, including education. This field is being under the focus of researchers who observe, analyze, and evaluate the process of ICT-enhanced instruction from various views. However, much less attention is paid to learners with special educational needs (SEN). Are the strengths of ICT exploited in SEN schools? In what way? Are these schools sufficiently equipped with hardware and software? Are the teachers qualified for teaching SEN learners? Do they know how to efficiently use ICT for them? Are the SEN learners able to exploit what technologies can offer them? These were the questions which should be answered in the near future, identically as they were monitored with learners without special needs.

S. K. S. Cheung et al. (Eds.): ICBL 2019, LNCS 11546, pp. 164–173, 2019.
https://doi.org/10.1007/978-3-030-21562-0_14

Therefore, the main objective of this paper is to introduce research results relating to the field of ICT at SEN schools in the Czech Republic.

2 Theoretical Background

2.1 SEN Learners

Some educators and experts may propose different definitions and use different terminology. What all of the definitions have in common is Special Educational Needs refer to learners having learning, physical, and developmental disabilities, behavioural, emotional, and communication disorders, and learning deficiencies [1, 12]. In this research, SEN education refers to teaching learners who for intellectual or medical reasons fall behind with their education when compared to most of their peers. This means the field of SEN does not include education of gifted learners, or economically and/or culturally disadvantaged ones.

In the world context, special educational needs schools and programmes are for children who have disabilities that interfere with learning. These schools provide support that is not normally provided in general education programmes, i.e. they tailor learning to address each child's unique combination of needs. Adaptations are made to allow learners to meet age-appropriate educational goals. They offer a wide range of approaches and services, e.g. small classes, individualized learning, one-on-one support, self-contained classrooms, resource rooms, and special learning aids. Learners with special needs are also entitled to an individualized education programme, which spells out a child's learning needs, services the school will provide, and how progress will be measured [2].

2.2 SEN Education in the Czech Republic

All the above mentioned also works in the Czech Republic, where the SEN instruction underwent a long history, and has undergone many transformations. Moreover, few years ago, the inclusive model of SEN learners' education was introduced.

The inclusive education is the process supporting equal chances for all children to meet the requirements of educational system. Children who are expected to need some support are defined as those with special needs by the School Act [3]. Inclusion is understood as a higher level of integration (i.e. the implementation of various groups into a whole, when the groups are distinguished according to the diagnostic criteria). This approach focuses on the handicap, impairment; and inclusion, reflecting the individuality, is its target. If the child fails in meeting the educational requirements, within integration, the fault is on child's site, whereas within inclusion, constraints against meeting the target are searched and removed from the curriculum, as stated by the School Act. To support the process of inclusion, the individual educational plan is designed for each child.

Common special needs include learning disabilities (such as dyslexia), emotional and behavioral disorders (such as ADHD), physical and developmental disabilities (such as autism spectrum disorders and intellectual disability). Learners with these special needs are likely to benefit from additional educational services such as different approaches to teaching, specifically adapted classes, and last but not least, the use of ICT. Main educational outcomes include hygienic habits, ability of self-service, work with objects of daily common use, acting in daily common situations, individualized development of physical and mental abilities and basic knowledge of reading, writing, counting so that they were able to engage in the society to maximum extent.

SEN learners' education is based on the Framework Educational Programme (FEP) for SEN schools [4] which is designed in two levels: (1) education of learners with moderate disorders and (2) education of learners with severe and combined disorders. Both levels include following topics: Language and language communication, Mathematics, Man and the world, Man and the society, Man and the nature, Man and the health (Physical education, healthy lifestyle), Arts (music, drawing), Man and the world of work, and Information and communication technologies. This subject in taught within the version 1 of FEP only. The process of teaching/learning is supported by the individualized approach to each learner, and also other benefits are available, e.g. psychologist, social worker, early intervention and therapy services, and a teaching assistant who accompanies the learner to all lessons providing common care and helping during the instruction.

As most of SEN learners are not able to reach a common level in motor development, the work with hardware is difficult and limited for them. However, if they succeed, ICT help them in everyday situations as to other people and also arose positive emotions with them [5].

Currently, in Czech SEN schools, interactive boards are widely exploited, and tablets are preferred to personal computers because of their main features (portability, weight). Moreover, special devices making the work with them easier are widely available, e.g. various types of stands for keeping the tablets in right positions, styluses (hand pointer, head pointer, mouth stick stylus etc.), ergonomic keyboard, coloured keyboard, one-button communicator, touch-, oral-, head-directed mouse. Selected applications are mostly designed by world and Czech IT specialists in cooperation with teachers. They are available for mathematics (Visual Math, Logicly, Number pyramid, Math Racing), language and communication, reading and writing (Alphabet for children, Slabikar [First Reader], Bitsboard, Book creator, Do as me), Man and the world, society, nature (My house, My play home stores, speech therapy, Songs, Rhymes, My mosaic, Foldify, Hello Color Pencil) [6].

The proposed categorization of expected outcomes of SEN learners in work with tablets focuses three fields:

(1) tablet operation (holding in hands, switch on/off of the tablet, adjust brightness, loudness, be oriented on the screen and keyboard, using the keyboard, switch on/off of applications, charging the tablet, keeping it clean and handling with care),
(2) working with provided applications,
(3) creating own content.

Learners are divided into four groups reflecting their disorders which limit them in work:

(I) independent user,
(II) used who needs partial teacher's support,
(III) user who is able to work with selected applications with teacher's support,
(IV) learners not interested/not able to work with ICT [7].

3 Methodology

3.1 Research Question and Objective

Annually, data dealing with SEN education are collected by the Czech Statistical Office. However, not the whole area has been covered and not all questions have been answered. The field relating to ICT exploitation in SEN schools can be structured into three parts:

1. what ICT equipment is available at schools and what teachers' skills are;
2. what teachers' and learners' favourite ICT are from teachers' view;
3. how the Framework Educational Programme is evaluated by the teachers to enable SEN learners to reach maximum learning outcomes.

The main research objective was to collect still unknown data, analyze them and get a deeper view into the field of ICT exploitation at SEN schools.

3.2 Methods and Tools

So as to answer these questions, the questionnaire was designed. It consists of 28 questions requiring answers of three types: closed (multiple-choice), semi-closed (multiple-choice and open-answer), and open-answer type. The first version of questionnaire was distributed in the printed form. It was piloted by 11 respondents (seven SEN teachers and four teaching assistants) and the validity was evaluated by five other SEN experts (members of the Moravian-Silesian district SEN board). As the answers were difficult to be read in seven questionnaires, it was decided to use the electronic form with typed answers. Five items were removed from the first version and other four were stylistically adjusted. The final version followed the above mentioned three research areas: ICT equipment and teachers' ICT skills, teachers' and learners' favourite ICT from teachers' view and their FEP reflection. Total amount of items in the questionnaire was twenty-eight.

3.3 Research Sample

Research sample consists of 882 respondents working in SEN schools in all regions of the Czech Republic: 511 teachers (58%); 266 class teachers (30%); 105 teaching assistants (12%). Reflecting this structure, findings discovered within this research can be generalized for the whole Czech Republic. Detailed data are displayed in Table 1.

Table 1. Research sample: distribution of respondents.

Region	Respondents (N)	Respondents (%)
capital Praha	63	7.1
Středočeský (Central Bohemia)	105	11.9
Jihočeský (South Bohemia)	16	1.8
Plzeňský (Plzen)	12	1.4
Karlovarský (Karlovy Vary)	13	1.5
Ústecký (Usti nad Labem)	64	7.3
Liberecký (Liberec)	65	7.2
Královéhradecký (Hradec Kralove)	35	4.0
Pardubický (Pardubice)	56	6.3
Olomoucký (Olomouc)	40	4.5
Moravskoslezský (Moravian-Silesian)	127	14.4
Jihomoravský (South Moravia)	79	9.1
Zlínský (Zlin)	126	14.3
Vysočina (Highlands)	81	9.3
Total	**882**	**100**

Within the total amount of 882 respondents, there were 89.6% female and 10.4% male ones. Other characteristics show that 80% of them were older than 40 years; 90% reached the required level of education (higher education specialized in teaching SEN learners), and 73% had teaching practice longer than 16 years. Reflecting the statistical data provided by the Czech Statistical Office [8], the sample is representative http://www.msmt.cz/vzdelavani/skolstvi-v-cr/statistika-skolstvi/genderova-problematika-zamestnancu-ve-skolstvi Detailed data are displayed in Table 2.

Table 2. Research sample: age and education.

Age (yrs.)	%	Education level	%	Teaching practice (yrs.)	%
18–25	0.7	Upper secondary	3.6	< 5 yrs.	4.4
26–30	1.4	HE-Bachelor, college	1.0	6–10	7.0
31–40	13.5	HE-master, without SEN specialization	3.5	11–15	15.6
41–50	40	HE-master, SEN specialization	90	16–20	23.0
50+	40	HE-master, SEN + primary school specialization	1.9	20+	50.0

HE: higher education

The questionnaire was distributed in two ways:

(1) All schools were addressed as listed in the catalogue of companies (www.firmy.cz – instituce – vzdělávání – základní škola – praktické a speciální školy (SEN schools); total amount was 273. SEN classes running under common primary and lower secondary schools were not included. The headmasters were informed that the questionnaire is available on social network Twitter.

(2) Teachers and teaching assistants participating in the SEN schools group on Twitter were asked to fill in the questionnaire. The questionnaire was anonymous, however, double submissions could be discovered and omitted from the final research sample.

4 Results

The occurrences of collected data are summarized and displayed in tables. Total amounts may be higher in some questions because more than one answer was allowed/required in some items. First, ICT equipment and teachers' skills for working with single devices were considered by respondents. Second, teachers' and learners' favourite ICT were listed. Third, teachers' experience and opinions with Framework Educational Programme for SEN schools were evaluated.

4.1 ICT Equipment and Teachers' Skills

The equipment of SEN schools with PC/notebooks, tablets, interactive boards) was considered by the respondents. The data show SEN schools are equipped with enough PC/notebooks for teachers (nearly 98%) and for learners (84%). This result means that any learner can have their own device to use (mind that some learners with severe and combined disorders are not able to work with ICT, or even keep it, but the others are), so the SEN schools are appropriately equipped.

As for teachers' skills, most of the respondents consider themselves not to be beginners in working with PC/notebooks (97%) and tablets (87%); however, 25% of them find themselves beginners in working with the interactive board. Detailed results are displayed in Tables 3 and 4.

Additionally, to gain latest information, teachers search for it on the Internet (50%), receive it from the school management (headmaster, deputies) and school IT coordinator (38.9%), or find it in professional literature (11.1%); others get inspiration in discussion groups within social networks (28%).

Table 3. ICT equipment and teachers' skills.

Equipment	%
PC, NB for teachers	97.6
PC, NB for learners	84.0
Tablets for teachers	54.8
Tablets for learners	69.9
Interactive board	85.7

PC: personal computer, NB: notebook, IAB: interactive board

Table 4. Teachers' skills in work with PC, NB, tablet and interactive board.

Teachers' skills: PC, NB	%	Teachers' skills: tablet	%	Teachers' skills: IAB	%
Beginner	3	Beginner	12	Beginner	25
Intermediate	37	Intermediate	44	Intermediate	31
Advanced	35	Advanced	25	Advanced	27
Proficiency	25	Proficiency	18	Proficiency	17

PC: personal computer, NB: notebook, IAB: interactive board

Moreover, 85% of IT teachers attend further education courses (on the voluntary basis).

4.2 Teachers' and Learners' Favourite ICT: Teachers' View

As displayed in Table 5, according to teachers' opinions, their most favourite devices are PC and tablet (34% each), compared to learners who prefer tablet (42%) and PC (37%). The strongest reason is they have these devices at home and they are used to working with them. Portability and availability of notebooks do not seem to play important role in this case. Large size of PC screen and a wide choice of applications for tablets are appreciated. Detailed results are displayed in Table 5.

Table 5. Teachers' and learners' favourite ICT

ICT	Preferred by teachers (%)	Preferred by learners (%)
PC + software	34	37
NB + software	7	4
Tablet + application	34	42
IAB	17	15
Other (e.g. mobile phone …)	8	3

PC: personal computer, NB: notebook, IAB: interactive board

4.3 Framework Educational Programme: Teachers' Feedback

Framework Educational Programme works as the core document for SEN schools. However, teachers' experience and opinions with it differ:

20% of respondents think FEP does not reflect current needs of SEN learners;
13% consider it helpful;
10% follow it in lessons;
10% do not mind it;
10% state updates are needed;
14% teach what they consider needed for learners;
12% cannot decide about its contribution;
10% use FEP, level 2 only.

If ICT can be exploited in the lesson, 59% of teachers replace the existing, usually used (traditional) learning material with the ICT version. It means they trust (hope) a special software or application can help learners to understand the topic, motivate them to learning. If the learning material is missing, 85% of teachers substitute it with ICT, i.e. software, application, as a powerful means.

Last but not least, respondents provided open answers to describe advantages and disadvantages the ICT can provide to SEN learners. The main advantages were listed as follows:

- multi-mediality giving more options additionally to other materials (textbooks, worksheets etc.) (92%);
- support to learners' weaker functions, compensation, substitution of partial deficits, and/or compensation or replacement learning materials (85%);
- they are considered to be a favourite means (77%);
- there exists wide portfolio of applications for tablets (27%);
- motivation to learning (24%);
- help in preparation for lessons (17%);
- individualization of teaching/learning (15%);
- entertaining the learner (5%) etc.

On the other side, main disadvantages are

- the danger of addiction to using PC/notebook/tablet (45%);
- the danger of damaging the device (43%);
- necessity of teacher's help (22%);
- screening off when standing in front of interactive boards (26%);
- cannot be used for learners with severe and multiple disorders (16%).

However, 48% of respondents stated they did not know any disadvantages.

To sum up, we can state that ICT are a potentially powerful tool for extending educational opportunities. Additionally to primary and lower secondary schools in the Czech Republic, the ICT equipment in SEN schools is adequate and corresponds to learning outcomes defined by FEP (e.g. [9, 10]).

5 Conclusions

When comparing the above presented advantages now and then [11, 12], multi-mediality always was at the top of the list when ICT in non-SEN schools were researched. And, ICT are logical and natural to be exploited to support and compensate health and mental disorders in SEN schools [13]. One quarter of respondents mention the work with ICT to be still motivating, but ICT is considered a means of entertainment by 5% of them only. The main disadvantage is the danger of addiction mentioned by 45% of respondents.

The quality and scale of equipment in SEN schools clearly determines their indisputable status as educational (not medical) institutions which are running as an equal partner of other, non-SEN schools. The feature of multi-mediality clearly votes for ICT as a didactic means towards increasing learners' literacy in this field, which is highly important if SEN school learners are expected to become equal members of the current e-society. Despite the learning content differs in quantity, but it is of equal quality, learners have the ICT available during their obligatory schooling period. Apart from this, it is strongly required to be aware of the fact that SEN learners are not able to apply appropriate self-control, which can result in different effects compared to non-SEN learners. Even though the SEN schools are sufficiently equipped with ICT, teachers working with them are permanently on a high wire which can break any time. Therefore, cooperation with psychologist and/or social pedagogue is necessary. If the work with ICT is to serve as learner's reward, it should be conducted under strict rules and in pre-defined and limited times. Never in this process, the SEN learner should be left without control. In such a case, teachers' fears of SEN learners' addiction on ICT use could be higher than stated 45%.

In further research activities, attention will be paid to the way(s) how ICT support the process of meeting learning outcomes expected by the FEP for SEN schools, what the contribution of individual educational plans is, whether the supportive aids are efficiently exploited by SEN teachers (and if so, to what extent), and last but not least, how the FEW is reflected in the whole process.

Acknowledgements. The paper is supported by SGS06/PdF/2018-2019 project Individualizace výuky na nižším stupni ZŠ pomocí mobilních dotykových zařízení [Individualization of instruction on the primary schools through mobile touch devices].

References

1. Delaney, M.: Special Educational Needs. Oxford University Press, Oxford (2016)
2. Children with special educational needs and disabilities (Send). https://www.ourkids.net/school/special-needs-schools-features. Accessed 30 Jan 2019
3. Act N. 561/2004 Coll. on pre-primary, primary, lower and upper secondary, higher and other education, §16. https://zakonyprolidi.cz/cs/2004-561. Accessed 28 Jan 2019
4. Rámcový vzdělávací program pro obor vzdělávání. Základní škola speciální [Framework Educational Programme for Education. School for Learners with Special Needs]. http://www.nuv.cz/file/134. Accessed 28 Jan 2019
5. Zikl, P.: Využití ICT u dětí se speciálními potřebami. [ICT use by SEN children]. Praha, Grada (2011)
6. Petit. http://www.petit-os.cz/. Accessed 29 Jan 2019
7. Gybas, V.: Individualizace výuky v zš speciální pomocí mobilních dotykových technologií. [Individualization of instruction at SEN schools through touch mobile technologies]. Dissertation thesis. Supervisor: Katerina Kostolanyova. University of Ostrava, Ostrava (2018)
8. Genderová problematika zaměstnanců školství [Gender data of teaching staff]. http://www.msmt.cz/vzdelavani/skolstvi-v-cr/statistika-skolstvi/genderova-problematika-zamestnancu-ve-skolstvi. Access 21 Mar 2019
9. Neumajer, O., Rohlíková, L., Zounek, J.: Učíme se s tabletem [Learning with tablets]. Wolters Kluwer, Praha (2015)
10. Burgerová, J., Adamkovičová, M.: Vybrané aspekty komunikačnej dimenzie e-learningu [Selected aspects of communication dimension in e-learning]. Prešov, Prešovská univerzita (2014)

11. Arkorful, A., Abaidoo, N.: The role of e-learning, advantages and disadvantages of its adoption in higher education. Int. J. Instr. Technol. Distance Learn. **12**(1), 28–42 (2015)
12. The advantages and disadvantages of using ICT for teaching and learning. https://miraesiwinaya.wordpress.com/2010/01/22/the-advantages-and-disadvantages-of-using-ict-for-teaching-and-learning/. Accessed 28 Jan 2019
13. Florian, L.: Uses of technology that support pupils with special educational needs. In: Florian, L., Hegarty, J. (eds.) ICT and Special Educational Needs. A Tool for Inclusion, pp. 7–20, https://www.mheducation.co.uk/openup/chapters/0335211968.pdf. Accessed 28 Jan 2019

Learning Style Preferences and Blended Learning Approach on Secondary Technical School Level

Irena Loudova and Dagmar El-Hmoudova(✉)

University of Hradec Kralove,
Rokitanskeho 62, 500 03 Hradec Kralove, Czech Republic
{irena.loudova, dagmar.elhmoudova}@uhk.cz

Abstract. This paper reflects upon the experience of the delivery of study materials tailored to preferred learning styles at the Secondary Technical School of Public-Law using blended learning. The study was conducted within winter and summer semesters in 2017–2018 with 205 students at the age of 16 to 18. To measure students' learning styles Felder's Index of Learning Styles was used, and achievement scores of students' summative tests were compared before and after blended learning was adopted. Students, most of whom had visual preferences for learning, were randomly divided into two groups. The statistic results showed that there was no significant difference in terms of academic performance between students working in traditional classroom (control group) and students working in blended learning environment (experimental group). On the other hand, the analysis of obtained data revealed statistically significant differences in achievement between the two groups, indicating that the experimental group with visual preference performed better than the control group with visual preference. Significant differences were also found in the respective groups' academic performance according to gender. Male students were more motivated and performance-oriented.

Keywords: Blended learning · Learning style preference · Academic performance

1 Introduction

Our paper attempts to address the issue of using technology in the teaching process on secondary technical school level. The Secondary Public-Law School TRIVIS educates students in the field of security legal activities. Students who study in the 4-year educational program graduate at the age of 19 and are predominantly employed in the bodies of the Ministry of Interior, Ministry of Defense, Ministry of Justice and Ministry of Finance. We were directing our research to this school as it is the only secondary school in the region, whose mission is to provide blended learning environment for students.

As all the students belong to so-called Generation Z, we can assume that they use the Internet since a young age and are comfortable with technology and social media. The need for a compromise between the conventional face-to-face sessions (which

S. K. S. Cheung et al. (Eds.): ICBL 2019, LNCS 11546, pp. 174–185, 2019.
https://doi.org/10.1007/978-3-030-21562-0_15

have been practiced as the main teaching strategy until recently) and online learning leads us towards a new approach to teaching and learning, the so-called hybrid or blended learning [1]. E-learning is a valuable tool to have at our disposal when building and delivering our educational programs, moreover, considering blended learning as the effective combination of different modes of delivery, models of teaching and styles of learning, we should be using it wherever appropriate to enhance our provision and offer tailored learning to meet the needs of our learners. In 2017, LMS Moodle was implemented into the educational programs of the school.

2 Learning Styles and Blended Approach to Learning

Within the context of the advance of the technology that is used in blended learning, the idea to adapt the teaching strategy according to the students' learning styles seems to be very challenging. For lots of students the traditional education system is no longer an option given the need to keep up with the advancing technology. The fast developing technologies and the wide range of students with various learning styles continuously provokes and inspires teachers. It is well known that a single instructional model cannot satisfy all students [2]. Initial research into learning style models highlights that the variety of the students' learning styles has considerable importance for the instructional process [3].

There are many studies that show the efficiency of combining multimedia with online technology within the instructional process [4]. Most of the studies in this category are based on the learning styles as they were classified by David Kolb [5] and Felder and Silverman [6]. In our research we used the Felder-Silverman model, which includes four dichotomous dimensions: active-reflective, sensing-intuiting, visual-verbal and sequential-global. The learning style preferences of the model are easy to assess with the Index of Learning Styles (ILS).

The questionnaire [7] includes 44 questions with two alternatives; 11 questions for each learning style dimension. As a result, the questionnaire tells which learning style is the most pronounced on each axis and how strong the preference is. As the axes are continua, the preference can be mild, moderate or strong. The results of our survey are described in more details in the following chapter.

Blended learning focuses on optimizing achievement of learning objectives by applying the appropriate learning technologies to match the personal learning style preference to transfer the required skills to students. In this respect, we can see the interconnection between learning style model and blended learning as natural. There are many definitions for blended learning, but they all have some aspects in common. They refer to two different learning environments—face-to-face (synchronous) and online (asynchronous); and they refer to combining those two learning environments in a complementary way to deliver a programme of study so that learners can be supported both within the classroom environment and outside of it. In other words, the term blended learning refers to any programme of study that is delivered by appropriately combining both, synchronous interactive study (usually face-to-face) and asynchronous (individual) study (usually online), [8]. The key to a successful blended learning approach is to use the strengths of each medium appropriately, combining the two different learning environments in an integrated way so that each medium complements the other.

3 Methodology

Contemporary learning environments are much more vibrant. A variety of studies have shown that blended learning methods, combining traditional teaching in the classroom with online learning tools, are more effective than a simple face to face instruction. This also applies to the area of secondary education that is very sensitive to new pedagogical approaches.

3.1 Research Objectives

The basic research problem of the presented work can be formulated as a question:

Can modified learning materials in an e-learning course, reflecting the detected preferences of learning styles, increase academic performance in teaching English?

Based on the research problem the following research questions were formulated:

1. What is the academic performance of the students with respect to the implementation of didactic materials modified according to their preferences of learning styles?
2. Does the academic performance differ according to gender depending on the implementation of didactic materials modified according to the preferences of learning styles?
3. Does the preferred learning style affect academic performance in students using didactic materials modified according to preferences of learning styles?

The main goal of the research was to find out whether modified study materials in the online course lead to increased academic performance. To achieve this objective, the following sub-objectives were formulated:

1. Identify preferences of learning styles in students of the full-time study.
2. Create four modified e-courses in the LMS Moodle for Professional English (each course relates to one year -grade of study).
3. Analyze the learning outcomes of students who have completed the course.

3.2 Research Methods, Tools and Hypothesis

Further to reach the sub-objectives, the following steps were taken:

1. Four modified e-courses in the LMS Moodle for Professional English Language were created.
2. Blended learning teaching strategy was implemented into the educational environment.
3. Academic performance in a selected group of students was investigated, evaluated and statistically analyzed.

To detect the students' learning style preferences we used Felders' Index of Learning Styles (ILS), standardized online questionnaire and to measure the students' academic performance, standardized pre-test (created by authors of Cambridge ESOL class book) and standardized post-test were administered to students within the Professional English language course. Both tests were paper based. Due to the protection of personal data; an identification number was used to identify students. During the experiment, students of control group were taught only in face-to-face (synchronous) learning environment, using traditional didactic materials, including visual aids, non-standardized didactic tests and standardized tests (pre-test and post-test). Students of experimental group combined traditional face-to-face lessons with instruction in the Moodle virtual learning environment, where visual materials including animations and video clips were implemented. The tests were primarily focused on examining language competencies, especially micro-skills (often also understood as grammar and vocabulary) and receptive macro-skills (listening and reading).

The pre-test was distributed to students in both groups at the beginning of 2017 school year. The test contained thirty questions of varying difficulty with a maximum total score of 100. Initial students' knowledge of language competencies was evaluated. The test was paper-based and it took forty-five minutes.

The post-test was administered in both groups at the end of 2018 school year. It included thirty questions of various difficulty with a maximum total score 100. Current knowledge of language competencies achieved after one year of teaching was tested and evaluated. The test was paper-based and it took forty-five minutes. The control and experimental groups were provided feedback after the results were assessed.

To reach the main research objective, i.e. to discover whether study materials, modified according to the learning style preference in the on-line course lead to increased academic performance, three hypotheses were set:

H1: Students working in synchronous English language-learning environment have a different academic performance compared to students working in a blended English language-learning environment.

H2: The academic performance of the male versus female students is different.

H3: Students of the control group with visual preference have a different academic performance compared to the academic performance of students with visual preference in experimental group.

3.3 Research Sample

The surveyed population is a set of units that we assume our conclusions are valid for. It is a random sample representing all known and unknown properties of the population. At the same time, we assume representability. The paper presents the results of the pedagogical experiment that took place in the years 2017–18 at the Secondary Public-Law School TRIVIS. The research sample included a total of 205 students, (85 males and 120 females). The control group N = 106 (62 female; 44 male - chosen randomly) worked only in face-to-face (synchronous) learning environment. Experimental group N = 99 (58 female; 41 male – chosen randomly) used blended learning (asynchronous) strategy, see Table 1.

Table 1. Research sample group of students

Group	Female	Male	Total
Control group	62	44	106
Experimental group	58	41	99
Total	120	85	205

We mapped the sample group's learning style preferences to provide the students with awareness of their own way to learn and of learning styles in general. The aim was also to encourage students to use and improve their learning styles that are less dominant. When providing a student with his/her learning style result, it should also be emphasized that no learning style instrument is infallible when applied to individuals [9]. The learning styles can also be utilized when planning education. Knowing the students' learning style profiles may motivate their instructor to find new ways to present material [9].

Our data includes 205 ILS questionnaire results. The distributions of the results are presented in Fig. 1. Divided in categories, there is a clear majority of sensors and visuals in our population: that is, 88% visuals, 70% sensors in control group, 89% visuals, and 73% sensors in experimental group. Figure 1 shows that those dimensions are the most skewed ones. On the active-reflective and sequential-global dimensions, the results were distributed more evenly and the distributions are more symmetric. There were 69% of actives and 31% of reflective students in control group, 66% of actives and 34% of reflective students in experimental group. Sequentials (59% in control group; 64% in experimental group) were the majority in both groups.

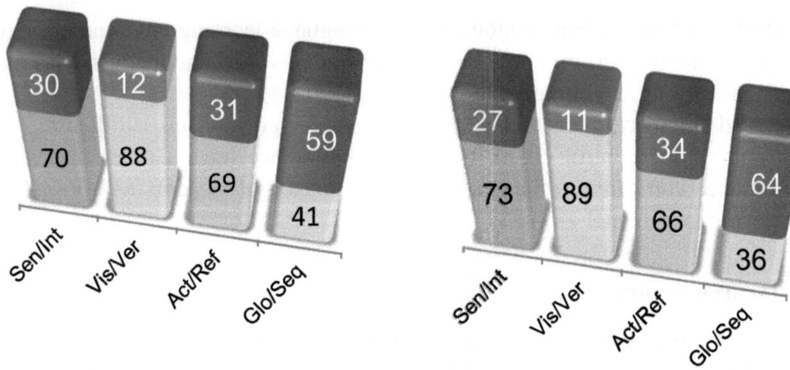

Fig. 1. Learning style preferences in control (left) and experimental (right) group of students in percentage.

Based on the learning style preferences, we modified learning materials in an e-learning course of Professional English language, which was used by the experimental group of students. The course was accessible 24/7, and included supporting study materials. We implemented the didactic materials into the e-course keeping in mind

Felder's characteristics of the individual preferences of the learning styles. Visual learners remember best what they have seen: images, diagrams, decision trees and demonstrations, while sensing learners are at their best when studying facts. From the standpoint of their memorizing and learning, it is important to see the connection between the subject under study and the real world. Students in control group used traditional visual materials, e.g. pictures, mind maps, graphs, posters, realia, charts, short video clips.

4 Results

The obtained data were processed by the statistical program NCSS 2007. Quantitative descriptive statistics were used, hypothesis testing was performed primarily at the significance level $\alpha = 0.05$. Given the type of data, the scatter analysis (Kruskal-Wallis test) and diametric conformity testing (t-test and Mann-Whitney test) were used. The normality of the data was determined using the Kolmogorov-Smirnov test. Results are structured into two parts: (1) descriptive statistics and (2) testing hypotheses.

4.1 Statistics Data

Results of descriptive statistics are displayed in Table 2 for control group and in Table 3 for experimental group. They present the values of total amount of respondents (N), Mean, Standard Deviation (SD), Minimum and Maximum score, Score range, Median, Mode and results of two tests of normality data distribution (Shapiro-Wilk W test and Kolmogorov-Smirnov test). The normality of data distribution was rejected by the statistic tests in pre-test and post-test in both groups. Reflecting this result, non-parametric test (Mann-Whitney test) was applied for verification of all hypotheses (Figs. 2, 3).

Table 2. Control group: Descriptive statistics of Pre-test, Post-test.

Heading level	Pre-test	Post test
N	106	106
Mean	0,695283	0,7431132
SD	0,1540452	0,1295734
Min	0,33	0,42
Max	0,92	1
Range	0,59	0,58
Median	0,735	0,75
Mode	0,81	
Normality: Shapiro-Wilk W	0,9208841(R)	0,9835326 (R)
Normality: Kolmogorov-Smirnov	0,1297755 (R)	0,05327712(R)

R: Rejected normality

Table 3. Experimental group: Descriptive statistics of Pre-test, Post-test.

Heading level	Pre-test	Post test
N	99	99
Mean	0,6247959	0,720202
SD	0,169877	0,1480208
Min	0,2	0,42
Max	0,92	1
Range	0,72	0,58
Median	0,62	0,72
Mode	0,62	
Normality: Shapiro-Wilk W	0,9629482(R)	0,9714637(R)
Normality: Kolmogorov-Smirnov	0,09688672(R)	0,08075114(R)

R: Rejected normality

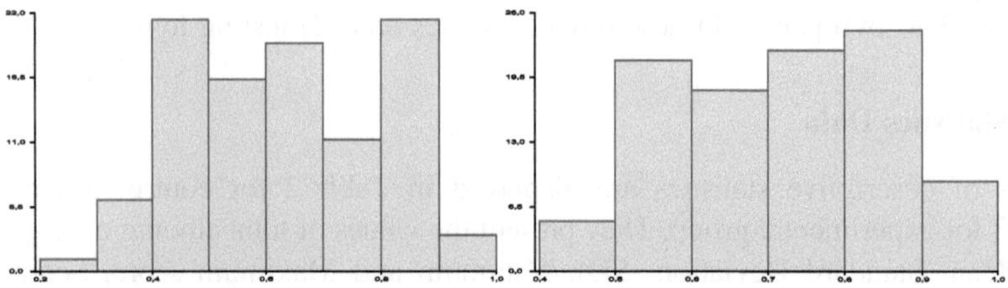

Fig. 2. Control group: Histogram - differences in test scores in pre-test (left) versus post-test (right).

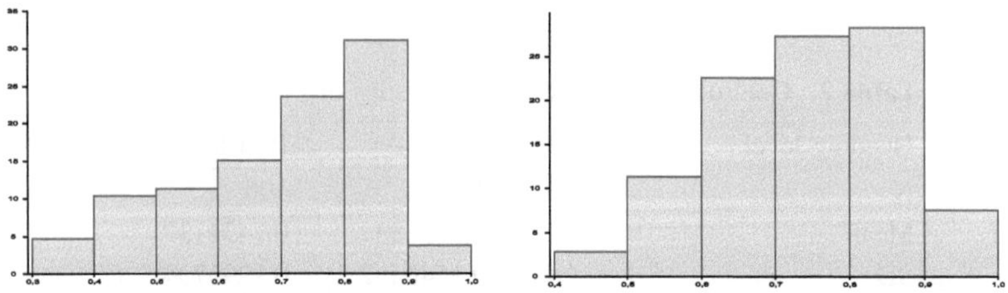

Fig. 3. Experimental group: Histogram - differences in test scores in pre-test (left) versus post-test (right).

4.2 Testing Hypothesis

First, the paired difference for pre-test and post-test score was calculated for control and experimental group by Mann-Whitney test. Reaching the Z-value = 1, 9364, the first hypothesis H1 was falsified ($\alpha = 0.05$; probability level = 0, 052815). This result means that statistically significant difference was not discovered between the pre-test and post-test scores in control versus experimental group, see Fig. 4. We can imply that in terms of study performance, simply participating in online activities, modified according to the learning style preferences, does not necessarily lead to significantly improved test scores.

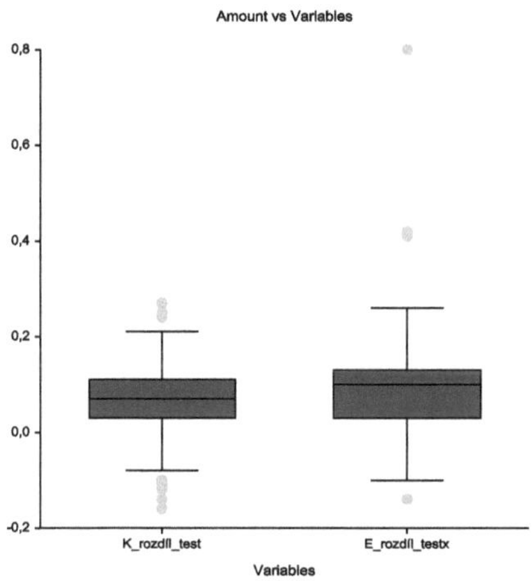

Fig. 4. Control group (left) vs. experimental group (right). Differences in test scores in pre-test versus post-test.

Second, the paired difference for academic performance of the male and female students was calculated by Mann-Whitney test. Reaching the Z-value = 1, 9671, the second hypothesis H2 was verified ($\alpha = 0.05$; probability level = 0, 049175). This result means that statistically significant difference was discovered between genders and their study performance, see Fig. 5.

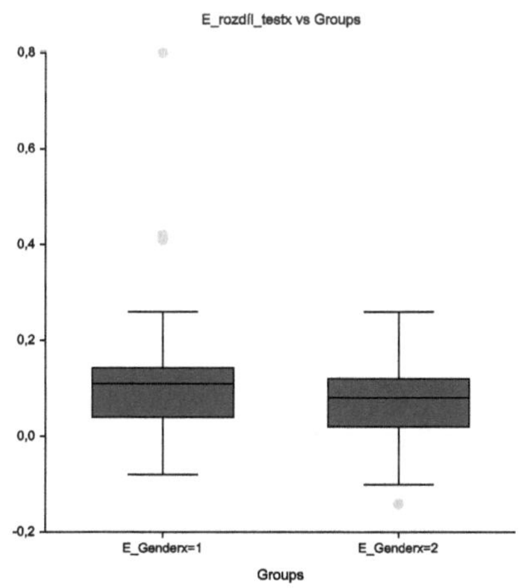

Fig. 5. Difference in academic performance in the view of genders (male – left; female – right).

With regard to the results of research on gender differences in academic performance, this result may seem surprising, but here we have to take into account that graduates of the above-mentioned school are employed in particular in security-law services or integrated rescue system. Students with an interest and learning background can continue their study at Police Academy or University of Defense, which is particularly attractive and motivating to the male students.

Third, the paired difference for academic performance of visual students in control group and visual students in experimental group was calculated by Mann-Whitney test. Reaching the Z-value = −3, 8509, the third hypothesis H3 was verified ($\alpha = 0.05$; probability level = 0, 000118). This result means that statistically significant difference was discovered between the academic performances of visual students in control group vs experimental group, see Fig. 6. The box graph clearly shows the higher study success in the visual students of the experimental group, whose learning style preference was enhanced by modified study materials in the virtual learning environment Moodle.

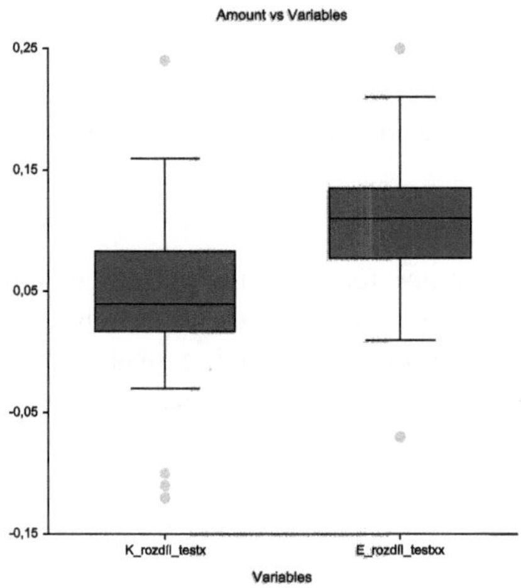

Fig. 6. Visual students' study success in control group (left) versus experimental group (right).

To sum up, hypotheses H2 and H3 were verified; hypothesis H1 was falsified.

5 Discussion and Conclusion

Reflecting the size and structure of the research sample, our research results cannot be generalized, they are valid for the sample groups only.

As displayed in Fig. 4. there was no significant difference in academic performance between control group of students, studying in the traditional learning environment and experimental group, instruction of which was blended and study materials modified according to the preferred learning style were uploaded in the virtual learning environment Moodle. Our findings may seem difficult to explain as it is generally assumed that the self-directed learning that occurs in online environments should result in deeper learning, and thus better academic performance.

However, an alternative explanation comes from Garrison [10], who notes that e learning is not synonymous with the collaborative and constructivist approaches that can foster deep learning. If so, perhaps the current findings reflect collaboration and constructivism in both modalities, but in regards to different aspects of the learner experience. Overall, performance across the two modalities is convergent, but the electronic and face-to-face pathways to that performance may be divergent.

The lack of relationship between preference and performance is a notable one. At least in the current study, it seems that a liking for a particular modality does not benefit performance in that modality. Importantly, these findings also suggest that asking students to engage in their non-preferred modality does not mean that poor performance will ensue. The implication is that educators can select delivery modality based solely on pedagogical reasons with confidence, rather than being concerned that a certain delivery method may disadvantage students who hold negative perceptions of that method [11].

Research also suggests that when online and face-to-face elements are combined, learners often place a greater value or emphasis on the face-to-face aspects of the experience [12]. This was confirmed by our long-standing practice across all levels of education.

The effectiveness of blended learning was, however, supported by the results shown in Fig. 6, where visual students of experimental group proved to reach much better academic performance than students who were studying in traditional, single-mode, lecture-style classroom program.

Many scientists have studied visual didactic materials and their impact on learning environment. From the point of language learning, Mayer [13], Callow [14], Paivio [15] and many others study the issue of visual materials, which have become an essential component of education process within a highly visual culture. Images and videos bring the real world in the classroom, allowing learners to see the context, body language, and facial expressions [16]. Visual materials have also an emotional impact; as the adage says, "a picture is worth a thousand words" [17].

There are, however, opponents, who refer to the fact that information overload has been created, which may result in shortened attention spans and superficial thinking in the future [18]. The variety and speed of digital information is affecting cognitive process, which suggests that teachers have a vital role in helping students to be selective [19].

Data consistently support the general hypothesis that girls outperform boys in almost every academic measure, e.g. Halpern [20], Lewin [21], Mickelson [22], Perkins, Kleiner, Roey and Brown [23]. Unlike universally acknowledged results in research of gender and academic performance, our research revealed a statistically significant difference between boys and girls. Male students in our research group had a better academic performance than female students. We believe that this is a specific sample of students where the higher motivation and better academic results of male students are closely related to the focus of the educational field and further employment possibilities in the special bodies of the power ministries (Ministry of the Interior, Ministry of Defence and Armed Forces).

We assume that learning is multimodal and the special thing about computer technology involved in learning process is that it allows students and teachers to manipulate the various modes and to break free of the linearity of traditional classroom instruction. This brings us to the question of teachers' role in the classroom. According to Dias [24], teacher in traditional classroom is controller, prompter, tutor, troubleshooter and participant, while Harmer [25] defined the roles as integrator (setting goals), negotiator, reporter (informing students about developments), and confidant.

We can conclude that teacher is the "strategist", directing students to resources that are appropriate for learning aims and students are "tacticians", using those resources in individual way to create a personalised learning pathway. Even though the outputs of our research did not confirm explicitly generally recognized benefits of blended learning in educational environment (in our case, in Professional English language course), we believe that it is necessary to continue and improve the virtual learning environment, bearing in mind that the role of teacher is irreplaceable as "*eLearning doesn't just "happen"! It requires careful planning and implementation.*"

Acknowledgements. The authors thankfully acknowledge the management of the University of Hradec Kralove, namely Dean's office of Pedagogical faculty, for supporting the work and granting permission to publish the paper from IP RVO funds. The data processed in our research was gained thanks to the European Union Project Literacy in Innovative way. Reg. no.: CZ.02.3.61 / 0.0 / 0.0 / 16_012 / 0000608, which was realized at the Secondary Technical School of Public-Law TRIVIS.

References

1. Richards, J., Rodgers, T.: Approaches and Methods in Language Teaching. Cambridge University Press, New York (2001)
2. Schaller, D., Borun, M., Allison-Bunnell, S., Chambers, M.: One size does not fit all: learning style, play, and online interactives. In: Research and Evaluation (2007). http://www.eduweb.com/onesize-full.html. Accessed 15 Jan 2019
3. Keefe, J.: Student Learning Styles and Brain Behavior. NASSP, Reston (1987)
4. Najjar, L.: Multimedia information and learning. J. Educ. Multimed. Hypermedia **5**(2), 129–150 (1996). http://www.medvet.umontreal.ca/techno/eta6785/articles/multimedia_and_learning.pdf. Accessed 16 Jan 2019
5. Kolb, D.: Experiential Learning. Prentice-Hall, Englewood Cliffs (1984)
6. Felder, R.M., Silverman, L.K.: Learning and teaching styles. Eng. Educ. **78**(7), 674–681 (1988)
7. Felder, R.M., Soloman, B.A.: Index of Learning Style Questionnaire (ILSQ) (1999). http://www.engr.ncsu.edu/learningstyles/ilsweb.html
8. King, A.: Blended Language Learning: Part of the Cambridge Papers in ELT Series. Cambridge University Press, Cambridge (2016)
9. Felder, R.M., Spurlin, J.: Applications, reliability and validity of the index of learning styles. Int. J. Eng. Educ. **21**(1), 103–112 (2005)
10. Garrison, D.R.: E-learning in the 21st Century: A Framework for Research and Practice. Routledge, New York (2012)

11. Brown, H.D.: Principles of Language Learning and Teaching. Addison Wesley Longman, White Plains (2000)
12. Arias, J., Swinton, J., Anderson, K.: Online vs. Face-to-Face: a comparison of student outcomes with random assignment. E-J. Bus. Educ. Sch. Teach. **12**(2), 1–23 (2018)
13. Mayer, R.E.: Cognitive theory of multimedia learning. In: Mayer, R.E. (ed.) The Cambridge Handbook of Multimedia Learning, pp. 31–48. Cambridge University Press, New York (2005)
14. Callow, J.: Classroom assessment and picture books - strategies for assessing how students interpret multimodal texts. Aust. J. Lang. Lit. **41**(1), 5–20 (2018)
15. Paivio, A.: Dual coding theory and education. In: Draft Paper for the Conference on "Pathways to Literacy Achievement for High Poverty Children". The University of Michigan School of Education (2006)
16. Goldstein, B.: Working with Images. Cambridge University Press, Cambridge (2008)
17. Keddie, J.: Images. Oxford University Press, Oxford (2009)
18. Persson, P.: Attention manipulation and information overload. Behav. Public Policy **2**(1), 78–106 (2018). https://doi.org/10.1017/bpp.2017.10
19. Carr, N.G.: The Shallows: How the Internet is Changing the Way We Think, Read and Remember. Atlantic Books, London (2010)
20. Halpern, D.F.: Sex Differences in Cognitive Ability, 3rd edn. Lawrence Erlbaum Associates, Mahwah (2000)
21. Lewin, T.: At colleges, women are leaving men in the dust. The New York Times, 9 July 2006
22. Mickelson, R.A.: Why does Jane read and write so well? The anomaly of women's achievement. Sociol. Educ. **62**, 47–63 (1989)
23. Perkins, R., Kleiner, B., Roey, S., Brown, J.: The High School Transcript Study: A Decade of Change in Curricula and Achievement, 1990–2000. NCES 2004-455. National Center for Education Statistics (2004)
24. Dias, J.: The teacher as chameleon: computer-mediated communication & role transformation. Teachers, learners, and computers: exploring relationships in CALL, Chubu Nihon Bunkakai, Nagoya, pp. 17–26 (1998)
25. Harmer, J.: The Practice of English Language Teaching, 4th edn. Longman, London (2007)

Teacher's Developmental Stages of Exploring Thinking Tools in a Blended Learning Environment

Xiao Hong Zhang[1(✉)], Kenichi Kubota[2], Mayumi Kubota[2], and Kedong Li[3]

[1] Graduate School of Kansai University, Kansai University, Takatsuki, Osaka, Japan
windyzhang0929@gmail.com
[2] Kansai University, Takatsuki, Osaka, Japan
[3] South China Normal University, Guangzhou, Guangdong, China

Abstract. The purpose of this study is to examine Chinese, primary school teachers' developmental stages in blended learning environments when exploring the use of thinking tools (TTs) for improving students' thinking skills. This study analyzed data using the Trajectory Equifinality Modeling (TEM). TEM is a new qualitative methodology of Cultural Psychology that explores the trajectory of multiple decision-making actions based on time and interaction between social direction and social guidance. TEM clarified that Chinese primary teachers went through the followings five stages: Stage 1: application of TTs, Stage 2: trials of improving students' reasoning, Stage 3: reflection of the usage of TTs in one year, Stage 4: "Aha" experiences of matching TTs with specific thinking skills (reasoning) and Stage 5: shifting the focus from TTs to reasoning. In Stages 1, 2, 3, and 5, online support was the major turning point and sustaining Lesson Study was the social guidance that promoted teacher inquiry. In Stage 4, face-to-face training triggered the "Aha" experience and multiple viewpoints from the teachers who had experienced using TTs in the training workshop and provided social guidance. Furthermore, attention needed to be paid to how the relocation of the principal and the director of the research group in the school affected teacher's decision-making.

Keywords: Developmental stages · Blended learning environment · Thinking skills · Thinking tools · Trajectory equifinality modeling

1 Introduction

With the development of globalization, many countries focus on nurturing children's thinking skills in primary education in the 21st century. A new teaching strategy using thinking tools (TTs) to improve children' thinking skills was introduced into some experimental primary schools in China based on China-Japan Collaborative Research Program [1, 2]. To support Chinese primary teachers exploring TTs, educators created blended learning environment by combining face-to-face training and online support.

S. K. S. Cheung et al. (Eds.): ICBL 2019, LNCS 11546, pp. 186–202, 2019.
https://doi.org/10.1007/978-3-030-21562-0_16

Many studies paid attention to the environment of face-to-face learning and online support in blended learning environment [3, 4]. However, Graham and Dziuban warned that a blended learning environment is not "just a linear combination" of face-to-face training and online support [5]. Li et al. pointed out that social and cultural factors related to the learners need to be explore [6].

In addition, teaching innovation is more easily influenced by the social and cultural factors in new educational environments. Kishi et al. indicates that teachers encounter difficulties when exploring new teaching strategies which they did not experience previously [7]. Social factors that influenced teachers' involvement seems to affect teachers' decision-making processes. To successfully implement teaching innovation, developmental stages in the teacher must be highlighted since professional development "must be seen as a process, not as an event." [8, 9].

Up to this point, the developmental stages of Chinese teacher, using TTs in the blended learning environment related to social factors, has not been examined. Therefore, the purpose of this study is to expand knowledge of developmental stages related to social factors for designing blended learning environment when teachers introduce TTs into classrooms.

2 Thinking Tools and Its Relationship to Blended Learning

2.1 A New Teaching Strategy by Exploring Thinking Tools

With the shift from knowledge acquisition to fostering students' thinking skills, how to nurture children's thinking skills became an important educational goal in Japan. However, it is difficult to nurture children's thinking skills because thinking is a complex process in their heads and cannot be observed. Furthermore, children cannot explain what they think or control what to think.

To achieve the new teaching goals in elementary school, teaching strategies, using thinking tools (TTs) to improve students' thinking skills, were developed. TTs can be described as special graphic organizers, which match with specific thinking skills [10]. Using thinking tools that "show one's thinking visually" in class was found to have educational benefits [11]. For example, Venn diagrams matched with comparison, and Pyramid chart matched with structure. Writing or talking about their thoughts using thinking tools could improve some specific thinking skills of students. It is crucial for teachers to decide what kinds of thinking skills to nurture and which TTs can be used to match with them [10, 11].

2.2 Innovative Teaching Strategy by Exploring TTs in China

To promote the quality of education, China's government called for promoting thinking skills from primary education in 2016 [12]. As a teaching innovation, the teaching strategies, using TTs was introduced into some experimental primary schools since 2012 in Guangdong Province, China [1, 2]. Miyake et al. surveyed how teachers used

TTs from 2015 to 2016 and discovered that some teachers used TTs as tools to show the result of students' thinking and motivated students to attain more knowledge [1, 13]. The survey showed that teachers encountered difficulties when shifting from knowledge teaching to thinking-training teaching. It also showed that using new strategy required time and effort to result in teachers changing. In 2017, Miyake et al. discovered that some teachers became focused on the thinking process of students through conversation analysis between teachers and students who participated in the lesson [14]. The studies mentioned above illustrated how Chinese teachers used TTs through face-to-face training at a certain period of time.

2.3 Supporting Chinese Teacher in Using TTs Through Blended Learning

To support teachers who were examining using TTs to be integrated in their own teaching strategy, Chinese educators used QQ, an online support to help teacher solve problems they encountered, in addition to face-to-face training class. QQ is a type of social networking service in China.

Blended learning is defined as "integrating face-to-face learning and online learning" [15]. Blended learning has some advantages over only face-to-face learning or online learning with its enriching interaction and information. The two types of blended learning are integrated structured learning and unstructured learning. Structured learning means that an educator controls the face-to-face learning and online learning during a certain period of time. Unstructured learning is learner-centered, with learning from uncontrolled online support, such as email and a social network system [16]. Blended learning is used to promote the professional development in targeted training led by educators or trainers [17]. An essential feature of teachers' learning is to solve problems in practice. Therefore, promoting problem solving with teachers through a combination of face-to-face training and online support is a useful component of teacher training. In this paper, teachers' blended learning was defined as "the training integrating face-to-face training and online support".

2.4 Problem Statement

Graham and Dziuban indicated that blended learning designed for teacher is not "just a linear combination of the two" [5]. They showed the importance of how teacher changed through face-to-face training and online support in the blended learning environment. In the practice of using TTs, improving thinking skills is the teaching goal not just the correct use of TTs. Teachers needs to use TTs flexibly, based on the situation and student needs, to improve students' specific thinking skills. This type of practice requires knowing when and which methods assist teachers' understanding and application of TTs better. Furthermore, it is crucial to critically rethink about what is and how best to design a blended learning environment.

3 Blended Learning Environment

3.1 Blended Learning Environment

To organize blended learning environments to support learning effectively is important. Yeh et al. indicated that blended learning is effective to promote pre-service teachers' professional development. Forty-four pre-service teachers participated in a 17-week experimental instructional program. Through the analysis of data collected, the blended learning environment promoted pre-service teachers' professional knowledge and personal teaching efficacy in their teaching of creativity [18]. Guzer and Caner analyzed the literature from 2010 to 2012 and identified that integrating the constructive model into the blended learning environment is crucial [19]. Furthermore in 2017, Li et al. analyzed the learners' change in the blended environment and indicated that cultural background should be explore in order to capture the dynamics of blended learning [6]. Kubota stated that teachers' change is inherently social and mediated by the cultural context in the teachers' educational environment [20]. Therefore, it is necessary to organize the blended learning environment by paying attention to the social and cultural factors of the teachers.

3.2 Social Factors in Blended Learning Environment

Shulman et al. indicated that teachers learned and developed "within a broader context of community, institution, polity, and circumstance" [21]. Kishi et al. suggested that social and cultural factors influenced teachers' decision making since teachers are easily in conflict with different social factors when they try to use new strategies from another country [7]. Zhao and Frank indicated that teachers encounter cultural pressure when they tried to explore new teaching strategies in their classroom in China [22]. This data showed that teachers have difficulty making a thorough inquiry into new practices. In contrast, to support teachers' professional development, professional development communities proved to help teachers continue inquiring, through Lesson Study. Lesson Study is a type of collaborative activity where teachers meet to discuss learning goals, plan an actual lesson, observe the lesson and report on the results [23]. Lesson Study has three levels with School-based, District-level and National-level lessons. Lesson Study has proven to help teachers to inquiry with implementation of a program. Akita indicated that Lesson Study could help teachers reflect deeply and has benefits to help teacher identify more problems and discuss new ways to improve lessons. From the studies mentioned above, it is crucial to analyze the interaction between social factors in the social and cultural context in which teachers are involved.

3.3 Developmental Stages in Blended Learning Environments

Blended learning is rooted in the idea that learning is not just a one-time event, but is a continuous process [16]. Furthermore, professional development of teachers involves making various choices and using the decision-making process [9, 23]. Kolb identified that teacher learned in the follow cycle: (1) having an experience, (2) reviewing the experience and reflecting, (3) theorizing about what happened and why, then exploring options and alternatives, and (4) planning what to do differently the next time [15, 24]. In the developmental process, Thorne suggested that it is important that teachers have a deep understand of new strategies, reflect on their experiences and have "Aha" experiences in the blended learning environment [15].

Teachers make choices with some options and alternatives that take them in different directions. The decisions that teachers make are dependent on what problems the teachers notice when they reflect on what they did [25]. Korthagen and Vasalos suggests that gaining awareness of essential aspects in practice is a big turning point in the change process [26]. The "Aha" experience is the stage or moment "when you realize that you know what everything means or why you have spent so long thinking about something" [27]. It often occurred with people who are greatly involved in doing something in the "right" environment at the "right" time [15, 28]. Reflection and the "Aha" experience are cognitive activities in a person that triggers teachers to change. In the blended environment of using TTs, teacher make decisions to move on regardless of face-to-face training or online support when using TTs. Decisions, that teacher make, depend on what they learned from face-to-face training or online support, and the their social environment. However, observing when face-to-face learning or online learning is effective in the developmental stages is difficult. Furthermore, the social factors that affect teacher in decision-making situations in the blended learning environment is also unclear.

Therefore, this study aims to expand knowledge of developmental stages in the blended learning environment including social factors, when Chinese teachers explore TTs. The study can provide valuable information for designing blended learning environments for teacher's professional development in the educational field of improving students' thinking skills.

4 Research Objective

Based on the above, in the practice of using TTs to improve students' thinking skills, the specific research questions driving this study are:

(1) What developmental stages did a representative Chinese teacher experience?
(2) What kinds of the social factors influenced the teacher's developmental stages in the blended learning environment?

Through clarifying the developmental stages and the social factors in the blended learning environment, the authors tried to propose some suggestions to design more effective blended learning environments to support Chinese primary teachers who use TTs in the future.

5 Research Methodology

This study was based on the framework of the Trajectory Equifinality Modeling (TEM). TEM is a new qualitative methodology of Cultural Psychology and has "two central features in its analytic scheme: time and the transformation of potentialities into actualities" [29]. "Transformation of potentialities into actualities" means people choose some options from many alternative options in the social and cultural context [29]. The chosen options become the developmental trajectories, and the options not chosen became the potential trajectories. From the results, it is possible to depict the variability of trajectories and the dynamics of social factors.

5.1 Trajectory Equifinality Modeling

To explore the trajectory of multiple decision-makings, some basic concepts of TEM are illustrated as follows in Fig. 1. *Equifinality Point* (EFP) are the given end states, that can be reached by many potential means but is not a goal point. If EFP is reached, EFP transforms to a new point to pursuit. *Polarized Equifinality Point* (F-EFP) is a potential EFP to "neutralizing implicit value system of research". *Bifurcation Point (BFP)* is a point, which has alternative options. While teachers go through the BFP, two kinds of social power, *Social Direction* (SD) *and Social Guidance* (SG), influence people's chosen options. SD is the power of inhibition leading to EFP. SG is the power of promotion to proceed to EFP [29, 30]. By clarifying the trajectory of how people reach EFP, researchers can identify what kind of social factors inhibit or promote teachers' decision-makings [29].

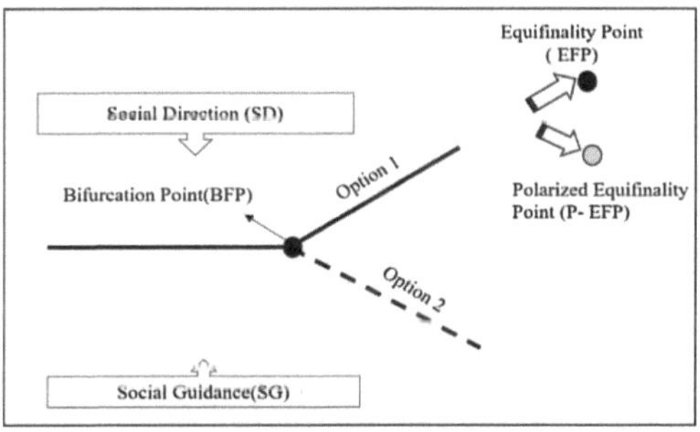

Fig. 1. Concepts of TEM (Based on Yasuda et al. 2015; Sato, 2017; Marsico and Valsiner, 2018)

5.2 Applying Concepts of TEM to the Study

Based on research objectives, the authors applied concepts of TEM to the study. The position in this study is shown in Table 1. Firstly, the authors utilized a teacher "using TTs to teach lesson for improving students' reasoning" as the *Equifinality Point* since reasoning was one higher order thinking skill of importance in mathematics [31]. In China, few teachers paid attention to improving students' thinking skills based on the subject content instead they focused on teaching knowledge to help student pass the College Entrance Examination [32, 33]. Therefore, this study "using thinking tools to teach lessons without improving students' reasoning" was taken as the *Polarized Equifinality Point* since it is possible goal for teachers in the Chinese society. Furthermore, the authors utilized the turning points in practicing TTs as *Bifurcating Point.* Next, the authors examined the social power, which inhibited teachers from using TTs for reasoning as *Social Direction*, or social power which promoted teachers go to EFP as *Social Guidance*.

Table 1. Concepts of TEM used in this study

Concepts	Definition	Positioned in this study
Equifinality Point (EFP)	A given end state that can be reached	Using TTs to teach lesson for improving students' reasoning
Polarized Equifinality Point (P-EFP)	A potential EFP	Using TTs to teach lesson without improving students' reasoning
Bifurcation Point (BFP)	Bifurcating point to acheive EFP	Bifurcating points in practing TTs to go to EFP
Social Direction (SD)	The social power of inhibition go to EFP	Social power inhibited teachers using TTs to achieve EFP
Social Guidance (SG)	The social power of promotion to go to EFP	Social power promotted teachers using TTs to acheive EFP

5.3 Historically Structured Inviting (HSI)

This study chose Teacher C as a research collaborator. Teacher C was a teacher who researchers thought could "use thinking tools to teach lesson to improve students' reasoning". Teacher C taught mathematics 5 years and 4 months. In addition, she took part in the training class provided by Chinese educators since September 2017. She used TTs for three years and four months until the final interview.

There are two reasons to choose Teacher C as a research collaborator. Firstly, TEM chose research collaborators based on Historically Structured Inviting (HSI). HSI occurs when required researchers invite representative collaborators who have experience achieved EFP to discuss how collaborators changed [34]. This is a new way to choose sample to understand human's developmental trajectory based on equifinality sampling in qualitative methodology of Cultural Psychology [29, 34, 35]. Secondly, choosing one teacher can depict the specific process of using TTs. Based on the 1/4/9 principle, where 1 or 2 persons can clarify the specific process, 4 ± 1 person can clarify the multiple experiences, and 9 ± 2 person can clarify the patterns of the developmental process [34, 35].

5.4 Data Collection

To ensure that the teacher remembered her experiences and to confirm what social factors influenced her usage, the researchers explained the research theme and defined TEM with simple terms. After Teacher C understood and accepted the research theme and TEM, researchers began the interviews. To ensure that Teacher C was relaxed and would talk freely, the authors went to her schools and interviewed her in a secluded room without others present. Based on Trans-view interview strategy, the authors collected data three times. Trans-view is an interview strategy in which researchers confirmed contents three times to establish agreements with the researcher collaborator [34]. The authors asked Teacher C about when and what she learned from face-to-face training and online support, how she used TTs, what options she chose or might choose when she encountered problems, and what social factors influenced her choice. The interview times for the first, second, and third time were about 83 min, 101 min, and 30 min, respectively.

5.5 Analysis Procedure

To draw TEM diagrams, the authors analyzed data using the steps in Fig. 2.

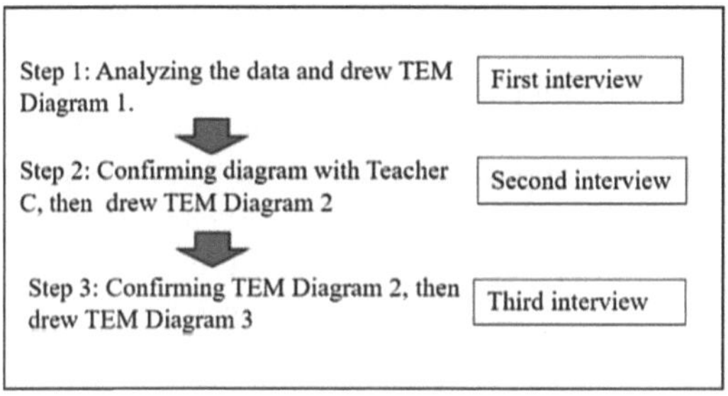

Fig. 2. Procedure of analysis and drew TEM diagram

First, the authors divided the data based on meaning, and wrote short titles for identification. The data was sorted by time, before drawing a TEM diagram that was shown to Teacher C. Second, Teacher C read her TEM diagram and talked in more detail about the learning from face-to-face training and online support and how she used TTs and the social factors. Then, researchers drew a TEM Diagram as in Diagram 2. Third, the authors showed the edited TEM again to Teacher C, and asked teachers for their opinions, before modifying it again. The authors quoted content of the TEM in *italic* type, and cited the interview data with "".

6 Result and Discussion

From the data, the authors drew a diagram in Fig. 3, which showed the developmental process of how Teacher C reached the point of using TTs to teach lesson for improving students' reasoning (EFP). Through the TEM diagram, the authors discovered that the developmental trajectory of Teacher C could be divided into five stages: application of TTs, trials of improving students' reasoning, reflection of the usage of TTs in one year, "Aha" experience of matching TTs with specific thinking skills and shifting the focus from TTs to reasoning.

6.1 Stage 1: Application of TTs

In Stage 1, the stage of application of *TTs, Teacher C took part in training classes for TTs* twice. An official working in the *Municipal Board of Education* (SG1) required Teacher C to hold a Lesson Study in the city when she received the second training class. She was given one-week to prepare for the Lesson Study.

In preparation for the Lesson Study, Teacher C quickly *downloaded materials about TTs from the QQ community* (BFP1). Due to the *lack of time* (SD1), Teacher C felt anxious to fulfill the "task" from her superiors and made great effort to *use TTs in class*. She might not have use TTs in the class if the official from the *Municipal Board of Education* (SG1) did not ask her to hold the Lesson Study. *However*, Teacher C found that *some student could not participate in group-thinking activities*.

She encountered great pressure of opposition from *senior teachers* in school (SD2) when she wanted to continue to use TTs. She might not have been able to modify the design of group activities without the suggestions from the researchers in the *first Lesson Study* (SG2). Then, she *modified the designs about group activities* and attempted to encourage all of students to think. As a result, she noticed that *using TTs easily trigger all of students to think* in the first stage.

In this stage, Teacher C *downloading materials about TTs from the QQ community* (BFP1) was the first bifurcating point. She accessed rich resource in a week through the QQ online community. This showed that QQ online had the advantage of supplying rich resources for teacher in a short time. From the perspective of social factors, the authors discovered *Requirement from Municipal Board of Education* (SG1) promoted Teacher C to use TTs in the class, but the deadline was too short. This illustrated the top-down power structure that was used when introducing TTs into the classroom. Furthermore, *opposition of senior teachers* (SD2) also created great stress for Teacher C. This phenomenon indicated that some teachers, especially senior teachers, who were comfortable using traditional strategies, did not favor the introduction of teaching innovations. This result was consistent with Zhao and Frank who identified traditional pressure in school worked against teaching innovation [22].

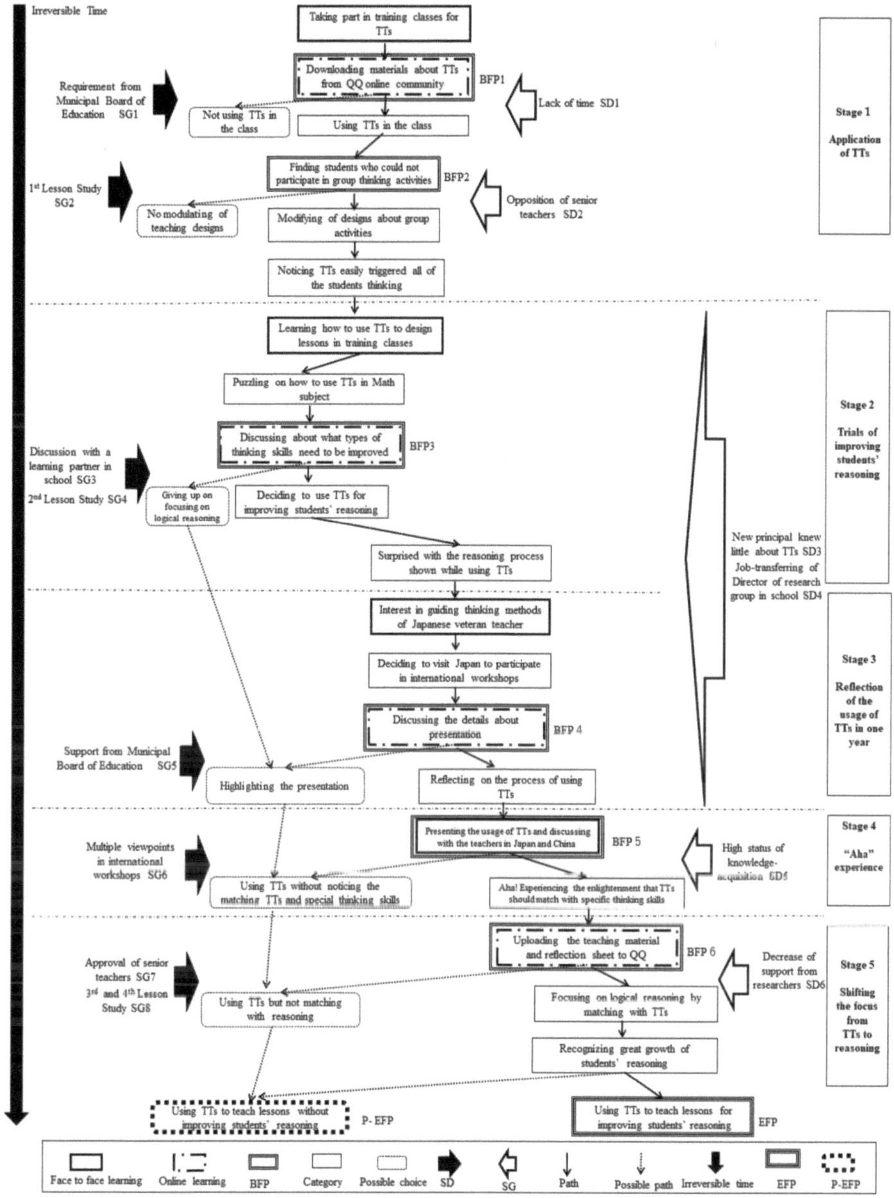

Fig. 3. The TEM of developmental trajectory of Teacher C

6.2 Stage 2: Trials of Improving Students' Reasoning

Stage 2 was the stage of the trials of improving students' reasoning. First, Teacher C realized her lack of understanding of TTs and *learned how to use TTs to design lessons in training classes*. However, she *was puzzled about how to use TTs in mathematics* and *discussed the types of thinking skills that needed to be improved* in mathematics with Chinese educators (BFP3) using QQ. She great difficulty using TTs since the *new principal at her school knew little about TTs* (SD3) and the *the director of the research group was transferred to a new school.* She said she felt "very sad" because of the lack of support from the management level in the school. After *discussion with a learning partner in the school* (SG3) and with approval from the *second Lesson Study,* Teacher C decided to use TTs in a lesson on students' reasoning, (SG4). She was *surprised with the reasoning process that students showed when using TTs* while she guided children's thought based on reasoning. She felt extremely happy about the results and wanted to learn more about how to guide students thinking. In Stage 2, online support, discussion about specific thinking skills (BFP3), was the bifurcation point after Teacher C encountered problems on how to use TTs in mathematics. Teacher C connected with Chinese educators to seek problem-solving methods.

In the Foshan area, the management level administrators in schools are relocated every three years. The relocation of the principal and the director of the research group in the school seems to create great social stress for Teacher C. In the study of Zhao and Frank, the management level in school influenced teachers using new strategies [22], but they did not mention how the relocation of personnel affected teachers' choice-making. In this study, the authors indicated that relocation of management level officials in school should be considered when teachers used TTs.

6.3 Stage 3: Reflection of the Usage of TTs in One Year

Reflection on the usage of TTs in one year was Stage 3. In this stage, the social directions were influenced by the *new principal who knew little about TTs* (SD3) and the *job-transferring of the director of research group in school* (SD4) which was the same as Stage 2. Teacher C was *interested in the guiding thinking methods of Japanese veteran teachers* in a training workshops and decided to visit Japan to participate in international workshops. She *discussed the details about presentation* through QQ online support (BFP4) and then *reflected on the process of using TTs.*

Some officials of Municipal Board of Education also took part in this international workshop. The *support from the Municipal Board of Education* (SG5) motivated the teacher to reflect deeply on the practice of her usage of TTs. After reflecting on the experience of using thinking tools in one year, Teacher C began to explain her usage of TTs in her own words. Without support from the *Municipal Board of Education* (SG5), to motivate her to improve her presentations, Teacher C might have only *highlighted the presentation but not reflection of the process.*

Akita identified that teachers easily reflected on what happened recently, but had difficulty reflecting on the entire process of activities over the long term [23]. However, Teacher C was able to do so, after she *discussed the details about presentation* (BFP4) with Chinese researchers through QQ online support. The social directions were the same as Stage 2, where she reflected on the entire process about how she used TTs because of the social guidance and *support from Municipal Board of Education* (SG5).

6.4 Stage 4: "Aha" Experience of Matching TTs with Specific Thinking Skills

Unduly *high status of knowledge-acquisition* (SD5) was expended on Stage 4 but this was the most important stage for Teacher C. In this stage, she *presented and discussed her usage of TTs with the teachers in Japan and China* (BFP5). Then, she experienced an "Aha" moment through communication with teachers who had also used thinking tools in Japan and China. A teacher who was listening, asked her: "why did you not use a flower (one kind of graphic organizers) to express the results of students' thought?" Teacher C was surprised with this question that she never considered, and then engaged in finding the answer at that moment. "Aha! TTs should match with specific thinking skills!!! I suddenly recognized it!" she talked about this "Aha" experience four times in the interview. Through these "Aha" experiences, she gained awareness of essential aspects of using TTs.

In Stage 4, the face-to-face workshop was the bifurcation point. Due to the *high status of knowledge-acquisition* (SD5), Teacher C had difficulty realizing that the teaching goal of using TTs was not for knowledge-acquisition but for improving thinking skills. Even if educators told her, she could not generate the meaning in her mind, in the international workshops, she was fully immersed in the presentation and discussion. She suddenly experienced "Aha!" moments and recognized that "TTs should match with specific thinking skills!!!" The "Aha!" moment often occurred in the activity with accompanying feeling of focus and involvement [27, 28]. The authors considered that teacher could easily experience "Aha" moments as follows. Firstly, Teacher C had long-term experiences of using TTs in blended learning environment in the Stage 1, 2 and 3. The "Aha" moments were the developmental stage but also the result of her experience. Secondly, she was fully immersed in the presentation and discussion in international workshop. Last but not least, the participants in the workshops were the teachers who also have experienced of exploring TTs. The environment of workshop made her easily to catch the essential aspects, including the problems teachers often met, why and how to use TTs.

6.5 Stage 5: Shifting the Focus from TTs to Reasoning

Stage 5 was when Teacher C shifted *focus from TTs to students' reasoning*. After returning to China, Chinese educators asked her to *upload teaching materials and reflection sheets* related to how to use TTs to QQ (BFP6). After that, the *support from researchers decreased* (SD6). However, Teacher C insisted on *focusing on the logical reasoning that matched with TTs* and modulated the guiding thinking methods in this stage because of two Social Guidance. The first SG was the *approval of a senior teacher* (SG7). At Stage 1, the senior teachers did not approval of introducing TTs in the school However, in Stage 5, senior teachers became accustomed to TTs. This kind of change encouraged Teacher C's inquiry to improve her use of TTs. The second SG is when Teacher C did Lesson Studies twice, in the *third and fourth Lesson Study* (SG8). She made an effort to improve the lesson on using TTs to improve students' reasoning since many teachers in the city were going to see how she used TTs to improve students' thinking skills. These two Lesson Study supplied goals in a certain period. Goal-setting in the teacher's mind was important to inquiry, using new strategies better [15]. Therefore, she analyzed what types of specific thinking skills were necessary based on teaching situations in mathematics. In addition, she analyzed and chose suitable TTs, including new TTs, to match with specific thinking skills depended on her own judgment. In BFP6, the possible choice was *using TTs but not with reasoning*. As a result, she recognized great growth of students' logical reasoning. Finally, she arrived at EFP where she could *use thinking tools to teach lessons to improve students' reasoning*. As mentioned by Kitamura, teachers have difficulty achieving the stage of focusing on specific thinking skills based on the situations in their subject [36]. In Stage 5, Teacher C used TTs to focus on reasoning of students because of the change of senior teachers' attitude (SG7) and goal setting to hold *Lesson Study* (SG8) motivated her to inquiry.

7 Overall Discussion

In the developmental trajectory of Teacher C, the authors discovered that four bifurcation points showing the decision-making were online support in Stage 1, 2, 3, and 5. Teacher required help from researchers when she found some problems were difficult to solve by herself when using TTs. As Kishi et al. indicated, teachers had difficulty using new strategies when they have no experience [7]. Therefore, they need efficient support from other educators. Through online supporting, educators gave Teacher C sustaining guidance to solve her problems.

However, some problems were not easy to even identify since using TTs is a new strategy to improve students' thinking skills. For example, Teacher C, did not have a clear understanding about improving specific thinking skills even if educators explained it. In Stage 4, face-to-face workshops became the bifurcation point that triggered her understand that TTs were used to match with specific thinking skills through an *"Aha" experience*. Kurokami et al. [10] and Kansai University Elementary School [11] pointed out that matching TTs with specific thinking skills in the subject matter is a key point to improve students' thinking skills. However, Kitamura said that teachers had difficulty focusing on the specific thinking skills based on the subject matter in the practice of using TTs [36]. The "Aha" experience only occurred in face-to-face learning where there were multiple viewpoints in learning environments. It showed she gained awareness of essential aspects that TTs should match with specific thinking skills through face-to-face training. This illustrates the importance and timeliness of workshops that offer multiple viewpoints.

The authors discovered the decision-making points after Teacher C learned from face-to-face training and online support, were strongly affected by the social factors that occurred in every stage. As Kubota [20] and Shulman [21] mentioned, a teacher's changing is social, and constructed by the social factors in the concrete situation. Teacher C's decision-making was consistent with the opinions of Kubota [20] and Shulman [21]. However, these two studies did not show what kinds of social factors affected teachers' decision making. This study indicated the specific interaction between social direction and social guidance in the decision-making point in the developmental stages.

Furthermore, in this case, some similar, social factors occurred in different stages that indicated the types of social consequences that need to be highlighted. For example, Lesson Study promoted Teacher C inquiry on how to use TTs in the Stage 1, 2 and 5. She decided to use TTs from the *first Lesson Study*, tried to use TTs for reasoning from the *second Lesson Study*, and shifted the focus from TTs to specific thinking skills from the *third and fourth Lesson Study*. Akita suggested that Lesson Study greatly benefited teachers to reflect and make lesson better in school-based lesson, district-lesson and national-level lesson [23]. In this study, the city-level Lesson Study promoted Teacher C to explore TTs better since this city-level Lesson Study provided goal-setting for her in some certain time. This indicates that Lesson Study is helpful for teachers' goal-setting and motivates them to inquire about how to nurture students' thinking skills.

In addition, this study found that the social factors in teacher' learning community was changeable, such as changing from social direction to social guidance. Teacher C felt great pressure from the *opposition of senior teachers* (SD2) in using TTs in school in Stage 1. However, in Stage 5, senior teacher started to use TTs. *Approval of senior teachers* (SG7) greatly motivated Teacher C to *focus on matching TTs with lessons on reasoning*. The changing of senior teachers' attitudes, from opposition to approval of using TTs, showed the possibility that changing social direction can provide social guidance for teacher' professional development.

8 Conclusions and Future Perspective

The purpose of this study is to examine Chinese primary school teachers' developmental stages in blended learning environments when exploring the use of TTs for improving students' thinking skills. By using TEM diagrams, a Chinese primary teacher went through the following five stages: Stage 1: application of TTs, Stage 2: trials of improving students' reasoning, Stage 3: reflection of the usage of TTs in one year, Stage 4: "Aha" experience of matching TTs with specific thinking skills (reasoning), Stage 5: and shifting the focus from TTs to reasoning. In Stage 1, 2, 3, and 5, online support provided the major turning points. In Stage 4, face-to-face training workshop was the transformation point that triggered the "Aha" experience. The importance of the two learning types, of online support and face-to-face training, were shown although the effectiveness occurred in different stages.

This study also found that social factors, such as the relocation of management level officials in the school, influenced what decisions the teacher made at the turning points in every stage. These social directions inhibited Teacher C from inquiry. The social guidance, such as sustaining Lesson Study and Multiple viewpoints in international workshop, encouraged her to continue to inquiry about how to use TTs for improving students' reasoning.

To help Chinese teachers use TTs that match with students' specific thinking skills, in the future, the authors proposes some suggestion that will design a blended learning environment in a professional developmental community as follows. Educators need to (1) provide sustaining online support for teachers' problem-solving, and create more face-to-face workshops to encourage professional dialogue with multiple viewpoints and to foster "Aha experiences", (2) eliminate or decrease the social directions, by creating explanation sessions and generating a manual about TTs to relieve the pressure from the relocation of management level officials occurring in schools, and strengthen the social guidance, such as creating different level Lesson Study to motivate teacher to inquire about how to use TTs at every developmental stage.

It should be noted that this study examined the specific developmental trajectory of one representative teacher in a blended learning environment. Based on Yasuda et al., examining 9 ± 2 persons could find the patterns of developmental process [34]. To this end, future studies are suggested to examine a larger number of teachers' developmental model to clarify the patterns of the change process in the blended learning environment when Chinese primary teachers use TTs to guide students' specific thinking skills.

Acknowledgements. This work was supported by the funding of the Japan Society for the Promotion of Science (Grant Number: 17H04572). We greatly thank for the methodological support from Yasuda Yuko, Ritsumeikan University, Japan.

References

1. Miyake, K., Kishi, M., Kubota, K.: International collaborative research on developing lesson for higher order thinking: how do Chinese primary school teachers apply practice developed in Japan into their lesson in China? In: Research Report of Japan Education Technology Conferences, vol. 15, no. 3, pp. 139–144 (2015)
2. Li, K.: Visualization learning action research. Educ. Inf. Technol. China **7–8**, 9–17 (2016)
3. So, H., Brush, A.T.: Student perceptions of collaborative learning, social presence and satisfaction in a blended learning environment: relationships and critical factors. Comput. Educ. **51**, 318–336 (2008)
4. McCarthy, H.: Blended learning environments: using social networking sites to enhance the first year experience. Australas. J. Educ. Technology. **26**(6), 729–740 (2010)
5. Dziuban, D.C., Picciano, G.A., Graham, R.C.: Conducting Research in Online and Blended Learning Environments: New Pedagogical Frontiers (2015)
6. Li, Y., Yang, H.H., Cai, J., MacLeod, J.: College students' computer self-efficacy, intrinsic motivation, attitude, and satisfaction in blended learning environments. In: Cheung, S.K.S., Kwok, L.-f., Ma, W.W.K., Lee, L.-K., Yang, H. (eds.) ICBL 2017. LNCS, vol. 10309, pp. 65–73. Springer, Cham (2017). https://doi.org/10.1007/978-3-319-59360-9_6
7. Kishi, M., Kubota, K., Ito, T.: A case study of implementing lesson study for pre-service training for education in Myanmar. J. Educ. Technol. Res. Jpn. Soc. Educ. Technol. **35**, 1–10 (2012)
8. Guskey, R.T.: Professional development and teacher change. Teach. Teach.: Theory Pract. **8** (3), 381–391 (2002)
9. Sato, K., Akita, K., Shimizu, K., Kotama, S., Kitamura, Y.: Teacher as learning professional expert. Iwanami Shoten, Tokyo (2016)
10. Kurokami, H., Kojima, A., Taizan, Y.: Teaching how to think with thinking tools, NPO Gakusyu Sozou Forum, Osaka (2012)
11. Kansai University Elementary School.: The guidebook of the method to nurture thinking skill. Sakura Sha, Tokyo, Japan (2015)

12. Ministry of Education of China.: The key competency of Chinese students (2016). http://jwc.lzu.edu.cn/upload/news/N20180803173448.pdf
13. Miyake, K., Kishi, M., Kubota, K.: The awareness of nurturing thinking skills in Chinese primary teachers. Jpn. Soc. Educ. Technol. **40**(Suppl), 53–56 (2016)
14. Miyake, K., Kishi, M., Kubota, K., Li, K.: The evaluation of the lessons with using thinking tools since 4 years: from the viewpoint of interaction between teachers and students. Jpn. Assoc. Educ. Media Study **24**(1), 43–56 (2017)
15. Thorne, K.: Blended Learning: How to Integrate Online and Traditional Learning. Kogan Page, London (2003)
16. Singh, H.: Building effective blended learning programs. Educ. Technol. **43**(6), 51–54 (2003)
17. Tucker, R.C.: Power up Blended Learning: A Professional Learning Infrastructure to Support Sustainable Change. Corwin, California (2019)
18. Yeh, Y., Huang, L., Yeh, Y.: Knowledge management in blended learning: effects on professional development in creativity instruction. Comput. Educ. **56**, 146–156 (2011)
19. Guzer, B., Caner, H.: The past, present and future of blended learning: an in depth analysis of literature. Procedia Soc. Behav. Sci. **116**, 4596–4603 (2014)
20. Kubota, K.: Applying a collaborative learning model to a course development project (1999)
21. Shulman, L.S., Shulman, J.H.: How and what teachers learn a shifting perspective. J. Curric. Stud. **36**, 257–271 (2004)
22. Zhao, Y., Frank, A.K.: Factors affecting technology uses in schools: an ecological perspective. Am. Educ. Res. J. **40**(4), 807–840 (2003)
23. Akita, K.: Research of lessons and learning of teacher: for Lesson Study, Akashi Syoten (2008)
24. Kolb, D.A., Rubin, I.M., McIntyre, J.M.: Organizational Psychology: An Experiential Approach to Organizational Behavior, 4th edn. Prentice Hall, London (1994)
25. Schon, D.: The Reflective Practitioner: How Professionals Think in Action. Basic Books, New York (1983)
26. Korthagen, F., Vasalos, A.: Levels in reflection: core reflection as a means to enhance professional growth. Teach. Teach.: Theory Pract. **11**(1), 4747–4771 (2005)
27. Garii, B.: That "aha" experience: meta-cognition and student understanding of learning and knowledge. **4**, 1–22 (2002)
28. Csikszentmihalyi, M.: Applications of Flow in Human Development and Education: The Collected Works of Mihaly Csikszentmihalyi. Springer, Heidelberg (2014). https://doi.org/10.1007/978-94-017-9094-9
29. Sato, T., Hidaka, T., Fukuda, M.: Depicting the dynamics of living the life: the trajectory equifinality model. In: Valsiner, J., Peter, M., Lyra, M., Chaudhary, N. (eds.) Dynamic Process Methodology in the Social and Developmental Sciences. Springer, New York (2009). https://doi.org/10.1007/978-0-387-95922-1_10
30. Sato, T.: Collected Papers on Trajectory Equifinality Approach. Chitose Press Inc., Tyoko (2017)
31. Richland, E.L., Begolli, N.K.: Analogy and higher order thinking: learning mathematics as an example. **3**(2), 160–168 (2016)
32. Gegen, S.: Comparative study of China and Japan elementary school Art textbook. Mod. Soc. Cult. Res. **58**, 75–91 (2014)
33. Ueno, S., et al.: Future and Schools Reformation in East Asia. Kitaooji-Shobo, Kyoutou (2015)
34. Yasuda, Y., Nameda, A., Sato, K.: TEA Theory: Let's Study Trajectory Equifinality Approach. Shinyo-Sha, Tokyo (2015)

35. Marsico, G., Valsiner, J.: Beyond the Mind: Cultural Dynamics of the Psyche. Informaion Age Publishing Inc., Scottsdale (2018)
36. Kitamura, T.: Using thinking tools to improve reading ability in Japanese literature. In: Research bulletin of Middle Education in Shika University, pp. 24–29 (2013)

Analytics and Evaluation for Blended Learning

The Analysis of Online Learning Behavior of the Students with Poor Academic Performance in Mathematics and Individual Help Strategies

Jiyou Jia(✉) and Jingrong Zhang

Department of Educational Technology, School of Education, Peking University, Yiheyuanlu 5, Beijing 100871, China
{jjy, zhjr}@pku.edu.cn

Abstract. It is crucially important that educational practitioners and researchers pay attention to the students with poor academic performance and help improve their learning. The behaviors of the students using online learning systems can be used as one important data source to analyze the students' learning behaviors. From the viewpoint of formative assessment, we define one student as a student with poor academic performance during one learning period if this student is classified into a student with poor academic performance in three quarters of all examinations during this period. After screening all students' mathematic exam scores from Grade One to Grade Three of one experiment class in a junior high school in China, six students are identified as students with poor academic performance in math education during nearly three years' study period. They performed worse in most examinations, but not bad in some examinations. Based on the OLAI (Online Learning Activity Index) model proposed by Jia and Yu (2017) to describe the students' online learning activities, we analyze the students' online quiz activity in a web-based interactive learning system by comparing the values of the OLAI dimensions of the students. The data analysis shows that every student had his or her own feature, and thus individual approaches to help each student are suggested. All the poor students had a bad performance in the starting point, i.e. the first exam. Their deficiency in previous study prevented them from understanding new knowledge and should be overcome at first. Overall, their online performance is positively correlated with the normal exam performance. The online quiz activities with instant feedback is helpful for the students with poor academic performance in their normal exams. The more challenging quizzes and the frequent help from teaching assistants online must not lead to better performance in normal exams.

Keywords: Poor academic performance · Formative assessment · Online learning behavior · OLAI (Online Learning Activity Index) · Learning analytics · Mathematics

S. K. S. Cheung et al. (Eds.): ICBL 2019, LNCS 11546, pp. 205–215, 2019.
https://doi.org/10.1007/978-3-030-21562-0_17

1 Concept Definition and Research Question

In educational practice and research, it is of crucial importance that educational practitioners and researchers to be concerned with the students with poor academic performance and to assist them to improve their academic performance. If one student in primary and secondary schools has poor academic performance, but cannot get timely help from the teachers and parents, he or she often has to receive remedial education before entering the ordinary higher education. How to identify a student as a student with poor academic performance remains to be discussed. The different cutoff scores used to identify poor academic performance often range from student examination performance at the 10th to the 45th percentiles. We define the student as a student with poor academic performance in one examination, if he or she has the score below the quartile in this exam (Geary and Hoard 2005). From the viewpoint of formative assessment, the student who just fails in one exam cannot be defined as a student with poor academic performance. We define one student as a student with poor academic performance during one learning period such as three school years, if he or she has poor academic performance in three quarters of all exams during this whole period.

In recent years, besides one-to-one tutoring and other traditional approaches, many intelligent or interactive online tutoring systems have been used to assist the students' learning. The automatically recorded behaviors of the students using online learning systems can serve as one important data resource to analyze the learning features and to explore the relation between online learning behavior and normal exam performance. In this paper the following two questions will be addressed regarding the students with poor academic performance in mathematics study:

What are the online learning features of those students?

What is the relation between their online learning feature and their performance in normal school exams?

2 Related Work

One student with poor academic performance has learning difficulties, and cannot improve his or her competence by self-regulated learning. A great number of researchers have studied the students' learning difficulties generally (Sweller 1994; Chappell 2000; Gustafsson et al. 2013) and in different school subjects including mathematics (Shalev 2007; Lewis 2014; Roschelle et al. 2016), language (Ellis 2006), science (Bahar et al. 1999; Sirhan 2007), and so on. Because mathematics is the foundation to learn other school subjects and very important to logical thinking, the learning difficulties in mathematics have been investigated for a long time. Many notions are used to describe the students with poor mathematic performance, such as mathematical learning disability (MLD), mathematical low achievement (MLA), mathematical learning difficulty (MLD), and mathematical struggling learner (MSL). The previous experience and basis, motivation, interest, habit, the attitude from parents, teachers and other students, and other factors all may contribute to learning difficulties in mathematics.

Educational technology has been used to help the students with poor academic performance, and the positive effect has been evidenced in many relevant studies (Burns et al. 2012; Ok and Bryant 2016; Roschelle et al. 2016; Satsangi and Bouck 2015; Zhang and Zhou 2014). However, the detailed analysis of the online behavior of the students with poor academic performance by using the learning systems and its relation with the normal exam performance has not been found in our literature review.

This study attempts to fill in this gap. We scrutinize the online learning behavior of one experiment class in China that regularly used one intelligent web-based mathematics instruction system, and explore the relation between their online learning behavior and the scores in regular exams.

3 The Students with Poor Academic Performance in the Experiment Class

The experiment class is one normal class in a junior middle school located in Chengdu City, Sichuan Province, one province in south-western China. This class existed between September 2015 and June 2018. In the first school year this class included 49 students. In the second and third school year, three students were absent in all exams, and are excluded in this analysis.

We collected the scores of 48 exams held between November second, 2015 and January 24th, 2018, including mid-term and final term tests. Not all students took part in every exam, as some were absent due to different reasons.

By the first screening, we set the exam score to zero for the absent students to examinations and calculate the quartiles for all examinations, just like the simple measuring regulation in school practice. The following result are found: none of the students had always been below the quartile in all 48 examinations; 11 students had never been below the quartile in any examination and belonged to 22.9% or near one quarter of all students; the students whose exam scores had at least once been below the quartile counted 35 and belonged to 77.1% or three-quarters of all students; the mean and median counts of all students with their exam score below the quartiles for all exams was 11.3 and 4, respectively. According to the previous definition, four students were classified as the students with poor academic performance during the study time between November second, 2015 and January 24th, 2018. The students are anonymously identified as Pu, Tang, Wen and Zhong, and had the poor academic performance in 47, 46, 41 and 43 examinations, respectively.

By the second screening, we exclude all the students who had not taken part in at least one exam for the sake of comparableness and then 28 students were included. After calculating the quartiles for all examinations, the following results are found: none of the students had always been below the quartile in all 48 examinations; seven students had never been below the quartile in any examination and belonged to 25% or just one quarter of all the students; the students whose exam scores had at least once been below the quartile counted 21 and belonged to 75% or three-quarters of all the students; the mean and median of all students' count with their exam score below the quartiles for all exams was 11.85 and 2.5, respectively. According to the previous definition, four students were classified as the students with poor academic performance during the study time between November second, 2015 and January 24th, 2018. The students are identified as Liang, Wang, Wen and Zhong, and had the poor academic performance in 39, 39, 44 and 46 examinations, respectively. Because in this screening all the students who did not write the exam were excluded, the score quartiles of all examinations were more than that in the first screening. The improved quartiles explain why the two students Wen and Zhong had poor academic performance in more exams than in the first screening. The other two students Liang and Wang had poor academic performance in 32 and 33 exams respectively in the first screening.

Through the two screening, we classify the six students into students with poor academic performance in the research period: Liang, Wang, Pu, Tang, Wen and Zhong.

The time series distribution of the regular exam scores of the six students with poor academic performance is shown in Fig. 1. It cannot be estimated from the figure when the students had a better performance or worse performance. The only common feature of the six students is that they all had worse performance in the first examination.

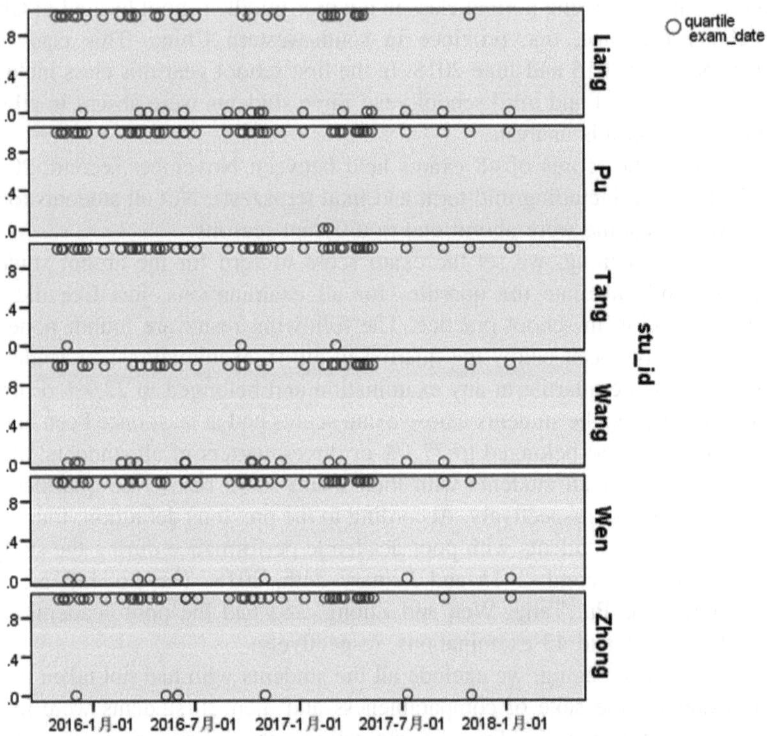

Fig. 1. The time series diagram of the score rank in normal exams of the six students with poor academic performance, with the top circle representing that the student is below the quartile and the down circle representing that the student is above the quartile.

Figure 1 shows that two students, namely Liang and Wen, performed better in the last exam of the whole period. From the point view of summative assessment, both should not be classified as students with poor academic performance in the last exam.

Because mathematics learning is a cumulative process, the score of one student in the first exam is the starting base point, and the score in the last exam is the end point, the six students' scores in the first and last exam are listed in Table 1. In the first exam, Pu performed the worst, and Wang performed the best. In the last exam, Laing and Wen performed the best, while Tang did not write the quiz.

Table 1. The scores of the six students in the first exam and the last exam

Student	First score	Last score
Liang	54	81
Pu	28	63
Tang	47	0
Wang	68	71
Wen	62	81
Zhong	62	71

In the next section we will analyze the students' online learning behavior based on the OLAI model.

4 The OLAI Analysis of the Students Using a Web-Based Interactive Learning System

"Lexue 100" (with the Chinese meaning Happy Learning for 100 Percent, http://www.lexue100.com) is a web-based intelligent instruction system for school mathematics, developed by Beijing Lexue 100 Online Education Co., Ltd. More than 6.8 Million quizzes have been designed for the different versions of mathematics textbooks that are used in different provinces and metropolis in China. Writing quizzes is the main learning activity in this system. Each quiz is composed of a series of gap-filling or single-choice questions with predefined standard answers. As soon as one student submits the trial answer to the system, the trial answer can be compared with the standard answer, and the corresponding quiz score and feedback are instantly provided to the student. Users are allowed to pass the quiz only if every answer gets right, meaning that if the first try of one student is wrong, the student will have to try again until the answer hits the point.

The OLAI (Online Learning Activity Index) model was proposed by Jia and Yu (2017) to describe the students' online learning activities. OLAI can be calculated by the summarization of standardized and dimensionless speed, quality and quantity to complete one activity, i.e. OLAI = speed + quality + quantity. This formula means that OLAI is also a dimensionless value and can comprehensively describe the learner's online learning behavior. Furthermore, the OLAIMAA (OLAI Mean of All Activities) can be used to measure one learner's online learning activities during a certain period on average and the OLAISAA (OLAI Sum of All Activities) can be used to measure one learner's online learning activities from a summative perspective. Similarly, the online learning performance of a specific learner group, such as a class or a school, can also be described by similar indexes such as OLAIMAAAP (OLAI Mean of All Activities of All Participants) and OLAISAAAP (OLAI Sum of All Activities of All Participants).

In Jia and Yu (2017), the concrete formulas to calculate the three dimensions of the OLAI for the quiz activity in the "Lexue 100" system was introduced in details. Based on those formulas, we calculated all the OLAI values for the 46 students in the experiment class during the study period between November the second, 2015 and January the 24th, 2018. The quartile for the quizzes number completed by all students is 1061. Like the scores in all regular school examinations, the percentiles for the OLAI dimensions are also calculated so that the corresponding position of the six students with poor academic performance in the experiment class regarding their OLAI values can be shown as in Table 2. The cell value is set to Yes, if the student's value is below the quartile among the 46 students in the class; otherwise the cell value is set to No. In addition, in order to compare the students' performance, the values of the OLAI dimensions of the six students, together with the mean and median value of the whole class, are listed in Table 3.

Tables 2 and 3 show that none of the six students performed poorly in all the eight OLAI dimensions. Among them, the student Pu and Zhong performed the worst in online activities with 6 dimensions below the quartiles. The student Tang and Wang performed worse with 4 dimensions below the quartiles. The student Wen performed better just with one dimension below the quartiles. The student Liang performed the best in online activities with all 8 dimensions above the quartiles. We depict the six students' online behavior in the following details.

Table 2. The positions of the 6 students with poor academic performance in the experiment class regarding the OLAI dimensions represented by whether the value is below the quartile in the class.

Student	OLAI SAA	OLAI MAA	Speed sum	Speed mean	Quality sum	Quality mean	Quantity sum	Quantity mean
Liang	No	No	No	No	No	No	No	No
Pu	Yes	Yes	No	Yes	Yes	Yes	Yes	No
Tang	Yes	No	No	No	Yes	Yes	Yes	No
Wang	No	Yes	Yes	Yes	No	Yes	No	No
Wen	No	No	No	No	No	No	No	Yes
Zhong	Yes	Yes	No	No	Yes	Yes	Yes	Yes

Table 3. The values of OLAI dimensions of the 6 students with poor academic performance

Student	OLAI SAA	OLAI MAA	Speed sum	Speed mean	Quality sum	Quality mean	Quantity sum	Quantity mean
Liang	3692.3	2.74	303.1	0.22	1222	0.91	2167.2	1.61
Pu	451.8	2.27	−37.5	−0.19	159.6	0.8	329.7	1.66
Tang	2077.3	2.72	49.67	0.07	636.5	0.83	1391.0	1.82
Wang	4424.8	2.19	−519.8	−0.26	1633.4	0.81	3311.2	1.64
Wen	4277.2	2.6	281.6	0.17	1538.6	0.94	2456.9	1.49
Zhong	1108.7	1.94	−43.8	−0.08	451.5	0.79	701	1.23
Class mean	3412.5	2.45	−54.7	−0.06	1235.0	0.89	2231.9	1.62
Class median	3870.2	2.52	16.2	0.02	1326.7	0.89	2472.3	1.61

Student Pu performed better in speed mean and quantity mean, but the quizzes he wrote counted below the quartiles of all students. This behavior means he completed totally 199 quizzes, much less than others, but the questions in the quiz quantity counted as usually, and the average speed to complete the quizzes was also satisfying. However, the quality to complete the quizzed was bad and should be improved. This student completed only fewer required quizzes fast. In normal examinations, this student performed the worst in the whole class from the first through the last exam except twice, and thus should be paid special attention by the teachers and the parents.

Student Zhong performed better in both speed sum and mean, but the quizzes he wrote counted below the quartiles of all students. This behavior means he completed totally 569 quizzes, less than others, but the speed to complete the quizzes on average and in sum was satisfying. However, both the quality and quantity to complete the quizzed were bad. This student completed only fewer required quizzes very fast, but the completion quality should be improved. This means he did the online quizzes just perfunctorily. In normal examinations, this student performed worse in all exams except six, and thus should be paid special attention by the teachers and the parents.

Student Tang performed better in both speed sum and mean, as well as quantity mean and OLAIMAA, but the quizzes he wrote counted below the quartiles of all students. This behavior means he completed less quizzes (totally 764) than others, but the quality to complete the quizzes on average and in sum was not satisfying. This student completed only fewer required quizzes with more questions very fast, and the fast speed on average and in sum plus the average quantity lead to better OLAIMMA. This means he did the online quizzes just perfunctorily. In normal examinations, this student performed worse in all exams except three, and thus should be paid special attention by the teachers and the parents.

Student Wang performed better in both quantity sum and quantity mean, as well as quality sum and OLAISAA, and the quizzes he wrote counted above the quartiles of all students. This behavior means he completed totally 2019 quizzes, more than others, and the quizzed contained more questions than usual and are more difficult for him. But the speed and quality to complete the quizzes on average were not satisfying. This student very slowly completed more required quizzes with more questions, and the quality for some quizzes was very good. The better quantity on average and in sum plus the quality sum lead to better OLAISAA. In normal examinations, this student performed worse in 33 exams, and thus should take acre about the exams with bad records.

Student Wen performed online worse just in the dimension of quantity mean, but better just in 6 normal exams. Student Liang performed better in all dimensions, but better just in 10 normal exams. These two students completed the required quizzes with both better quality and speed on average and in sum, thus the OLAISAA and OLAIMAA were also satisfying. But they performed worse in most normal exams than the other average students in the class, though better than the other five students with poor academic performance. The reason may be that they did not complete the online quizzes by themselves, but with others' help. This guess was just verified in half by checking the online questions-answering records. While writing the quiz online, the student can call for instant help from the distant teaching assistant. Through chatting the assistant can answer the student's questions about the current quiz. The question-answering log data show that Student Wen had more times' question-answering online than usual, but the Student Liang had usual question-answering. Through the online help, the student Wen could complete the quiz, but this help did not result in better performance in regular classroom exams.

The time series distribution of the OLAI and its three dimensions' values including speed, quality and quantity for all online quiz activities of the six students is shown Fig. 2. Obviously, the student Pu had taken part in much less activities than others, and the student Zhong had fewer quizzes from July 2017 to January 2018. Except the winter vacations in January and February 2016 and 2017, as well as the summer vacations in July and August 2016 and 2017, the other four students continued to write quizzes. The OLAI and its three dimensions' values of the six students varied not much. But exceptionally the student Wen had three very low and negative values in the dimension speed and corresponding OLAI values. A negative speed in one quiz means that this student completes this quiz slower than the average students.

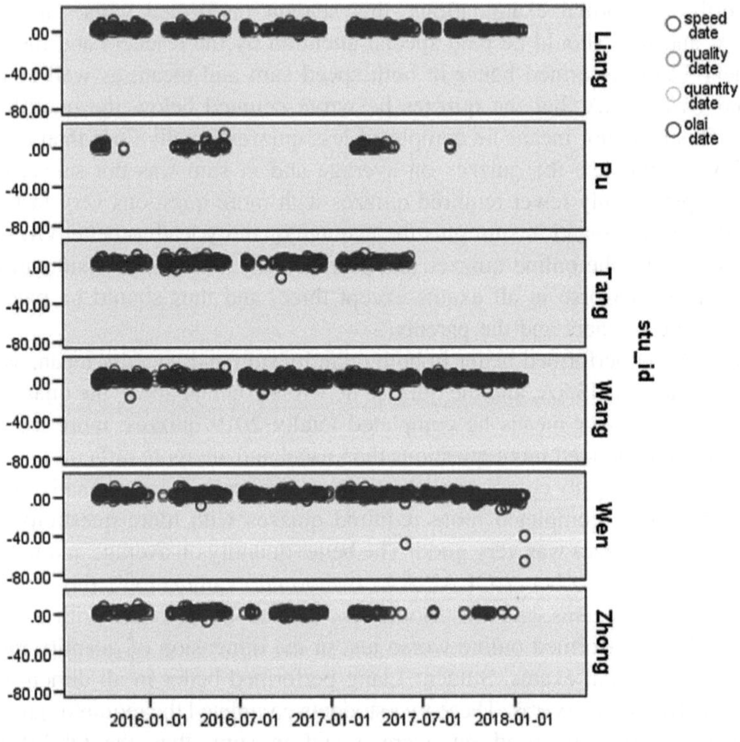

Fig. 2. The time series distribution of the OLAI and its three dimensions' values of the six students with poor academic performance.

If the student Wen's three exceptional values are excluded, the time series distribution is shown in Fig. 3 with greater clarity. The student Liang had the most stable online performance with less activities whose speed and OLAI value were below zero. This phenomenon confirms the quartile analysis that Liang has less activities whose OLAI values were below the quartiles of all students. This student's better online performance corresponds to the better performance in normal exams among all the six students.

The student Wang and Wen constantly participated in most quizzes. Although they completed some quizzes very slowly so that the speed was negative enough to lead to the negative OLAI value, the speed of most quizzes was positive enough so that the speed mean and sum were above the quartile of all students. The Student Wen's better online performance on average did not result in better performance in normal exams. The reason may be that the online quizzes were completed with the help of online teaching assistants. If this student could not get instant help, he or she might spend much longer time on completing the difficult quizzes.

The students Pu, Tang and Zhong could not completed the most quizzes, and so had also worse performance in normal exams.

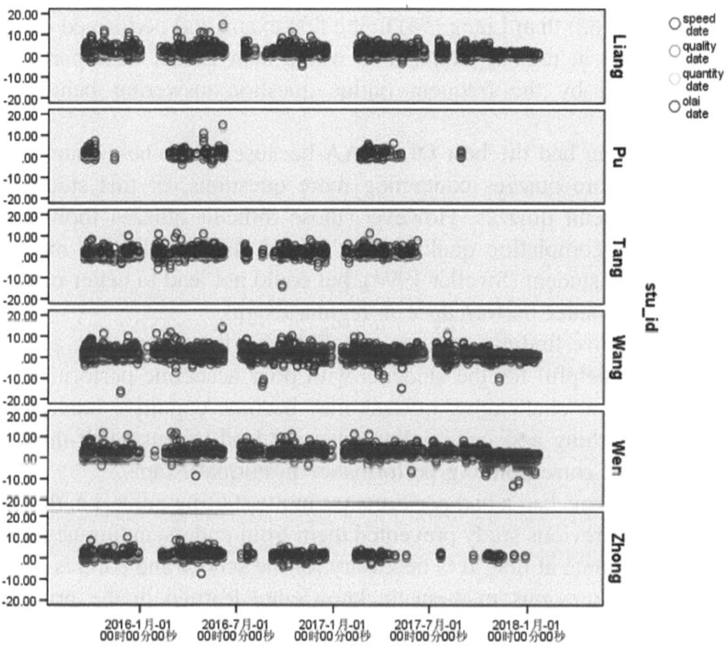

Fig. 3. The time series distribution of the OLAI and its three dimensions' values of the six students with poor academic performance excluding three exceptional values.

5 Findings and Conclusion

After screening all students' exam scores from Grade One to Grade Three of a class in a junior high school, we identified six students as students with poor academic performance during the study time. The quartile analysis of their exam scores show that their chance to get the worse scores, i.e. the scores below the quartiles was randomized. They performed worse in most examinations, but not bad in some examinations. It could not be predicted in which exam they could performed better.

The students' online quiz activity analysis using the OLAI model shows that two students Liang and Wen performed better in the online quizzes, the student Tang and Wang performed at the intermediate-level, while the other two Pu and Zhong performed worse in the online quizzes. Among the six students, Liang was the best one in normal exams, Pu and Zhong performed the worst in normal exams. In the last exam of the research period, the scores of both Liang and Wen were above the quartile of all students, and were the best twos among the six ones. Considering that the performance of both Liang and Wen was not the best twos among the six ones on the first exam, but their online learning activities' quality and quantity on average represented by OLAIMAA and in sum represented by OLAISAA were the best twos, we can infer that the online performance is positively correlated with the normal exam performance, at least from the point view of summative assessment.

The two students Liang and Wen had some difference. The student Wen had a better starting point (62) than Liang (54) in the first exam, and performed better online, but the performance in regular exams was worse than Liang. This paradox can be somewhat explained by the frequent online question-answering behavior of this student.

The student Wang had the best OLAISAA because of the best quantity sum, i.e. Wang completed more quizzes containing more questions, or this student liked to challenge more difficult quizzes. However, those difficult quizzes took this student more time, and the completion quality wasn't good. This hard work might become cognitive load to the student (Sweller 1994), but could not lead to better mastery of the learned content and better performance in regular exams.

Based on the above findings, we can conclude that the online quiz activities with instant feedback is helpful for the students with poor academic performance in their normal exams, but too challenging quizzes may become cognitive load, and the frequent help from teaching assistants online must not lead to better self-thinking about learning content and corresponding performance in normal exams.

All the poor students had a bad performance in the starting point, i.e. the first exam. Their deficiency in previous study prevented them from understanding new knowledge and should be overcome at first. It is necessary for the school and parents to help them with reviewing the previous mathematic knowledge learned in the primary school before they began the learning in the junior high schools.

6 Limitation and Further Studies

This paper just studied six students with poor academic performance in one experiment class in a junior high school. In the future we will investigate more students in more classes to validate the findings from this study. With a bigger sample, statistical approaches like ANOVA, Pearson correlation analysis, and regression analysis could be adopted to determine how significant the difference between the students' online behavior is, and what the correlation between the school exam and online behavior is.

The analysis method used in this paper, i.e. formative assessment based on the students' learning behavior measured by the OLAI, may be also suitable for good and medium students. We will analyze the behavior of good and medium students and explore the behavior difference among them in the further studies.

Acknowledgement. This research is supported by the project "Lexue 100, Smart Education" of Beijing Lexue 100 Online Education Co., Ltd. The authors thank also all the teachers and students who have participated in the program, especially the teachers and students in the experiment class.

References

Jia, J., Yu, Y.: Online learning activity index (OLAI) and its application for adaptive learning. In: Cheung, S.K.S., Kwok, L., Ma, W.W.K., Lee, L.-K., Yang, H. (eds.) ICBL 2017. LNCS, vol. 10309, pp. 213–224. Springer, Cham (2017). https://doi.org/10.1007/978-3-319-59360-9_19

Burns, M.K., Kanive, R., Degrande, M.: Effect of a computer-delivered math fact intervention as a supplemental intervention for math in third and fourth grades. Remed. Spec. Educ. **31**(3), 184–191 (2012)

Geary, D.C., Hoard, M.K.: Learning disabilities in arithmetic and mathematics: theoretical and empirical perspectives. In: Campbell, J.I.D. (ed.) Handbook of Mathematical Cognition, pp. 253–267. Psychology Press, New York, NY (2005)

Gustafsson, J.E., Hansen, K.Y., Rosén, M.: Effects of home background on student achievement in reading, mathematics, and science at the fourth grade. I. Timss and Pirls 2011 Relationships Report (2013)

Lewis, K.E.: Difference not deficit: reconceptualizing mathematical learning disabilities. J. Res. Math. Educ. **45**(3), 351–396 (2014)

Ok, M.W., Bryant, D.P.: Effects of a strategic intervention with iPad practice on the multiplication fact performance of fifth-grade students with learning disabilities. Learn. Disabil. Q. **39**(3), 1–11 (2016)

Roschelle, J., Feng, M., Murphy, R.F., Mason, C.A.: Online mathematics homework increases student achievement. AERA Open **2**(4), 1–12 (2016)

Satsangi, R., Bouck, E.C.: Using virtual manipulative instruction to teach the concepts of area and perimeter to secondary students with learning disabilities. Learn. Disabil. Q. **38**(3), 174–186 (2015)

Shalev, R.S.: Prevalence of developmental dyscalculia. In: Berch, D.B., Mazzocco, M.M.M. (eds.) Why is Math so Hard for Some Children? The Nature and Origins of Mathematical Learning Difficulties and Disabilities, pp. 49–60. Paul H. Brookes, Baltimore (2007)

Zhang, Y., Zhou, X.: Building knowledge structures by testing helps children with mathematical learning difficulty. J. Learn. Disabil. **49**(2), 1–11 (2014)

Sweller, J.: Cognitive load theory, learning difficulty, and instructional design. Learn. Instr. **4**(4), 295–312 (1994)

Chappell, A.L.: Emergence of participatory methodology in learning difficulty research: understanding the context. Br. J. Learn. Disabil. **28**(1), 38–43 (2000)

Ellis, R.: Modelling learning difficulty and second language proficiency: the differential contributions of implicit and explicit knowledge. Appl. Linguist. **27**(3), 431–463 (2006)

Bahar, M., Johnstone, A.H., Hansell, M.H.: Revisiting learning difficulties in biology. J. Biol. Educ. **33**(2), 84–86 (1999)

Sirhan, G.: Learning difficulties in chemistry: an overview. J. Turk. Sci. Educ. **4**(2), 2–20 (2007). https://doi.org/10.5334/jime.ai

Mobile Blended Learning and Evaluation of Its Effectiveness on Students' Learning Achievement

Blanka Klímová[1](✉) and Pavel Pražák[2]

[1] Department of Applied Linguistics, University of Hradec Kralove, Hradec Kralove, Czech Republic
blanka.klimova@uhk.cz

[2] Department of Informatics and Quantitative Methods, Faculty of Informatics and Management, University of Hradec Kralove, Hradec Kralove, Czech Republic
pavel.prazak@uhk.cz

Abstract. This study provides a new view on blended learning. It describes successful mobile blended learning, which is based on the combination of traditional, face-to-face classes and the use of mobile app, which was exploited as support for the retention and practice of new English words and phrases at the Faculty of Informatics and Management of the University of Hradec Kralove, Czech Republic. The purpose of this article is to evaluate the effectiveness of the use of mobile app on students' learning achievement in the university Course of Practical English Language. The methodology is based on an experiment and statistical analysis of students' achievement results. The findings of this study confirm that the use of mobile app is effective in learning new words and phrases, which is in line with other studies on this topic. In fact, the use of app in informal settings extends and enriches student's learning environment and enhances student's learning potential. Future research should continue in order to obtain more subject samples. It will be also important to see if the success rate of students who use the mobile app while studying changes or remains the same over time. In addition, the authors might research students' motivation and attitude towards the use of mobile app.

Keywords: Mobile blended learning · English learning · Vocabulary learning · Mobile app · Effectiveness

1 Introduction

Nowadays, young generation cannot imagine their life without using a mobile phone, respectively a smartphone, on a daily basis. Almost 90% of young people at the age of 18–29 years own a smartphone [1]. Therefore, mobile learning, as a branch of e-learning [2], has inevitably become a new approach to teaching and learning, especially in institutions of higher learning [3–5]. The reason is that mobile learning enables students to learn anywhere and at any time thanks to the easy portability of mobile devices, students can proceed according to their own pace ubiquitously. However,

S. K. S. Cheung et al. (Eds.): ICBL 2019, LNCS 11546, pp. 216–224, 2019.
https://doi.org/10.1007/978-3-030-21562-0_18

in comparison, with e-learning, learning phases are shorter, but occur more often [6]. Therefore, there is a chance that such repetitive learning will have a positive effect on the retention of new knowledge in students' long-term memory. Furthermore, since smartphone displays are smaller than those of laptops or tablets, the content must be adjusted accordingly.

Mobile learning is usually conducted as support to traditional teaching and more recently, the so-called mobile blended learning started to be used. In this study the concept of mobile blended learning (MBL) is perceived as a combination of traditional, face-to-face formal learning with the use of mobile application (app) in informal settings, outside the traditional classroom. Compare with [3, 7]. In such environment, the learner has a greater control over his/her learning as formal and informal learning converges and greater opportunities for collaboration emerge. In this context, the teacher must be much more aware of how to support their students' learning in order to potentialize it in the most effective way.

At present, MBL is also used in English language teaching (ELT) [8–10]. In fact, pure mobile applications are the most widely used applications in the English m-learning context [11]. Although MBL is used to increase all four language skills, i.e. listening, reading, speaking, and writing, research studies reveal that it is especially effective in vocabulary learning [12–17]. This is primarily due to the small display and therefore the content of an app is designed in small segments, which is suitable for learning new words, possibly phrases.

This study describes successful MBL, which is based on the combination of traditional, face-to-face classes and the use of mobile app, which was exploited as support for the retention and practice of new English words and phrases at the Faculty of Informatics and Management (FIM) of the University of Hradec Kralove, Czech Republic. The purpose of this article is to evaluate the effectiveness of the use of mobile app on students' learning achievement in the university Course of Practical English Language.

2 Materials and Methods

2.1 Participants

Altogether 59 students attended the Course of Practical English Language in their third year of study of Management of Travel and Tourism at FIM. 31 students were involved in this course in the winter semester of 2017 and 28 students in the winter semester of 2018. They were all full-time students. Their level of English according to the Common Reference Framework for Languages (CERF) was B2-C1 [18]. Both courses lasted 12 weeks, from the end of September to the middle of December. The face-to-face classes were held regularly once a week for 90 min. Out the total number of students, 41 students (experimental group) used the mobile app outside the classes and 18 students (control group) did not use it.

2.2 Study Design and Hypothesis

The mobile app was designed according to students' needs, which were analyzed at the beginning of the winter semester of 2017. This analysis revealed that students needed to learn and retain English vocabulary and phrases. The mobile app, called Anglictina TODAY [19], comprises two application parts and one server part. The first application part is designed as a web interface for the teacher (Fig. 1) and the second application part is presented with a mobile app for students (Fig. 2). This app is available both for the Android operating system and iOS.

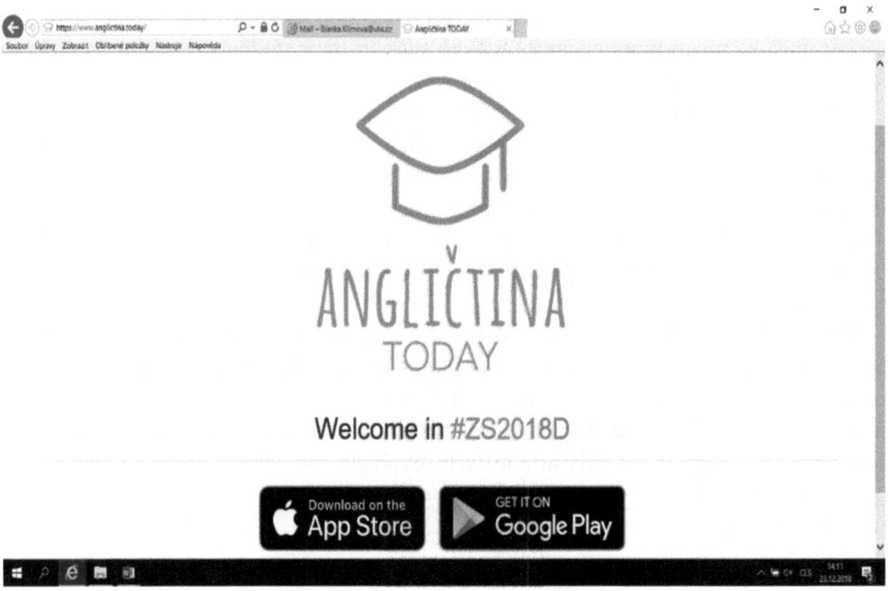

Fig. 1. Teacher's interface

Altogether, there are ten parallel lessons of vocabulary and phrases. The content of each lesson is physically completed with words and phrases by the teacher. The students must translate the word or the phrase from their native language into English. Each lesson is done as a test and comprises on average of 15–18 new words and 10 new phrases. The selected words and phrases are always those discussed in the face-to-face classes so that the students who do not use the mobile app can write them down and practice then from their notes. All the words and phrases are related to their field of study, i.e., tourism, the topics generated by the needs analysis. Furthermore, the teacher tries to encourage the students to revise and practice the new words and phrases via notifications sent to them on their smartphones at least twice a week.

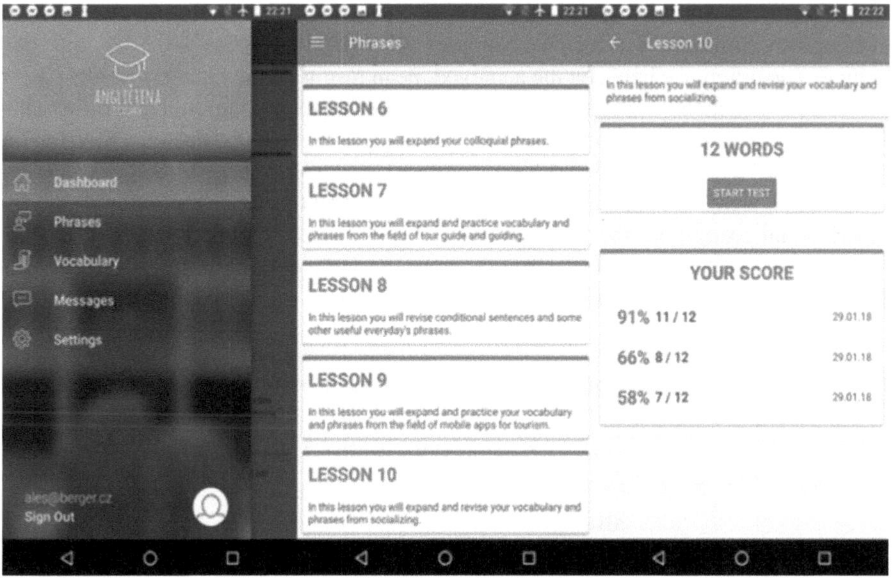

Fig. 2. Mobile app screen

The methods also included methods of analysis and evaluation of the results of students' achievement tests were used, including a statistical analysis. The pass mark for doing the final achievement test was 50%, i.e., 30 points. All the results were recorded and statistically analyzed. The authors set the following hypothesis:

H: Students who use mobile apps in their studies have significantly higher learning outcomes than students who do not use this app.

3 Results

In the statistical analysis of the impact of the use of the mobile application on students' learning achievements, a sample of 31 students from the year of 2017/18 and 28 students from the year of 2018/19 was used. The sample size is therefore n = 59. The results of their final test were recorded in the range of 0 to 60 points. The following calculations were made using the IBM SPSS Statistics 25 software. The descriptive statistics of both volumes are shown in Table 1 below.

Table 1. Descriptive statistics for variable results of the final test in points with 95% confidence interval for mean (authors' own processing)

Year	Mean	Lower bound	Upper bound	Median	Std. deviation	Min	Max
2017/18	39.23	35.55	42.91	40.50	10.03	21	56
2018/19	35.52	31.91	39.13	37.00	9.32	17	54

In order to verify that both grades of students can be run in one sample, Kolmogorov-Smirnov test for two samples ($Z = 0.910$, p-value = 0.379) was performed. The difference between the achieved mean results of the final test results can be considered statistically insignificant, as confirmed also by the Mann-Whitney test ($U = 340.5$, p-value = 0.156). At the significance level of 0.05, the selection for the years of study can be considered homogeneous.

Students were randomly assigned to two independent groups. The study group (an experimental group), the size of which was $n_1 = 41$, used a mobile application in their study. The second group, whose size was $n_2 = 18$, was a control group and did not use the mobile app. Table 2 below provides an overview of this division.

Table 2. Division of students into an experimental group (students who use mobile application) and a control group (students who do not use the application)

Year	Control	Experimental	Total
2017/18	12	19	31
2018/19	6	22	28
Total	18	41	59

The box diagram of the score results from the test is for the two groups of students shown in Fig. 3 below.

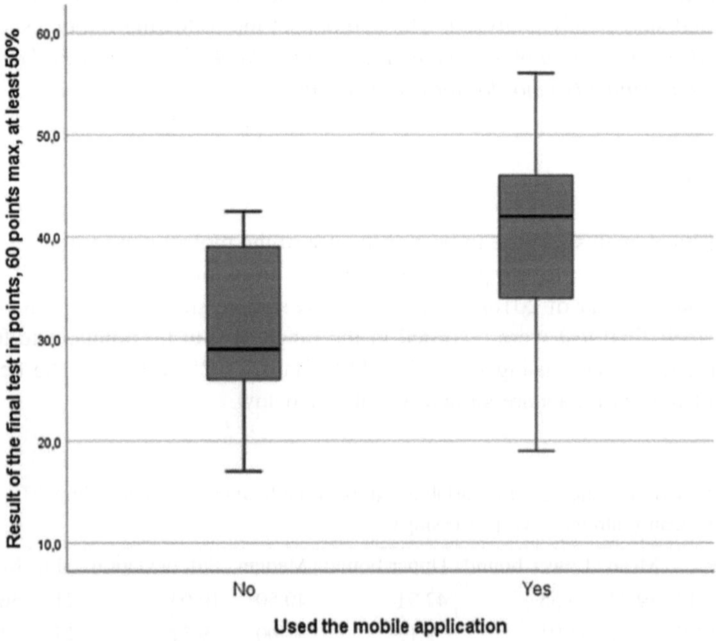

Fig. 3. A box diagram of students' results

From Fig. 3, it could be concluded that the students of the research group achieved higher results as it has been expected. However, this observation is further confirmed by the calculation. The descriptive statistics for both groups of students is provided in Table 3 below.

Table 3. Descriptive statistics of the results of the final test in points divided into experimental group of students and control group of students with 95% confidence interval for mean (authors' own processing)

Group	Mean	Lower bound	Upper bound	Median	Std. deviation	Min	Max
Control	30.47	26.40	34.55	29.00	8.20	17.0	42.5
Experimental	40.54	37.73	43.34	42.00	8.88	19.0	56.0

As it is shown by the Kolmogorov-Smirnov test, at the significance level of 0.05, we cannot reject the hypothesis that the scores achieved by the students in the experimental group ($Z = 0.110$, $df = 41$, p-value = 0.200) and the control group ($Z = 0.129$, $df = 18$, p-value = 0.200) come from normal distribution.

For the difference of average gain of final test points for both groups of students, a two sample t-test with the same variance was performed ($F = 0.066$, p-value = 0.799). For this test, $t = -4.100$, d.f. = 57 and p-value < 0.01 were found. At the significance level of 0.01, there was a statistically significant difference between the average results achieved by students who use the mobile app and those who do not use it when studying English. In other words, the observed difference in the gain of points in the test in the experimental and control group is not random. In this way, the set hypothesis that students who use mobile apps in their studies have significantly higher learning outcomes than students who do not use it can be accepted.

4 Discussion

The findings of this study confirm that the mobile app is an effective tool in learning new words and phrases. The data obtained in both years of 2017/18 and 2018/19, during which the mobile app was used, show (compare Table 1 and the results of the nonparametric tests) that its positive effect on study success is comparable in both years. However, the effect of time will also be monitored in the following years to confirm or modify this observation.

Human learning is very individual, and it is not possible to adapt to all the requirements, to the objectives and the tempo of all the students within the framework of teaching. Implementing the mobile app into the classroom allows students to adapt their studies to their personal needs and abilities. Thanks to the used platform, the app is also very accessible. This all results in the improvement of the student's learning outcomes.

The results of this study are thus in line with other research studies on this topic [12–17, 20, 21]. For instance, Wu [12, 13] maintains that students using a smartphone app for learning English words can retain more words, around 89 words more than the students who do not use it. Mahdi [15] in his meta-analysis illustrates a medium effect of using mobile devices on both receptive and productive vocabulary learning (g = .67). In addition, he indicates that adult students benefit from using mobile devices in vocabulary learning more than young learners. Rezaei et al. [16] point out that it is also important to present the contents through graphics to show the meaning of words, which helps students remember these words. Furthermore, the results of their study also revealed that when students had used the mobile apps, their motivation for vocabulary learning had increased.

The authors found only one study [22] whose results showed no significant difference between the experimental and control group in their post-tests on vocabulary knowledge. However, there was a positive effect on vocabulary learning in the delayed post-test in the experimental group.

Although the words and phrases are learned via the mobile app in isolation, they are practiced in class in context for their better retention (cf. [23, 24]). Furthermore, this app is used as support to formal in-class learning and in fact, it extends and enriches students' learning environment outside the traditional classrooms [25].

In addition, there are other benefits of MBL. One of the benefits of the designed mobile app Angličtina TODAY is its personalized approach. Firstly, students can learn at their own pace ubiquitously. Secondly, they learn the words and phrases they need. And thirdly, they get instant feedback on their progress.

Another benefit is also the fact that teacher has a chance to discover what his/her students know before they enter their face-to-face lessons because s/he can see from the mobile app statistics which words or phrases are the most problematic. Figure 4 below illustrates students' activity on practicing new words and their correct and incorrect answers, as well as percentage of the correct answers.

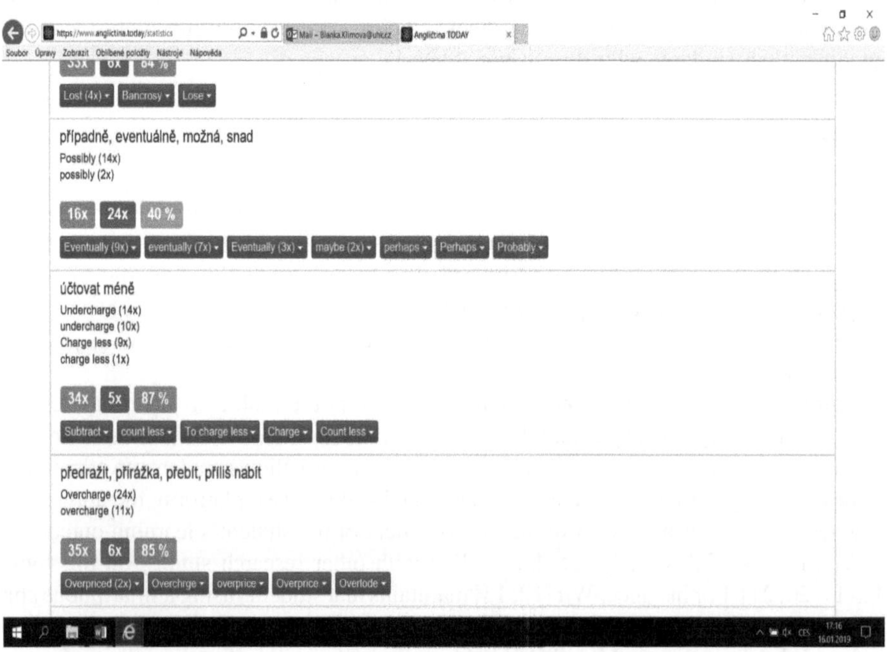

Fig. 4. Statistical analysis of student's knowledge of the practiced words

In class, s/he can revise these words/phrases with students again in order to retain them. In addition, continuous repetition in small chunks can help students remember the vocabulary more easily and effectively. In addition, students can remember the words better because they must write the word, they can hear its pronunciation, they can repeat it, and see its correct form. All these facts might then increase students' motivation to use the app and practice the new words and phrases [26].

Overall, it is important to plan and control the whole pedagogical process, react to students' immediate needs and their language level and implement appropriate teaching and learning methods. It is the teacher's encouragement enhanced through different methods (such as feedback or notifications) that is essential for students' motivation to use the mobile app and study the new words and phrases outside the formal learning settings.

5 Conclusion

The results of this study indicate that the mobile apps are appropriate learning tools, which thanks to their unique features (e.g. interactivity, ubiquity, or portability) and with teacher's encouragement motivate students to learn and they have a positive effect on their learning outcomes. For further research on mobile devices and mobile communication see Pikhart [27, 28].

Future research should continue in order to obtain more subject samples and thus, more conclusive results. It will be also important to see if the success rate of students who use the mobile app while studying changes or remains the same over time. In addition, the authors might research students' motivation and attitude towards the use of mobile app.

Acknowledgments. This study is supported by the SPEV project 2104/2019, run at the Faculty of Informatics and Management, University of Hradec Kralove, Czech Republic. The authors thank Josef Toman and Ales Berger for their help with the data collection.

References

1. Smith, A.: Record shares of Americans now own smartphones, have home broadband (2017). http://www.pewresearch.org/fact-tank/2017/01/12/evolution-of-technology/
2. Pachler, N., Bachmair, B., Cook, J.: Mobile Learning: Structure, Agency, Practices, 1st edn. Springer, New York (2010). https://doi.org/10.1007/978-1-4419-0585-7
3. Avci, H., Adiguzel, T.: A case study on mobile-blended collaborative learning in an English as a foreign language (EFL) context. Int. Rev. Res. Open Distrib. Learn. **18**(7), 1–14, https://files.eric.ed.gov/fulltext/EJ1163180.pdf (2017)
4. Morris, N.P., Lambe, J., Cicconet, J., Swinnerton, B.: Mobile technology: students perceived benefits of apps for learning neuroanatomy. J. Comput. Assist. Learn. **32**, 430–442 (2016)
5. Klimova, B., Pulova, P.: Mobile learning in higher education. Adv. Sci. Lett. **22**(5/6), 1111–1114 (2016)
6. Mauer, M.: Mobile blended learning with eSqirrel (2015). https://eproceedings.epublishing.ekt.gr/index.php/openedu/article/viewFile/62/52

7. Lai, K.W., Khaddage, F., Knezek, G.: Blending student technology experiences in formal and informal learning. J. Comput. Assist. Learn. **29**(5), 414–425 (2013)
8. Kukulska-Hulme, A., Shield, L.: An overview of mobile assisted language learning: from content delivery to supported collaboration and interaction. ReCALL. **20**(3), 271–289 (2008)
9. Teodorescu, A.: Mobile learning and its impact on business English learning. Procedia – Soc. Behav. Sci. **180**, 1535–1540 (2015)
10. Balula, A., Marques, F., Martins, C.: Bet on top hat – challenges to improve language proficiency. In: Proceedings of EDULEARN15 Conference 6–8 July 2015, pp. 2627–2633. Spain: Barcelona (2015)
11. Elaish, M.M., Shuib, L., Ghani, N.A., Yadegaridehkordi, E., Alaa, M.: Mobile learning for English language acquisition: taxonomy, challenges, and recommendations. IEEE Access **5**, 19033–19047 (2017)
12. Wu, Q.: Learning ESL vocabulary with smartphones. Procedia – Soc. Behav. Sci. **143**, 302–307 (2014)
13. Wu, Q.: Designing a smartphone app to teach English (L2) vocabulary. Comput. Educ. https://doi.org/10.1016/j.compedu.2015.02.013
14. Basal, A., Yilmaz, S., Tanriverdi, A., Sari, L.: Effectiveness of mobile applications in vocabulary teaching. Contemp. Educ. Technol. **7**(1), 47–59 (2016)
15. Mahdi, H.S.: Effectiveness of mobile devices on vocabulary learning: a meta-analysis. J. Educ. Comput. Res. **56**(1), 134–154 (2017)
16. Rezaei, A., Mai, N., Pesaranghader, A.: The effect of mobile applications on English vocabulary acquisition. https://www.researchgate.net/publication/261246911 (2014)
17. Song, M., Chen, L.: A review on English vocabulary acquisition and teaching research in recent 30 years in China. Sci. J. Educ. **5**(4), 174–180 (2017)
18. Common European reference framework for languages (2019). https://en.wikipedia.org/wiki/Common_European_Framework_of_Reference_for_Languages
19. Anglictina Today (2017). https://www.anglictina.today/
20. Klimova, B.: Mobile phones and/or smartphones and their apps for teaching English as a foreign language. Educ. Inf. Technol. **23**(3), 1091–1099 (2017)
21. Klimova, B., Prazak, P.: Evaluation of the effectiveness of the use of a mobile application on students' study achievements – a pilot study. In: Al-Sharhan, S.A., et al. (eds.) I3E 2018. LNCS, vol. 11195, pp. 37–44. Springer, Cham (2018). https://doi.org/10.1007/978-3-030-02131-3_5
22. Alemi, M., Sarab, M.R.A., Lari, L.: Successful Learning of academic world list via MALL: mobile assisted language learning. Int. Educ. Stud. **5**(6), 99–109 (2012)
23. Celik, O., Yavuz, F.: The effect of using mobile applications on literal and contextual vocabulary instruction. IJLT **10**(2), 126–136 (2017)
24. Heil, C.R., Wu, J.S., Lee, J.J., Schmidt, T.: A review of mobile language learning applications: trends, challenges, and opportunities. EuroCALL Rev. **24**(2), 32–50 (2016)
25. Glahn, C., Gruber, M.R., Tartakovski, O.: Beyond delivery modes and apps: a case study on mobile blended learning in higher education. In: Conole, G., Klobučar, T., Rensing, C., Konert, J., Lavoué, É. (eds.) EC-TEL 2015. LNCS, vol. 9307, pp. 127–140. Springer, Cham (2015). https://doi.org/10.1007/978-3-319-24258-3_10
26. Goz, F., Ozcan, M.: An entertaining mobile vocabulary learning application. EPESS **7**, 63–66 (2017)
27. Pikhart, M.: Intercultural linguistics as a new academic approach to communication. In: SHS Web of Conferences, vol. 26, p. 01005 (2016)
28. Pikhart, M.: Theoretical foundations of intercultural business communication and their practical consequences. In: SHS Web of Conferences, vol. 26, p. 01006 (2016)

Data Analysis Model of Wearable Devices in Physical Education

Qian Dong[1,2(✉)], Ximei Qu[1,2], and Rong Miao[1,2]

[1] Department of Educational Technology, Graduate School of Education, Peking University, Beijing, China
st16625m@gse.pku.edu.cn
[2] Zhejiang Radio and Television University, Zhejiang, China

Abstract. At present, the physical health of primary and secondary school students is declining while physical education plays an important role in improving students' physical quality. However, how to judge scientifically and accurately students' exercise load and ensure students' exercise safety have become one of the constraints in physical education. The application of wearable devices can help teachers to understand students' exercise data in time, but the analysis procedure is complicated. Based on this, this paper puts forward a data analysis model of wearable devices in physical education. The four steps are as follows: (1) understand the whole (2) compare and observe (3) analysis and hypothesis (4) calibrate and test. And then taking Binhe Primary School in Zhejiang as an example, we apply this model to analysis the data.

Keywords: Wearable devices · Physical education · Data analysis model

1 Background

In recent years, it shows a trend of continuous decline on the level of Chinese students' physical health [1]. Physical education, a compulsory course for students, plays an important role in training students' participating in physical exercise, improving students' physical quality and promoting their all-round development. In December 2017, Ministry of Education has issued a notice on the issuance of management standards for schools in compulsory education, which clearly stated that each school need to ensure their students to exercise for one hour a day and have enough physical education classes [2].

However, how to give a good PE course in a scientific way is difficult to solve in the current traditional education. Safety is also one of the main factors restricting the development and reform of policy in PE class [3]. On one hand, many teachers worry that the exercise load exceeds the students' physiological limitation. Some students are easy to produce sports fatigue and body's metabolism disorder, and some even cause severe sports injury or sudden death. On the other hand, if the exercise load is too low, it is hard to achieve the teaching effect in class. Therefore, it is of great importance to know every student's physiological limitation. However, with limited teaching place and method, it is hard to provide accurate guidance for students in traditional education.

S. K. S. Cheung et al. (Eds.): ICBL 2019, LNCS 11546, pp. 225–238, 2019.
https://doi.org/10.1007/978-3-030-21562-0_19

Currently many teachers mainly rely on empirical observations, such as students' face color, expression, sweating or panting condition to judge their exercise load. But because of the large number of students and their individual differences, it is difficult for teachers to know about every student and give scientific, comprehensive and real-time judgement. For assessment, teachers often use a single resultant evaluation method as the main tool for evaluating students, which leads to lack of concern about students' individual learning process and scientific educational evaluation.

In recent years, wearable devices have played an active role in improving students' learning interest, helping teachers understand students' learning process, optimizing teaching design. Besides, the impact of information technology on school education has been expanding. With the development of mobile Internet and the continuous evolution of sensors, information encryption and other technologies, the performance of wearable devices has been continuously improved and the application scenarios have been more extensive, such as medical treatment, military, entertainment, design and other fields [4, 5]. People are curious about a deep integration of wearable technology in education.

Wearable devices can collect and record students' physiological representation and other data in time, which can help meet people's potential demand for educational data and accelerate the data-based research and application process in education. By collecting learners' data and analyzing learners' individual learning process, students' learning process and individual differences can be understood more accurately and scientifically. On this basis, teachers can provide students with targeted guidance, so as to optimize the teaching process and improve teaching quality.

2 Literature Review

2.1 The Application of Wearable Devices in Education

Wearable devices are tools that combine multimedia, radio, sensor and other technologies. It can be easily carried by users in the form of accessories. According to different ways of wearing, wearable devices can be divided into four types, that is head-worn, wristband, portable and wearable (worn on body) [6].

With the increase of wearable products and the expansion of application in new areas, educators begin to think about the application of wearable devices in education [7]. Christine believes that wearable technology can help cultivate students' ability of teamwork, communication, problem solving and autonomous learning. She has summarized seven applications of wearable devices in education, including Autographers camera, Key gloves, GoPro camera, Google Glass etc [8]. The increase of wearable devices in education has provided infinite possibilities for their application. Some researchers have started the experiment to develop and apply wearable devices in different courses.

From the perspective of functions of wearable devices, current applications can be roughly divided into two categories. Firstly, wearable devices are used for augmented interaction. For instance, teachers' teaching plans can be photographed and archived by Autographers cameras. Secondly, wearable devices can help collect, record students' physiological indicators and know the learning process. Zhao [9] has developed a wearable device to detect galvanic skin response of online learning.

In terms of subjects, wearable devices are applied in courses such as language and PE. For example, Elena et al. [10] have introduced IoT (Internet of Things) and wearable technologies into task-based language learning for young children to help students focus on the implementation of interaction and track to record students' interaction behaviors. Lindberg et al. [11] have developed a sports game called Running Othello 2 (RO2) to solve the problem of the increasing number of obese and overweight on children, using wearable devices to record movements and heart rates. Lee et al. [12] have used wearable devices to obtain students' activity data in PE, analyzed sports data and heart rate, quantified students' rest time, and compared the steps of tall and short students.

In addition to the experimental research, researchers also studied the application prospect of wearable devices in PE. Zhao and Xu [13] have analyzed the application of wearable devices in PE based on SWOT model. They believe the advantage of wearable devices in PE of primary and secondary schools lies in helping students build long-term sports database, which is beneficial to the scientific guidance of teachers. The disadvantage is that the price is high and some functions cannot fully meet the daily education.

Arlen et al. [7] believe that application of wearable devices in education has both problems and challenges. The application is good for students' participating in the curriculum, carrying out all-round learning design, understanding physiological needs, and helping schools establish student archives. But wearable devices may also bring privacy and security issues, such as exposing too much personal information. Moreover, the introduction of wearable devices may lead to the reform of schools' teaching environment and teachers' teaching strategies.

At present, wearable devices can record students' heart rate, breath and steps in real time in PE, which not only helps students understand their personal exercise state, but also helps teachers make more scientific judgment. In other subjects, wearable devices are often used to record data and enhance interaction. But the analysis of the collected data is still insufficient, and mature application model has not been formed.

2.2 Exercise Load and Its Measurement

Exercise load is a quantitative description of the internal and external physical activity process over a given period [14]. Exercise load in PE is the degree to how much students' physical exercise stimulates the body [15]. The exercise load in this study refers to the quantitative description of students' status in the physical training process of PE in primary and secondary schools.

Exercise load is an important index of students' physical health development and class evaluation. If exercise load is high, it is easy to exceed the limitation of physiological function, make students feel wearisome, and even cause muscle strain and faint, which is not beneficial to the development of students' physical quality and the achievement of teaching objectives. If exercise load is too low, it is difficult to meet the instructional goal and make students feel the sense of achievement, pleasure and the inherent charm of sports. So reasonable exercise load is very important in PE.

As an important physiological index to understand students' learning status, the measurement of exercise load faces three problems: what to measure, how to measure and how to express the measurement results [16]. Now there are two kinds of data on exercise load: one is physical data, such as speed, distance while the other is physiological data, such as heart rate and oxygen consumption during exercise [17]. In practice, some use sports achievement to calculate the intensity of exercise load, and some take heart rate as the main evaluation index. When using sports achievement, it is generally necessary to distinguish different items and measure their training results and best results. The measurement accuracy is close to professional training. While the heart rate as the evaluation index can reflect exercise load more accurately, and it is also convenient to collect and measure. Now schools often use heart rate as an evaluation index to evaluate the physical exercise load.

According to the "Health Standard of Physical Load in Athletic Training for Middle and Primary School Students" (WS/T 101-1998), the measurement of exercise load is to measure the heart rate of each student at 10 s immediately after each activity in the basic part of physical education class or extracurricular activities. And 10-second heart rate will be converted to one-minute heart rate. In one class, according to the physical exercise class's structure, the heart rate needs to be measured three times, that is preparing part, basic part, and ending part. The appropriate average heart rate is between 120–200 times/min for exercise load.

Technical Specifications of Monitoring and Evaluating Exercise Load in Physical Education of Dongcheng District of Beijing Primary and Secondary School (trial) raised indexes of athletic intensity in physical education class, including average heart rate, heart rate in basic part, maximum heart rate, heart rate index, supplemented by the heart rate curve, students' and teachers' evaluation scales.

It should be noted that different types of PE classes have different requirements for exercise load. In addition, in order to ensure students' attention after class, scholars proposed that the average heart rate should be controlled at 120–130 times/min for the PE courses before those courses hard to concentrate, such as physics and math. However, for PE before those easy to concentrate, such as music and art, the average heart rate should be controlled at 130–140 times/min [18, 19].

3 Data Analysis Model

To help teachers know students' exercise load, it carries out verification experiments based on the WST model applied to PE [20], and constructs a data analysis model.

The data analysis in WST model needs to solve the following three problems: (1) What kinds of data shall we collect? (2) What kind of information can be obtained from the data (3) What are the steps of data analysis?

3.1 Types of Data Collected

When using this model to carry out experiment, with the help of wearable devices, scale and other tools, a total of four kinds of data are collected: wearable device's collection of heart rate data (maximum, minimum, average and heart rate curve), data of students' subjective feelings, teachers' observation data, teaching contents recording table.

3.2 Data Information

1. **Wearable device data (bracelet data)**
   Each student wears a wearable device (bracelet) before class. In class, heart rate data of each student is collected by the bracelet, including maximum heart rate, minimum heart rate, average heart rate data reflecting the concentration degree of students' heart rate and the heart rate curve describing the changes of students in the whole course.
2. **Students' subjective feelings**
   According to students' comprehension ability, the study adjusts the RPE scale proposed by Brog Gunner and designs the scale of students' subjective feelings. The scale has levels from 1 to 5 defined that corresponds to no feeling, not too tired, moderate, a little tired and very tired. Students fill out the subjective feeling scale fills out to help students understand their subjective feeling changes in different stages of class (PE class can be divided into preparation part, basic part and ending part).
3. **Teachers' observation**
   The teacher chooses a proper number of students in class and completes teachers' observation scale. In this scale, the number from 1 to 5 represents the exercise load from very low, a little low, moderate, a little high to very high. Teachers use traditional ways to judge students' exercise load in different stages of PE class, like observing students' facial expression and sweating degree.
   In PE class, the teaching assistant helps them record the course teaching content according to the time sequence accordingly.
   In addition to getting information from a single type of data, different types of data can also be compared and calibrated.

3.3 Data Analysis Model

From the above, it can be seen that a variety of information can be obtained through the comparison of different types of data collected according to the WST model, and a variety of information can be obtained. Accurately, there are 15 types by calculating mathematical formula $C_4^1 + C_4^2 + C_4^3 + C_4^4 = 15$. This includes not only individual data, but also overall data. It includes not only the information obtained by a single type of information, but also the information obtained by comparative analysis of different types of data. In order to help teachers better apply wearable devices for data analysis, understand students' sports load, optimize teaching design, provide targeted guidance for students and improve teaching quality, we construct a data analysis model of wearable devices in physical education (Fig. 1).

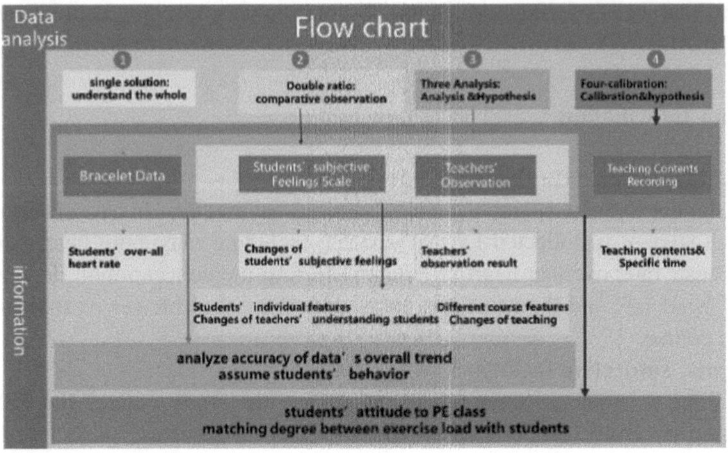

Fig. 1. Data analysis model of wearable devices in physical education

The data analysis model of wearable devices in PE is divided into two dimensions, that is flow and information. From the perspective of flow, it includes: (1) understand the whole (2) compare and observe (3) analysis and hypothesis (4) calibrate and test. For information, the obtained information is from the surface layer to deep layer, and the analysis object is from the whole to the individual. Detailed explanations are as follows.

(1) **understand the whole**
By analyzing the bracelet data of all the students and the chosen students, we can know the whole and individual heart rate.

(2) **compare and observe**
On the basis of the first step, horizontal and vertical comparisons are made through students' subjective scales and teachers' observation table. The horizontal analysis is about one student's analysis in different classes, which helps teachers know students' individualized characteristics and the changes of teachers' understanding of students. The vertical analysis is an analysis of the same course for different students, from which we can get the teaching characteristics of physical education and the change of teaching attitude of teachers.

(3) **analysis and hypothesis**
Then, the bracelet data is verified with the subjective observation scale of students and the observation records of teachers, so as to further judge the accuracy of the overall trend of the data of the key observation objects and propose hypotheses.

(4) **calibrate and test**
Finally, through the analysis and comparison of the bracelet data of the key students and the teaching contents recording table, the behavior characteristics of students in the process of class can be understood, and then, the attitude of students towards PE and the exercise load can be judged to be in line with their physical endurance limitation.

The above data analysis model diagram can help teachers understand the data analysis process of wearable devices used in physical education and obtain relevant information.

4 Experimental Procedure

4.1 Participants

In this research, 21 pupils from grade 3 of Binhe Primary School in Hangzhou, Zhejiang Province, were selected as subjects. All the students wear wearable bracelet, in which five students are randomly selected as the key observation objects.

The selection of key observers follows two principles: first, the selected students need to be healthy. According to the definition of "Health Standard WS/T 101-1998 for Physical Exercise Load in Primary and Secondary Schools", healthy students refer to those who can take PE classes according to the requirements of physical education syllabus and often do physical exercise. Secondly, the proportion of male and female is appropriate. Among the 21 students in this class, there are 13 boys and 8 girls. The key observers were 3 boys and 2 girls.

4.2 Measure Tools

According to the application mode of wearable devices in PE, we design measure tools. In addition, by comparing the teacher's experience observation table, the student's subjective feeling scale and the student's movement data collected by wearable devices, a tripartite comparison and mutual evidence is formed as below (Fig. 2).

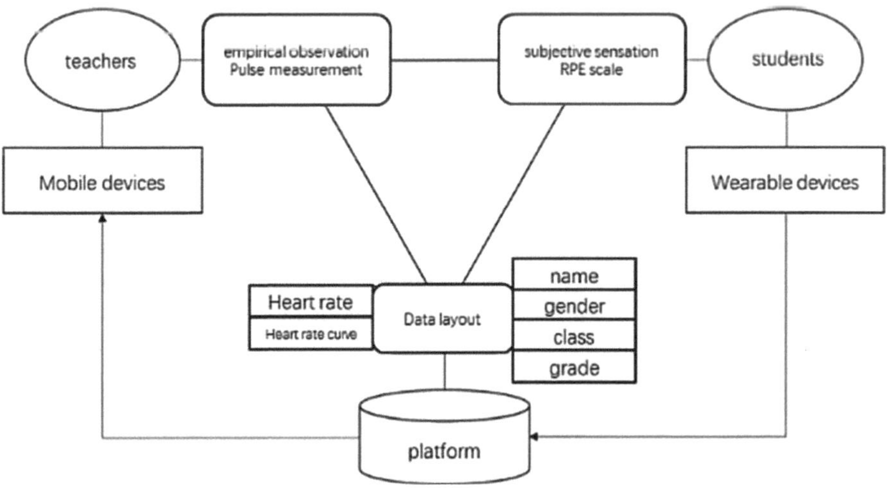

Fig. 2. Research tools design

4.2.1 Heart Rate Measurement

The wearable device measures the heart rate data of students through sensors. According to technical specifications for monitoring and evaluation of exercise load in primary and secondary schools in Dongcheng District, Beijing [21], the specific measurement data and standards are as follows.

Average heart rate: the average heart rate refers to average heart rate in the whole PE class, and it is appropriate in 130–170 times/min in exercise period. Average heart rate $= \frac{\frac{x_1 + x_n}{2} + x_2 + x_3 + \cdots + x_{n-1}}{n-1}$. x_n means the nth real time heart rate for 3 min.

Maximum heart rate: the maximum heart rate refers to the maximum heart rate of students in the whole PE class, generally not more than 200 times/min.

Heart rate curve: the system platform can generate a student's heart rate curve of the class and 10 min after class. The diagram takes time as a horizontal coordinate, and the heart rate is a longitudinal coordinate. According to the change of the curve, it is easy to evaluate whether the exercise load is suitable. It is qualified that the peak of the heart rate curve appears in the middle part of the basic part in class [22].

4.2.2 Procedure

According to the school PE class arrangement, the research carried out three experiments, in total, one per week like the following.

(1) Before class, students wear bracelets 5–10 min to measure the quiet heart rate.
(2) On the basic teaching stage, all students complete a 45 min course in accordance with the requirements of the PE teacher. Teachers' observation scale, course teaching record table are used as the reference and contrast basis for students' exercise load.
(3) After class, students continue to wear wearable devices (bracelet) for about 10 min and fill in the RPE scale.

5 Data Analysis

Next, the data analysis model proposed in this paper is applied to analysis.

(1) **understand the whole**

The heart rate of the whole class. In order to understand the whole of PE classes, first of all, we analysis data of the whole class, which includes the lowest heart rate, average heart rate and maximum heart rate below (Table 1).

Table 1. Heart rate of three courses in PE Class

Whole class	First: hop			Second: shuttle run			third: hop		
	Min heart rate	Avg heart rate	Max heart rate	Min heart rate	Avg heart rate	Max heart rate	Min heart rate	Avg heart rate	Max heart rate
min	41	75	112	42	70	102	43	79	116
avg	52	88	147	56	87	135	56	90	143
max	69	102	171	102	103	171	78	121	171

Longitudinal comparison results of the min minimum heart rate, the avg average heart rate and the max maximum heart rate in three PE courses of class are shown. It can be found that the min minimum heart rate, avg average heart rate and max maximum heart rate of the whole class in three PE classes are close to each other. The min minimum heart rate is 41–43 times/min, the avg average heart rate is 87–90 times/min, and the maximum heart rate is 171 times/min.

The heart rate of key observers. On the basis of understanding the data of the whole class, we analysis the heart rate of key observers. The following Table 2 focuses on the heart rate data of five students, including the min heart rate, average heart rate etc.

Table 2. The key observers' heart rate data from bracelet

key observers		First: hop			Second: shuttle run			third: hop		
No	gender	Min heart rate	Avg heart rate	Max heart rate	Min heart rate	Avg heart rate	Max heart rate	Min heart rate	Avg heart rate	Max heart rate
1	M	56	94	171	62	102	138	64	99	163
2	F	45	90	138	42	70	116	52	84	116
3	F	59	89	159	63	88	133	57	95	150
4	M	60	89	156	54	87	171	65	85	116
5	M	59	92	156	56	90	150	65	94	125
MIN		45	89	138	42	70	116	52	84	116
AVG		56	91	156	55	87	142	61	91	134
MAX		60	94	171	63	102	171	65	99	163

Longitudinal comparison results of the min minimum heart rate, the avg average heart rate and the max maximum heart rate in three PE courses of the five observers are shown in the figure.

It can be seen that the min minimum heart rate, avg average heart rate and max maximum heart rate of the whole class in three PE classes are close to each other. The min minimum heart rate is 42–52 times/min, the avg average heart rate is 87–91 times/min, and the maximum heart rate is 163–171 times/min.

(2) **compare and observe**

After analysis the key observation data from the bracelet, in order to compare the data of the bracelet, students' subjective feelings and teachers' observation, the followings are the students' subjective scales and teachers' observation records of three PE class (Tables 3, 4 and 5).

Table 3. Students subjective scale and teachers' observation record in Course1

Course 1	Students subjective scale				Teachers' observation record		
Name	Preparation part	Basic part	End part	10 min after the end	Preparation part	Basic part	End part
SM1	1	4	1	1	2	3	2
SF2	1	4	2	1	2	4	2
SF3	1	3	1	1	3	4	2
SM4	4	5	2	1	3	4	2
SM5	1	2	1	1	3	3	2

Table 4. Students subjective scale and teachers' observation record in Course2

Course 2	Students subjective scale				Teachers' observation record		
Name	Preparation part	Basic part	End part	10 min after the end	Preparation part	Basic part	End part
SM1	2	3	1	1	3	4	2
SF2	4	3	2	1	3	4	2
SF3	4	4	2	1	3	4	2
SM4	4	5	4	2	4	5	2
SM5	2	1	1	1	3	4	2

Table 5. Students subjective scale and teachers' observation record in Course3

Course 3	Students subjective scale				Teachers' observation record		
Name	Preparation part	Basic part	End part	10 min after the end	Preparation part	Basic part	End part
SM1	2	3	1	1	3	4	2
SF2	4	3	2	1	3	4	2
SF3	4	4	2	1	3	4	2
SM4	4	5	4	2	4	5	2
SM5	2	1	1	1	3	4	2

The above figure can be compared and analyzed in two dimensions. Horizontally, the same student shows certain characteristics of individual exercise load intensity in different PE class. For example, SM1 usually think the exercise load is low from the preparation part. With class deepening, the heart rate of the basic part gradually increases. SM5 may have good physical fitness or general interest in PE because his three subjective feelings of exercise load are no feeling, not too tired. While in the basic part, SM4 usually feel exercise load is high. There are also some similarities among different students. For example, SF3 and SM4 think the exercise load trend of PE class from the preparation to the basic and then the end part is low-high-low.
Through the above analysis, PE teachers can better understand students' subjective feelings in the process, infer their personalized characteristics, and provide certain teaching improvements. For example, SM4 have low endurance of exercise load. In the high exercise load part, teachers need to focus on observing its performance in to avoid sports safety problems. It also needs to observe SM5's learning attitude and whether he is serious enough to complete the training according to the requirements.
Longitudinally, the characteristics of three PE courses can be found. In the first course, students' subjective perception increases first and then decreases from the preparation part to the basic part and then to the end part. Teachers' judgments vary slightly, but the trend is the same. While students in the second course have a relatively big difference, but their heart rate in preparing part is usually higher than that in the first course. Maybe because the teaching place is an outdoor playground which is far from the teaching building, students have come to the teaching place by jogging and walking before the preparation part. In the third

course, the students' subjective feelings show great difference at the end of the last part. It can be inferred that, due to the intensity of the basic part, the requirement of the end part of the exercise load is still rising, some students can continue to complete, while some students are difficult to complete, so they give up.
So teachers can predict students' physical condition according to the differences of teaching places, and adjust the arrangement of teaching in time. For example, outdoor courses can appropriately shorten the time of preparation, exercise-loaded courses should observe students' state at any time, so as to avoid students being too tired to complete tasks according to standard actions.
Teachers of the three courses judge all the students' exercise load from the preparatory part to the basic part, and then to the end part. The trend of students' heart rate increases first, then decreases. However, this is not how students actually feel. Moreover, the coincidence between teachers' experience observation and students' subjective judgment tends has declined, teacher can adjust their instructional design and attitude accordingly.

(3) **analysis and hypothesis**
In order to further understand the students' movement process, taking SM5 as an example in course 1, this paper tries to explore the relationship among students' subjective feelings, teachers' observation records and heart rate data of bracelet. Below is the heart rate curve of SM5's first course. The abscissa represents time (time: minutes: seconds) and the ordinate is heart rate (times/minutes). In order to make the relationship between the structure of PE class and the heart rate more clear, yellow blocks are marked, which are the preparation part, the basic part, the end part and the heart rate after the end (Figs. 3 and 4).

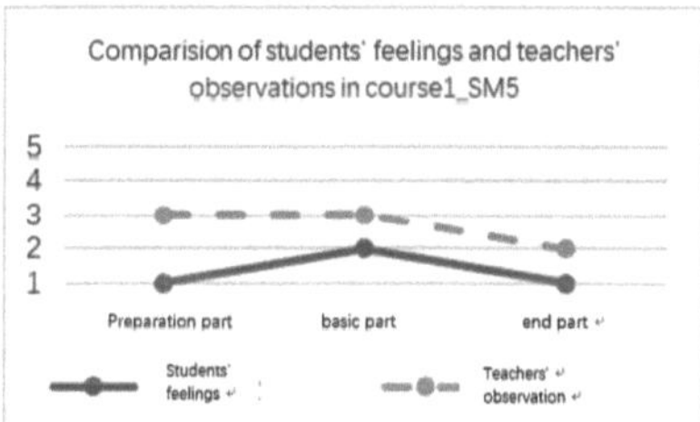

Fig. 3. Comparison of students' feelings and teachers' observations in Course1_SM5

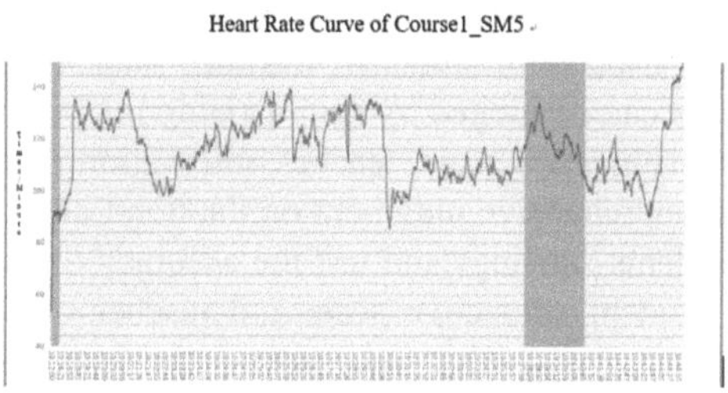

Fig. 4. Heart rate curve of Course1_SM5 (Color figure online)

Through the second graph of SM5's first course students' subjective feeling, teachers' observation and heart rate curve, it showed the trend of teachers' observation and students' subjective feeling is basically the same, but teachers think students' exercise load is higher than students' subjective feeling. The overall situation of heart rate data presented by heart rate curve is also consistent with the form filled out by students.

(4) **calibrate and test**

Next, it is the step that make further exploration with the records of teaching segments. Taking the first physical education class, single leg jumps as an example. The total teaching time is 30 min, from 10:10 to 10:40. The preparation part is 10:10–10:15, the basic part is 10:15–10:36, and the end part is 10:37–10:40, totaling 4 min.

The heart rate curve corresponds to the teaching content basically, for instance, in the warming up preparation part, students' heart rate rises gradually, and then heart rate restores steadily when interpreting instructions in basic part. With exercise difficulty increasing, heart rate rises continuously. However, it can be found that from 10:26 to10:28, although the difficulty of one-leg jumping in teacher's teaching content is constantly increasing, the heart rate of student is declining, in addition to students' heart rate. The subjective feeling of the basic part of PE is not too tired, so it is speculated that SM5 may not be serious enough in this stage of practice.

We can infer SM5 is relatively excited at the beginning. With the course going on, the attention may not be enough in the second half, and the practice is not serious enough through the heart rate curve. But when he has a short rest, he is more active after class. Teachers need to care more about students' attention in the second half of the course in order to help students improve the effect of exercise.

6 Conclusion and Discussion

There are four steps of Data Analysis Model of Wearable Devices in PE: (1) understand the whole (2) compare and observe (3) analysis and hypothesis (4) calibrate and test. Using four steps, it helps teachers get data from the whole to the individual, from the surface to the depth, thus helping them better understand students' exercise load, optimize teaching design, and enhance the teaching effect.

Through the comprehensive analysis and comparison of experimental data,such as bracelet data, student subjective scale and teacher observation record table, we can understand the different aspects of students' learning state. For example, the overall exercise load of students can be judged by summarizing the bracelet data. Through the mutual confirmation of subjective scale, teacher observation record table and bracelet data, we can make a comprehensive judgment on the trend of class students' exercise. We can understand students' feelings and test the accuracy of teachers' judgments on students through the student subjective scale and teacher observation record table. Horizontal analysis of the same student's in different courses can help to understand the characteristics of students' individualized learning. Through the longitudinal analysis of two forms of different students in the same course, we can know the load intensity of the same PE curriculum. The horizontal and vertical comprehensive judgment is helpful to understand students' personalized learning characteristics, make more accurate and scientific judgment on the matching degree between teaching content and students' exercise load, so as to optimize teachers' instructional design and improve the teaching efficiency. By comparing the bracelet data, teachers' observation records and students' subjective scales, we can know the students' learning attitude and physical fitness. For the same student, for example, whether the exercise load of physical education classroom teaching content is too much beyond the limits of physical endurance, or whether the students are lazy because they don't want to finish the training subjectively, etc.

The data analysis model of wearable devices in PE proposed can help teachers better understand students' exercise load and make more scientific and accurate judgments. However, at present, the application of wearable devices in physical education is still in the initial exploratory stage. It is necessary to calibrate the accuracy of its data through scales and other measures to obtain more dimensional information, so as to promote the better application of wearable devices in the field of education.

To sum up, the data analysis model of wearable devices can help teachers understand students' exercise load in time, conduct learner analysis and teachers' self-evaluation, and make more scientific judgments on students' learning behavior, so as to optimize the instructional design and promote the scientific and accurate evaluation of education. Furthermore, with the support of data, teachers can arrange more reasonable exercise load according to learners' characteristics, so then stimulate students' learning motivation, maintain students' learning state, promote students to develop the habit of participating in physical exercise actively and consciously, and improve students' health level comprehensively. In addition, the normal application of wearable devices can establish student files without interrupting students' normal learning, promote teachers' individualized guidance to students, and promote more scientific and multi dimensional teaching evaluation.

References

1. Yang, C.: Discussion of reasons and countermeasure of continuous decline of Chinese students' physical health in recent years
2. Ministry of Education of the People's Republic of China: The Notice on the insurance of management standards for schools in compulsory education [EB/OL]. http://www.moe.gov.cn/srcsite/A06/s3321/201712/t20171211_321026.html. Accessed 5 Dec 2017
3. Sun, C.: Research of safety problem and strategy of physical education in middle schools and primary schools. Sports Vis. (13), 63 (2011)
4. Nanxiang, Y., Dongyi, C., Houshiji, X.: Wearable computer technology and new development of its application. Digit. Telecommun. **39**(4), 13–20 (2012)
5. Johnson, L., Adams Becker, S., Cummins, M., Estrada, V., Freeman, A., Ludgate, H.: NMC Horizon Report>2013 Higher Education Edition, The New Media Consortium, Austin, Texas (2013)
6. Sun, X., Feng, Z.: Study on interactive design of wearable devices. Decoration (2), 28–33 (2014)

7. Borthwick, A.C., Anderson, C.L., Fitness, E.S., et al.: Special article personal wearable technologies in education: value or villain? J. Digit. Learn. Teach. Educ. **31**(3), 85–92 (2015)
8. Christine, K.: Are wearables the next big innovation in classroom tools? [EB/OL]. https://www.varinsights.com/doc/are-wearables-the-next-big-innovation-in-classroom-tools-0001
9. Zhao, N.: design and research of wearable affective computing device for online learning. Zhejiang University (2016)
10. Elena, D.L.G., Camacho, V., Orozco-Barbosa, L., et al.: Introducing IoT and wearable technologies into task-based language learning for young children. IEEE Trans. Learn. Technol. 366–378 (2016)
11. Lindberg, R., Seo, J., Laine, T.H.: Enhancing physical education with exergames and wearable technology. IEEE Trans. Learn. Technol. **9**(4), 328–341 (2016)
12. Lee, V.R., Drake, J., Williamson, K.: Let's get physical: K-12 students using wearable devices to obtain and learn about data from physical activities. Techtrends **59**(4), 46–53 (2015)
13. Zhao, S., Xu, X.: Application of wearable devices in physical education-based on SWOT model analysis. Contemp. Sports Technol. **6**(34), 111–112 (2016)
14. Wang, G., Hu, J.: Localization and analysis of exercise load and physiological load. J. Chengdu Phys. Educ. Inst. (4), 96 (1996)
15. Shen, J.: Physical Education in Schools, p. 118. Higher Education Press, Beijing (2010)
16. Sun, Q.: Physical Education Measurement and Evaluation, pp. 15–16. Higher Education Press, Beijing (2010)
17. Wang, C.: Ideas and practice about students' physical education exercise load. Educ. Explor. (10), 29–30 (2008)
18. Zhu, L.: Preliminary discussion on the relationship between the exercise load of physical education course and students' cultural learning. Phys. Educ. Chin. Sch. (1) (1984)
19. Ma, X.: A preliminary discussion on the relationship between the sports load of PE class and students' cultural learning. Acad. J. Kaifeng Med. Coll. (2), 79 (2000)
20. Miao, R., Dong, Q., Weng, W.Y., Yu, X.Y.: The application model of wearable devices in physical education. In: Cheung, S.K.S., Kwok, L.-F., Kubota, K., Lee, L.-K., Tokito, J. (eds.) ICBL 2018. LNCS, vol. 10949, pp. 311–322. Springer, Cham (2018). https://doi.org/10.1007/978-3-319-94505-7_25
21. Exercise load monitoring project group in Dongcheng District. Technical specification for monitoring and evaluation of exercise load in primary and secondary schools in Dongcheng District [EB/OL]. https://wenku.baidu.com/view/c939dae4336c1eb91a375df5.html. Accessed 29 Sept 2015
22. Song, Y., Ma, J.: Guidance for Physical Education Classes and Extracurricular Activities for Children and Adolescents, pp. 17–20. Peking University Medical Publishing House, Beijing (2013)

Research on the Hotspots and Trends of Learning Analytics Based on CiteSpace

Yinghui Shi[1], Shimeng Wang[1], Yanqiong Ma[1], Jason Macleod[2], Min Chen[1], and Harrison Hao Yang[1,3](✉)

[1] Central China Normal University, 430079 Wuhan, China
{yhshi,minchen}@mail.ccnu.edu.cn
[2] D'Youville College, Buffalo 14201, USA
jason.w.macleod@gmail.com
[3] State University of New York at Oswego, 13126 Oswego, USA
harrison.yang@oswego.edu

Abstract. Learning Analytics has become a hot research topic in the field of ICT in education in recent years. Based on 623 journal papers (published from 2011 to 2018) about learning analytics in Web of Science Core Collection, this study explored research hotspots and trends of learning analytics by the bibliometric method and mapping knowledge. Time range, region distribution, main research directions of the literature, and mapping knowledge were used to explore the main trends of the learning analytics. A further summary and reflection were given to provide the reference for deep study and practical exploration of learning analytics.

Keywords: Learning analytics · Visualization analysis · CiteSpace · Hotspots · Trend

1 Introduction

As an emerging, relatively new, and rapidly developing discipline [1], learning analytics is the progress of measuring, retrieving, analyzing and presenting of data about learners and their backgrounds in order to understand and optimize learning and the environment in which it occurs [2, 3]. Since 2011, the New Media Consortium has made *learning analytics* as one of the main trends and key technologies that influencing education development for three consecutive years in *New Horizon Report* [4–6]. In October 2012, the US Department of Education pointed out that the application of big data in education mainly relies on the support of educational data mining and learning analytics [4]. In addition, nearly half of the top 10 IT issues in 2017 proposed by the EDUCAUSE rely on prediction and analysis of data [7]. Learning analytics is being pushed to an important height by educators and researchers. As a result, learning analytics has become a research focal point throughout the world in recent years [8].

A growing body of educators and researchers have applied learning analytics in educational contexts, such as assessing students' learning behavior, estimating the

S. K. S. Cheung et al. (Eds.): ICBL 2019, LNCS 11546, pp. 239–248, 2019.
https://doi.org/10.1007/978-3-030-21562-0_20

cognitive value, improving students' interaction and engagement. However, little research has been carried out regarding the hotspots and trends of learning analytics. According to Chen (2014), CiteSpace was designed to carry out quantitative and qualitative studies in the field of scientific subject, which was considered as a useful approach for the detection and visualization of emerging trends and transient patterns of literature [9].

A great deal of studies which use CiteSpace to analyze trend has been published [10]. Thus, in the present study, the CiteSpace software, especially its functions like citation analysis and mapping knowledge in combination with the bibliometric method, was used to discover the main trends and hotspots of the learning analytics over the last decade by analyzing literature about the learning analytics retrieved from the Web of Science, and more detailed information for deep research and practical exploration of learning analytics was provided.

2 Materials and Methods

The data was collected from the Web of Science Core Collection. Key concepts and search term were developed to capture literature about learning analytics from international perspectives. Relevant studies were located through a comprehensive search of publicly available literature published from 2011 through 2018. We chose 2011 as a starting point for the literature search because IWBs was prevalent and became widely available in instruction around that time. We selected the Web of Science Core Collection data origin, because this database could provide a wide multidisciplinary lens, while also controlling the intellectual rigor of identified publications. The search was restricted to articles written in English and published in peer-reviewed journals, which were seen as a useful criterion for selecting studies of sufficient quality [11]. The specific search phrase utilized in this study was as follows: "learning analytic" or "learning analytics" or "learning analysis technique". SPSS, CiteSpace 5.3 and EndNote were used to analyze the literature in this study. SPSS 21.0 was applied to generate diagrams. Then, CiteSpace 5.3 was utilized to conduct the visualized network. In the end, we compared the results with that in CiteSpace 5.3 and EndNote, in order to verify the agreement of the subject terms results.

3 Results

3.1 Time Range

According to the retrieval results of Web of Science Core Collection, the sum of eligible papers was 677, and the publications about learning analytics per year in Web of Science were obtained during 2011–2018. As is exhibited in Fig. 1, it shows an upward trend over the past eight years in the publications of learning analytics literature.

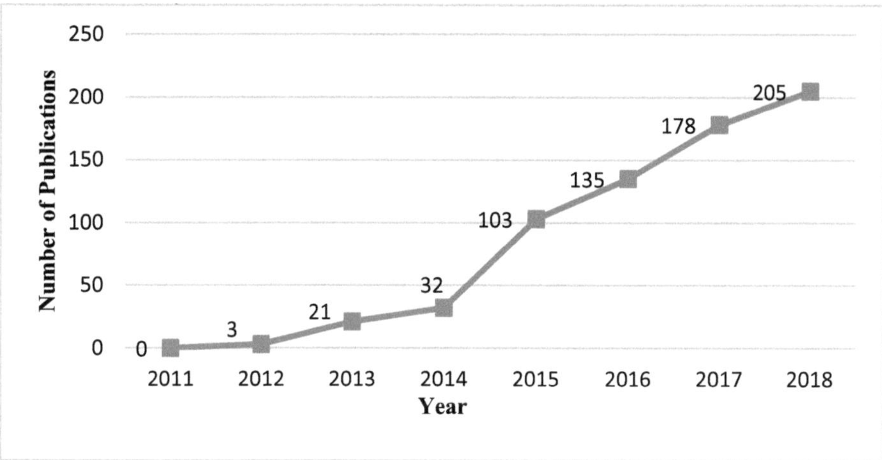

Fig. 1. The number of publications on learning analytics per year from 2011 to 2018.

Although learning analytics came into the spotlight as early as in 2011, not enough attention has been paid by the researchers as there was no publication in that year. After that, the number of publications was increased slowly from 3 papers in 2012 to 32 papers in 2014, which reflected that research on learning analytics was at the exploratory stage during this period. Since 2014, however, the number of publications was increased dramatically and exponentially from 32 papers in 2014 to 205 papers in 2018, which indicated that the funding of research for learning analytics increases, and the learning analytics catches a growing number of researchers' eye around the world since learning analytics was seen as one of the main trends and key technologies from 2011 to 2013 in *New Horizon Report*. Moreover, along with the rapid development of relevant theories, more researchers are involved in the study of learning analytics.

3.2 Region

Regarding the authors' nationality of the targeted papers, the USA (25%) accounts for more than a quarter of the total ranking, followed by Spain (19%) and Australia (12%), China ranks in the fifth place (9%). Figure 2 illustrates the percentages of papers across countries and regions from 2011 to 2018 in details. A large amount of USA literature is closely related to high attention for using learning analytics in education, including online learning and learning communities. Although China is at the top of the list, well behind that of USA, it also needs to carry out the researches on learning analytics in depth, aiming to promote the development of education in China by better understanding and predicting students' personal learning needs and performance [12].

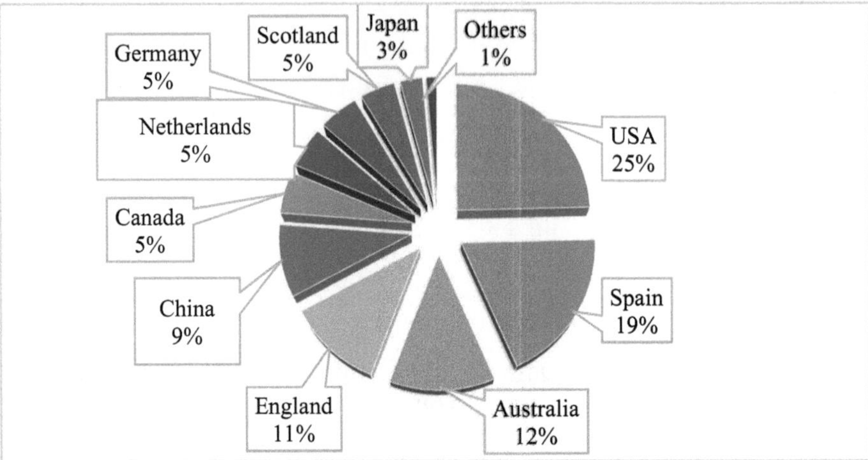

Fig. 2. The percentage of publications by country and region, 2011–2018.

3.3 Research Direction

With the help of the analysis function of the Web of Science, the top ten research directions of the learning analytics were obtained during 2011–2018. It is worth to note that because some papers contain more than one research directions, so the sum of publications are more than 667. As we can see from Table 1, the most popular research directions are education and educational research, which contributes more than half of the total. Computer science is another popular research direction, and it makes up about one-fifth of the total. Other hot directions, including psychology, engineering, information science library, telecommunications, social sciences, science technology, business economics, health care sciences services and linguistics, claim approximately 1/4 of the total.

Table 1. The top 10 research directions of the learning analytics, 2011–2018

Research direction	Number of Publications	Percentage (%)
Education/Educational Research	436	53.83
Computer Science	167	20.62
Psychology	67	8.27
Engineering	62	7.65
Information Science Library	21	2.59
Telecommunications	12	1.48
Social Sciences	11	1.36
Science Technology	10	1.23
Business Economics	8	0.99
Health Care Sciences Services	8	0.99
Linguistics	8	0.99

These findings highlight that learning analytics are used primarily in the field of education and educational research. In addition, the application field and scope of learning analytics is not only limited to education but also extending to other non-education areas, such as engineering and health care sciences services.

3.4 Citation Analyses

CiteSpace 5.3 was utilized to carry out the visualized analysis on the data. Firstly, articles were selected as the document type from all 677 papers on Web of Science; secondly, the search records were arranged by times cited from the highest to the lowest. Finally, 623 records were exported first as our data source. Several CiteSpace 5.3 options were selected, which includes the time range (2011–2018), years per slice (1 year) and pruning (pathfinder). The best knowledge mapping will be obtained by adjusting the parameter size of TOP N, TOP N% and article labeling [13]. Through the co-journal analysis, the knowledge mapping network of co-journal literature was shown in Fig. 3.

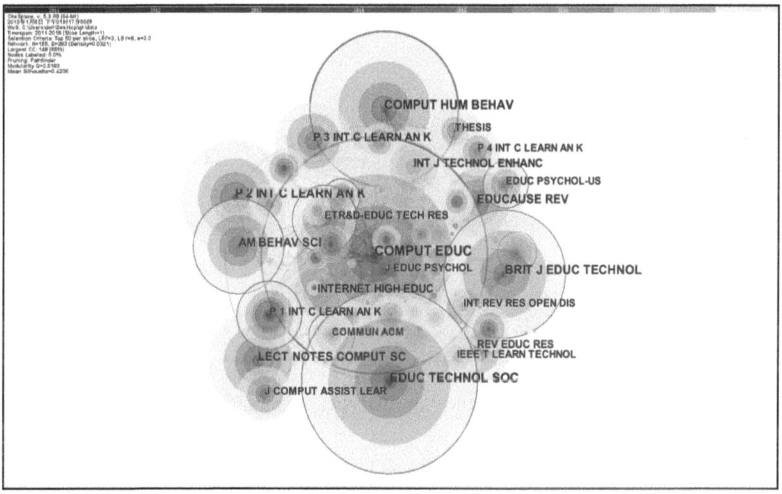

Fig. 3. A network of co-journal learning analytics papers (2011–2018, one-year slices). Abbreviations: COMPUT HUM B, Computers in Human Behavior; INT J TECHNOL ENHANC, International Journal of Technology Enhanced Learning; EDUC PSYCHOL-US, Educational Psychology; ETR&D EDUC TECH RES, Educational Technology Research and Development; AM BEHAV ACI, American Behavioral Scientist; COMPUT EDUC, Computers & Education; BRIT J EDUC TECHNOL, British Journal of Educational Technology; INTERNET HIGH EDUC, Internet and Higher Education; INT REV RES OPEN DIS, International Review of Research in Open and Distance Learning; IEEE T EAEN TECHNOL, IEEE Transactions on Learning Technologies; EDUC TECHNOL SOC, Educational Technology & Society; J COMPUT ASSIST LEAR, Journal of Computer Assisted Learning.

One kind of journal corresponds to one node. The frequency cited is expressed by the radius. The line between nodes represents a co-occurrence relationship, and its thickness indicates the strength of the co-occurrence. Chen (2014) explained the citation ring in his article [9]. The thickness of a ring is scaled based on the number of references in a given time slice. As is exhibited in Fig. 3, the highest cited journal is *Computers & Education*, followed by *Educational technology & society* and *Computers in Human Behavior*. It was found almost the journals cited as the top 5 are from the field of educational technology, which had great relevance to the application of learning analytics at all levels of education, especially in higher education.

Figure 4 illustrates a network of co-words of the papers. As is exhibited in Fig. 4, it's obvious that the highest frequency term is learning analytics. The specific search phrase utilized in this study was "learning analytics", thus the node of learning analytics is the largest. Combined with other words, such as performance, education, student, higher education, MOOC, it can be inferred that the research of the learning analytics emphasizes the application in education.

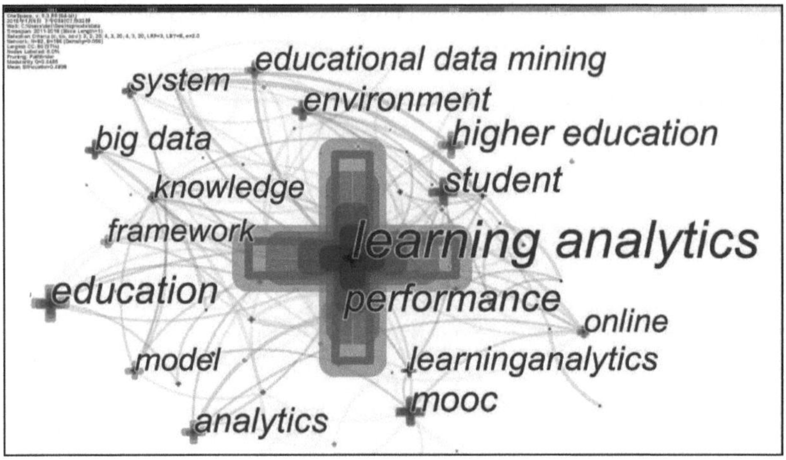

Fig. 4. A network of co-words of learning analytics papers (2011–2018, one-year slices).

Learning analytics can be exploited to improve the learning outcomes of students in higher institutions towards attaining sustainable education by analyzing students' performance in the process of education [14]. At the same time, types of the term such as educational data mining, big data, environment, and online indicate that learning analytics becoming more concerned with big data in the process of learning, especially online learning.

From Table 1, we clearly observe that publications about education and educational research occupy for more than half of the total. In order to further discover keywords of education and educational research, we exported all the records, which were sorted by times cited from the highest to the lowest. Figure 5 illustrates a network of co-words in the educational field. Compared to Fig. 4, the keywords in Fig. 5 are almost the same as that in Fig. 4, such as learning analytics, education, and performance. However, some words' appearance frequency becomes higher than that in Fig. 4, such as education, higher education, and MOOC.

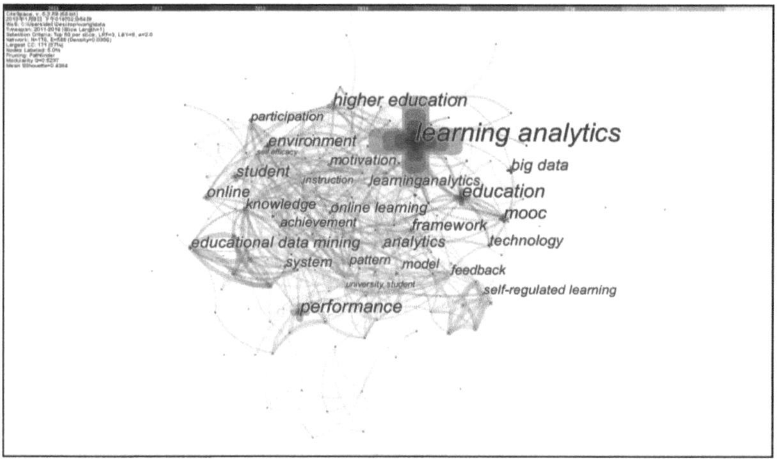

Fig. 5. A network of educational field co-words of learning analytics papers (2011–2018, one-year slices).

4 Discussion

In this study, a visualization analysis was conducted to explore research hotspots in the field of learning analytics regarding the publication time range, country, research direction, and citation analysis of the papers published relating to the learning analytics from 2011 to 2018 based on CiteSpace 5.3. To some extent, it reveals the general trends and research hotspots of learning analytics.

From the aspect of the time range, the concept of learning analytics was put forward in 2011, but the researches of learning analytics began in 2012. This happens because the NMC successively released the *Horizon Report* in 2012 and in 2013, and predicted that learning analytics would become the mainstream in the next three to five years [5]. Scholars were more concerned about the researches of learning analytics. Since 2012, more and more researchers launched applied studies on learning analytics, and the publications of that showed an upward trend up to 2018.

From the aspect of research direction, it was found that education and educational research are the hottest directions. However, many non-education fields such as psychology and engineering infiltrate the research of learning analytics, which reflects that scholars were more concerned about research and application of learning analytics, which will facilitate the extension of learning analytics to other fields. The development of any individual and field depends on a perfect understanding of themselves for making the adjustment and improve performance to ensure them getting better.

At the same time, analytical tool in EndNote was used for analyzing the dataset, which was similar to that of the co-word analysis. For this, fields including "title", "short title", "keywords", and "abstract" were selected to get subject terms in the EndNote. Finally, Table 2 displays the top 20 terms and their records. Comparing Table 2 with Fig. 4, it's obvious that most of the subject terms in Table 2 also present in Fig. 4. What's more, the more records of subject terms are, the bigger the size of the corresponding node is. Thus, it indicates that EndNote and CiteSpace 5.3 agree well with the subject terms results.

Table 2. The top 20 subject terms from EndNote

No.	Terms	Records	No.	Terms	Records
1	Learning analytics	395	11	Model	32
2	Performance	73	12	Online	31
3	Education	66	13	System	30
4	Student	51	14	Framework	30
5	Higher education	51	15	Knowledge	29
6	MOOC	50	16	Technology	26
7	Analytics	45	17	Motivation	25
8	Environment	42	18	Pattern	24
9	Educational data mining	37	19	Online learning	23
10	Big data	37	20	Design	22

International conference on learning analytics and knowledge (LAK) is committed to cutting edge research in the field of learning analytics. By analyzing systematically, the theme reports and papers of the conference in 2017, it was found that MOOCs and higher education would become the hotspots of research in this field in the next few years [15]. Combining Figs. 4 and 5, it is shown that our findings are in accordance with [15]. In this study, the application of learning analytics in MOOCs and higher education is considered as the hotspots. However, research in this paper has not only included this two themes, but covered other themes, such as performance, students, environment, educational data mining and big data, possibly associated with the social environment. The advent of the era of big data brings opportunities for the development of learning analytics, not only in data source but also in the data analysis method. Obtaining data in the process of learning is the foundation for learning analytics. The era of big data provides massive learning data. Thus, how to get necessary educational data from the mass data for learning analytics is a problem. The emergence of educational data mining technology provides a solution to this problem. Educational data mining and big data will be bound to become the hotspots in the coming years, which is consistent with our findings. However, although multiple similar subject terms were selected to expand the searching, for the precision of which a small part of the publications sacrificed. We had better do further work to optimize the searching strategy. In addition, only one database, the Web of Science Core Collection, was used as the data source, which possibly has little impact on the diversity of results. To conclude, researchers have identified learning analytics as a dynamic and important issue [2, 16], while the research direction of learning analytics will be still blurred in the future.

5 Conclusion

With the coming of the era of internet, information technologies and big data, how to use learning analytics to transform big data in education into information and knowledge serving education and to provide decision-making and learning optimization services for education, has become a common concern of educators and learners [17]. The emergence of learning analytics provides an important basis for the development of education in the era of big data. This study analyzed the publication time range, country, research direction, and citation analysis of the papers published in the field of learning analytics, so as to draw the attention of researchers on learning analytics, and carry out more in-depth studies. With the coming of the era of big data, learning analytics will play an increasingly important role. The focuses of future study on learning analytics will be how to effectively use learning analytics, fully explore the value behind the data, and promote and optimize students' learning effect of personalized learning.

Acknowledgement. The work was supported by the National Key Research and Development Program of China (2018YFB1004504).

References

1. Rienties, B., Boroowa, A., Cross, S., Kubiak, C., Mayles, K., Murphy, S.: Analytics action evaluation framework: a review of evidence-based learning analytics interventions at the Open University UK. J. Interact. Media Educ. **2016**(1), 1–11 (2016)
2. Zhu, Z.T., Shen, D.M.: Learning analytics as scientific strengths for smart education. e-Educ. Res. **34**(5), 5–12 (2013)
3. Siemens, G. http://www.learninganalytics.net/?p=126
4. Johnson, L., Adams, B.S., Freeman, A.: The NMC Horizon Report: 2011 Museum Edition. Report, New Media Consortium (2011)
5. Johnson, L., Adams, B.S., Cummins, M.: The NMC Horizon Report: 2012 Higher Education Edition. Report, New Media Consortium (2012)
6. Johnson, L., Adams, B.S., Cummins, M., et al.: The NMC Horizon Report: 2013 Higher Education Edition. Report, New Media Consortium (2013)
7. EDUCAUSE. https://www.educause.edu/~/media/files/articles/2017/1/erm1712.pdf
8. He, K.K.: The new development of "learning analytics technology" in China. e-Educ. Res. **37**(7), 5–13 (2016)
9. Chen, C.: Citespace II: detecting and visualizing emerging trends and transient patterns in scientific literature. J. Assoc. Inf. Sci. Technol. **57**(3), 359–377 (2014)
10. Zhu, S., Yang, H.H., Feng, L.: Visualizing and understanding the digital divide. In: Cheung, S.K.S., Kwok, L.-F., Yang, H., Fong, J., Kwan, R. (eds.) ICHL 2015. LNCS, vol. 9167, pp. 394–403. Springer, Cham (2015). https://doi.org/10.1007/978-3-319-20621-9_33
11. Korpershoek, H., Harms, T., De Boer, H., Van Kuijk, M., Doolaard, S.: A meta-analysis of the effects of classroom management strategies and classroom management programs on students' academic, behavioral, emotional, and motivational outcomes. Rev. Educ. Res. **86** (3), 643–680 (2016)
12. Greller, W., Drachsler, H.: Translating learning into numbers: a generic framework for learning analytics. J. Educ. Technol. Soc. **15**(3), 42–57 (2012)

13. Li, J., Chen, C.M.: Text Mining of Science and Visualization on Citespace. Capital University of Economics and Business Press, Beijing (2016)
14. Popoola, S.I., Atayero, A.A., Badejo, J.A., John, T.M., Odukoya, J.A., Omole, D.O.: Learning analytics for smart campus: data on academic performances of engineering undergraduates in a Nigerian Private University. Data Brief. **17**, 76–94 (2018)
15. Wu, Y.H., Li, R.C., Wang, H.N.: The development, status, and challenges of learning analysis: a review of the 7th international conference on learning analytics and knowledge. Open Educ. Res. **23**(5), 44–58 (2017)
16. Sergis, S., Sampson, D.G.: Teaching and learning analytics to support teacher inquiry: a systematic literature review. In: Peña-Ayala, A. (ed.) Learning Analytics: Fundaments, Applications, and Trends. SSDC, vol. 94, pp. 25–63. Springer, Cham (2017). https://doi.org/10.1007/978-3-319-52977-6_2
17. Wei, S.P.: Learning analytics: mining the value of education data under the big data era. Mod. Educ. Technol. **23**(2), 5–11 (2013)

Open Educational Resources

Promoting High-Quality Teachers Resource Sharing and Rural Small Schools Development in the Support of Informational Technology

Mingzhang Zuo[1], Wenqian Wang[2], and Yang Yang[1](✉)

[1] School of Educational Information Technology, Central China Normal University, Wuhan, China
mzzuo@mail.ccnu.edu.cn, aerbeisiyang@mails.ccnu.edu.cn

[2] Educational Information Technology Collaborative Innovation Center, Central China Normal University, Wuhan, China
wenqianwang@mails.ccnu.edu.cn

Abstract. Rural small schools in China have characteristics including remote location, small scale and poor conditions in infrastructure, quality of teaching and teacher. The shortage of teacher resources is the biggest problem in rural small schools compared with other resources. To address the problem and help offer sufficient and high-quality courses in rural small schools, the sharing of high-quality teacher resources are the most significant way to achieve it. In this paper, synchronous interactive hybrid classroom and synchronous interactive special delivery classroom teaching are put forward to facilitate the sharing of high-quality teacher resources in experimental areas. This article introduces a case of practicing the sharing of high-quality teacher resources by information technology from the urban school to the rural school in Xian'an district, Hubei province. The article concludes with a discussion of the findings for sharing teacher resources to provide equal educational opportunities between urban and rural areas.

Keywords: Resource sharing · High-quality teacher resources · Educational informatization · Small schools in rural areas

1 Introduction

In September 2015, General Secretary Xi proposed "National Training Initiative for Primary and Secondary Teachers (2014)" pointing out that to complete the building of a moderately prosperous society in all respects by 2020 is the most arduous task in poor areas. The prime task of poverty reduction lies in education. It is an important task of poverty reduction to enable children in poor areas to receive a good education, and it is also an important way to block the transmission of poverty across generations.

As an important way to promote the poverty reduction in education, Education informatization in rural schools in China is still at the initial stage of groping and start-up. It faces the development problems including a shortage of funds, poor quality of teachers and teaching as well as unavailable environment [1]. Teachers are the primary

S. K. S. Cheung et al. (Eds.): ICBL 2019, LNCS 11546, pp. 251–264, 2019.
https://doi.org/10.1007/978-3-030-21562-0_21

resources of education and the uneven allocation of teacher resources is an important reason for the gap between urban and rural education [2–4]. Hubei Collaborative Innovation Center (HCIC) for information technology and balanced development of K-12 education is an organization aiming for achieving the balance between rural area and urban area, especially in the aspect of education. It aims at reviving rural small schools, complementing the weak points of balanced development of compulsory education, promoting equal educational opportunities, improving and realizing educational equity effectively.

Rural small schools in China are different from other countries. According to "Educational Statistics Yearbook of China" published in 2016(latest), there are 86800 small schools in rural areas. It is defined as the school with combined instruction as the main method, which adapts to the development of education in rural areas, especially in the sparsely populated and scattered remote areas [5]. Combined instruction in China refers to an organizational form in which students of two or more grades are combined into one class with one or two teachers. The main problem in rural small schools is a shortage of teachers, especially high quality teachers.

The purpose of the study is to identify how information technology promotes the sharing of high-quality teacher resources and the development of rural small schools. The survey results were discussed involving the following questions. (1) What is the effect of information technology alleviating the problems existing in rural small schools? (2) What is the sharing mechanism of high-quality teacher resources in the support of information technology? Our intent was not to answer experimental hypotheses, but rather to begin to focus on developing research questions.

In this article, we describe the practice of the transferring and sharing of teacher resources from urban schools to rural small schools to balance the education between urban and rural areas for facilitating the balanced development and equity of education in Xian'an district, Hubei province. As will be described, study context is illustrated to explain the background of rural small schools in the process of urbanization. The next section of the article describes the practice of the transferring and sharing of teacher resources in small schools in rural areas. Then, the discussion of the practice is followed by illustrating the preliminary effects and the mode of sharing teacher resources. The article concludes with a presentation of the implications of the case for promoting the balanced development and equity of the education in rural areas by the transferring and sharing of teacher resources.

2 The Context of the Study

In Victoria, Australia, rural small schools refer to the schools having an enrollment of 100 students or less being 70 km or more from Melbourne, the state capital, or 25 km from a regional center [6]. Rural small schools already include many of the characteristics identified in the "effective schools" research including interpersonal relationships, shared expectations, and a safe learning environment [7].

As small and incomplete schools, the rural small schools are set up to adapt to the development of rural areas in China, especially the sparsely populated and scattered remote areas [8], aiming for facilitating the school-age children in remote rural areas to go to the school nearby. According to "Outline of National Medium-and Long-Term Education Reform and Development (2010–2012)" [9], it is clear that school layout can be rationally planned to meet the development needs of urban and rural areas, and rural small schools should be arranged so as to facilitate students to go to school nearby. At the meantime, it points out that information technology has a revolutionary impact on education and must be highly valued.

However, with the advancement of new urbanization, a large number of people flow from rural areas to cities, resulting in a decrease in the number of students in rural schools year by year. Many rural small schools gradually disappear, and a large number of schools become rural small schools due to the reduction in size [10]. The number of rural small schools has dropped sharply, leading to the students in remote rural areas being too far away from school, increasing traffic risks and economic burden on families. Rural small schools have become the "last mile" for the stable development of China's compulsory education.

2.1 Problems Caused by the Advancement of Urbanization

The advancement of urbanization puts great pressure on the education in urban school. The situation in which rural students go to cities to receive compulsory education leads to the difficulty in adapting the layout and capacity of urban schools, resulting in a shortage of urban education resources and insufficient number of schools. This puts forward higher requirements for urban school infrastructure investment, education funds, teachers and education resource allocation.

In contrast, the fact that a large number of students are leaving the school leads to the vacancy of school buildings and waste of resources in rural small schools.

2.2 Why Rural Small Schools Can't be Cancelled

Rural small schools are indispensable parts to ensure that school-age children in remote rural areas attend school nearby. It is convenient for children to go to school by setting up rural small schools near villages, which can save the cost of children going to school and ensure children' safety, thus promoting the equality of educational opportunities for school-age children in remote rural areas to the greatest extent. According to the results of 10,903 valid student questionnaires of the research group on the reasonable layout of rural primary and secondary schools in central and western China [11], the average distance for students to go to school if cancelling rural small schools is 4.8 km, and the farthest distance is 100 km. Therefore, the rural small school has the vitality, and will exist for a long time in the rural remote area.

2.3 The Role of Rural Small Schools in the Balanced Development of Compulsory Education

Firstly, the rural small school is the key to the development of the compulsory education. According to statistics calculated by Education Statistics Yearbook of China, the number of ordinary primary schools nationwide in 2016 was 177,633. And the number of rural small schools was 86800, accounting for 48.86% of the total number of primary schools, which is relatively large. As an important part of compulsory education, the rural small school plays an irreplaceable role in solving the problem of nearby school enrollment of school-age children in sparsely populated and scattered rural remote areas, and it will still exist for a long time in the future.

Secondly, the rural small school is the weakest link in the balanced development of compulsory education. At present, there are many forms including central primary schools, complete primary schools and rural small schools in the vast rural areas of China, especially in the remote central and western regions. Due to the characteristics including remote geographical location and small size, rural small schools are the smallest "shortcoming" in the development of compulsory education. The establishment of rural small schools is conducive to ensuring the balanced development of compulsory education.

Thirdly, the rural small school is an effective organizational form to ensure the quality of education. The quality of education is the core of the balanced development of compulsory education. Although rural small schools have a small number of students with small scale, they can completely guarantee and improve the quality of education. Moreover, the teachers in rural small schools are mostly native people. So they are very familiar with the students, which is conducive to the communication and interaction between teachers and students. In addition, rural small schools are convenient to use multiple teaching methods, so as to facilitate the performance of the students' learning.

2.4 Problems Exist in Rural Small Schools: a Shortage of Teachers

There is a serious shortage of teaching staffs in rural small schools, especially high quality teachers [10]. According to our investigation, in the Midwestern regions of rural primary schools, teachers of Music, Art, Physical Education and Information Technology are less than one respectively per school. As a result, most rural small schools are unable to offer courses required by compulsory education completely. At present, the shortage of teaching staffs is a common phenomenon in rural small schools, and also a key factor restricting the improvement of teaching quality.

The structure of teachers in rural small schools is unreasonable. On the whole, the proportion of substitute teachers in rural small schools is much higher than other schools. According to the research data of 2014 "Construction Status of Rural Primary and Secondary School Teachers" made by the research group, the proportion of public teachers and substitute teachers in rural small schools is 75.4% and 23.0% respectively. In other public schools, the proportion of public teachers is 88.3%, that of substitute teachers is 7.7%, and that of special post teachers is 2%. Due to the shortage of insufficient numbers, teachers are busy from morning till night. Some rural school teachers must responsible for boarding student accommodation problems. Heavy mental and manual pressures exhaust their body and mind. What's more, the teachers in these rural small schools have little chance to go out for training. Thus, their teaching skills have stagnated for years.

The number of teachers in rural small schools equals the number of grades, that's to say, each teacher is responsible for all the courses of a grade, including Chinese, Maths, English, Music, Art, Sports, etc. Some teachers even are responsible for multiple grades. These rural small schools seem to have basically offered all the courses stipulated by the national compulsory education stage. But due to the limitation of teachers' professional quality, the teaching of English, music, fine arts, physical education and many other disciplines still cannot be carried out normally. For example, the music class only teaches to sing several songs. The art class teaches the child to draw some simple pictures. It can be seen that the lacks of teachers and high-quality courses are still common problems in rural small schools.

3 Sharing the Teacher Resources in the Support of Information Technology to Balance Development of Compulsory Education

3.1 "Internet Plus Rural Small Schools"

With the rapid development of Internet, a new concept called 'Internet Plus' is becoming more and more popular among the last several decades. Internet Plus, similar to Information Superhighway and Industry 4.0, is proposed by China's Prime Minister Li Keqiang in his Government Work Report on March 5, 2015 so as to keep pace with the Information Trend. "Internet Plus" refers to the application of the internet and other information technology in conventional industries. It is an incomplete equation where various internets (mobile Internet, cloud computing, big data or Internet of Things) can be added to other fields, fostering new industries and business development in China.

In rural small schools, it's hard to recruit high-quality teachers because of their poor conditions. Rural small schools are indispensable parts to ensure that school-age children in remote rural areas attend school nearby. It is convenient for children to go to school by setting up rural small schools near villages, which can save the cost of children going to school and ensure students' security, thus realizing the equality of educational opportunities for school-age children in remote rural areas to the greatest extent.

The mode of "Internet Plus rural small schools" is proposed to overcome the problems of rural small schools by applying the internet and other information technology in rural small schools.

3.2 The Practice in Xian'an

Located in Xianning, Hubei province of China, Xian'an district was half urban and half mountain areas. The teaching environment of urban areas is quite different from that of rural areas. It is located in the southeast of Hubei province. Xian'an district covers an area of 1,501 km^2 and has a total population of 547,408. By 2018, there are 106 primary schools in Xian'an primary and secondary schools, among which 19 are rural small schools. There are 45,439 primary school students in the district, among which 750 students are in rural small schools.

As shown in Table 1, in terms of age distribution, the number of teachers under 40 years old is only 3 in 2013. However in 2018, the number of teachers increase to 37, with the growth ratio of 11.3%. The number of teachers between 40 and 50 years old increased slightly between 2013 and 2018. The number of teachers over 50 years old dropped by 58% from 2013 to 2018.

Table 1. The age distributions of teachers in rural small schools in Xian'an district.

Age	<40	40–50	>50
Number in 2013	3	11	31
Number in 2018	37	12	13
Growth ratio	11.33	0.09	−0.58

In terms of educational background, in 2013, the number of teachers below Secondary Vocational School Education level is 6, increased to 12 in 2018. The number of teachers with Secondary Vocational School Education is dropped by 48%. In 2013, the number of teachers above Secondary Vocational School Education is only 6. However, in 2018, the number is increased to 36 with the growth ratio of 46.7% (see Table 2), which demonstrates the improvement of number and quality of teachers in rural small schools in Xian'an district after the practice.

Table 2. The educational backgrounds of teachers in rural small schools in Xian'an district.

Educational background	Below secondary vocational school education	Secondary vocational school education	Above secondary vocational school education
Number in 2013	6	33	6
Number in 2018	12	16	34
Growth ratio	1	−0.52	4.67

Since 2013, the problem of poor quality of teaching and insufficient teacher in rural small schools has been highlighted. HCIC has been researching, developing the experimental zones, exploring to facilitate the high-quality and balanced development of rural small schools by "Internet Plus" mode.

Combined with educational management departments, primary and secondary schools as well as relevant educational informatization enterprises in Xian'an, HCIC innovate the teaching structure and teaching mode by means of informatization. It helps rural small schools set up well-organized and well-developed courses, improving teachers' professional quality and teaching level.

In terms of technology environment, HCIC adopts cloud platform to build a consortium of resource construction. In this process, there are shared public resources, characteristic resources and local resources. What cannot be ignored is the quality of teachers.

In terms of institutional mechanism, a dual-track digital school is built first, which uses the digital platform organization to offer sufficient classes. And the teaching management is in line with the urban schools.

In terms of management rules, the Education Bureau of Xian'an district has specially established the corresponding regulations of the digital school. It takes information technology as the support, innovation system and mechanism as the breakthrough, following the construction idea of "based on network, entity operation and two-level management". It also adopts the mode of "independent establishment and hierarchical management" concerning operation.

In the functional framework of the digital school education cloud platform, HCIC is trying to establish a mode of county centered, with the town as the node, and the teaching small school as the terminal of the digital school system, while the main portal is established in the province.

HCIC provides two different forms of synchronous interactive classroom teaching forms solve problems of a shortage of teacher resources and insufficient and low-quality courses offered by rural small schools. It can be divided into synchronous interactive hybrid classroom teaching and synchronous interactive special delivery class teaching.

In synchronous interactive classroom teaching forms, teachers in urban schools are selected as main lecturers, while teachers in rural small schools play the role of assistant teachers to help organize the management and implementation of the class. The work distribution is demonstrated as Table 3.

Table 3. The work distribution of teachers and students in urban and rural small schools

Activities	Main lecturers in urban schools	Assistant teachers in rural small schools	Students in rural small schools
Before class	Prepare teaching materials and contents for the class and deliver it to the rural small schools	Communicate with the lecturer and receive the teaching materials and contents	Preview the teaching contents delivered from urban schools
During class	Carry out teaching activities and conduct comprehensive and unified guidance of organization and management of the whole class	Assist the main lecturer to carry out teaching activities and meet the collaborative needs of classroom teaching organization and management. Record the teaching process	Interact with the lecturer and answer the questions proposed by them
After class	Assign the homework Reflect on the whole class according to the feedback sent by assistant teachers Correct students' homework	Provide class feedback and send it with students' homework to the lecturer and communication with each other	Do homework and communicate with assistant teachers about their questions and feelings about the class

3.2.1 Synchronous Interactive Hybrid Classroom Teaching

Synchronous interactive hybrid classroom teaching refers to a teaching form that realizes the interconnection between urban and rural areas through the network.

It transmits the classroom from urban schools where main lecturer teachers are located to the "live telecast classroom" in rural small schools where the resident teachers are located. It aims at realizing the communication between the local classroom and the classroom in other different places, between teachers and students, between students and students, truly promoting the sharing of high-quality educational resources. The interaction during synchronous interactive hybrid classroom teaching is shown in Fig. 1. There are several characteristics of this teaching mode: (1) the same teaching materials are provided between urban and rural schools; (2) real-time interaction between students and teachers in urban and rural small schools are realized; (3) a mix of local and remote teaching forms has been achieved.

It is possible to help offer the curriculums of music, art without additionally increasing the working hours and tasks of the teachers in urban schools.

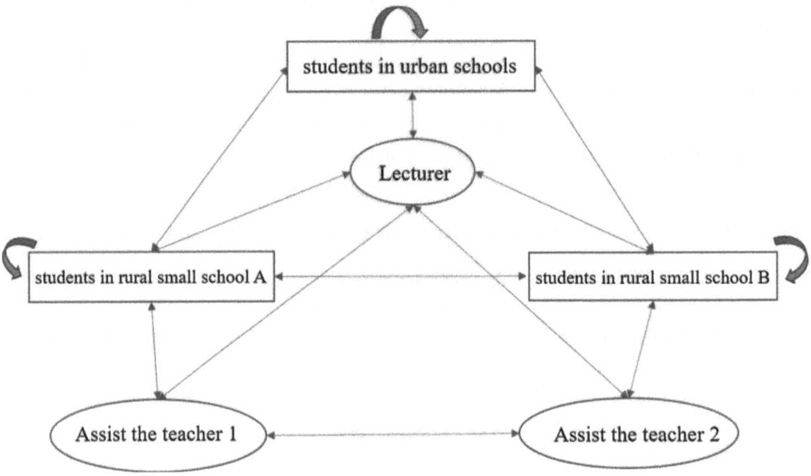

Fig. 1. A figure of interaction during synchronous interactive hybrid classroom teaching

Synchronous Interactive Special Delivery Class Teaching

Synchronous interactive hybrid classroom requires teachers to teach between the urban school and multiple rural small schools at the same time. It is difficult to take into account the learning needs of students in urban and rural schools. And differences between students of urban and rural schools are harder to be considered comprehensively, which affects the teaching effect to a certain extent.

At the same time, taking into account the learning activities of students in urban and rural schools, teachers are inevitable to encounter many emergencies. Therefore, the maintenance of classroom teaching order has also become an important factor affecting synchronous hybrid classroom teaching.

Synchronous interactive special delivery class teaching can alleviate the above problems to some extent. Similar to the synchronous interactive hybrid classroom, it's also the realization of the interaction between urban and rural teachers as well as students with teachers from urban schools as main lecturers to teach students in rural small schools. The difference is that there are no students in the class where the lecturer is, that is, the lecturer is only required to teach the students in the corresponding rural small schools. On the one hand, the synchronous interactive special delivery classroom can provide the high-quality teachers in the urban school into the rural small schools. And it realizes the two-way interaction between lecturers from urban schools and the students in rural small schools.

On the other hand, teachers can design the courses according to the actual situation of students in the rural small schools, so as to better pay attention to the cognitive characteristics, knowledge basis and learning needs. The teaching mode of synchronous interactive special delivery class is demonstrated in Fig. 2.

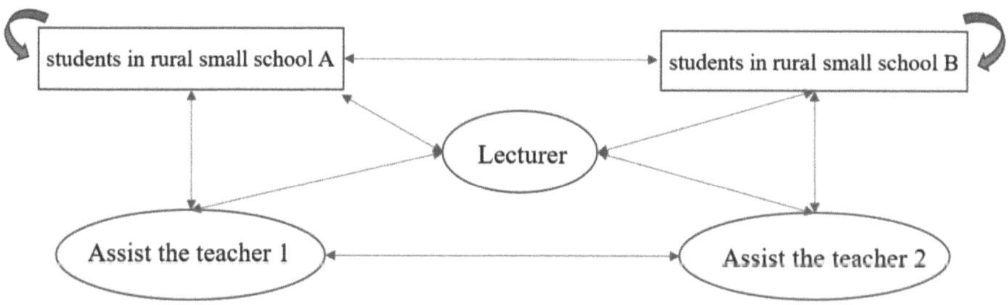

Fig. 2. A figure of the teaching mode of synchronous interactive special delivery class

4 Outcome

The data collected during the research period include the statistical data of the development of rural small schools, relevant management systems, teachers' and students' attitudes towards the synchronous classroom.

The purpose of this study is to identify how information technology promotes the sharing of high-quality teacher resources and the development of rural small schools. The survey results were discussed involving the following questions:

(1) What is the effect of information technology alleviating the prominent problems including a shortage of teachers, especially high-quality teachers?
(2) What is the sharing mechanism of high-quality teacher resources in the support of information technology?

As introduced in the practice, HCIC has implemented practice in to Xian'an, including aspects of technical environment, institutional mechanism, management rules, functional framework of the digital school and teaching method. The whole practice has achieved the following preliminary results.

4.1 Preliminary Results

The Number of Teachers and Students is Increasing in Rural Small Schools
In this case, the practice in Xian'an and other rural small schools has turned out to alleviate the realistic problems of poor quality of education and teacher. It has been proved that the implementation of this project has increased the number of both teachers and students.

At the end of 2013, there were 30 rural small schools in Xian'an district, with a total number of 45 teachers and 773 students. The ratio of students to teachers in rural small schools was about 17:1, and the average number of students in each rural small school was about 26 [12]. According to the data calculated by the Education Bureau of Xian'an district, at the end of 2018, there are 19 rural small schools in Xian'an district, with 62 teachers and 750 students in total. The ratio of students to teachers in rural small schools is about 12:1, and the average number of students in each rural small school is about 39.

The Phenomenon of Insufficient and Low-quality Courses is Alleviate
Both synchronous interaction hybrid class and synchronous interaction special delivery class are designed for solving the practical problem of insufficient and low-quality courses in rural small schools.

This can not only help offer courses of English, Music, Fine arts that previously unable to offer well, but also reduce the workload of teachers in rural small schools. At the meantime, rural students can enjoy the high-quality teacher resources of urban schools, making up for the lack of quality teachers in rural small schools. Thus effectively narrowing the educational gap between schools and promoting the fairness of the education process.

From 2013 to the end of 2018, in terms of Xian'an digital school, the scale of the school has developed from three rural small schools including Xian'an Biguiyuan Foreign Language primary school, Fushan primary and secondary school and No. 2 Bridge primary school to more than 10 rural small schools covering all rural areas in the whole region [10]. According to the statistical results of the Education Bureau of Xian'an district, in terms of National Compulsory Education Curriculum Standards, the current curriculums offered in rural small schools are complete, with 98% high-quality curriculums [13].

Students' Interest in Learning has been Significantly Improved
At present, the information technology-based teaching in rural small schools in experimental areas is to present various teaching information in the form of hypermedia and hypertext. It has the characteristics including fast transmission speed, clear sound and image, vivid picture, bright color. It can present the knowledge content that is difficult to be presented in written textbooks.

According to the survey, after the practice of synchronous interactive hybrid class and synchronous interactive special delivery class, 92.2% of the teachers in rural small schools agree that the students in rural small schools have a broader vision and know more things. 87.1% of students believe that their interest in learning is stronger. 85.5% of students believe that they have more communication with teachers and peers [13].

Information Technology Abilities of Teachers in Urban and Rural Schools are Significantly Improved
Information technology ability training for primary and secondary school teachers were carried out in the experimental area, adhere to the combination of school-based training and off-campus training, centralized training and self-study. Great importance has been attached to the process of evaluation of the learning effect of the teachers involved in the training. The overall effect of teachers' information teaching ability training lasting three years is good, among which 30% of the teachers have reached the excellent level, 50% have reached the good level, and only 10% of the teachers have not fully mastered the training content due to poor knowledge foundation or incomplete homework [13].

4.2 The Construction of High-Quality Teacher Resources Sharing Mode

In the practice of Xian'an, the synchronous classroom including synchronous interactive hybrid classroom, synchronous interactive special delivery classroom promotes the sharing of teacher resources.

Synchronous interactive hybrid classroom teaching adopts the mode of 1 + M (M⩽3 rural small schools). That is, each urban school in the experimental area directly provides high-quality synchronous interactive teaching to the rural small schools under its jurisdiction through the network.

In the synchronous interactive classroom, the teacher in urban school is served as main lecturer while the teacher in rural small school plays the role of assistant teacher. The lecturer needs not only interact with the students in the urban school, but also communicate with the students in the rural small schools through the synchronous network, so as to keep pace with each other.

Teachers in rural small schools need to change their roles and cooperate closely with the teachers in urban schools. They are specifically responsible for students' pre-class preparation, classroom order maintenance, feedback, and homework correction. Students in urban and rural schools jointly answer the lecturer's questions. In the process of interaction and collaboration, the students of the two areas continuously deepen their understanding of each other and cultivate their interpersonal skills, information technology skills, and broaden their horizons. Problems also exist that the lecturers are hard to pay attention to the urban and rural students at the mean time. Students in rural small schools may feel isolated.

In order to avoid the shortcomings of synchronous interactive hybrid classroom, synchronous interactive special deliver classroom teaching is proposed. It is the network synchronous interactive teaching between the main lecturer and students in rural small schools, and the teaching objects are only rural teaching students. It is specially designed for the characteristics of students in rural small schools. It provides the high-quality teachers of the urban school to rural small schools through network to realize the two-way interaction between the main lecturer and rural students. It effectively avoids the disadvantages of synchronous interactive hybrid classroom that is difficult to take into account the different learning needs of students in the two schools.

Through network synchronization, the teaching of high-quality teachers in urban areas can be transferred to the classroom of rural small schools, so as to realize the sharing of high-quality teacher resources. Before the beginning of each semester, teachers shall jointly negotiate the curriculum plan of the synchronous class. The course plan is carried out in strict accordance with the syllabus and curriculum standards of each subject. The teacher will design the teaching plan according to actual situation of rural small schools. Curriculum evaluation standards are issued by the teaching and research group of the Education Bureau, and are evaluated according to the actual situation of teachers and students in the rural small schools.

Although the sharing of teacher resources between urban and rural areas has achieved, problems also emerge during the practice.

First of all, it is difficult for the lecturers in urban schools to effectively balance the teaching in their schools and the two or three rural small schools under their jurisdiction. They may pay more attention to students face-to-face in urban schools and ignoring students in rural small schools.

In addition, due to a lack of contact between students in rural small schools and the lecturer, the students are not active in answering questions, which will directly affect the teaching effect of the urban and rural classroom.

Thirdly, it is difficult for students in rural small schools to maintain attention. As the digital schools generally have two or three rural small schools under their jurisdiction, the students can only learn from the live video, which lacks the face-to-face interaction between teacher and students. It may lead to divergence of attention.

Thus, we suggest that the main lecturer and the assistant teacher should fully communicate with each other about the teaching content before class, including what to teach, what teaching aids are needed in class, what should be paid attention to, and so on. During the class, the assistant teacher and the students should participate in the interaction together to improve the participation of students in the rural small schools. After class, the lecturer gets feedback and suggestions from the assistant teachers. In addition, the main lecturer can go to the rural small schools once a month, increasing the contact with the students there.

5 Conclusion

Information technology enables poor and remote rural schools to enjoy the high-quality teacher resources without changing the allocation of teachers. From the perspective of educational equity, it can be found that the two teaching methods are to enable children in poor areas to enjoy the same opportunities of quality resources as children in cities, and to guarantee the educational process equity as described by Husén [14, 15], a Swedish educator. Among all the teaching resources, teachers are the primary resources of education and the uneven allocation of teacher resources is an important reason for the gap between urban and rural education [2–4].

In this article, we describe the practice of the transferring and sharing of teacher resources from urban schools to rural small schools to balance the education between urban and rural areas for facilitating the balanced development and equity of education in Xian'an district, Hubei province. And most importantly, we discuss the preliminary results after the practice in Xian'an district. The construction of high-quality teacher resources sharing mode is also illustrated in the paper.

In the process of using information technology, appropriate technologies and means should be chosen according to local conditions. And different methods should be adopted in different scenarios to solve teaching problems and improve the quality of education. Secondly, the concept of community should be established. By means of "regional pairing, school grouping and teacher cooperation", the community of teaching practice should be established to form a co-construction and sharing mechanism of high-quality resources.

Education authorities should fully mobilize various social forces such as the state, local government, enterprises, educational organizations, teachers and students to form a multi-party coordination mechanism of "government-guided, enterprise-constructed, university-supported, and school-applied". Guided by market application, advanced theories from universities and advanced technologies from companies should be provided. Through government funds and management support as well as active participation of primary and secondary schools, education authorities should jointly seek appropriate strategies and implementation paths of education informatization.

There are also some limitations. Firstly, the main purpose of the case study methodology is to dig deeply into the areas where hypotheses are uncertain and contextual commonalities among the participants are stressed, rather than differences [16, 17]. Secondly, we only illustrate one case of practice in one experimental area, so the universality should be enhanced.

Acknowledgement. We want to appreciate the financial support from The National Education Sciences Planning Project (ACA170010). We would like to express our sincere and heartfelt thanks to the editors and reviewers.

References

1. Wei, M.: Obstacles in Informationization Development of Rural Small Schools and the Solutions–Based on Field Research in Eight Cities in Hubei Province (2016). (in Chinese)
2. Knamiller, G.: The effectiveness of teacher resource centre strategy. Educ. Res. Papers **128**, 68–69 (1999)
3. Brent, B.O., Roellke, C.F., et al.: Understanding teacher resource allocation in New York state secondary schools: a case study approach. J. Educ. Financ. **23**, 207–233 (1997)
4. Lee, J.: Educational equity and adequacy for disadvantaged minority students: school and teacher resource gaps toward national mathematics proficiency standard. J. Educ. Res. **105**, 64–75 (2012)
5. Bray, M.: Are Small Schools the Answer? Cost Effective Strategies for Rural School Provision. ERIC (1987)
6. Starr, K., White, S.: The small rural school principalship: key challenges and cross-school responses. J. Res. Rural Educ. **23**, 1 (2008)
7. Lemke, J.C.: Teacher induction in rural and small school districts (1994)
8. Fan, X., et al.: Balanced development of compulsory education and construction of rural teaching stations. Educ. Res. (2011). (in Chinese)
9. Anonymous Outline of China's medium - and long-term education reform and development plan (2010–2020) (2010)

10. Wang, J., Feng, S., Wu, X.: Internet plus rural small-schools: practice research on the balanced development of compulsory education in the process of new urbanization. China Educ. Technol. (2016). (in Chinese)
11. Fan, X., Guo, Q.: Effects, Problems and countermeasures of adjustment of layout in rural primary and secondary schools—based on the survey and analysis in 6 provinces/autonomous regions in central and western regions. Educ. Res. (2009). (in Chinese)
12. Wang, J., Chen, W.: Observation and evaluation of student development in small rural schools promoted by information technology—taking Xian'an experimental area as an example. China Educ. Technol. (2018). (in Chinese)
13. Fu, W., Wang, J., Zuo, M.: Informatization and the development of small schools in rural areas: effects, problems and countermeasures. J. Central China Normal Univ. (2016). (in Chinese)
14. Husén, T.: Educational research at the crossroads? An exercise in self-criticism. Prospects **19**, 349–360 (1989)
15. Husén, T.: The Swedish school reform-exemplary both ways. Comp. Educ. **25**, 345–355 (1989)
16. Yin, R.K.: Case study research: design and methods. J. Adv. Nurs. **44**, 108 (2010)
17. Recker, M.M., Dorward, J.: Nelson LM discovery and use of online learning resources: case study findings. J. Educ. Technol. Soc. **7**, 93–104 (2004)

An Empirical Study on the Usefulness, Effectiveness and Practicability of Vocational and Professional Education and Training's (VPET) Open Educational Resources (OER) in the Hotel Industry

Ricky Yuk-kwan Ng[1], Kwan-Keung Ng[2(✉)], and Brian Liu[3]

[1] Centre for Learning and Teaching, Vocational Training Council, Hong Kong, China
rickyng@vtc.edu.hk
[2] University of Sunderland, Hong Kong, China
steven.ng@sunderland.edu.hk
[3] Hong Kong, China

Abstract. Open educational resources (OER) is increasingly popular amongst all levels of educational institutions. However, it is noticed that adaptability of OERs for in-service training in specific industry is a major factor. Training managers, trainers and trainees also have concerns on the training packages' practicability developed by vocational and professional education and training's (VPET) subject teachers and academics. Although advice and consultancy were obtained from industry practitioners during the development of the training packages, it is always an issue of generalisation and adaptability because of the difficulty for one jacket to fits all. Each organisation has its training practices in terms of organisational culture, protocol and standard. This empirical study looks into the aforementioned factors with a hope to provide solutions and insights on future development, and application of OERs in the hotel industry. Using the concept of expert judgement, feedback and comments were gained from trainers and trainees on the following areas (1) instructional design, (2) user interface and (3) functionality as well as qualitative feedback on the usefulness and adaptability to suit industry's training needs to examine the effectiveness and practicability of the training packages developed for a VPET OER Project. Findings revealed that trainers and trainees in the hotel industry well accepted the OERs and regarded they are practical, comprehensive and well designed to meet their needs. Feedback also showed that the training materials are very useful especially for those learners who are new to the hotel industry.

Keywords: Vocational and professional education and training (VPET) · Open educational resources (OER) · Expert review · Hotel industry · In-service training

---

B. Liu—Independent Researcher

S. K. S. Cheung et al. (Eds.): ICBL 2019, LNCS 11546, pp. 265–276, 2019.
https://doi.org/10.1007/978-3-030-21562-0_22

1 Introduction

Open educational resources (OER) is increasingly popular amongst all levels of educational institutions around the world over the last decade [1]. Online OER learning has become one of the youngsters' most preferred learning activities because of the self-paced, self-regulated and flexible nature of the courses [2, 3]. Studies also revealed that OER and online learning are the future of education for they opened up a lot of opportunities and choices for the less privileged [4]. Kearney, Schuck and Burden [5] asserted that online learning opened up a third learning space (trains, café etc.) in addition to the first (educational institutions) and second (libraries, museums, field trips) learning spaces. Ng [6] elaborated the concept and asserted that technology enabled learning opened up a new dimension of omniscience learning space not bounded by space and time. Students can preview and review the online materials at their own pace and time while teachers can also keep track of students learning process [7–10]. Given majority of the online video source OERs are designated for the learning of knowledge and theories, they are more suitable for the higher education sector. However the application on vocational and professional education and training's training (VPET) is less favourable because of several reasons. Ng and Lam [11] found out that within VPETs training institutions, teachers and instructors' reluctance towards OER rests on the perception and practicability because a number of teaching are hands-on and conducted in workshops with specific facilities and settings. It is also noted that they are skeptical about the effectiveness of the online learning mode especially on students' motivation and their efforts on self-regulated learning. It is also noted that adaptability for in-service training in specific industry is another major factor. Training managers, trainers and trainees also have concerns on the training packages' practicability developed by VPET's subject teachers and academics. There are always issues of generalisation, adaptability and discrepancies between institutional groomed and workplace trained practitioners. In view of the above, the authors of this paper, Ng, R. has 25-year experience in education and training with a speciality in developing VPET learning resources; Ng, S. has 30-year experience in education sector while Liu, B. has over 35 years of sector experience and is currently a human resources director in a multi-national hotel in Hong Kong. The authors are also researchers, contributors, subject experts and project assessors in a Hong Kong Government funded Quality Enhancement Support Scheme (QESS) project 'Development of Effective Pedagogical Practices and a Cross-institutional Online Sharing Platform for Hong Kong's VET'. The Project aimed to identify suitable VPET pedagogical practices to devise suitable e-learning means for more effective learning and teaching. The deliverables are a series of OER online learning packages for VPET stakeholders uploaded on an online platform. Using the OER packages developed for the hotel sector from the platform, this empirical study looked into the application of OER packages with a hope to provide solutions and insights on future development of OERs for the hotel industry.

2 The Tripartite Collaboration in VPET

VPET or in another commonly used term technical and vocational education and training (TVET) has gained much attention in the past decade [12–16]. VPET or TVET comprises "education, training and skills development relating to a wide range of occupational fields, production, services and livelihoods" ([17], p. 2) and aims to generate manpower by nurturing professionals and skilled technicians. UNESCO has been studying the needs and strategies to revamp and better develop vocational training [17]. Studies revealed that the reformation of TVET in Asia is essential because of the advancement of technologies, rapid economic and societal changes as well as the needs of new skills and competencies required at work [18, 19]. As early as 2010, the SkillsFuture Singapore (SSG) initiative purports to "promote culture and holistic system of lifelong learning through the pursuit of skills mastery, and strengthen the ecosystem of quality education and training in Singapore" [16]. The SSG initiative showed that tripartite collaboration between government, industry sectors and educational institutions is the essential factor to devise policies and mechanism to cope with the fast changing needs in industries. OECD's report further indicated that TVET's sustainable development rely on "the effective partnership between government, employers and unions to ensure that the world of learning is connected at all levels with the world of work" [20, 21]. Diep and Hartman [18] stressed on TVET teachers' competence of linking real work process with professional learning process and asserted that "teachers need to understand the process of work in real workplaces" and "consider the cooperative learning places and the content of the curriculum" (p. 9). That requires a good application of pedagogical content knowledge (PCK) so that teachers and trainers can transform the subject contents into teaching and training practices [22–24]. In view of the above, the urgent needs remain on closer collaboration between TVET institutions and industries to benefit learners and trainees in TVET institutions and workplaces.

3 The Hong Kong Experience

TVET in Hong Kong has also gained the government's attention to cope with the global trends. The Task Force on Promotion of Vocational Education was formed in 2014 by the HKSAR Government to conduct studies and advise the Secretary for Education on strategies and concrete proposals to raise the awareness and recognition of vocational education in Hong Kong. After a series of public engagement activities with the stakeholders on their perceptions towards TVET, the Task Force recommends a three-pronged strategy to promote TVET. Firstly, Rebranding VET: the Report suggests "to rebrand VET in Hong Kong as Vocational and Professional Education and Training (VPET)" to further enhance the professional knowledge, professional recognition and articulation pathways of vocational and professional education and training [25]. Secondly, Strengthening Promotion: to promote and to raise awareness and recognition of vocational education in Hong Kong through a range of publicity campaigns and organisation of large-scale skills competitions together with applied research to exhibit students' achievement and professionalism, thus to raise the professional image of VPET. Thirdly, Sustaining Efforts: the Report "recommends the government to encourage the senior government officials to seize every opportunity to promote and support VPET on different occasions so as to demonstrate the government's support and recognition of VPET as an integral part of the community" ([26], p. 102). Furthermore, to seek the major chambers of commerce's support regarding recruitment and promotion to foster career progress of VPET.

In addition, the Education Bureau of HKSAR funded a Quality Enhancement Support Scheme (QESS) Project to engage four VPET institutions to collaborate on a 3-year Project "Development of Effective Pedagogical Practices and a Cross-institutional Online Sharing Platform for Hong Kong's VET" to study the needs of VPET and to develop a series of innovative OER teaching and learning packages in the four selected programme areas (Hotel and Catering, Health Care and Community Services, Business and Management and Servicing) on a sharing platform named VPETCity. The study report suggested that technology enhanced learning (TEL) would be the most appropriate innovative pedagogical practices to accommodate VET students, teachers and workplace mentors' learning and teaching needs. The report also recommended making use of new technologies to blend face-to-face teaching with e-learning or mobile learning to further enhance students' motivation and interaction [26]. A series of 13 learning and teaching packages in the four aforementioned programme areas were developed after consultancy from industry practitioners, VPET teachers, instructional designers and multi-media programmers. Taking this opportunity, this study aimed to find out the hotel industry practitioners' views on the packages' usefulness, effectiveness and practicability of the OER packages.

4 Research Methodology and Design

This empirical study adopted the "expert judgment" concept by Dempster [27]. Using structured expert review form, data was collected from experts from the hotel industry. Using expert review form that contained eight structured criteria referencing closed-ended questions on the respective areas (1) instructional design, (2) user interface and (3) functionality on a Likert scale from 1 to 4 (where 1 is the least favourable and 4 is the most favourable) and a section to collect overall qualitative comments from trainers and trainees. The items in the questionnaire were used to examine the usefulness, adaptability, effectiveness and practicability of how the OER training packages able to suit industry's training needs and they were as follows:

(1) Instructional Design
   a. Clarity of objectives to learners: realistic, achievable, operational
   b. Clarity of information structure: amount of information, clear structure, logical flow of content
   c. Comprehensibility of content: clear and easy to understand
(2) User Interface
   a. Visual structure: consistency, memory load
   b. Aesthetics of interface
   c. Legibility of text

(3) Functionality
  a. Navigation: Ease and effectiveness
  b. Use of graphics/media: Meaningful and functional

A total of 15 participants (6 trainers and 9 trainees) in one of Hong Kong's multinational hotel participated in this study. The participants were asked to log on the VPETCity website to trial test the four teaching and packages (Wine and Spirits Studies, Principles of Foods and Beverages, Front Office Operations and Housekeeping Operations) developed for the hotel industry. All the learning materials, activities and assessment items that including lecture videos, animated PowerPoint presentations, online quizzes and examinations were being tested by the participants. Both feedback and responses to the items in the expert review form were collected after a two-week's trial period and regarded as expert reviews.

5 Findings

Responses to the items in the expert review forms were analysed while the open-ended feedback from the open-ended question was further examined to explore emerging issues. Six trainers trial tested the respective teaching and learning packages (one for Wine and Spirits Studies, one for Principles of Foods and Beverages, one for Front Office Operations and three for Housekeeping Operations). Nine trainees also trial tested the Front Office Operations and Housekeeping Operations teaching and learning package.

5.1 Responses from Trainers

Wine and Spirts Studies
In terms of Instructional design, the trainer rated 4 on the scale and contented that objectives of the module are operational, specific, realistic and catered for learners' achievement while leaners need to take effort to discern the content structure and the flow of logic is sometimes illogical (rated 2 on the scale). The trainer rated 1 on the scale and also concerned that the content is not clearly written and learners may have difficulties to understand the technical terms at ease. Responses for the item on *User interface* revealed that the trainer consented that the use of navigation tools and graphic layouts are in consistency (rated 3 on the scale) while some icons and buttons are user-friendly and take times to memorise their functions (rated 3 on the scale). The trainer agreed that some part of the package (colours and fonts design) would able to gain learners' attention while there are still rooms for improvement (rated 3 on the scale). For *Functionality*, the trainer admitted that the navigation design and learning strategies are ease of use and enable learners to navigate between screens and have control of when to quit a particular part or the whole programme (rated 4 on the scale). Apart from the above, it is found that many graphics/media are decorative but some can enrich textual message (rated 2 on the scale). Qualitative feedback on the usefulness and adaptability to suit industry's training needs are summarised as follows:

- "The Programme Team puts effort in ensuring references are in line with the learning content and that relevant and up-to-date references are adopted as far as possible. The Programme Team will review and update references as appropriate".

Principles of Foods and Beverages
Responded to the item on *Instructional design*, the trainer rated 3 on the scale and contented that objectives of the module are generally realistic and achievable but still need fine-tuning to make it more specific. The information given is of appropriate amount and presented in a logical way for learners to easily discern the content structure (rated 4 on the scale). The trainer also agreed that the content is clearly written and learners can understand the technical terms at ease (rated 4 on the scale). Responses for the item *User interface* revealed that the trainer consented that the visual structure is very clear and consistency while icons and buttons are user-friendly and learners can easily adapt to the interface design (rated 4 on the scale). The trainer also agreed the whole interface is comfortably looked and the package is aesthetically pleasing and learners will be attracted by the visuals used to enhance memory of the contents (rated 4 on the scale). Text is also easy to read because of the design of font size and type (rated 4 on the scale). For *Functionality*, the trainer admitted that the navigation design and learning strategies are ease of use and enable learners to navigate between screens and have control of when to quit a particular part or the whole programme (rated 4 on the scale). Lastly, it is found that mostly graphics/media are functional and carry meanings. They can enrich textual message in order to enhance and reinforce learners' learning (rated 4 on the scale). Qualitative feedback on the usefulness and adaptability to suit industry's training needs are summarised as follows:

- "The programme structure is designed in such a way that individual Module can be offered as standalone programmes to meet with various demands in coming years".
- "The programme is designed to meet the needs of in-service personnel to enhance their competitiveness and employability by improving their professional knowledge, skills and management capability".
- "It is also intended that the programme content would act as a foundation for graduates to pursue further studies".
- "Furthermore, in comparison with other available programmes in the market, this programme provides a wider scope and breath with its focus not only on wine but also on other beverages, such as coffee, Chinese tea and beer".
- "The competitiveness of this programme should not be underestimated".
- "Nevertheless, according to different needs of students, they may choose to pace their own learning and complete the required modules within maximum registration period; or to exit the programme with exit award given that he/she has passed the required modules".
- "The programme is designed with multiple intermediate awards and exit awards based on module accumulation which would provide flexibility for the students to obtain different professional qualifications suitable to their needs".
- "To enhance students' interpersonal and communication skills, group work and presentation are used for assessments".

- "Group work gives students the chance to interact with each other, discuss ideas, compromise and reach consensus. Presentations, on the other hand, help students build up their confidence and ability in presenting and explaining ideas clearly and effectively".

Front Office Operations

In response to the item *Instructional design*, the trainer rated 4 on the scale and contented that objectives of the module are operational, specific, realistic and catered for learners' achievement while the information given is of appropriate amount and presented in a logical way for learners to easily discern the content structure (rated 4 on the scale). The trainer also agreed that the content is clearly written and learners can understand the technical terms at ease (rated 4 on the scale). Responses for the item *User interface* revealed that the trainer consented that the use of navigation tools and graphic layouts are in consistency (rated 3 on the scale). Although some icons and buttons are user-friendly, learners need to take times to memorise their functions (rated 3 on the scale). The trainer agreed that some part of the package (colours and fonts design) would able to gain learners' attention while there are still rooms for improvement (rated 3 on the scale). For *Functionality*, the trainer opined that although a consistent navigation design can be found that the navigation design between are still not so user-friendly and limited learners to navigate between screens (rated 3 on the scale). Lastly, the trainer found that many graphics/media carry meanings and can enhance textual message (rated 3 on the scale). Qualitative feedback on the usefulness and adaptability to suit industry's training needs are summarised as follows:

- "Both training materials are very useful especially for those learners who are new to this hotel industry. The contents are comprehensive that consisting of the essential knowledge for these two operational departments".
- "Overall, it is a great learning material for new staff and student to learn the basic, and for experienced staff, it is an amazing opportunity to refresh the crucial knowledge".
- "Recommend putting a summary at the end of each week to recap the key takeaway and vocabularies list in order to maximise the learning outcome".

Housekeeping Operations

Three trainers trial tested the teaching and learning packages and their responses are summarised as follows:

In terms of *Instructional design*, one trainer rated 3 on the scale and asserted that objectives of the module are generally realistic and achievable but still need fine-tuning to make it more specific. Two trainers rated 4 on the scale and contented that objectives of the module are operational, specific, realistic and catered for learners' achievement. One trainer opined that information given is of appropriate amount but learners will get lost occasionally (rated 3 on the scale) while the other two trainers agreed that the information given is of appropriate amount and presented in a logical way for learners to easily discern the content structure (rated 4 on the scale). One trainer rated 3 on the scale and opined that although content is written in a clear way but there are occasional technical terms that learners may take times to understand. Two trainers agreed that the content is clearly written and learners can understand the technical terms at ease (rated

4 on the scale). Responses for the item *User interface* revealed that one trainer consented that the use of navigation tools and graphic layouts are in consistency (rated 3 on the scale) while other two trainers rated 4 on the scale consented that the visual structure is very clear and consistent while icons and buttons are user friendly and learners can easily adapt to the interface design. One trainer found no or little aesthetical sense in the package (rated 2 on the scale) while the other two trainers found the whole interface is comfortably looked and the package is aesthetically pleasing. Learners will be attracted by the graphic or animation used and the use of colour in text and graphics are likely to enhance learners' memory (rated 4 on the scale). One trainer rated 3 on the scale found learners can read the text in general and the font size and type used are appropriate but with rooms for improvement. Two trainers agreed that text is easy to read because of the colour and design of font size and type (rated 4 on the scale). For *Functionality*, one trainer opined that although a consistent navigation design can be found that the navigation design between is still not so user-friendly and limited learners to navigate between screens (rated 3 on the scale). Two trainers admitted that the navigation design and learning strategies are ease of use and enable learners to navigate between screens and have control of when to quit a particular part or the whole programme (rated 4 on the scale). Lastly, one trainer rated 2 on the scale found many graphics/media are decorative but in-turn can enrich textual message. Two trainers found that most graphics/media are functional, carry meanings and can enrich textual message in order to enhance and reinforce learners' learning (rated 4 on the scale). Qualitative feedback on the usefulness and adaptability to suit industry's training needs from the three trainers are summarised as follows:

- "Videos are the most useful resources as they are practical. They do suit for the industry's training needs as can be used for training up newcomers".
- "I agreed it is really the practical program that student can have the very deep understanding the overall condition of the industry as well as the more in-depth aware the details of the job position".
- "Moreover, it is also very useful for industrial training usage since the quality of the training video is not possible for the hotel itself to make for their own training usage".
- "It is best use as the new join training & refreshment training to existing employee.
- I am personally will definitely to use it as our departmental training tool for our new join & existing employee".
- "It is most welcome to have the same co-operation or contribution in the future which may have the mutually beneficial impact to both education aspect & industrial aspect".
- "It is very useful, easy to understand and helpful to me. It is also a good training tool for the department".

5.2 Responses from Trainees

Nine trainees trial tested the Housekeeping Operation package. The reason that only this particular package was tested rested on the large proportion of housekeepers in the participated hotel and their availability at the time of this study. Interestingly, all nine trainees rated 4 on the scale for the eight structured criteria referencing closed-ended questions and generally agreed that the package is useful and helps them a lot in familiarise the procedures and applying knowledge in housekeeping. They also agreed that the package reinforces their prior knowledge and allows better understanding of their professions. The responses from the trainees were very similar and it might reflected the collective organisational culture in hotel industry. Furthermore, in-house training was a basic requirement in that sector that all employees need to fulfil; and hence the qualitative feedback from them were limited, reserved and mostly rested on the positive side. In comparing to the trainers, the trainees were more in a passive position and they may need to know the aims and objectives of introducing the OER training packages before they make further meaningful responses. There may be a further needs to seek trainers' help to further explain those to the trainees for follow ups to obtain additional views by conducting group interviews to triangulate the responses.

6 Discussion

In general, the trainers and trainees well accepted the teaching and learning packages and regarded that they are practical, comprehensive and well designed to meet their needs. Feedback also showed that the training materials are very useful and effective especially for those learners who are new to the hotel industry. It is interesting to learn that all the trainees found the housekeeping operations package useful and helps them to familiarise the procedures and applying knowledge in their daily practices. The package further reinforces their prior knowledge and allows better understanding of their daily work. The well acceptance of the packages by both trainers and trainees may result from several reasons. Firstly, the packages were developed after extensive consultation from the hotel industry practitioners, subject teachers, instructional designers, multimedia programmers and assessed by industry experts to minimise discrepancies of what the VPET institution teaches and what the industry needs in workplaces. As the OER training materials aimed for self-learning, the content arrangement, instructional design, user interface design and the functionality were discretely structured to accommodate the learners' learning needs. Secondly, different kinds of media and representations, such as text, graphics, tables, audio, videos, animations, and interactive dynamic visuals were used in the packages to help learners to retain information and engagement. Thirdly, innovative TEL pedagogy was adopted to enable mobile, flexible and timely learning to suit the learners' work schedule in the workplaces. Fourthly, as the OER packages are regarded as a new training concept to the industry practitioners that the trainers can save time on developing the materials and they can easily adapt particular sections to accompany their training; the convenience and practicability well addressed their needs. Wong, Li and Wong [28] found that e-learning and online resources play significant role in continuing professional development (CPD) and becomes a viable way to support CPD in the near future. For the trainees, the flexible self-learning packages enable them to learn and review the lessons anytime and anywhere and thus free up a lot of physically bounded in-house training hours. Lastly, the OER packages help the industry to save up huge amount of money since the content development, preparation and production process is time-consuming and requires a lot of resources. Nevertheless, there are concerns about the overly positive feedback from the trainers and trainees. One salient point may rest on the excitement of the new. As the OER packages are considered as the very first attempt to change the concept of in-house training, the halo effect may override the actual usefulness, effectiveness and practicability of the packages. The packages may need to be tested over time instead of a relatively short two-week trial period. The other question remains on the absolute positive feedback from the trainees. The trainees find the packages useful because most of them are fresh in their jobs and the effectiveness may subside when their experiences grow. It is also commonly known that in-house training is the least favourite activity for staff, the self-learning enables them to self-regulate their learning rather than physically bounded by in-house training sessions.

7 Conclusion

Using the OER packages developed by the EDB funded QESS Project, this study adopted the expert judgement method to examine the usefulness, effectiveness and practicability of the OER packages developed for the hotel industry. Implications of this study are: 1. close collaboration and contribution of the stakeholders are essential to derive of quality and practical OER. It is noticed that feedback from the trainers were more keen than the trainers and it may result from their lack of engagement during the OER developing process and hence, a loss of trainees' views and ownership which led to the limited qualitative feedback; 2. flexible and self-learning suits workplace learning and training well for it enables flexible and timely learning without physical boundaries; 3. technologies are constantly under rapid changes, development of technology enhanced OER must not solely rely on technologies but more attention shall be given on pedagogies and instructional design; 4. this study has its own limitation and it is of certain that across hotels wide trial would help to test generalisability; 5. only the Housekeeping Operations package was trial tested because of the availability of participants, hence the validity is under challenge. Nevertheless, this study served as a pilot test of the OER packages and their application in the hotel workplaces; further studies of the OER packages developed for other industries will be able to generate views and data for multi-dimensional comparison between stakeholders, organisations and industries for knowledge and practice advancement.

References

1. Towey, D., Ng, R., Wang, T.: Open educational resources (OERs) and technology enhanced learning (TEL) in vocational and professional education and training (VPET). In: IEEE International Conference on Teaching, Assessment, and Learning for Engineering (TALE 2106), Dusit Thani Bangkok Hotel, Thailand, 7–9 December 2016 (2016)
2. Ng, R., Lam, R., Ng, K., Lai, K.: A cross-institutional study of vocational and professional education and training (TVET) students and teachers' needs of innovative pedagogical practices. In: Proceedings of 2016 International Symposium on Educational Technology (ISET), Beijing, pp. 101–105 (2016)

3. Ng, R., Lam, R., Ng, K., Lai, K.: A study of vocational and professional education and training (TVET) students and teachers' preferred support for technology based blended learning. In: Proceedings of the International Symposium on Educational Technology, Hong Kong, 27–29 June 2017 (2017)
4. Mtebe, J., Raisamo, R.: Challenges and instructors' intention to adopt and use open educational resources in higher education in Tanzania. Int. Rev. Res. Open Distrib. Learn. **15** (1), 249–272 (2014)
5. Kearney, M.; Schuck, S., Burden, K.: Exploring Mobile Learning in the Third Space. Taylor Francis Online (2016). https://www.tandfonline.com/doi/abs/10.1080/1475939X.2016.1230555?src=recsys&journalCode=rtpe20. Accessed 25 Jan 2019
6. Ng, R.: Omniscience learning space: a new dimension of learning. In: VPET Conference Series in the Learning and Teaching Expo 2017, Hong Kong Convention Centre, 13–15 December 2017 (2017)
7. Cheung, S.K.S.: A study on the pattern and trend of students' typical usage of mobile devices in learning activities. In: Cheung, S.K.S., Lam, J., Li, K.C., Au, O., Ma, W.W.K., Ho, W.S. (eds.) ICTE 2018. CCIS, vol. 843, pp. 89–100. Springer, Singapore (2018). https://doi.org/10.1007/978-981-13-0008-0_9
8. Cheung, S.K.S.: A case study on students' attitude and acceptance of mobile learning. In: Li, K.C., Wong, T.L., Cheung, S.K.S., Lam, J., Ng, K.K. (eds.) ICTE 2014. CCIS, vol. 494, pp. 45–54. Springer, Heidelberg (2014). https://doi.org/10.1007/978-3-662-46158-7_5
9. Cheung, S., Yuen, K., Tsang, E.: A study on the readiness of mobile learning in open education. In: Proceedings of IEEE International Symposium on IT in Medicine and Education, pp. 133–136. IEEE Press (2011)
10. Lam, J., Yau, J., Cheung, S.K.S.: A review of mobile learning in the mobile age. In: Tsang, P., Cheung, S.K.S., Lee, V.S.K., Huang, R. (eds.) ICHL 2010. LNCS, vol. 6248, pp. 306–315. Springer, Heidelberg (2010). https://doi.org/10.1007/978-3-642-14657-2_28
11. Ng, R., Lam, R.: Student learning preferences for and perceptions of blended learning: a case study in MOOCs for vocational education in Hong Kong. In: Hong Kong International Conference on Education, Psychology and Society (HKICEPS), Eaton Hotel, Hong Kong, 14–16 December 2016 (2016)
12. National Centre for Vocational Education Research: Australian Vocational Education and Training Statistics: Young People in Education and Training 2009 (2010). http://apo.org.au/node/23745. Accessed 30 Oct 2018
13. Thomson, A.: Global trends in vocational education and training. Paper presented at the National Conference for TAFE Directors Australian: Balancing the Big Issues, Sydney, Australia (2011)
14. BBC News: Vocational exams on the increase. BBC News, 23 June 2009 (2009). http://news.bbc.co.uk/2/hi/uk_news/education/8290470.stm. Accessed 30 Oct 2018
15. NCVER: National Centre for Vocational Education Research, Australian Vocational Education and Training Statistics: Young People in Education and Training 2009 (2010). http://apo.org.au/node/23745. Accessed 30 Oct 2018
16. Singapore Government: About SkillsFuture Singapore (2018). http://www.ssg-wsg.gov.sg/about.html?activeAcc=1. Accessed 30 Oct 2018
17. UNESCO: Proposal for the Revision of the 2001 Revised Recommendation Concerning Technical And Vocational Education. UNESCO, Paris (2015)
18. Diep, P.; Hartman, M.: Green Skills in Vocational Teacher Education-A Model of Pedagogical Competence for a World of Sustainable Development (2016). www.tvet-online.asia. Accessed 10 Jan 2019
19. Pavlova, M.: Regional Overview: What is the Government's Role of Greening in TVET? (2016). www.tvet-online.asia. Accessed 10 Jan 2019

20. OECD: Learning for Jobs (2010). http://www.oecd.org/edu/skillsbeyond-school/Learning%20for%20Jobs%20book.pdf. Accessed 10 Jan 2019
21. Orleans, L.: Professional Manpower and Education in Communist China, National Science Foundation, Washington, DC (1961)
22. Shulman, L.: Those who understand: knowledge growth in teaching. In: Education Researcher, vol. Fe. 1986, pp. 4–14 (2016)
23. Koehler, M., Mishra, P.: What is technological pedagogical content knowledge. Contemp. Issues Technol. Teach. Educ. **9**(1), 60–70 (2009)
24. Kosinar, J.: Profseeionalisierungsverlaufe in der Lehrerausbidung, pp. 4–23. Barbar Budrich, Berlin (2014)
25. HKSAR EdB: Education Bureau of the Hong Kong Special Administrative Region. Report of the Task Force on Promotion of Vocational Education (2015). https://www.edb.gov.hk/en/edu-system/other-edu-training/vocational-other-edu-program/promotion-vet.html. Accessed 30 Oct 2018
26. Ng, R.: "A report on the cross-institutional study of vocational education and training (VET) students' learning needs as well as teachers and workplace mentors' teaching practices" for the Quality Enhancement Support Scheme (QESS) Project: Development of Effective Pedagogical Practices and a Cross-institutional Online Sharing Platform for Hong Kong's VET (2016). https://vpetcity.vtc.edu.hk/doc/8_study_report.pdf. Accessed 30 Oct 2018
27. Yager, R.R., Liu, L.: Classic Works of the Dempster-Shafer Theory of Belief Functions. Springer, Heidelberg (2008). https://doi.org/10.1007/978-3-540-44792-4
28. Wong, B.T.-M., Li, K.C., Wong, B.Y.-Y., Yau, J.S.-W.: The e-learning trends for continuing professional development in the accountancy profession in Hong Kong. In: Cheung, S.K.S., Lam, J., Li, K.C., Au, O., Ma, W.W.K., Ho, W.S. (eds.) ICTE 2018. CCIS, vol. 843, pp. 258–266. Springer, Singapore (2018). https://doi.org/10.1007/978-981-13-0008-0_24

Study on the Instructional Design of a STEAM Course with Chinese Characteristics – Take "Making Handmade Wood-Burning Ceramic Cups" as a Case

Liuhui Huang[1], Yangyang Han[1], Kedong Li[1], Yunxiang Zheng[1(✉)], and Lihong Liu[2]

[1] South China Normal University, Guangzhou 510631, China
zyx@scnu.edu.cn
[2] Guangdong ZhiHaoLe Education Technology Co., Ltd., Guangzhou 510032, China

Abstract. In China, the disadvantages of disciplinary differentiation are increasingly emerging, while STEAM education emphasizes the application of interdisciplinary knowledge and the cultivation of innovative talents. With project learning as the core to help students master knowledge and skills, STEAM education emphasizes the use of scientific inquiry methods to stimulate students' interest in exploring the knowledge hidden behind the problem, and focuses on the adoption of engineering design to propose a solution. Combining the existing instructional design theory through literature review with the instructional design elements of some emerging learning styles, this study designed a STEAM course called "Making Handmade Wood-burning Ceramic Cups". A lesson was selected as a case to illustrate the details of this course, followed by the teaching effect to verify its feasibility and effectiveness. Together with the previous introduction about current STEAM projects in China, this paper provides reference for the construction of a STEAM course in primary and middle school with local characteristics.

Keywords: STEAM education · Instructional design · Wood-burning Ceramic Cups

1 Introduction

STEAM is the abbreviation of science, technology, engineering, arts and mathematics. At present, there is no clear definition of STEAM education and researchers mostly define it from a certain aspect in combination with their own research content. This study considers STEAM education as to help encourage learners to try in all manner of ways (e.g. engineering design, scientific inquiry, mathematical methods, technical making or artistic description) to solve real-world problems. In STEAM education, students use interdisciplinary knowledge and methods to enhance their innovative ability and even overall development [1]. Literature review shows that foreign articles mainly focus on STEAM education standard, engineering education, science education,

S. K. S. Cheung et al. (Eds.): ICBL 2019, LNCS 11546, pp. 277–288, 2019.
https://doi.org/10.1007/978-3-030-21562-0_23

STEAM course implementation, STEAM educators, and the like [2]. Among them, the practical exploration on STEAM courses receives the most concern in developed countries, such as the United States, Germany, Japan, etc. However, STEAM education has not been fully developed in China. The earliest relevant research can be tracked back to 2008, discussing some Chinese scholars' opinion and analysis on the status and policies of STEM/STEAM education in the United States. The number of research articles has increased dramatically during 2013–2016, focusing on the development status and policy interpretation of STEAM education abroad, the theory of STEAM (its connotation, characteristics and functions), as well as some STEAM practice including interdisciplinary integration, curriculum system construction and specific disciplinary application. Nevertheless, there are few researches on STEM/STEAM technology support and STEM/STEAM teacher professional development [3].

At present, STEAM education has been included in the National Education Development Policy of China, which accelerates the exploration of STEAM localization in China. More and more university researchers started to cooperate with primary and secondary school teachers in the field of interdisciplinary integration and innovative talent training. At the same time, the Chinese Ministry of Education issued a national plan called "the Guideline for Comprehensive Practical Activity Courses in Primary and Secondary Schools" [4], stating new requirements for students' overall development. That is, the courses should start with the problems in students' real life or associated with their needs. Instead of telling them about these problems directly, teachers should try to assist them to identify these problems by themselves, and help transform them into some project themes (or activity themes). Most importantly, teachers should encourage students to find solutions through investigation, experience, hands-on making, etc. Similarly, STEAM education emphasizes providing students with realistic learning situations, encouraging them to solve a complex problem step by step under the framework of Science, Technology, Engineering, Art and Math, and paying attention to the importance of students' high-level thinking and collaborative participation. In this way students will benefit a lot and improve in all-round ways [5]. As can be seen from above that both Comprehensive Practical Activity Courses and STEAM education share the same ideology in training students' abilities: (1) learning by solving real problems through hypothesis claiming and proving; (2) experiencing failure and success during the course of exploration; (3) gaining communication skills and self-regulating ability in collaborative situations [6]. Accordingly, STEAM education is considered to be the most suitable way to design and implement Comprehensive Practical Activities Courses in China.

In this context, more and more distinctive STEAM cases have emerged in China. The followings are some examples: (1) Shanghai Nanyuan Primary School, a "National Meteorological Science Model School" [7], develops some regional meteorological resources from interdisciplinary point of view and establishes a multi-dimensional learning environment (e.g. meteorological wind chime garden, plant nursery, meteorological science electronic screen, etc.) to support students' experiential and inquiry learning. After years of practice, three types of STEAM course have been formed gradually: basic type (e.g. "Knowledge for Meteorology and Life" based on language subjects), extended type (e.g. "Meteorology and Agriculture") and inquired-based type (e.g. "The impact of temperature changes on campus plants"). (2) Shenzhen Moon Bay Primary School develops a STEAM course called FEG (Finding-Engineering-Genius) smart car. Students first learn the shape of car body and its assembly method through scientific inquiry, and then experience the engineering design process through assembling and driving the car, and finally creatively design with a 3D modeling software called "SolidWorks". In this project-based learning, their overall promotion can be anticipated. (3) The Pei Dao Middle School in Macau develops a telescope-themed STEAM course, in which students learn the types of lenses and imaging features. Together with the calculation and measurement of the focal length, diameter, thickness and magnification of the lens, students learn how to make a telescope through draft design, work piece fabrication and assembly, and testing. (4) Hong Kong Leshantang Yu Jinqing Middle School takes the fish and vegetable symbiosis system, a mutual symbiotic ecosystem of aquaculture combined with hydroponic cultivation, as the topic for students from the first to third grades. Students can experience the engineering design process by taking tasks like "making a simple water filter model", "making a fish and vegetable symbiosis mobile vehicle", etc. Implied by these courses, this paper took "Making Handmade Wood-burning Ceramic Cups" as an example to provide reference for the construction of STEAM courses with local characteristics by discussing its instructional design and implementation in detail.

2 Course Design

2.1 Course Introduction

Wood-burning, a ceramic firing craft using wood as fuel, is the oldest ceramic firing technique in China. It is quite difficult to burn a kiln, and the quality of wood-burning works depends on the control of clay, fire, firewood, and kiln. That is to say, the type of clay, the variety of wood, the time of firing, and the control of temperature all affect the final product. This is a typical case that tiny changes make a huge difference, which serves as an entry point for students to explore. Therefore, the wood burning craft is very suitable for the topic of a STEAM course.

The goals of this STEAM course are: (1) Through experiential learning and exploration, students will learn about the environment, process, factors affecting the firing effect, together with its history and culture. (2) By visiting Foshan Nanfeng ancient stove as a field trip, students will learn how to test the temperature and understand the chemical changes of the clay under high temperature. (3) By exploring the influencing factors of pottery firing through experiments, students will master the solution and gain the ability to make a test. (4) Students are supposed to design and make a wood-burning plan, tune the temperature and position of the wood burning according to the test results, and make a personalized hand-cranked ceramic cup. (5) Students will learn how to showcase their works and exchange ideas with their partners.

The segmentation of its teaching objectives under the framework of STEAM is shown in Table 1.

In this paper, the term "S/T/E/A/M Knowledge" is used to represent Scientific Knowledge, Technical Knowledge, Engineering Knowledge, Artistic Knowledge and Mathematical Knowledge mentioned in the first column of Table 1, while "S/T/E/A/M Ability" is used to represent those abilities shown in the same column.

Table 1. Segmentation of the teaching objectives of "Making Handmade Wood-burning Ceramic Cups".

Dimension	Teaching objectives
Scientific knowledge and the ability to use scientific methods (S)	Students should learn: (1) the history, principle and process of wood-burning; (2) the composition of clay and its material changes at different temperatures; (3) dragon kiln size and structure; (4) how to use temperature-measuring tool; (5) the simulation experiment of pottery firing explosion; (6) the formation process and principle of the three elements of pottery and glaze
Technical knowledge and the ability to make with technology (T)	Students should learn or gain: (1) the ability to look up and make records; (2) how to use temperature-measuring cone; (3) the hand making procedure of ceramic cups; (4) the selection and application of survey methods
Engineering knowledge and design (E)	Students should learn: (1) to draw a dragon kiln structure diagram and identify its components; (2) to make a temperature measurement plan; (4) to make prototype test and modification; (5) to design wood-burning schedule; (6) to do product finalization
Artistic knowledge and the ability to describe in art (A)	Students should learn: (1) to evaluate different wood burning works; (2) to design visually the shape and function for ceramic cups; (3) to redesign according to the products investigated within the field trip
Mathematical knowledge and the ability to model in math (M)	Students should learn: (1) to measure, record and compare experimental data related to temperature, time and size; (2) the data representation for ceramic cups; (3) group coding for ceramic cups

2.2 Procedures and Activities

The instructional design of this course mainly consists of the following five procedures: Scenario Entering and Questions Raising, Scientific Inquiry and Mathematical Application, Engineering Design and Technical Making, Knowledge Expansion and Creative Design, and Multi-evaluation and Learning Reflection. For our STEAM course, the authors designed 14 teaching activities to specify these five procedures, as well as pertinent learning resources, student worksheets, and evaluation forms. These activities are shown in Table 2.

Table 2. Teaching activities of the course.

Activities	Description
Project introduction	Students learn about ceramics, wood burning history, and various firing methods of pottery in various ways (e.g. reading materials, watching videos, science resources, etc.), and reconstruct their knowledge structure through discussion

(*continued*)

Table 2. (*continued*)

Activities	Description
Scientific inquiry I	After on-site investigation of Nanfeng ancient stove in Foshan City, students are required to draw and mark the structure and size of the dragon kiln through measurement
Scientific inquiry II	Students are encouraged to find out the main components of pottery and its making procedure, mark down any temperature changes during the ceramic firing process, and explore possible effects caused by different wood burning temperatures
Technical making I	To design and make simple test cups
Mathematical practice	To learn the principle and usage of the temperature-measuring cone through some mathematical task, and compare the range of commonly used temperature-measuring tools
Thematic practice I	Students use the temperature-measuring cone to measure the temperature of different places in the dragon kiln and calculate the time required for firing, and further test the firing effect of the pottery in each place of the dragon kiln according to the results
Scientific inquiry III	To explore the influencing factors of a successful ceramic firing
Thematic practice II	To find the reason of explosion in the process of pottery firing by using existing tools to conduct experiments on ceramic balls and balloons
Engineering planning	To make a detailed work plan for hand-making ceramic cups
Technical making II	To modify the prototype according to the experimental results of the test cup, and make creative improvements
Thematic practice III	To knead the ceramic cup according to the draft, adjust the plan according to the actual measuring data, and then fire the ceramic cup
Knowledge expansion	To understand the three elements of pottery (mud, glaze, and fire), and the formation process and principle of glaze
Social connection	To investigate other kilning ways from nearby factories, and to learn how to identify and appreciate the handmade products of wood burning in other burning ways
Discussion and sharing	To show their own wood burning works and exchange opinions on the firewood culture

Each of these 14 teaching activities links with the above five procedures as follows:

Scenario Entering and Questions Raising. Project Introduction;
Scientific Inquiry and Mathematical Application. Scientific Inquiry I\II\III, Mathematical Practice;
Engineering Design and Technical Making. Technical Making I\II, Engineering Planning, Thematic Practice I\II\III;
Knowledge Expansion and Creative Design. Technical Making II, Knowledge Expansion, Social Connection;
Multi-evaluation and Learning Reflection. Discussion and Sharing.

In the following, one of the teaching activities (Thematic Practice I) is selected for the detailed presentation of the instructional design in Sect. 2.3, and the teaching effect of the course is analyzed to verify its feasibility and effectiveness in Sect. 3.

2.3 Instructional Design of Thematic Practice I as a Case

As is mentioned above, procedure "Engineering Design and Technical Making" includes one Engineering Planning activity, two Technical Making activities and three Thematic Practice activities. In the engineering design process, students firstly optimize the firewood plan and design draft, then select materials or components, and finally make and test the firewood ceramic cup model by solving the problems discovered in the previous learning process of scientific inquiry and technical making. In addition, students are required to record the whole inquiry and practice process, and share opinions with each other.

Again, the following is the decomposition of the teaching goals of this case under STEAM framework: (1) S (see Table 1 for abbreviations): According to the planning steps, students carry out the temperature-measuring experiment to measure the temperature of different places in the dragon kiln and calculate the time required for firing, and further test the firing effect of the pottery in each place of the dragon kiln. (2) T: Students learn to choose tools, components and methods. (3) E: Students complete the engineering steps in a planned manner: temperature measuring, time calculation, firing trial and prototype testing. (4) A: Students summarize the artistic effect by organizing their products together and discussing possible shapes in groups to share with others. (5) M: Students record the temperature variation of different places in the dragon kiln and calculate the time required for firing.

Here is the instructional design of Thematic Practice I:

(1) The focus is to test the temperature, time and effect difference between wood burning and electric kiln firing on pottery.
(2) Key knowledge of this practice is the different firing effects of pottery at various places in a dragon kiln.
(3) Teaching activities (90 min) include:

- Guidance: In the last lesson, students have known about the temperature-measuring cone and how to use it. In this lesson, they are supposed to use it in practice.
- Preparation before class: Students review the table of "Models of different temperature-measuring cone and their softening points" and the instruction of "How to use the temperature-measuring cone".
- Testing the temperature-measuring cone: Students use the temperature-measuring cone to find out the highest temperature in the firewood kiln and electric kiln respectively (see Fig. 1 for illustration), and the temperature of each place in the dragon kiln; and then calculate the time required for firing. The test results should be marked down.
- Testing with test cups: Based on the above results, students test the firing effect of the pottery in each place of the dragon kiln with test cups (see Fig. 2 for

illustration), and mark down the temperature and effect on the worksheet (completeness, foaming, crack, whitening, gloss, etc.).

- Discussion and sharing: Students discuss and exchange opinions on the artistic characteristics of firewood ceramics in groups, and make a summary.

(4) Tools and equipment: Temperature-measuring cone, test cups, pen, and paper.
(5) Reading materials: The table of "Models of different temperature-measuring cone and their softening points" and the instruction of "How to use the temperature-measuring cone".
(6) Student worksheet: Designed for students to mark down the shape of the temperature-measuring cone in two kinds of kiln, compare their temperature and time difference, and summarize the artistic characteristics as well.
(7) PMIQ (Plus, Minus, Interest, Questions) Table: Students use the PMIQ Table to mark down what they learn, what they miss, what they are still interested in and questions remaining.

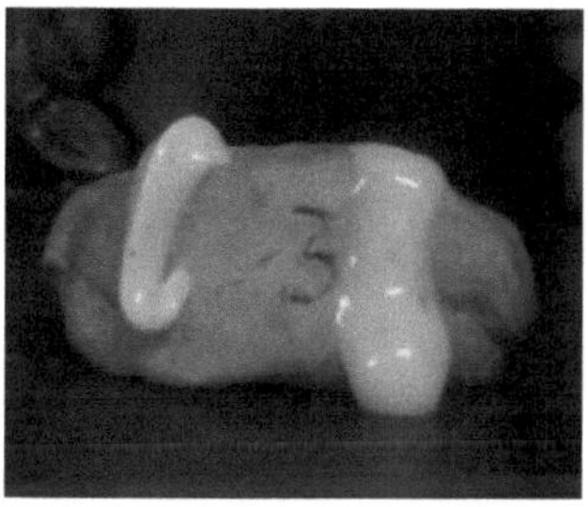

Fig. 1. Testing the temperature-measuring cone

Fig. 2. Testing with test cups

3 Methodology and Results

Participants and School Background. The participants were 40 students in the 7th grade from the 14th Middle School of Foshan City (divided into 8 groups). The response rate of complete and valid surveys was 100%. The school is the capital of ceramic art and has a strong cultural atmosphere. Wood-burning works can be seen everywhere, so it is not strange to these students. What's more, the school has a provincial ceramic demonstration base with pottery equipment and setting, which lays a good foundation for experiments.

Instrumentation. Pre-test and post-test questionnaires, teacher evaluation form, student self-assessment form and student worksheet were included as the instrumentation in our experiments. Specifically, (1) the questionnaires were adapted from [8] and [9]. The pre-test one consisted of 24 multiple-choice questions to investigate students' learning attitudes, teachers' teaching methods, students' learning effects, students' ability and STEAM literacy, while the post-test one added two open questions to check students' opinions on the relation between STEAM and the associated subjects. The pre-test questionnaire is shown in Table 3. (2) The teacher evaluation form was designed according to the characteristics and requirements of the STEAM course, and the needs of student learning were taken into account. The teacher evaluation form covered 14 activities mentioned above to comprehensively evaluate student's performance and work completion. The rates were divided into three levels: A, B and C. So the full score was 14As, where 13As or 14As were considered as Excellent. (3) The student self-assessment form was similar to the teacher evaluation form, but was filled out by students to make self-assessment with PMIQ form. (4) The student worksheet was a kind of teaching aid, where students filled in the blanks to test knowledge acquisition, make discussion notes, mark down experimental data, draw charts, and the like. That is to say, the students made a record for all they experienced on the worksheet, and their reflection as well. So that teacher or course leader could make assessment to check their learning effect. This course had totally 13 worksheets, with a score of 10 points each.

Table 3. Pre-test Questionnaire.

Components	Survey purpose	Item description
Learning attitude (Q1–Q4)	The influence and function of the instructional design on students' learning attitude	1. I like this course
		2. I usually like to watch books or videos about firewood
		3. I usually like to visit the ceramic museum, dragon kiln or ceramic exhibition
		4. I will explore independently when I have questions about firewood
Teaching methods (Q5–Q8)	Students' feeling of the changing of teaching methods	5. I identify teacher's teaching method as "learning and practice dominant"
		6. I like the teacher's teaching method
		7. I think the teaching method can improve the classroom efficiency
		8. I hope the teacher will continue to teach in this way
Learning result (Q9)	Students' self-cognitive changes in their own learning effects	9. I am active and earnest in class, and I've got productive learning results
Multidimensional ability (Q10–Q14)	The influence and function of the instructional design on students' collaborative learning ability, hands-on ability, verbal ability, problem solving ability and creativity	10. I like to cooperate with my classmates
		11. I like to make things by myself
		12. I would present my opinions in class

(*continued*)

Table 3. (*continued*)

Components	Survey purpose	Item description
		13. I'm good at solving problems I encounter
		14. I have a flexible mind in class and often break the routine to be creative
STEAM literacy and Ability (Q15–Q24)	The influence and role of the instructional design on students' mastery of S/T/E/A/M knowledge and S/T/E/A/M Ability	15. I've learned a lot by visiting the museum
		16. I can realize that the pottery explosion is caused by the heating difference between gas and solid
		17. I can make the ceramic cup according to the design
		18. I can use the temperature-measuring cone correctly
		19. I can draw a structure sketch of the dragon kiln and mark each part of it
		20. I can design a reasonable plan for explosion experiment
		21. I know how to identify and appreciate the wood-burning works
		22. I can design a creative and practical ceramic cup
		23. I can measure the size of the kiln as accurately as possible
		24. I can figure out the temperature change in firing pottery

Data Collection and Analysis Procedure. This study used action research method to conduct two rounds of experimental research. In the first round, we observed in the classroom and made records (how the students acted in the class). In the end, the pre-test was conducted, together with the assessment by teacher evaluation form, student self-assessment form and student worksheet. After that, we proposed strategies based on the analysis of the teaching effect of the first round to make improvement in the second round. Similarly, in the second round, we observed and made records, followed by the post-test and the assessment by those two forms and worksheet. Note that all responses were entered into Microsoft Excel for statistical analysis.

3.1 Analysis of the Questionnaire Results

Table 4 compares the questionnaire results to see the difference between the teaching effect of both rounds.

Table 4. Analysis of the Questionnaire Results.

Q	Pre-test	1st Post test	2nd Post test	Survey results
Q1	52.5%	75.0%	87.5%	To a certain extent, it has enhanced the students' learning interest, triggered their curiosity, and widened their access to knowledge. For example, the number of students who liked this course rose from 52.5% in pre-test to 87.5% in post-test (hereinafter the former percent refers to the result in pre-test and the latter refers to that in post-test). When confronting questions about firewood burning, the number of students who chose to ask for help (or decided to explore by himself/herself) rose from 12.5% (30%) to 20% (67.5%) respectively
Q2	20.0%	35.0%	50.0%	
Q3	47.5%	60.5%	65.0%	
Q4	30.0%	52.5%	67.5%	
Q5	5.0%	75.0%	90.0%	The change in teaching methods was recognized and appreciated by the students, and more than half of the students believed that the current teaching methods could improve the efficiency to a certain extent. For example, the number of students who identified teachers' teaching method as "learning and practice dominant" increased from 5% to 90%. At the end of the course, the number of students who liked the teaching method increased from 7.5% to 77.5%
Q6	7.5%	72.5%	77.5%	
Q7	12.5%	65.0%	67.5%	
Q8	5.0%	75.0%	80.0%	
Q9	45.0%	67.5%	77.5%	To a certain extent, it stimulated students' interest and formed an active classroom atmosphere. For example, the number of students who followed the course carefully through to the end and performed actively grew from 45% to 77.5%, and the number of students who could hardly complete the course reduced from 12.5% to 0
Q10	42.5%	65.0%	77.5%	To a certain extent, it helped the students expand ways to acquire knowledge, and cultivate students' collaborative learning ability, hands-on ability, verbal ability, problem solving ability and creativity. The number of students who liked to work with their classmates, make things on their own, make presentation in class, and solve complex problems increased steadily
Q11	12.5%	42.5%	55.5%	
Q12	37.5%	57.5%	62.5%	
Q13	7.5%	10.0%	15.0%	
Q14	22.5%	25.0%	25.0%	
Q15	0.0%	17.5%	25.%	(1) The students ability to apply scientific knowledge and methods was improved. For example, 95% of the students attained knowledge by visiting museums, and 100% realized that the blow-up of a pottery was caused by the heating difference between gas and solid (2) The students gained technical knowledge and the ability to make things with technology (selecting materials, tools, methods, etc.). For example, the number of students who could complete the handmade ceramic cup according to the draft increased from 40% to 87.5% (3) The students gained engineering knowledge and the ability to conduct engineering design. For example, both the number of students who could draw a brief structural sketch of the Shiwan Dagon Kiln and identify each part of it and that of students who could make a feasible experiment plan increased from 0% to 95% (4) The students' artistic appreciation, creation and the ability to describe in art were improved. For example, the number of students who knew how to identify and appreciate firewood burning works increased from 2.5% to 75%; and the number of students who could design creative and practical ceramic cups increased from 40% to 70% (5) The students' ability to calculate, measure, and perform mathematical modeling were improved. For example, the number of students who could accurately measure the size of the kiln rose from 32.5% to 65%; and the number of students who could use digits to describe the temperature change of the fired ceramic rose from 0% to 95%
Q16	2.5%	12.5%	15.0%	
Q17	7.5%	25.0%	27.5%	
Q18	0.0%	15.0%	15.0%	
Q19	0.0%	20.0%	22.5%	
Q20	0.0%	32.5%	32.5%	
Q21	0.0%	7.5%	10.0%	
Q22	2.5%	10.0%	15.0%	
Q23	32.5%	50.0%	62.5%	
Q24	0.0%	25.0%	25.0%	

3.2 Analysis of the Teacher Evaluation Form

After each round, the teacher used the teacher evaluation form to rate the students. The excellent rate of the first round was 55%, while in the second round it reached 75%. Among them, the number of students who achieved full mark increased significantly. It can be seen that the second round saw a certain degree of improvement over the first round. That is to say, the teachers gave higher praise for students' classroom performance, task completion and worksheet quality in each procedure, indicating that this instructional design helped to improve students' academic performance and cultivate various abilities.

3.3 Analysis of the Student Self-evaluation Form

Results showed that the excellent rate of the first round was 42.5%, while in the second round it reached 65%. It can be seen that the students' scores on their classroom performance, task completion and worksheet quality were improved to a certain extent in each procedure, indicating that they had more rigorous self-requirements and accepted their own learning outcomes and performance.

3.4 Analysis of the Student Worksheet Results

According to the analysis of the students' worksheets collected in the first round, students generally performed well. The students scored high in the sections of "Basic Knowledge", "Terminology Analysis", "Data Recording", "Site Investigation", "Design and Making", but relatively low in the sections of "Measurement", "Design and Implementation of the Simulation " and "Visiting Pottery Studio". For instance, when measuring the structure and size of the dragon kiln, the students were not well organized due to unclear task allocation. When visiting the pottery studio, they felt a little bit awkward due to lack of mastery of interview skills.

In the second round of teaching and learning, we made targeted improvements to avoid reoccurrence of the above problems. Therefore, compared with the scores of the first round, statistical analysis showed that the scores of the second round were higher. Besides mastering basic knowledge, the students improved a lot in many aspects, including collaborative learning ability, hands-on ability, problem solving ability and creativity. In a nutshell, after two rounds of teaching practice, the students benefited a lot by attending this course.

4 Conclusion

In conclusion, through the analysis of questionnaires, teacher evaluation form, student self-evaluation form and student worksheets, the teaching practice of our STEAM course named "Making Handmade Wood-burning Ceramic Cups" positively promoted the students' learning attitude, enhanced their acceptance of teachers' teaching methods and improved their learning effects. Moreover, the students' abilities were enhanced significantly, including collaborative learning ability, hands-on ability, verbal ability, problem solving ability, and creativity. And it had a good effect on the cultivation and improvement of STEAM literacy and ability as well. As few researches have been done on the instructional design of STEAM courses, this paper proposed the instructional design and practice of a STEAM course in primary school, aiming at providing reference for the construction of STEAM courses with local characteristics.

Acknowledgments. This work was supported by "Entrusted Project by the Policy and Regulation Department of the Ministry of Education of China" under grant Jybzfs2018115.

References

1. Li, K.D., Li, Y.: Integration of STEM education and interdisciplinary curriculum. J. Educ. Inf. Technol. **10**, 3–10 (2017). in Chinese
2. Brown, J.: The current status of STEM education research. J. Stem Educ. Innovations Res. **13**, 7–11 (2012)
3. Shi, Y.X., Qiao, A.L.: A survey of domestic STEM education research based on content analysis. J. China Educ. Technol. Equip. **16**, 16–19 (2017). in Chinese
4. Notice of the Ministry of Education on Printing and Distributing the Guideline for Comprehensive Practical Activity Courses in Primary and Secondary Schools. http://www.gov.cn/xinwen/2017-10/30/content_5235316.htm
5. Sanders, M.E.: STEM, STEM education, STEMmania. Technol. Teacher **68**(4), 20–26 (2008)
6. Xie, Q.: A brief talk on the integration of STEAM education and comprehensive practice activities. J. ChengCai. **6**, 5–7 (2016). in Chinese
7. Qian, X.Q., Lu, L.F.: Exploration of STEAM course based on meteorological research. J. Chinese Teacher. **18**, 66–69 (2016, in Chinese)
8. Lamb, R.L., et al.: A computational modeling of student cognitive processes in science education. J. Comput. Educ. **79**(C), 116–125 (2014)
9. Hunterdoniger, T., Sydow, L.: A journey from STEM to STEAM: a middle school case study. J. Clear. House **89**(4–5), 1–8 (2016)

Diagnostic Evaluation of MOOCs Based on Learner Reviews: The Analytic Hierarchy Process (AHP) Approach

Yanjiao Nie and Heng Luo(✉)

School of Educational Information Technology,
Central China Normal University, Wuhan 430079, China
luoheng@mail.ccnu.edu.cn

Abstract. The evaluation of MOOCs (massive open online courses) is needed to improve their design quality and to inform learners regarding course selection. In this paper, we proposed and validated an Analytic Hierarchy Process (AHP) Approach based on standardized rubric, expert feedback, data mining and emotion detection to systematically and diagnostically evaluate the quality of MOOCs. Using this approach, we analyzed review comments of three popular MOOCs on the Coursera Platform. The results indicate that the AHP approach is a feasible MOOC evaluation method that can provide accurate ratings as well as in-depth analysis of course design and learning outcomes. It is concluded that this new approach can supplement the existing user rating system with automated formative and summative evaluations.

Keywords: MOOCs · Quality assurance · Learners' comments · Diagnostic evaluations

1 Introduction

Massive Open Online Courses (MOOCs) are a new form of online instruction that is transforming and reshaping the landscape of higher education [1]. Since 2008, numerous MOOCs have been offered by high-profile universities to global learners on platforms such as Coursera, edX, and Udacity. These courses serve as an outlet for worldwide university outreach by making education accessible to the general public [2], and thus are expected to promote life-long learning beyond the brick-and-mortar educational contexts [3]. However, the rapid proliferation of MOOCs also raised concerns regarding their quality. For instance, Margaryan et al. [4] systematically analyzed the instructional design of 76 MOOCs and found that "although most MOOCs are well-packaged, their instructional design quality is low" (p. 77). The poor completion rates and critical reviews indicate potential issues in MOOC design and implementation and highlight the need for more accurate and meaningful evaluation of MOOCs [5].

There are three major approaches for evaluating the quality of MOOCs: expert-based approach, standardized approach, and learner-rating approach, albeit each is limited in certain aspects. Expert-based approach has subject-matter experts (SMEs) and instructional design (ID) professionals work together to thoroughly examine a MOOC and offer

S. K. S. Cheung et al. (Eds.): ICBL 2019, LNCS 11546, pp. 289–299, 2019.
https://doi.org/10.1007/978-3-030-21562-0_24

summative and formative feedback, but can be highly costly and time-consuming [6]. Standardized approach utilizes well-established rubrics such as Quality Matters (QM) or Quality Assurance (QA) as the evaluating criteria [7, 8], but the actual experiences of learners are often overlooked and dismissed. Learner-rating approach values the voices of MOOC learners, but the user ratings are summative and over-simplified [9], failing to identify key reasons behind the success or failure of the MOOC in evaluation. The absence of evaluation approach that is comprehensive, sophisticated, accurate, and easy-to-use hampers learners from making informed decisions regarding MOOC selection, and makes it difficult to prescribe formative modifications to the existing MOOCs.

To address this research need, this study proposes a MOOC evaluation approach informed by the Analytic Hierarchy Process (AHP), which integrates expert opinions, standardized rubrics, and learner feedback into the evaluation algorithm. The AHP approach is guided by the theoretical assumptions of course design and is based on the mining of learner reviews. By evaluating three selected MOOCs on the Coursera platform, this study seeks to validate the overall accuracy, diagnostic utility, and usability of the proposed AHP approach. More specifically, the following questions guided our research design:

1. What are the primary and secondary criteria for MOOC evaluation? How should they be weighted in the AHP approach?
2. How are those indicators commented in learner reviews? What are the emerging patterns of learner comments?
3. How accurate is the AHP approach in terms of overall course rating and problem diagnosis?

2 Literature Review

2.1 Principles and Standards of Quality Online Instruction

Despite the difficulty to conceptualize the term quality for online instruction, many researchers and organizations have prescribed principles and standards to assure the quality of online programs and courses. For example, Margaryan et al. [4] applied and tested a 10-principle framework for MOOC evaluation, and argued that well-designed MOOCs should be problem-centered, enable activation of existing experience, allow demonstration and application, promote knowledge integration and transfer, encourage collected knowledge and collaborative learning, support diverse learning needs, and support expert feedback. Many academic institutions and organizations have specified standards for quality online courses. Take the international organization of Quality Matters (QM) for example, it proposed and validated a course review rubric with 8 standards regarding course overview and introduction, learning objectives, assessment and measurement, instructional materials, learning activities and learner interaction, course technology, learner support, accessibility, and usability [8]. The Pennsylvania State University (PSU) expanded the list of standards to include course navigation, syllabus, instructor availability, and student input into the review rubric for PSU online courses [10]. Similar quality assurance processes can be seen in universities and colleges around the globe [11].

2.2 Analytic Hierarchy Process (AHP)

AHP is a structured decision-making technique developed by Professor Saaty of University of Pittsburgh in the 1970s. Users of AHP break a problem down and then aggregate the solutions of all sub-problems into a conclusion. The key is to establish a hierarchical analysis model composed of three layers (i.e., objective layer, criteria layer, and alternatives layer), and then determine the relative weight of each criterion by constructing a consistency judgment matrix. Rather than comparing all elements at once, AHP makes prioritizing judgements by conducting a series of pairwise comparison of elements at lower-level. Using the 1–9 scale, each judgement seeks to answer two questions: "which of the two elements is more important with respect to a higher-level criterion, and how strongly" [12] (pp. 82–83). AHP then synthesizes the judgements to calculate the overall priorities of the elements in the hierarchy. AHP has been widely used in the field of education quality assessment. Researchers have applied it to e-learning system assessment to make decisions regarding the best IT tools for students and determine adult learning preferences [13, 14]. However, applications of AHP in MOOC quality evaluation are still lacking in the literature.

3 Specifics of the AHP Approach for MOOC Evaluation

3.1 Evaluation Index

Selection of evaluation index is particularly important for the design of MOOC evaluation system. We modified QM rubric for online course evaluation to include a few standards offered by Quality Assurance rubric for PSU online courses. Since learning outcomes are a vital dimension in quality assurance of open education [15], we also added *acquisition of knowledge and skills* and *acquisition of learning method* in to our evaluation and finally concluded the following MOOC evaluation system (Table 1). In this system, we have identified 9 secondary indicators, and classified them into 4 main dimensions of *course planning*, *course content*, *instructional process* and *learning outcomes*.

Table 1. MOOC evaluation system and its indicators

Primary indicators	Secondary indicators	Evaluation criteria
B1. Course planning	B11. Course overview and introduction	Whether to have clear teaching target, course program
	B12. Accessibility and usability	Whether the course is free or not
B2. Course content	B21. Content organization	Arrangement of teaching time, course content, learning objectives are reasonable
	B22. Learner support	The usability of course technology, the rationality and richness of teaching resources and materials
	B23. Learning media	The sound is clear, the video is clear and fluent, and the subtitles are correct

(continued)

Table 1. (*continued*)

Primary indicators	Secondary indicators	Evaluation criteria
B3. Instructional process	B31. Teaching method	Whether the teacher's teaching style is accepted by learners
	B32. Course activities	Reasonable arrangement of course activities (including exercises, tests and assessment etc.)
B4. Learning outcomes	B41. Acquisition of knowledge and skills	Whether learners can acquire knowledge from the course instruction
	B42. Acquisition of learning method	Whether learners can learn from the course to solve problems and acquire learning methods

3.2 Weight Assignment by AHP

Combined with experts' judgment on the relative importance of impact factors, this study uses Analytic Hierarchy Process (AHP) to calculate the weight of each indicator on the basis of the MOOC evaluation system we have developed. The process of using AHP to determine the weight for each indicator is shown below (Fig. 1).

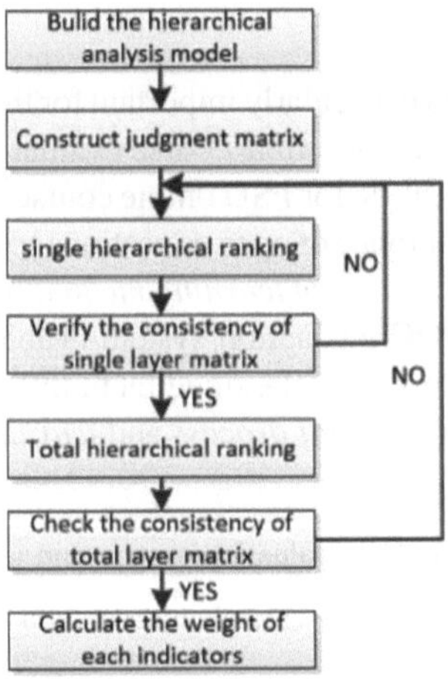

Fig. 1. The process of using AHP to determine the weight of indicators for the evaluation system

This process can be divided into three phases: (1) First of all, a hierarchical analysis model consisting of objective layer, criteria layer, and alternatives layer should be built to determine the hierarchical relationships. (2) Judgment matrix is constructed based on the experts' judgment on the relative importance of each primary indicator in 1–9 scale method. Single hierarchical ranking is to calculate the relative importance of the child elements relative to the previous element by normalizing the maximum eigenvalue and eigenvector of the numerical judgment matrix. The purpose of total hierarchical ranking is also to calculate the weight of relative importance of elements and the method is the same. The only difference between is that the single hierarchical ranking only calculates the weight of the child elements relative to the previous element, while the total hierarchical ranking needs to calculate the relative weight of all elements to objective layer and it proceeds down from the objective layer. (3) Consistency of single layer and total layer matrices are checked to ensure the degree of inconsistency is limited to the allowable range. By means of consistency checking, it can solve the conflicts between objective measurement data and human subjective judgement [16]. When the consistency tests are passed, the weight of each indicator in AHP can be determined.

The problem of this study is to evaluate the quality of a MOOC course and we can break this problem into 4 sub-problems. Following the analytical process of AHP, this study used Yaahp10.1 to determine the weight of each indicator. Yaahp10.1 is a widely used software that can conveniently construct the hierarchical model and judgment matrix, and can automatically adjust the consistency of the judgment matrix. Firstly, a hierarchical analysis model was built in Yaahp10.1 software according to the MOOC evaluation system we built. The objective, primary, and secondary indicators were listed in the objective layer, criteria layer, and alternatives layer in the hierarchical analysis model respectively. After this model was successfully constructed, a 9-point scale expert questionnaire designed by AHP were administered to seek expert's judgement on model hierarchy. In this study, we distributed questionnaires to five experts who are experienced in distance education and course design and evaluation to determine the relative weight of each indicator affecting the quality of MOOCs.

All collected questionnaires were later imported into Yaahp10.1 software to check the consistency of the constructed judgment matrix and automatically select the algorithm to adjust the matrix to meet the conditions. Finally, by using the group decision function of the software, the judgment matrix which had passed the consistency tests could be carried out. The arithmetic average operation by the calculating the aggregation of the results and the judgment weight of each indicator for the objective layer could be obtained (Fig. 2).

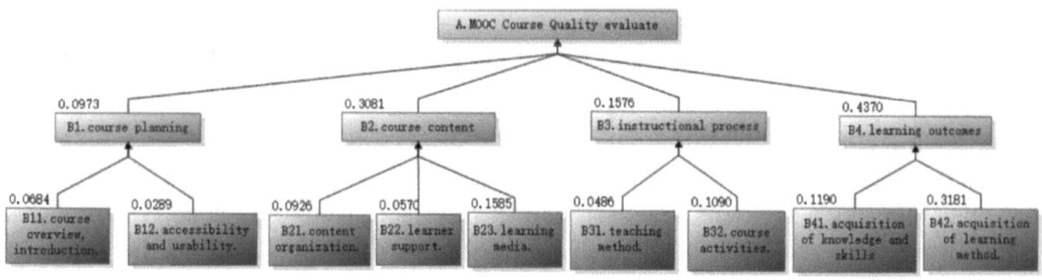

Fig. 2. Weight assigned to each indicator in the AHP approach

Table 2. Key words for positive and negative emotions towards each indicator

	Positive emotions	Negative emotions
B12. Accessibility	Free	Payment/pay/purchase/cost, not worth money
B21. Organization	Good/great/nice/excellent/amazing/informational/effective/easy/super/incrediable/wonderful/like/love/awesome, highly recommended, consequent, well designed/structured	Errors/mistakes/wrong/weak, too hard/easy/basic/simple, very hard/easy/basic, extremely hard/easy/basic, not good, too repetitive, incomplete, misrepresents, terrible, not friendly/professional, very/too slow
B22. Support	Illustrated with pictures, excellent course material, material is well done	Little/lack of/absence of/not give practice/example/materials
B23. Media	/	Audio/recording/video not work/no sound, no subtitles
B31. Method	Good/clearly/well explanation, enjoy the teacher, a nice way, remarkable/nice/great/interesting/encourage/lively/engaging/fabulous/teacher/tutor/instructor/professor	Not interesting/like/engaging, boring, monotonous, bad teacher/tutor/instructor/professor
B32. Activities	Great/good/excellent/well planned/practice/exercises/assignment	Without/little/few/not enough practice/exercises/assignment, tests/quizzes too simple/easy/hard
B41. Knowledge and skills	Useful/helpful/helped/beneficial/valuable, learn something/a lot, improved	Not helpful/valuable, not learn, learn anything/nothing

3.3 Emotion Detection of Learner Reviews

The primary data source is the texts of learner reviews towards MOOCs. In this study, we examined the learner reviews of 10 MOOCs on Coursera platform, and identified a list of key words as signifiers for positive and negative emotions towards each indicator. The words that learners often used in review comments are summarized in Table 2.

In addition to adjective words, we also paid attention to special sentence patterns in the comments. If a positive emotional word is preceded by "would be" or "could be", then this sentence expresses dissatisfaction. For example, a comment "it would be great if this course gives more exercises" indicates the course provided poor learning activities. However, these emotional expressions cannot all be listed, the variant forms of these words should also be taken into account when using these phrases to evaluate the quality of MOOCs.

For each learner review comment, it can be divided into different segments which can then be mapped to relevant indicators. We assigned "+1" if there were only positive emotions regarding a segment, and assigned "−1" if there were only negative emotions. If there were both positive and negative emotions, we assigned "0" to the segment. Then, plenty of tags would gather underneath each indicator: rating "1" means learner thinks this course is very good in this aspect, while "0" means it's good but not good enough to be specifically mentioned in review, and "−1" means the course still has some defects in this aspect.

4 Application of AHP Approach: Evaluating 3 Coursera MOOCs

We have selected three MOOCs (i.e., Learn Chinese, Grammar and Punctuation, Programing for Everybody) from different disciplines on Coursera platform, covering topics in language study, social sciences, and computer science respectively. Each MOOC has more than 1,000 review comments. The selected courses are denoted as MOOC A, MOOC B, and MOOC C respectively. The average learner ratings for these courses are 4.7, 4.6 and 4.8. When learners commented on a course, they also rated it using the five-star rating method. We can see from the course ratings that the quality of these courses is considered high with the number of high-rating comments greatly exceeding the low-rating comments. As a result, stratified sampling was utilized to extract a total of 303 learner comments from 1- to 5-star reviews for computing AHP scores in this study.

Emotion detection was conducted manually for exploratory purposes in this study on the selected learner comments. In order to diagnose MOOC design problems, we calculated the percentage of "+1" comment segments towards each indicator and use the percentage number as the unweighted rating score for the indicator. If there are no corresponding comment segments under a certain indicator, the indicator score is 0. For example, if the indicator *B23-learning media* has 100 related comment segments, 70% are positive, 30% are negative, then the unweighted rating score for B23 is 70. Finally, the weighted score can be obtained by summing each indicator score multiplied by the assigned judgment weight, as indicated in Fig. 1.

The results of weighted scores calculated by AHP for the three MOOCs are 29.47, 22.48 and 38.16, and the detailed scores for each indicator are shown in Fig. 3. The constitution of the AHP scores can reveal useful information regarding the shortcomings and strengths of the three MOOCs. Informed by the detailed AHP scores and learner review contents, We diagnosed the problems of the selected MOOCs as follows: MOOC A falls short in *course activities* and *learning media* because the exercise and test format is monotonous and the audio quality for lecture is poor. MOOC B performs poorly in *accessibility and usability* and *learner support*, since the it requires payment to complete the course and some support services are unavailable. MOOC C can further improve in areas of *course activities* and *learning media*. The main problems of this course are that the learning content and tasks are not completely consistent and subtitles are missing in the lecture videos. On the other hand, we can see that MOOC A does well in *content organization* and *acquisition of knowledge and skills* because of its good range of topics and content. MOOC B performs excellently in *teaching method* and *acquisition of knowledge and skills* because the instructor explains complex concepts in a systematic way and makes it easy to understand; learners are satisfied about what they have learned from the course. MOOC C is doing well in *teaching method*. The instructor makes this course enjoyable and uses the appropriate methods for developing knowledge and skills for the learners.

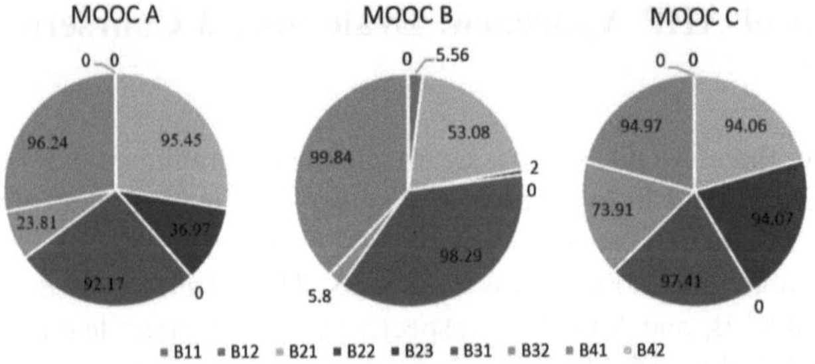

Notes: B11.course overview and introduction; B12.accessibility and usability; B21.content organization; B22.learner support; B23.learning media; B31.teaching method; B32.course activities; B41.acquisition of knowledge and skills; B42.acquisition of learning method.

Fig. 3. Detailed scores for each indicator for the three MOOCs.

To verify the overall accuracy of the weighted score, we invited an associate professor in instructional design to grade the three MOOCs and offer expert opinions. The maximum expert grading score for each course is 100 and the minimum is 0. The five-star learner ratings, AHP weighted scores, and expert ratings are converted to 0–1 standardized scores for comparison. As can be seen in Fig. 4, there is a general agreement between learner ratings and AHP scores, which rated MOOC C highest and MOOC B lowest in course quality. Interestingly, while the expert agrees on the high quality of MOOC C, he disagrees on the ranking of MOOC A and B.

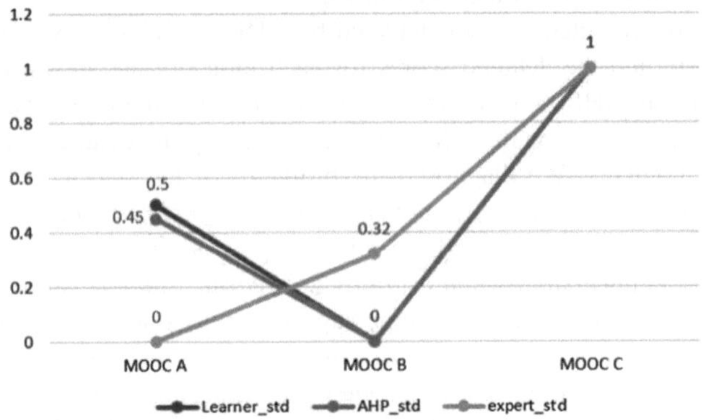

Fig. 4. Standardized scores from 3 approaches for MOOC A, B, and C

5 Discussion

5.1 Discussion for Research Question 1

The primary and secondary indicators for MOOC evaluation (Table 1) are identified, but the evaluation criteria are still subject to interpretation during the data mining process. The requirements for course quality are likely to change along with the needs of the society, and thus the indicators and assigned weights might still change for different courses. As seen in Fig. 2, the weight of each indicator is calculated based on expert opinions. While course content and learning outcomes are considered by the experts to be key factors of quality assurance, MOOC learners seemed to have different perspectives as they are mainly interested in course content rather than learning outcomes, evidenced in more review comments directed to the content indicator.

5.2 Discussion for Research Question 2

Learners' review comments are found to focus mostly on *content organization.*, but little on *course overview and introduction* and *acquisition of learning method.* This phenomenon indicates that learners may not value those criteria despite the presumed importance lauded by the experts. Considering the importance of learner experience in course evaluation, we suggest deleting the two indicators that learners do not value in order to further improve the accuracy and applicability MOOC evaluation.

From learner reviews, we also find that learners' comments on course difficulty are sometimes contradictory. One possible explanation for such contradiction is that MOOC learners are quite heterogeneous with varying educational background, prior knowledge, and motivations. According to Vygotsky's zone of proximal development theory, teaching will be more effective if MOOC difficulty can be adjusted for different student groups to ensure it is slightly beyond their current level [17]. Thus, MOOC instructors and designers should consider the levels of potential learners and divide courses into different difficulty tracks to provide individualized learning experience with the optimal difficulty.

5.3 Discussion for Research Question 3

Though the standard scores of three courses obtained by learner rating, AHP score and expert rating (Fig. 3), AHP approach is in general consistent with learner rating and expert, indicating its accuracy. The only prime difference is that expert gave higher rating to MOOC B, in contrast to AHP score and learner rating. Take MOOC B for example, as seen in Fig. 5, the biggest discrepancies lie in *B11-course overview and introduction*, *B12-accessibility and usability*, *B22-learner support*, *B23-learning media*, *B32-course activities* and *B42-acquisition of learning method.* In AHP approach, *B11-course overview and introduction* and *B42-acquisition of learning method* received zero rating because there are no review comments relevant to those indicators. *B12-Accessibility and usability* received poor rating from learners because MOOC requires payment to complete the course instruction. Because several course facilitators and assistant volunteered in MOOC B, the expert gave high score to *B22-learner support.* However, learners cared more about the experiences related to learner support services. Some support services were linked to external sites and were not easy to access. Learner dissatisfactions were mainly due to the broken links and inaccessible applications. Regarding *B23-learning media*, learners commented this course had poor visual communications and suggest adding some animations. The indicator of *B32-course activities* gained a high rating from the expert because the expert thought that activities were well designed, but learners seemed to have poor experience participating in course exercises.

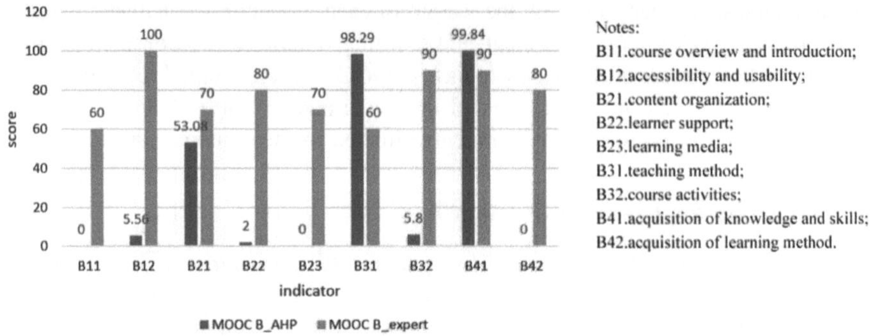

Fig. 5. Detailed scores of MOOC B generated by AHP and the expert

6 Conclusion

In this study, we proposed a MOOC evaluation approach informed by AHP and explored its accuracy, diagnostic utility, and usability with empirical evidence collected from three Coursera MOOCs. Compared to the five-star learner rating system and expert rating, this approach is more feasible and less costly, and still draws upon the input from experts, learner experience, and standardized evaluation rubric. The results of the AHP approach provide reference for learners to choose MOOCs and can also detect the existing problems for future revision. Based on the empirical results, we suggest MOOC instructors and designers should divide MOOCs into different tracks with varying difficulty levels and guide learners to select the track for optimal difficulty. In order to improve the accuracy of AHP approach, we suggest deleting two indicators (i.e., *course overview and introduction* and *acquisition of learning method*) in the evaluation system and recalculate the weights of the remaining indicators using AHP in future research.

There are still some limitations in this study. Firstly, for explorative purposes, we only selected a small portion of the comments for manual analysis in this study. In future research, we can utilize computer programs to automatize text mining and emotional detection processes so that more courses with complete review comments can be analyzed for validation and comparison of the AHP scores. However, through manual analysis of learner comments, we managed to identify a list of key words for positive and negative emotion detection, which lays a foundation for program writing in the future. Another limit is that there are some indicators receiving no corresponding reviews, indicating problems of indicator selection for the AHP approach. The results of this study can inform the future revision of the evaluation index with addition, deletion, and modification of indicators.

Acknowledgment. This study has been supported by the self-determined research funds of Central China Normal University from the colleges' basic research and operation of MOE (CCNU19TD023) and the Basic Research Funding Grant of Central China Normal University (CCNU18QN023).

References

1. Waldrop, M.: Campus 2.0. Nature **495**(7440), 160–163 (2013)
2. Rhoads, R.A., Camacho, M.S., Toven-Lindsey, B., Lozano, J.B.: The massive open online course movement, xMOOCs, and faculty labor. Rev. High. Educ. **38**(3), 397–424 (2015)
3. Shapiro, H.B., Lee, C.H., Roth, N.E., Li, K., Çetinkaya-Rundel, M., Canelas, D.A.: Understanding the massive open online course (MOOC) student experience: an examination of attitudes, motivations, and barriers. Comput. Educ. **110**, 35–50 (2017)
4. Margaryan, A., Bianco, M., Littlejohn, A.: Instructional quality of massive open online courses (MOOCs). Comput. Educ. **80**, 77–83 (2015)
5. Pursel, B.K., Zhang, L., Jablokow, K.W., Choi, G.W., Velegol, D.: Understanding MOOC students: motivations and behaviours indicative of MOOC completion. J. Comput. Assist. Learn. **32**(3), 202–217 (2016)
6. Dick, W., Carey, C.: The Systematic Design of Instruction, 4th edn. Longman, New York (1996)
7. Parscal, T., Riemer, D.: Assuring quality in large-scale online course development. Online J. Distance Learn. Adm. **13**(2), 7 (2010)
8. Wright, R.: Quality matters. Distance Learn. **15**(3), 41–49 (1978)
9. Gillmore, G.M., Kane, M.T., Naccarato, R.W.: The generalizability of student ratings of instruction: estimation of the teacher and course components. J. Educ. Meas. **15**(1), 1–13 (1978)
10. Penn State Quality Assurance e-Learning Design Standards. https://weblearning.psu.edu/resources/penn-state-online-resources/penn-state-quality-assurance-e-learning-design-standards/. Accessed 16 Feb 2019
11. Chua, A., Lam, W.: Quality assurance in online education: the universitas 21 global approach. Br. J. Edu. Technol. **38**(1), 133–152 (2010)
12. Saaty, T.L.: How to make a decision: the analytic hierarchy process. Eur. J. Oper. Res. **24**(6), 19–43 (1994)
13. Lin, T.C., Ho, H.P., Chang, C.T.: Evaluation model for applying an e-learning system in a course: an analytic hierarchy process-multi-choice goal programming approach. J. Educ. Comput. Res. **50**(1), 135–157 (2014)
14. Lee, D., Mccool, J., Napieralski, L.: Assessing adult learning preferences using the analytic hierarchy process. Int. J. Lifelong Educ. **19**(6), 548–560 (2000)
15. Stracke, C.M.: The quality of MOOCs: how to improve the design of open education and online courses for learners? In: Zaphiris, P., Ioannou, A. (eds.) Learning and Collaboration Technologies. Novel Learning Ecosystems, LCT 2017. LNCS, vol. 10295, pp. 285–293. Springer, Cham (2017). https://doi.org/10.1007/978-3-319-58509-3_23
16. Saaty, T.L., Vargas, L.G.: Models, Methods, Concepts & Applications of the Analytic Hierarchy Process. Springer, Boston (2001). https://doi.org/10.1007/978-1-4615-1665-1
17. Wass, R., Golding, C.: Sharpening a tool for teaching: the zone of proximal development. Teach. High. Educ. **19**(6), 671–684 (2014)

Pedagogical and Psychological Issues

Use of Fitness Trackers in Fitness Running Classes to Enhance Students' Motivation

David Chaloupský, Dagmar Hrušová(✉), and Pavlína Chaloupská

University of Hradec Králové,
Rokitanského 62, 500 03 Hradec Králové, Czech Republic
{david.chaloupsky, dagmar.hrusova,
pavlina.chaloupska}@uhk.cz

Abstract. The aim of the research was to examine the possibilities of use of fitness tracking applications in smartphones, for students to enhance their motivation to run, and for teachers to coach, monitor and evaluate the training process and its outcomes. The core of the study was to design and implement a model of fitness tracker-supported running classes. A two-year survey among university students (n = 133) was carried out to analyse and evaluate the usability and possible benefits of the applied blended learning methods. The number of students who passed the assignment criteria of fitness running increased and the percentage of drop-outs decreased in the experimental group. The results indicated enhanced motivation of students to enroll and participate in fitness running. The highest rated formal benefit of the designed model of fitness tracker-supported running was found in individual choice of time and place.

Keywords: Physical activity · Motivation · Education · Running · Fitness tracker

1 Introduction

Regular physical activity helps develop health-oriented physical fitness, focused on harmonious motor development and positive motion experiencing. A current trend in the field of leisure physical activity emphasizes sport activities that combine positive and meaningful experiences, proving one's own physical and mental strength, and satisfaction of performance. A need to bring students to regular physical activity [1–5], is a current topic under discussion not only at the Czech universities. In wider context it is recommended [1] that college administrators, clinicians and public health education promoters should collaborate in motivating students to offer and accept modules relating to sustainable lifetime physical fitness and wellness for a healthy lifestyle. Physical activity classes or course, occur in study curriculum both as compulsory and optional subjects. However, quite a high percentage of students might not participate in physical activity (PA) lessons, despite a wide range of various sports activities offered within optional physical education. Such an example can be seen at the Faculty of Informatics and Management, University of Hradec Králové (FIM UHK) in the Czech Republic. Physical activity is included in the curriculum at FIM UHK as an optional subject. The attendance of all the physical activity lessons (including various fitness activities, sport games, outdoor sports and courses) is around 600 students each

S. K. S. Cheung et al. (Eds.): ICBL 2019, LNCS 11546, pp. 303–315, 2019.
https://doi.org/10.1007/978-3-030-21562-0_25

semester, which may seem quite a lot, but relatively, this figure represents only about 35% of the total number of all the students at the faculty.

When analyzing physical activity classes and their attendance at FIM UHK, it was found out that in classes with low attendance, such as fitness running, the greatest obstacle was in time availability of individual lessons and its time overlapping with other subjects. This study deals with the problem of how to enhance students' motivation and participation in physical activity on the example of fitness running. Searching for a possible solution an innovation of fitness running was suggested by means of blended learning methods through external motivation in external resources of technical support and feedback. Using wearables has become a modern way of runner's self-regulatory support [5]. Fitness trackers and fitness apps are seen as modern wearables to technically support runners by providing quantified information about their exercise behavior via an online data analysis platform [6]. FIM UHK has been involved in the design and implementation of e-courses for more than twenty years and developed an international reputation [7]. Both students and teachers are familiar with working in virtual platforms as their daily routine at school, which provided a friendly environment for the research.

2 Theoretical Framework

Running has been popular in recent years and participation in distance running has grown [8, 9]. An increase in people engaged in fitness running can be seen in the Czech Republic, in the case of Hradec Králové [10]. Running provides an opportunity for personal development, not only in terms of physical, but also psychological and social aspects. Runners are characterized by performance [11] in a recreational level (beginner amateurs), a level of performance (advanced amateurs), or a top level (professionals). Within the given categories, the student runners who participated in the research belonged to the category of amateur runners. The subject of the research is referred to as the physical activity (PA) subject of fitness running, or simply fitness running. Running can be recommended as a leisure time sport activity to wide public not only for its physical health benefits, but as a means to enhance quality of life through positive experience [12], like other fitness activities [13]. Feelings of happiness can be induced by experiencing the present moment [14]. Optimal experience is described in the theory of "flow" [15].

2.1 Motivation to Run

The issue of motivation in sport has been addressed by a number of researches. Commonly used approach to study exercise motivation is based on a self-determination approach [16]. It is characterized by fulfilment of three basic needs: autonomy (to feel in control of one's behaviour), competence (to feel effective and successful in one's behaviour) and relatedness (to feel that one belongs to somewhere) [17]. Research into running motivation provides different perspectives on individual motivational categorization but basically they cover psychological, achievement, social and physical concerns. The main categories of running motivations are based on MOMS

(Motivations of Marathoners Scales) [18] and contain the following subcategories: weight concerns and general health orientation (physical motivation), recognition and affiliation (social motivation), competition and personal goals achievement (achievement motivation) and life meaning, self-esteem and psychological coping (psychological motivation) [18]. In the investigation of the needs of amateur runners, main design themes were suggested in: festival, competition, practicalities, togetherness, and support [19]. Amateur runners are often being motivated through common extrinsic motivational factors such as health concerns or external reward system [19] e.g. a medal for every half marathon finisher. Running USA [20] reported the most consistent year-to-year themes in running motivators, which are examined annually in the 2017 National Runner Survey (n = 6800+). Among primary motivation to start running there were exercise (24%) and weight concerns (14%). Among primary motivation to continue running there was staying healthy (77%), staying in shape (73%), relieving stress (62%) and training for a race (62%). The findings indicate that each runner has his or her individual set of motivational factors needed to start and keep practicing physical activity regularly.

A lack of motivation can cause inconsistency. Runners often make various excuses and drop out within a few months. In supervised running programs the rate of drop out among beginner runners was studied and the reported percentage to quit was 50% within 6 months [21]. The percentage is reckoned to be even higher among the beginners of unsupervised programmes [18]. Drop out can occur more frequently in runners who tend to be more externally motivated when they do not feel enough external resources, such as social support or feedback on their behaviour [22]. Differences in running motivation between online fitness community users and non-users were studied [16]. Online fitness community users were more achievement-oriented. Their primary focus was on self-regulatory features, whilst social features, such as sharing on external social media platforms, were used less often. Concerning the importance of goal achievement in students' motivation to run, low task-oriented and low ego-oriented students were found to be at greater risk of lower motivation and lower performance level [4]. The findings can have an implication in physical education teaching. The level of competitiveness in PE is likely to promote ego orientation and the learning environments should be structured to adopt a high task orientation [4]. This can be supported by implementing a blended model in teaching physical activity while maintaining high standards of learning process [23].

2.2 Wearables and Fitness Data Analysis Platforms

Self-monitoring is an important part of a sport training and is needed for a runner to be able to make some progress [24]. According to National Runner Survey [20] 82% of runners like to have and track all of their running statistics, and 65% say it helps them train better. Recording, analyzing and monitoring of physical activity can be done via online social networks, or the so called online fitness communities [25]. Self-monitoring is a key element of self-regulation, especially in a short term running goal achievement.

The wearables provide quantified information about training that can be further visualised, analysed, summarized, saved or shared via a data analysis platform.

Wearable devices can be understood as a daily convenient device combined with multimedia, radio, sensor and other technologies [5]. Smart technologies worn or carried for running are represented by a smartphone, sports watch or a GPS item. Fitness tracking apps in smartphones tend to be used more often by younger recreational runners, compared to the use of sports watches [26].

Commercially available platforms have emerged that enable their users to upload data from various brands of wearables [16]. The records of fitness trackers are based on real-time GPS measures. There exist a wide range of free apps with different quality of functions and features. Commonly used fitness trackers aimed at running monitoring are for example Endomondo RunKeeper, Strava or Runtastic. During physical activity a fitness tracker displays quantified data about distance, duration, actual and average speed, actual and average pace, calories burnt and other. In history of records a user can display additional data for example about altitude, ascending and descending, splits in kilometers, basic or satellite maps. Concerning physical education, an application of wearables can contribute to the formation of students' profiles, from the group evaluation to individual evaluation, from summarized evaluation to formative education [5]. Therefore, it has a potential to effectively promote the educational process in PE classes.

3 Methods

3.1 The Aim

The aim of the research was to examine the possibilities of use of fitness trackers (FT) in mobile applications, for students to enhance their motivation in running, and for teachers to coach, monitor and evaluate the training process and its outcomes.

Fitness trackers, which belong to running activity wearables, can support the athletes in physical exercise by providing detailed and quantified records of their physical activity [6]. The core of the study was to design a model of FT-supported, teacher-coached running classes, which would substitute the traditional running lessons. The designed model was implemented and examined. A survey was carried out in two consecutive academic years (four semester, September 2016–August 2018) to analyse and evaluate the usability and possible benefits of the applied blended learning methods.

3.2 Research Sample

The basic sample comprised 179 students of the Faculty of Informatics and Management, University of Hradec Králové, who enrolled in the physical activity optional subject of fitness running and started their attendance in the period of September 2016 to August 2018. The period covered two academic years, four consecutive semesters. The students engaged in one of the following fields of study in Economics and management: Applied informatics, Information management, Financial management or Tourism management. The participants were included based on listing in the university electronic evidence system STAG. The research sample then included 133 participants

(89 men and 44 women, aged 19–23) who started the attendance and fulfilled all the assignment criteria of the subject of PA fitness running (introductory tutorial, consultation with the teacher to set individual goals and methods, FT-monitored running, weekly reports, final evaluation). Neither age nor gender differences were subject of the research, the above mentioned data are given only for descriptive purpose. All the participants can be simply referred to as university students. Major participant's characteristics were described in terms of a preceding running experience, performance level, track preference (city/nature) and motivation. 71% of students had been running before, with the most common frequency of once a weekly. 14% started running after they enrolled in the subject of fitness running. Most participants preferred to run in nature (76%). 82% of students indicated fitness running to be their most favorite sport within the range of all the offered PA classes at Faculty of Informatics and Management. As to the motivation for regular training, 66% were always looking forward to running, regardless of the weather and other external conditions. 19% were driven by the compulsory assignment to send their weekly reports to the teacher. Detailed motivations are provided further in the results of the questionnaire survey.

3.3 Data Collection, Procedures and Analysis

Main methods of data collection were content analysis and synthesis, testing, and inquiry. Data were proceeded by methods of both quantitative (descriptive statistics) and qualitative (comparison, assessment) analysis.

Quantitative data were collected for both control and experimental group in terms of fitness running attendance. The course participation and successful completion of credit assignments in the monitored period indicated a development in student motivation to engaged and continued participation between the experimental (September 2016–August 2018) and control (September 2014–August 2016) period.

An indicator of the student enhanced motivation was the development of attendance in the monitored period of September 2016–August 2018, concerning the number of students who enrolled to regular running lessons and passed the assignments of the subject of fitness running. The mentioned period was compared to a control period of September 2014–August 2016. The results from four semesters of traditional face-to-face fitness running classes were compared to four semesters with a blended learning model. The specific differences between course instructional model in the control and experimental group were in the use of wearable fitness monitoring devices and in the intervention of the teacher. In control group the lessons consisted of weekly traditional group organized face-to-face running trainings outdoors in the terrain. However, that was very demanding for the teacher as there were runners of different fitness or performance levels and the training efficiency was low. In experimental group the blended learning model was used, further also referred to as a model of FT-supported (fitness trackers), individualized, teacher-coached running classes. The lessons included introductory tutorial (a group session in the classroom with the teacher), individual introductory consultation with the teacher to set individual goals and methods, students' weekly running (individual trainings) with fitness tracker recording, students' sending weekly reports (email), final consultation with the teacher and final evaluation. The suggested benefit of this model is seen in an individualized approach to set and adjust the goals, training plan and training times to fit individual needs of every runner, either beginner or advanced.

For both experimental and control group there was the same coach all the time – an experienced PE teacher who has guaranteed outdoor physical activities, namely running, at FIM UHK for more than fifteen years.

Qualitative data were collected for the experimental group to search for motivational factors among the runners using wearable fitness monitoring devices and also to find out fitness tracker applicability. The main technique was a questionnaire, distributed to the participants personally as a part of the final evaluation of the monitored semesters. The main categories of running motivations correspond with MOMS [18] and contain items characterizing physical, psychological, achievement and social motivation (see chapter 4.5).

The collected data were evaluated in quantitative analysis by means of descriptive statistics (relative frequency) to get major characteristics. In addition, qualitative analysis was proceeded by the teacher to deeper understanding of students' motivation and individualized approach in running coaching.

4 Results

4.1 Fitness Tracker Data Analysis

The starting point of the research was to select a suitable fitness tracking app. Three teachers tested the apps of Endomondo, Runtastic, Runkeeper and Strava and agreed to select Endomondo to be applied in the model of fitness tracker-based running classes. The teachers defined and tested key requirements, which were best met in Endomondo. The most useful functions and features are described as follows. The app is free and multiplatform, thus available for any smart phone. Running data are recorded easily in an online training diary. There are graphs analysing running speed and elevation and altitude profile in dependence on distance or time. Figure 1 shows an analysis of a 9.7 km run of one of the participants.

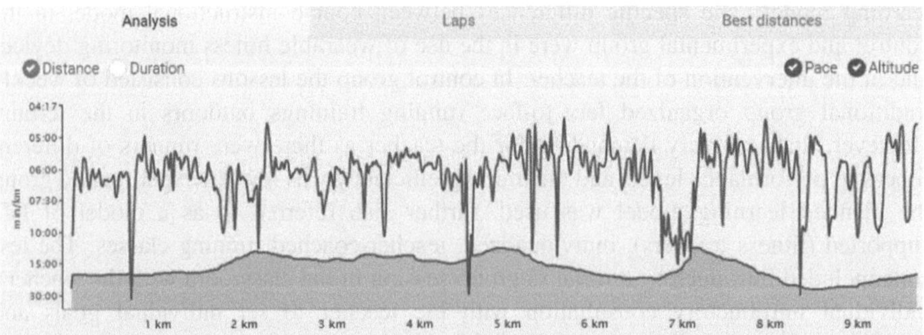

Fig. 1. A screenshot of a 9.7 km run displaying pace in dependence on the distance and elevation

Graphs are supplemented with easily readable maps. There is a switch between basic and satellite map (see Fig. 2), which is useful for the teacher to track if the training was in nature or in an anthropogenic environment.

Fig. 2. A screenshot of a 9.7 km run displaying physical activity data and a course on a satellite map

Users can paste their own pictures. Individual records can be shared easily. Teacher checks weekly reports based on the links sent by students by email. Teacher can enter users' accounts as a non-registered user and browse all the students' records. This is considered the most important feature for the teacher to get an objective overview of students' trainings in terms of frequency, volume and intensity. All the trainings are saved and easy to find in the calendar. Additional attractions for students were found for example in the following features: to import data or to input them manually, to draw a running course in the map, to choose as existing course, to compare personal records. Different types of trainings can be selected: common running, setting goal-achievement (distance, time or calories burnt), beating a time record, a 3 km run to measure the fitness level. Endomondo can be used to measure not only running but also other sport activities.

4.2 The Model of Fitness Tracker-Supported Fitness Running

Goals of the Designed Model

- Formal – to include the innovative blended model of fitness running as an optional (or compulsory, in the future horizon) subject of physical activity in the study curriculum.
- Educational – the students should acquire bases of specialized knowledge and skills in sport training.
- Health – to develop condition motor abilities in terms of health-oriented fitness, to support and drive the students to include regular physical activity as an important part of both their study and leisure time.

- Motivational – to make use of fitness trackers as a helpful technical tool for students in getting in the habit of running regularly and consistently, to enhance positive experiences and satisfaction.
- Diagnostic/control – to provide input, continuous and output assessment.
- Preparatory – to prepare the students to be able to set the training goals and methods on their own and thus be able to carry on running after the end of the semester.

Content. Fitness running with the given minimal training parameters of a volume: ten training units, duration: 60 min and frequency: once a week, with an emphasis on regularity. Introduction to the theory and practice of sport training.

Structure. Introductory tutorial (Endomondo functions, technical training parameters, setting personal profiles for sharing the records with the teacher, consultation with the teacher to set individual goals and methods), fitness tracker-monitored running trainings, weekly sent students' reports, final consultation with the teacher and evaluation (meeting the goals, adjusting the training for the upcoming transitional period between semesters, motivation to carry on running in future).

Form. A combination of a group face-to-face session in the classroom (introductory tutorial) and individual consultations with parallel individual running trainings, which allow all the students to fulfil the assignments choosing when and where they go running (time and place flexibility). The final evaluation takes the form of an individual one-to-one session.

Methods. A continuous peer-evaluation support by the teacher, using expository, motivational, and diagnostic teaching methods, combined with a heuristic method, based on students' self-discovery approach to the training. The key technical element for implementing blended methods in running is the fitness tracking app of Endomondo, a tool used as a part of diagnostic and control process. The suggested benefit of this model is seen namely in an individualized approach to set and adjust the goals, training plan and training times to fit individual needs of every runner, either beginner or advanced.

4.3 Fitness Tracker Applicability

Fitness tracker applicability assessment is based on the questionnaire data collected at the end of each semester in the monitored period as a part of final evaluation. Students most appreciated the ability to store individual records in the calendar (90%), to monitor the parameters such as mileage (90%) and speed (86%), and to compare their own individual performances (82%). 63% of runners did not use GPS navigation. On the other hand, only 11% preferred to keep the same track and course. This correlate to the findings that the students tried to discover new terrains and places when running (76%). This is greatly recommended by the teacher as the so called "running at random" and this method adds a discovery value to simple running.

The highest rated formal benefit of the designed model of fitness tracker-supported running was found in individual choice of time (98%) and place (96%). Self-paced and partly self-managed training process enabled the runners to be independent from the others, which may have helped to solve a major problem in low attendance in group face-to-face trainings. The independence is seen not only in terms of time and place choice, but also in different goal-achievement orientation and performance level.

4.4 Development of Fitness Running Attendance

The development of students' attendance in the optional subject of fitness running was analyzed in four academic years of September 2014–August 2018 (eight consecutive semesters). In the period of September 2016–August 2018 (FT-group) the use of fitness tracking apps on smart phones was being in progress and the research was carried out to evaluate the applicability of fitness trackers in running classes. The preceding period of September 2014–August 2016 was selected as a control period (control group) to evaluate the effect of fitness tracker-supported classes to enhance motivation in students. The running classes in the control period were held in a traditional form and no wearables or other technical support were used. The indicator was the development of attendance.

There was an increase in attendance between the monitored periods. In the control group the total of 65 students enrolled and started the attendance, out of which 38 fulfilled the assignments successfully. In the FT-group the total of 179 students enrolled and started the attendance, out of which 133 fulfilled the assignments successfully. The number of students who passed the subject of fitness running increased more than three times in FT-period. Also the percentage rate of successfulness in fulfilling the credit assignments increased, which means that fewer students dropped out. In the control sample the drop out was 42% whilst in the FT-group the drop out was 26%.

4.5 Students' Motivation for Running

The results provided major runners' characteristics in the categories of physical, psychological, achievement and social motivation (see Table 1). The participants were asked to mark if the items motivated them to run, or not, or if they could not decide in terms of perceived motivation.

Table 1. Motivation to run.

Students' motivation to run	%
Stay in shape	98
Stay healthy	90
Have fun/enjoy the activity	86
Improve state of mind/mood	84
Relieve stress/relax	82
Achieve a goal	71
Meet a personal challenge	69
Self-esteem/self-respect	66
Respect of friends/family	55
Control weight	50
Socialize with a running community	38
Compete with other runners	23

In summary the highest percentages were found out in physical health concerns of staying in shape and healthy, followed by psychological motivation of enjoyment, relaxing and better mood. Weight concerns were relatively lower rated compared to staying healthy and in shape. Competitiveness was the least influential motivator, which corresponded to self-regulatory approach. Students preferred to compete in beating their own individual performance, in meeting a personal challenge.

5 Discussions

Engagement in regular physical activity of college or university students and the need to increase motivation and participation has currently been discussed. The issue has been approached in recent studies [1–3, 27]. There is a recommendation for physical education to be a compulsory subject or a course to help in educating students in physical activity before their graduation, to maximize their future motivation, and, last but not least, to prevent them from cardiovascular related diseases [1]. The aim of physical education is above all to develop motor abilities, to acquire motor skills and stereotypes that can be transferred, brought to life and continued after the studies. If students get used to practice some sport regularly during their university studies, they are more likely to be consistent with it even after they graduate.

The authors of this study agree that compulsory physical activity can be a solution. However, as supported by the results, with optimal motivation, physical activity in university education may work and have an effect on health despite being "just" an optional, not compulsory, subject of the study curriculum. Thi was shown in the technical motivation applied in this research in the case of fitness running. The problem of motivation tor regular physical activity is not only to start, but especially to carry on in a long-term horizon [3, 21]. Concerning the use of fitness trackers to support beginner runners, a key condition is a regular and systematic repetition of the physical activity despite the possible resistance of the body. Usual phases in beginners are an initial excitement accompanied by a quite fast minor progress, especially if the person had not been running before, followed by resistance and discomfort. In the latter phase the role of the teacher is very important to support the students and help them to overcome the feelings of discomfort, uneasiness and doubts. With regularly repeated running trainings, the discomfort usually changes in positive perception of the movement and physical load, and over time can emerge to a desirable phase when the runner is driven by an intrinsic need of body (and mind). This phase should be a goal of physical education process not only at universities. If a regular physical activity becomes a common part of students' lifestyle, external motivation, such as the reward system of credits or grades, may not be needed anymore. The above-mentioned importance of the role of a teacher in physical activities is supported by the research of supervised participation in physical activities, examining determinants relating to adoption and maintenance of physical activity [21]. Supervised running programs had fewer drop-outs [18]. Similarly, there were fewer drop-outs in the fitness tracker-based, running classes.

Hand in hand with motivations like keeping in shape, health concerns, having fun, relieving stress and relaxing, technical motivation based on fitness tracking seems to be an efficient means to increase students' interest and participation in physical activity classes. Use of innovative means is recommended in physical education [2]. Hybrid or blended approach, using the benefits of online instruction in combination with face-to-face interaction, seems to be a convenient approach not only in classroom teaching, but also in physical activity [23]. Fitness trackers are seen to be a helpful tool in getting in the habit of a regular exercising. However, it is also recommended not to rely on the technology too much because an intense focus on data, their quantification and statistics can move the runner away from the experience of running as such [24]. In self-monitoring, the runners can make use of the benefits of getting fitness tracking objective data on one hand, whilst listening to their body on the other hand.

6 Conclusion

Regular physical activity is recommended to be included in study curriculum as a compensatory tool to develop health-oriented fitness and to support healthy lifestyle in practice. The core of the research is an innovated model of the subject of fitness running, which has been in progress at the Faculty of Informatics and Management, University of Hradec Králové, Czech Republic, for four semesters. The designed blended model uses a combination of fitness tracking apps support and individualized teacher-coached running classes. Since the implementation 179 students have enrolled fitness running and 133 passed the assignments.

The number of students who enrolled and passed increased three times and at the same time the rate of drop-outs decreased from 42% to 26%, compared to the control group. The results indicated that the use of fitness tracking apps and data analysis platform enhanced motivation in students to run. A key condition for an efficient implementation of wearables in running classes is the role of a teacher who should help to set goals and methods of their achievement, and to coach, monitor and evaluate the training process and its outcomes.

From the point of view of fitness tracker applicability in training analysis, students most appreciated the ability to store individual records in the calendar, to monitor the parameters such as mileage and speed, and to compare their own individual performances. Self-paced and partly self-managed training process enabled the runners to be independent from the others, which may have helped to solve a major problem in low attendance in group-organized face-to-face training sessions. The independence is seen not only in terms of a time and place choice, but also because in different goal-achievement orientation and performance level. In the case of fitness running, technical motivation with fitness tracking seems to be an efficient means to increase students' interest and participation in physical activity classes.

References

1. Bebeley, S.J., Laggao, S.A., Gendemeh, C.: Physical activity epidemiology of college students physical exercise self-efficacy: motivational drive for health education promotion. J. Phys. Educ. Res. **5**(4), 33–40 (2018)
2. Martin, J.T., Tubera, J.G., Von Monta, B.D.: Motivation and physical activity participation of Filipino college students. Asia Life Sci. **25**(1), 245–254 (2016)
3. Kilpatrick, M., Hebert, E., Bartholomew, J.: College students' motivation for physical activity: differentiating men's and women's motives for sport participation and exercise. J. Am. Coll. Health **54**, 87–94 (2005)
4. Xiang, P., Liu, Y., McBride, R.E., Bruene, A.: Longitudinal goal patterns and their effects on students' motivation in running programs. J. Exp. Educ. **79**, 295–317 (2011). https://doi.org/10.1080/00220973.2010.486809
5. Miao, R., Dong, Q., Weng, W.Y., Yu, X.Y.: The application model of wearable devices in physical education. In: Cheung, S., Kwok, L., Kubota, K., Lee, L.K., Tokito, J. (eds.) ICBL 2018. LNCS, vol. 10949, pp. 311–322. Springer, Cham (2018). https://doi.org/10.1007/978-3-319-94505-7_25
6. Patel, M.S., Asch, D.A., Volpp, K.G.: Wearable devices as facilitators, not drivers, of health behavior change. JAMA **313**, 459–460 (2015)
7. Černá, M., Svobodová, L.: Development of computer competence courses in seniors – shift from learning space with computer-based activities to virtual platform - case study. In: Cheung, S., Kwok, L., Kubota, K., Lee, L.K., Tokito, J. (eds.) ICBL 2018. LNCS, vol. 10949, pp. 416–425. Springer, Cham (2018). https://doi.org/10.1007/978-3-319-94505-7_34
8. Hanc, J.: Sometimes half is better than whole. New York Times (2008). https://www.nytimes.com/2008/07/24/fashion/24fitness.html. Accessed 09 Sept 2018
9. Deaner, R.O.: Distance running as an ideal domain for showing a sex difference in competitiveness. Arch. Sex. Behav. **42**, 413 (2013). https://doi.org/10.1007/s10508-012-9965-z
10. Hrušová, D.: Development of running races and their attendance: a study of Hradec Králové. In: Bekirogullari, Z., Melis, M.Y. (eds.) 7th icCSBs 2018 Annual International Conference on Cognitive - Social, and Behavioural Sciences, Abstract Book, p. 72. Future Academy (2018). http://dx.doi.org/10.15405/iccsbs2018(2357-1292)
11. Dovalil, J., Choutka, M.: Sport. In: Olympismus. Olympia, Praha (2004)
12. Sato, M., Jordan, J.S., Funk, D.C.: The role of physically active leisure for enhancing quality of life. Leisure Sci. **36**(3), 293–313 (2014)
13. Hrusova, D., Hrusa, P., Chaloupska, P., Chaloupsky, D.: Effect of fitness sport activities on subjective experiencing and psychological states. In: Bekirogullari, Z., Melis, M.Y. (eds.) International Conference on Sport, Education & Psychology, icSEP 2017, EpSBS, pp. 36–42. Future Academy (2017). http://dx.doi.org/10.15405/epsbs.2017.06.5
14. Killingsworth, M.A., Gilbert, D.T.: A wandering mind is an unhappy mind. Science **330** (6006), 932 (2010)
15. Bonaiuto, M., et al.: Optimal experience and personal growth: flow and the consolidation of place identity. Front. Psychol. **7**, 1654 (2016). https://doi.org/10.3389/fpsyg.2016.01654
16. Stragier, J., Abeele, M.V., De Marez, L.: Recreational athletes' running motivations as predictors of their use of online fitness community features. Behav. Inf. Technol. **37**(8), 815–827 (2018). https://doi.org/10.1080/0144929x.2018.1484516
17. Deci, E.L., Ryan, R.M.: Cognitive Evaluation Theory. In: Deci, E.L., Ryan, R.M. (eds.) Intrinsic Motivation and Self-Determination in Human Behavior. Perspectives in Social Psychology. Springer, Boston (1985). https://doi.org/10.1007/978-1-4899-2271-7_3

18. Masters, K., Ogles, B., Jolton, J.: The development of an instrument to measure motivation for marathon running: the Motivations of Marathoners Scales (MOMS). Res. Q. Exerc. Sport **64**(134), 143 (1993)
19. Knaving, K., Woźniak, P., Fjeld, M., Björk, S.: Flow is not enough: understanding the needs of advanced amateur runners to design motivation technology. In: Proceedings of Conference on Human Factors in Computing Systems, pp. 2013–2022 (2015). https://doi.org/10.1145/2702123.2702542
20. Running USA: The 2017 National Runner Survey (2017). http://cdn.trustedpartner.com/docs/library/RunningUSA2012/RunningUSA_NRS_2017.pdf
21. Dishman, R.K., Sallis, J.F., Orenstein, D.R.: The determinants of physical activity and exercise. Public Health Rep. **100**, 158–171 (1985)
22. Teixeira, P.J., Carraça, E.V., Markland, D., Silva, M.N., Ryan, R.M.: Exercise, physical activity, and selfdetermination theory: a systematic review. Int. J. Behav. Nutr. Phys. Act. **9**, 78 (2012). https://doi.org/10.1186/1479-5868-9-78
23. Bachman, Ch., Scherer, R.: Promoting student autonomy and competence using a hybrid model for teaching physical activity. Int. J. Instr. **8**(1), 3–18 (2015)
24. Miller, J.A.: Can a fitness tracker help you run a better race? The New York Times, 21 December 2017. https://www.nytimes.com/2017/12/21/well/move/can-a-fitness-tracker-help-you-run-a-better-race.html
25. Stragier, J., Mechant, P., De Marez, L., Cardon, G.: Computer-mediated social support for physical activity: a content analysis. Health Educ. Behav. **45**(1), 124–131 (2015). https://doi.org/10.1177/1090198117703055
26. Janssen, M., Scheerder, J., Thibaut, E., Brombacher, A., Vos, S.: Who uses running apps and sports watches? Determinants and consumer profiles of event runners' usage of running-related smartphone applications and sports watches. PLoS ONE **12**, e0181167 (2015). https://doi.org/10.1371/journal.pone.0181167
27. Sekot, A.: Sport and physical activities in the Czech Republic. Phys. Cult. Sport Stud. Res. **48**, 44–65 (2010). https://doi.org/10.2478/v10141-010-0006-0

A Study on Acceptance of Educational Games for the Students in the Stage of Compulsory Education

Yu Jiang[1(✉)], Yongle Zhao[2], Ying He[2], Lizhen Jiao[3], and Ximei Qu[4]

[1] National Center for Educational Technology, Beijing 100031, China
jiangy@moe.edu.cn
[2] Honghe University, Mengzi 661100, Yunnan, China
[3] Tsinghua University, Beijing 100084, China
[4] Zhejiang Radio and Television University, Hangzhou 310012, Zhejiang, China

Abstract. In order to study the students' acceptance of educational games in the stage of compulsory education, and to understand the relevant factors that affect their acceptance, the study used self-educated educational games technology acceptance questionnaires as the main tool and surveyed 16,757 students in the compulsory education period from the first to the ninth grade. The results show that students generally have a higher acceptance of the educational games. This acceptance is affected by many factors, including grade level, family location, parental education, time of parents' accompanying, academic level, and related technical experience all have impact on students' technical acceptance. However, regression analysis found that students' acceptance is not enough to predict whether they would actually use educational games, for parents and teachers may play a greater role in it. However, the technical acceptance of students can still be used to predict the effectiveness of use of educational games. In order to understand the rules and mechanism of educational games, researchers should consider the situation of students, parents and teachers comprehensively.

Keywords: Educational games · Students in the stage of compulsory education · Technology acceptance

1 Introduction

Educational games have received much attention in recent years and are thought to bring change and innovation to education. By using educational games for teaching activities, it is possible to stimulate learning motivations, improve creativity, and promote students to develop positive emotional attitudes (Shang et al. 2014). There have been many academic studies to prove its effectiveness, but the successful application of them is still mainly concentrated in the fields of business, health and special education, except for basic education. Among them are the reasons for the cautious attitude towards new technologies in the field of basic education, and the lack of acceptance and cooperation of the users.

S. K. S. Cheung et al. (Eds.): ICBL 2019, LNCS 11546, pp. 316–326, 2019.
https://doi.org/10.1007/978-3-030-21562-0_26

Since the introduction of the Technology Acceptance Model (TAM) (Davis 1989), user acceptance of information technology has been used to predict the application prospects of the technology. As an emerging educational technology, educational games are no exception. Teachers and students are the main users in the implementation of educational technology, and the process of technology acceptance has always been a concern of researchers. However, in the research related to educational games, the acceptance of teachers is relatively more important, and there are fewer studies on the acceptance of students. This is not in line with the trend of student-centered reform in contemporary education, and it is also possible to cause the related technologies failing to perform as they were expected. This problem has been changed in recent years, and the researchers have begun to pay attention to the role of students' attitude factors in the application of educational games. Empirical studies have confirmed that students' acceptance of educational games would affect the application (Çankaya and Karamete 2009). Meanwhile, in application with high students' acceptance, such as learning disabilities and health behavior modification, the success rate of educational games is also significantly higher (Marino et al. 2013). Recognizing that students' acceptance is closely related to the effectiveness of educational games, some researchers have recently suggested acceptance should be treated as a direct indicator of the actual effectiveness of educational games (Malaquias et al. 2018).

However, the results of these post-tests can't predict whether students will actually use educational games to learn. If we can obtain the acceptance characteristics of students before applying and take appropriate intervention, or choose the right types of educational games, we can improve the success rate and stability of the technology. This stability is especially important in basic education. It is necessary to quantify the student's technical acceptance. To achieve this, we must not only understand the current status of students' acceptance of educational games, but also analyze the relevant factors that influence the acceptance. At the same time, due to the large number of primary and middle school students in China, the degree of internal consistency is difficult to guarantee, and a large number of samples are needed as the basis for data analysis to obtain more reliable conclusions. To this end, this research conducted a large-scale sampling survey of students in compulsory education in China, and tried to understand students' acceptance of educational games, analyzed the relevant factors affecting technology acceptance process.

2 Research Design

2.1 Research Tools

Before survey, we revised the questionnaire according to our trial test which more than one thousand students from grades 3rd to 9th were participated. A set of Likert scale(7-point)questionnaires containing 13 items was compiled. The questionnaire has good reliability and validity indicators, which are divided into three factors: "usefulness cognition", "use and recommendation tendency" and "others' objection". The three-factor aggregation validity AVE index was 0.634, 0.770 and 0.518. The discriminant validity CR index was 0.896, 0.909, 0.842, and the internal consistency coefficient

Cronbach α coefficients were 0.894, 0.883, 0.832, and the overall Cronbach α coefficient was 0.889. In addition, a subscale is added to the actual questionnaire distribution to reflect the students' negative evaluation of the quality of educational games. The subscale consists of three 7-point options with a Cronbach alpha coefficient of 0.756.

The questionnaire is suitable for measuring the students' acceptance of educational games. In order to explore the various factors affecting students' acceptance tendency furtherly, besides adding to collect the demographic variables, other items related to the use educational games are supplemented. For example, the experience of other technologies, including video games and learning platforms, personal academic performance, etc.

2.2 Research Participants

Although the questionnaire is mainly for students in grades 3rd–9th, the item's description is relatively simple and can be used for students in lower grades. The students in 2nd grade can complete independently. Most of the 1st year students can also read and answer independently. Random sampling is conducted nationwide by surveying on several educational web platform and delivering the electronic questionnaire that is generated by one open survey tool in different ways. The sampling time is continuous two months in 2018.

A total of 17,309 samples were collected from the system. We deleted the invalid questionnaires which are answered in a too short time, including invalid or contradictory content or with extreme score and incomplete information. A total of 16,757 valid samples from grades 1st–9th were obtained. The efficiency is 96.8%. Data processing is implemented by using the SPSS software package.

3 Data Analysis

3.1 Students' Acceptance and Tendency to Use of Educational Games Is Relatively High

The standardized questionnaire has four subscales, which respectively reflect the cognition of advantages of educational games (5.215 ± 1.398), the actual tendency to use (4.525 ± 1.424), the negative opinions or use resistance (3.932 ± 1.414) from teachers and parents, and the negative evaluation of the quality of the educational games (3.413 ± 1.493). Overall, students in the compulsory education stage have higher recognition of the advantages of educational games, and fewer negative evaluations.

3.2 The Relationship Between the Demographic Variables of Students and Their Acceptance

Gender differences are common influencing factors in various measurements, but in this survey, gender differences are reflected between tendency to use and negative evaluation. Boys are more inclined to use educational games than girls. At the same time, boys are more critical about the quality of educational games and have more negative reviews. However, the difference is small, and the Cohen'd index is 0.1 and 0.06. It indicated that the gender difference has an impact, but not significant.

Whether the one-child has a significant impact on the growth environment, but the impact of this factor in the survey is very small, too. The difference is in the resistance of students to use, and this resistance is mainly from parents. In the survey of parents which is conducted in the same period, whether the one-child is a factor that significantly affects the attitude of the parents (Table 1).

Table 1. Gender difference

Gender (N = 16757)	Recognition of advantages M ± SD	Tendency to use M ± SD	Use resistance M ± SD	Negative evaluation M ± SD
Boys (6919)	5.225 ± 1.424	4.615 ± 1.467	3.926 ± 1.456	3.462 ± 1.556
Girls (9838)	5.208 ± 1.379	4.463 ± 1.390	3.936 ± 1.383	3.379 ± 1.447
Significant difference (*t*)	0.770	6.764***	0.450	3.483**

Note: **$p < 0.01$, ***$p < 0.001$.

Although gender and whether or not the one-child has little effect separately, there was a significant interaction between the two dependent variables of cognition of advantages and tendency to use ($F = 7.837$, $p < 0.001$). The simple effect test found that in the recognition of advantages, the boys' of the one-child family score (5.298 ± 1.419) was significantly higher than the not only child family (5.200 ± 1.425), also significantly higher than the one-child (5.170 ± 1.404). The girls' is not much different between One-child and not only child family. In terms of tendency to use, the boys' in the One-child family was significantly greater than that of not only children (4.672 ± 1.443, 4.595 ± 1.475), while girls were just the opposite (4.398 ± 1.407, 4.475 ± 1.386).

In contrast, the two highly relevant factors of age and grade ($r = 0.83$) have a greater impact. Students' scores showed significant differences in the three scoring dimensions of recognition of advantages, tendency to use, and negative evaluation. However, there is no linear relationship between age or grade factors and students' scores. The correlation coefficient between age or grade and each dimension score is less than 0.1. The reason is that the acceptance of students is greatly improved by the 5th grade, but it will fall back along the grades' increasing to the 9th grade. Therefore, along with the age or grade increases, students' acceptance of educational games generally shows an inverted U-shaped curve (Tables 2 and 3).

Table 2. Grade differences

Grade (N = 16757)	Recognition of advantages M ± SD	Tendency to use M ± SD	Use resistance M ± SD	Negative evaluation M ± SD
Grade 1 (1363)	5.070 ± 1.399	4.498 ± 1.264	3.900 ± 1.211	3.531 ± 1.229
Grade 2 (1369)	4.938 ± 1.505	4.332 ± 1.426	3.959 ± 1.324	3.479 ± 1.345
Grade 3 (2069)	5.029 ± 1.484	4.460 ± 1.438	3.901 ± 1.414	3.434 ± 1.520
Grade 4 (3172)	5.141 ± 1.481	4.487 ± 1.507	3.913 ± 1.453	3.313 ± 1.571
Grade 5 (3722)	5.279 ± 1.404	4.613 ± 1.465	3.943 ± 1.498	3.315 ± 1.551
Grade 6 (2774)	5.417 ± 1.274	4.602 ± 1.404	3.970 ± 1.464	3.428 ± 1.474
Grade 7 (1089)	5.405 ± 1.233	4.564 ± 1.337	3.934 ± 1.366	3.519 ± 1.383
Grade 8 (923)	5.413 ± 1.123	4.567 ± 1.308	3.946 ± 1.308	3.591 ± 1.377
Grade 9 (276)	5.240 ± 1.189	4.313 ± 1.281	3.778 ± 1.177	3.664 ± 1.493
Significance test (*F*)	27.703***	7.798***	1.002	8.591***

Note***p < 0.001.

Table 3. Age differences

Age (N = 16757)	Recognition of advantages M ± SD	Tendency to use M ± SD	Use resistance M ± SD	Negative evaluation M ± SD
6–7 years old (933)	4.932 ± 1.442	4.437 ± 1.280	3.980 ± 1.167	3.583 ± 1.214
8–9 years old (2363)	5.012 ± 1.442	4.414 ± 1.351	3.923 ± 1.294	3.492 ± 1.332
10–11 years old (5155)	5.136 ± 1.484	4.473 ± 1.476	3.939 ± 1.434	3.312 ± 1.533
12–13 years old (5911)	5.337 ± 1.472	4.616 ± 1.463	3.941 ± 1.491	3.377 ± 1.573
14–15 years old (2053)	5.400 ± 1.365	4.565 ± 1.330	3.896 ± 1.386	3.558 ± 1.442
16–17 years old (291)	5.383 ± 1.187	4.465 ± 1.236	3.862 ± 1.264	3.471 ± 1.386
Significance test (F)	38.346***	10.242***	0.72	15.511***

Note: ***p < 0.001.

Most students reported their parents' academic qualifications. The Spearman correlation coefficient of the two (father's academic qualification and mother's academic qualification) was as high as 0.723, indicating that the parents' education backgrounds in many families were possible at the same level.

However, the impact of these items on the acceptance of educational games is also lacking in a linear relationship. The correlation coefficient between the parental education backgrounds and each dimension is below 0.05. However, the parental education backgrounds still have a significant impact on the acceptance score. From the distribution of the mean scores, there is also an inverted U-shaped relationship.

Students whose parents have low education have low acceptance of educational games. Students with highly educated parents are more cautious about the advantages of the educational games, and the attitude is more open and willing to try. Among them, the students who have parents with postgraduate education showed low recognition and high resistance, but the tendency to use is high.

The location of the student's family reflects the differences in the macro social environment. This factor has a general impact on the students' scores, and there are significant different among the four dimensions (Table 4).

Table 4. Impact of student family location

Family location (N = 16757)	Recognition of advantages M ± SD	Tendency to use M ± SD	Use resistance M ± SD	Negative evaluation M ± SD
Provincial capital (1402)	5.063 ± 1.565	4.462 ± 1.566	3.686 ± 1.497	3.410 ± 1.541
Prefecture-level city (1610)	5.262 ± 1.428	4.462 ± 1.375	3.878 ± 1.346	3.376 ± 1.444
County town (3668)	5.302 ± 1.374	4.524 ± 1.431	3.872 ± 1.409	3.345 ± 1.476
Country (10077)	5.197 ± 1.375	4.545 ± 1.408	3.997 ± 1.409	3.444 ± 1.500
Significance test (F)	11.460***	2.631*	24.246***	4.303**

Note: *$p < 0.05$, **$p < 0.01$, ***$p < 0.001$。

We found that students' recognition of advantages of educational games in rural is lower than that in county towns and prefecture-level cities. The use resistance is greater than that in provincial capital cities. The negative evaluation is also significantly higher than that of prefecture-level cities and county towns. However, students' tendency to use in rural area is more than the students in provincial capitals and prefecture-level city.

3.3 The Influence of Various Behavioral Characteristics of Students and Their Family Members on Acceptance

There are also links between the various behavioral characteristics of students and their family members and their attitudes. We surveyed some related things that may affect the acceptance of educational games. The survey divided the time of parents' daily accompanying into four levels, and found that there were significant differences in the acceptance scores of students with different time of parental companion (Table 5).

Table 5. Differences in time of parents' companying

Time of parents' companying, (N = 16757)	Recognition of advantages M ± SD	Tendency to use M ± SD	Use resistance M ± SD	Negative evaluation M ± SD
Less than 1 h (3549)	5.132 ± 1.438	4.440 ± 1.452	4.056 ± 1.325	3.945 ± 1.379
1–2 h (2548)	5.201 ± 1.323	4.508 ± 1.311	3.991 ± 1.314	3.918 ± 1.272
2–3 h (1936)	5.207 ± 1.330	4.526 ± 1.342	3.913 ± 1.407	3.998 ± 1.325
3 h + (8694)	5.254 ± 1.415	4.567 ± 1.458	3.864 ± 1.544	3.917 ± 1.483
Significance test (F)	6.530***	6.924***	1.926	17.618***

Note: ***$p < 0.001$.

The survey also allowed the students to evaluate their academic achievement by themselves. The items designed ask the students to compare with their own classmates, and then assess the level of academic achievement. The levels is divided into four, including excellent/fine/common and poor. This data does not necessarily reflect the student's objective performance level, but reflects their satisfaction and sense of accomplishment in their own learning behaviors. The results showed that it has a significant impact on the acceptance of educational games.

Overall, students with better self-assessment are more open-minded and more inclined to use educational games. Post-mortem examinations found that students with good academic performance had higher score than common and poor students in recognition of advantages. Their tendency to use was higher than students who were poor. In terms of resistance, students who are unsatisfied about their own learning performance are significantly higher than students with high self-efficacy. The worse the self-assessment of the achievement, the more negative evaluations. The differences between the different levels are significant.

Experience in applying technology platforms has been an important predictor of technology acceptance (Legris et al. 2003). In the trial test, we found that most students are accustomed to accessing to the internet on mobile devices, and with 65.7% of students tending to use software products on mobile devices. It seems that the acceptance of mobile devices play an important indicator for predicting the acceptance of educational games. Two indicators used in this questionnaire reflect this tendency: whether you are accustomed to using mobile phones, tablets or other mobile terminals, and whether you are accustomed to using applications. It was found that students who are accustomed to using mobile devices have higher acceptance and tendency to use in educational games, and also less resistance and negative evaluation. Students who are accustomed to using mobile applications also exhibit similar characteristics.

3.4 Logistic Regression Analysis for Predicting the Use of Educational Games for Students

Predicting whether students will use educational games is also an important goal of research. To this end, an open question was set in the questionnaire to ask if the students actually used the educational games and whether it was rewarding. Manual analysis of the qualitative content of the answer confirms whether it is actually used educational games or not. In the end, a total of 11028 samples were identified, and other samples could not confirm. Among them, 4,204 students explicitly reported that they have used or are using educational games. These students have significant differences in the acceptance and evaluation of educational games to other students. They have higher recognition and using tendency, including recommendation tendency, less resistance to use, and lower negative evaluation. In addition, there is a high biserial correlation between the three criteria, including cognition of advantage, tendency to use and negative evaluation and the actually usage. It may be an effective predictor (Table 6).

Table 6. The differences between whether to use educational games or not

(N = 11003)	Recognition of advantages M ± SD	Tendency to use M ± SD	Use resistance M ± SD	Negative evaluation M ± SD
Y (4201)	5.362 ± 1.357	4.700 ± 1.399	3.788 ± 1.456	3.215 ± 1.556
N (6802)	4.931 ± 1.420	4.232 ± 1.379	3.959 ± 1.383	3.607 ± 1.447
Significant difference (t value)	15.909***	17.171***	6.304***	13.972***
Quadratic correlation coefficient	0.190***	0.206***	−0.080*	−0.171***

Note: *$p < 0.05$, ***$p < 0.001$.

Other demographic variables and behavioral variables have basically no significant linear relationship with whether or not used educational games before. Age and grade factors are more significantly relate correlation to predict to use. These two variables have high homogeneity corrclation. In order to avoid collinearity, the grade that can better reflect the changes of physiological and social environment is selected. The grade and the scores from the three subscales, including cognition of advantages, tendency to use and negative evaluation, were treated as an independent variable for logistic regression analysis to explore the predictive ability of the questionnaire to the use educational games actually. It was found that the logistic regression model consisting of four independent variables has a minimum tolerance of 0.713 and a maximum VIF of 1.402, which is within the acceptable range, but the Condition Index is up to 13.159, indicating that there is still a certain multiple collinearity. The main problem is that the tendency to use and cognition of advantages have a high correlation. To solve this problem, the collinearity can be reduced to an acceptable range by stepwise regression and by choosing to eliminate the cognition of advantages factor. The process is as follows (Table 7):

Table 7. Whether to use the logistic regression model of educational games

Model		B	SE	Wald	Significant	OR
Model 1	Grade	−.173	.010	291.089	.000	.841
	Constant	.228	.045	25.066	.000	1.256
Model 2	Grade	−.180	.010	305.281	.000	1.293
	Tendency to use	.257	.015	297.823	.000	.835
	Constant	−.890	.079	125.747	.000	.411
Model 3	Grade	−.180	.010	299.096	.000	1.288
	Tendency to use	.253	.015	285.610	.000	.825
	Negative comment	−.193	.014	177.450	.000	.835
	Constant	−.214	.094	5.156	.023	.808
Model 4	Grade	−.187	.010	317.930	.000	1.144
	Recognition of the advantages	.134	.017	59.162	.000	1.203
	Tendency to use	.185	.017	114.614	.000	.839
	Negative evaluation	−.175	.015	143.931	.000	.829
	Constant	−.631	.110	33.151	.000	.532

After adding the cognition of advantages variable, the coefficient of the tendency to use changes greatly, and there may be high collinearity between the two. Therefore, using model 3 and testing, the highest condition index is less than 10, and the collinear feature no longer appears. However, the Cox & Snell R and Nagelkerke R values of the model were 0.07 and 0.10. The Hosmer and Lemeshow test results were not satisfactory, $p < 0.05$. The degree of acceptance and students' grade can explain whether students have tendency to use or not partly, but it is of little significance in predicting their use in the actual environment. Acceptance should mainly be used to predict the degree of cooperation and efficiency when their teachers are using educational games.

4 Discussion

4.1 Students' Acceptance of Educational Games and Important Factors

The survey found that students accepted educational games generally. Relative to parents, most students tend to be positive about the function of educational games, and the proportion of willing to try is higher. It is found that many demographic variables and behavioral variables have an impact on the acceptance of students, and the ways are more complicated. A significant difference test on the four dimensions shows that few variables have a linear effect, but often appear as an inverted U-shaped trend. This data feature makes most variables not significantly related to the student's acceptance score, but in fact the differences between students with different characteristics are very significant, and there may be interaction between the factors.

Most of these influencing factors are related to the students' growth environment, especially the family-society environment, and the physiological-related variables are not significant. For example, although the impact of gender differences is significant, it is extremely weak, and the environmental and cultural factors such as family location and parental education are relatively significant, similar to some similar surveys in the past (Cheung and Lee 2011). The age and grade factors seem to be related to physiological maturity, but the data does not show a clear linear relationship. For elementary school students, the acceptance degree has increased obviously from the age of 10, and then maintained at a stable level. This is likely to be the result of qualitative changes in the learning environment, technical reserves and technical acceptance of students at this stage, as well as the learning autonomy. This factor also plays an important role in the subsequent logistic regression model because of the large variation.

In general, the behavioral of the students themselves and their parents have a more important distinction. The survey showed that time of parents' daily companying, academic self-assessment and student's pre-technical (mobile devices use) have high predictive value for students to accept educational games, which are consistent with the results of previous similar studies (Martins and Kellermanns 2004). It is suggested that we should pay more attention to individual behavior characteristics, family parenting style, and socialized living environment when predicting students' using tendency. At the same time, teachers also play an important role in this process. A recent meta-analysis study found that educational games are not independent variables for students' learning outcomes, but a mediate between teacher teaching and student learning outcomes (Lamb et al. 2018). Therefore, to fully understand the process of educational games, it is necessary to comprehensively analyze students, parents and teachers.

4.2 The Predicted Value of Students' Acceptance of Educational Game Technology

The classical Technology Acceptance Model believes that the technical acceptance of an object can predict whether it will use the technology, and the explanatory power is usually around 30% or even higher. In a similar survey of college students, the results are basically consistent with the assumptions of the Technology Acceptance Model (Al-Adwan et al. 2013; Park 2009). However, This survey showed that although students' subjective attitudes and other factors have certain predictive effects on whether to use educational games, they can only explain about 10% of the overall variation. According to the analysis of the survey of teachers and parents conducted in the same period, both of them have higher explanatory powers for the actual use of educational games. Therefore, the factors that influence whether students actually use educational games or not may depend on the attitudes of parents and teachers. To confirm this, it is also necessary to combine the data of students, parents and teachers.

Although the degree of acceptance of students does not predict whether or not they actually use educational games, this measurement still has other value. The degree of technical acceptance can be used to predict whether the use of technology will achieve goals or not. Studies have repeatedly confirmed that the degree of acceptance and cooperation of students in educational games is a key factor in predicting their use (Bourgonjon et al. 2010). This kind of acceptance affects the degree of student participation and subjective pleasure, which in turn affects the cooperation of students with teaching activities, thus affecting the implementation effect of educational games. In areas where students' strong demand, recognition and acceptance are high, it has always a high success rate. For example, educational games are used to counsel students with dyslexia (Franceschini et al. 2013). Therefore, before applying educational games in teaching, students should be surveyed in advance to know the technical acceptance level, and cognitive intervention should be carried out for students with lower acceptance to enhance their understanding of the advantages of educational games to ensure the effective. The survey also found that most students who were used to use educational games have a higher evaluation and a willingness to continue using them. Therefore, it is helpful to try to improve the acceptance of students by using the related platforms in advance and trying out educational games that are easy to use.

In the future, we should also investigate the technical acceptance and other relevant situations of parents and teachers, and compare the effects of the three with the actual implementation of educational games. That would be helpful for us to fully understand how to effectively apply educational games in the instruction system.

References

Al-Adwan, A., Al-Adwan, A., Smedley, J.: Exploring students acceptance of e-learning using technology acceptance model in jordanian universities. Int. J. Educ. Dev. Using Inf. Commun. Technol. **9**(2), 4–18 (2013)

Bourgonjon, J., Valcke, M., Soetaert, R., Schellens, T.: Students' perceptions about the use of video games in the classroom. Comput. Educ. **54**(4), 1145–1156 (2010)

Çankaya, S., Karamete, A.: The effects of educational computer games on students' attitudes towards mathematics course and educational computer games. Pro.-Soc. Behav. Sci. **1**(1), 145–149 (2009)

Cheung, C.M., Lee, M.K.: Exploring the gender differences in student acceptence of an internet-based learning medium. In: Technology acceptance in education, pp. 183–199. Sense Publishers (2011)

Davis, F.D.: Perceived usefulness, perceived ease of use, and user acceptance of information technology. MIS Q. **13**, 319–340 (1989)

Franceschini, S., Gori, S., Ruffino, M., Viola, S., Molteni, M., Facoetti, A.: Action video games make dyslexic children read better. Curr. Biol. **23**(6), 462–466 (2013)

Lamb, R.L., Annetta, L., Firestone, J.: A meta-analysis with examination of moderators of student cognition, affect, and learning outcomes while using serious educational games, serious games, and simulations. Comput. Hum. Behav. **80**, 158–167 (2018)

Legris, P., Ingham, J., Collerette, P.: Why do people use information technology?: a critical review of the technology acceptance model. Inf. Manag. **40**(3), 191–204 (2003)

Malaquias, R.F., Malaquias, F.F., Hwang, Y.: Understanding technology acceptance features in learning through a serious game. Comput. Hum. Behav. **87**(5), 395–402 (2018)

Marino, M.T., Israel, M., Beecher, C.C., Basham, J.D.: Students' and teachers' perceptions of using video games to enhance science instruction. J. Sci. Educ. Technol. **22**(5), 667–680 (2013)

Martins, L.L., Kellermanns, F.W.: A model of business school students' acceptance of a web-based course management system. Acad. Manag. Learn. Educ. **3**(1), 7–26 (2004)

Park, S.Y.: An analysis of the technology acceptance model in understanding university students' behavioral intention to use e-learning. Educ. Technol. Soc. **12**(3), 150–162 (2009)

Shang, J.J., Xiao, H.M., Jia, N.: The overview of the empirical research from worldwide: 2008-2012. Res. Educ. Technol. **1**, 71–78 (2014)

A Study of Primary School Pupils' Motivation, Emotional Intelligence and Attentional Control Ability

Ruonan Hu, Junjie Shang(✉), and Qi Xia

Graduate School of Education, Peking University, Beijing 100871, China
jjshang@gse.pku.edu.cn

Abstract. It's up to students themselves whether to engage in learning or not no matter in what kind of learning model. Blended learning has higher requirements on effectively selecting and processsing information, due to the application of multiple media and methods. While Multitasking capacity and information handling capacity of human brain is limited. Three important mechanisms–attention, emotion and motivation – contribute to the prioritization and selection of information. Therefore, how to improve attention, positive emotion and motivation is of vital importance. Attentional control ability decides attention level and emotional intelligence decides emotional state. This study investigated the attentional control ability level, motivation level and emotional intelligence of 1860 primary school pupils in China and relationship among them. The result found that: there's significant differences among different groups in motivation, emotional intelligence and attentional control ability and significant relationship was found among them. This research facilitates us to have a deeper understanding of factors that influence students' cognition process and help to provide better learning experience in blended learning.

Keywords: Chinese student · Motivation and engagement · Attentional control ability · Emotional intelligence

1 Introduction

Learning has experienced different forms in different times. For example, imitation in primitive society, class teaching in the printing era, distance education in the electronic communication era, blended learning and personalized learning in the digital era. Whatever imprints of learning methods and learning concepts induce by the times, the personalized characteristics of the learners themselves never change. Although we have entered the industrial 4.0 era characterized by intelligence, we still retain the collective teaching with the feature of large-scale industrial age, but our understanding of learning has changed from black-box theory of brain to in-depth understanding of human brain mechanism, and plenty of scientific empirical researches have been done on the influencing factors of learning. For example, John Hattie took 15 years to make a comprehensive meta-analysis of more than 800 meta-analysis of 52,637 studies and hundreds of millions of students. 138 factors affecting academic achievement were extracted. The greatest influencing factor among the six major influencing factors are

S. K. S. Cheung et al. (Eds.): ICBL 2019, LNCS 11546, pp. 327–338, 2019.
https://doi.org/10.1007/978-3-030-21562-0_27

family, students, schools, teachers, teaching and curriculum. As Hattie said in the conclusion, "ultimately it is the students themselves, not the teachers, who decide what to learn." (Hattie 2015) Neuroscience has proved that there is no exactly the same brain in the world. Although everyone's basic brain structures are the same, the sizes of brain structure are different, and the organization and intensity of cell connections are also different. Therefore, we should pay attention to the individual characteristics of students no matter in traditional learning or in blended learning.

Whether in the classroom or home, students tend to be distracted when confronted with interfering information, especially in such smart phone prevailing society. And the ability of the brain to process information is limited (Klingberg 2011), which makes it very important for our brain to decide which to select and which to ignore. Attention, emotion and motivation are three systems that serve as important roles in prioritizing and selecting information, and interact with each other (Raymond 2009). Attention is decided by attentional control ability and emotional state directly influenced by emotional intelligence. Therefore, how to improve the level of attentional control ability, emotional intelligence and motivation is of critical significance. The level and interaction of all above three simultaneously influence students' attitude and behavior to learn, affect whether students focus on the right information. The main purpose of this study is to find out the existing level and relationship of attentional control ability, emotional intelligence and motivation level among Chinese primary school pupils.

2 Literature Review

2.1 Attention and Attentional Control Ability

From the perspective of the brain mechanism of attention, attention system involves three networks: (1) alert network, which keeps us awake and conscious; (2) orientated network, which prioritizes input sensory information; (3) The executive network, used to detect the target, selectively pay attention, and to hold the attention undisturbed (Petersen and Posner 2012).

Attentional Control Ability is the ability of individuals to choose what to pay attention on and what to ignore, that is, to achieve the directing, concentrating, switching, allocating and continuous controlling of attention. Attention control can be regarded as the control of two modes of attention: bottom-up stimulus-driven mode and top-down goal orientation mode. In recent years, the neural mechanisms of these two modes have also been experimentally confirmed (Katsuki and Constantinidis 2014). The prefrontal lobe mainly controls the top-down attention mode and achieves attention orientation according to previous experience, plans and goals. Bottom-up process is also affected by prefrontal lobe. Dorsolateral prefrontal lobe, sub parietal cortex and temporal epithelium are also involved in attention regulation (Müller and Kleinschmidt 2003).

2.2 Emotion and Emotional Intelligence

Emotion is the subjective experience of the human brain in processing the information. Emotion affects attention (Vuilleumier 2005), learning and memory (Um et al. 2012), reasoning (Jung et al. 2014) and problem solving (Isen et al. 1987).

Emotional Intelligence (EI) is the ability of individuals to recognize their own and other people's emotions, and to use, manage and adjust their emotions to adapt to the environment or achieve goals. As early as in the 20th century, Thorndike divided intelligence into abstract intelligence (the ability to understand ideas), mechanism intelligence (the ability to understand different mechanisms and abstract things), social intelligence (the ability of human self-management and to behave appropriately in interpersonal relationships), in which social intelligence is similar to emotional intelligence. At present, it is generally believed that emotional intelligence is a combination of cognitive factors and non-intellectual factors. Daniel Goleman put forward in his book *Emotional Intelligence* that emotional intelligence includes: self-awareness and evaluation of self-emotion; social awareness, understanding of other people's emotion; self-management, proper management of self-emotion; relationship management, influence on others and interpersonal relationships (Goleman 2001).

2.3 Learning Motivation

There are various motivation theories. At the beginning of the 21st century, Martin put forward Motivation and Engagement Wheel, which synthesized various motivation theories. In his theory, motivation is the force that promotes students' learning behavior, and engagement is the behavioral expression of students' learning motivation. Positive motivation and engagement can promote students' drive to learn, while negative motivation and engagement harness their drive to learn. Ideas, feelings and behaviors that enhance motivation and engagement are called Positive motivation and engagement factors. Ideas, feelings and behaviors that reduce motivation and engagement are negative motivation and engagement factors. In order to improve students' motivation and sense of engagement, it is necessary to increase positive factors, and reduce negative factors.

2.4 Research Hypothesis and Research Model

Attention, emotion and motivation are closely related. Attention select external stimulus and decides whether to enter the working memory system or the conscious system. Motivation and emotion determine the choice and orientation of attention (Raymond 2009). The emotional system generates motivation. At the same time, motivation appears in the mode of emotion, attitude and will. From the perspective of brain mechanism, anterior cingulate gyrus has many connections with the visual processing area of the brain, and coordinates emotional, motivational and attention processes. In addition, the orbitofrontal cortex plays an important role in emotional value judgment. It interacts with the visual cortex and acts as a mediator in the visual cortex and motor system. The amygdala sends signals to the visual cortex and receives signals from the orbitofrontal cortex, including the orbitofrontal cortex. The processing of emotional signals is coordinated by attention.

Correspondingly, we assume that attention control, emotional intelligence and motivation also interact. From neuroscience perspective, as we can see from Fig. 1, part of the external stimulus signal directly reaches the sensory cortex and part enters the reticular structure of the brainstem to activate and arouse emotion and attention. When it reaches the sensory cortex, the prefrontal cortex is involved in attention regulation and emotional processing regulation. The anterior cingulate cortex is involved in both emotional processing regulation and attention regulation. The amygdala, thalamus, hypothalamus and hippocampus in the limbic system are interrelated and participate in emotional processing and recognition. The striatum receives dopamine signals about reward, judges reward and activates motivation. It can be seen that motivation, attention and emotion are interrelated in the neurological mechanism, while attention control ability, emotional intelligence and motivation system are stable mechanisms formed by multiple strengthening of their respective production mechanisms, so they also have mutual relations. Motivation helps individuals to adjust their attention actively, control their attention level independently. Emotional intelligence, emotional recognition and regulation, is the basis of ensuring the maintenance of attention and motivation level. The level of motivation and attention control affects the generation of emotions, or requires the promotion of emotional intelligence.

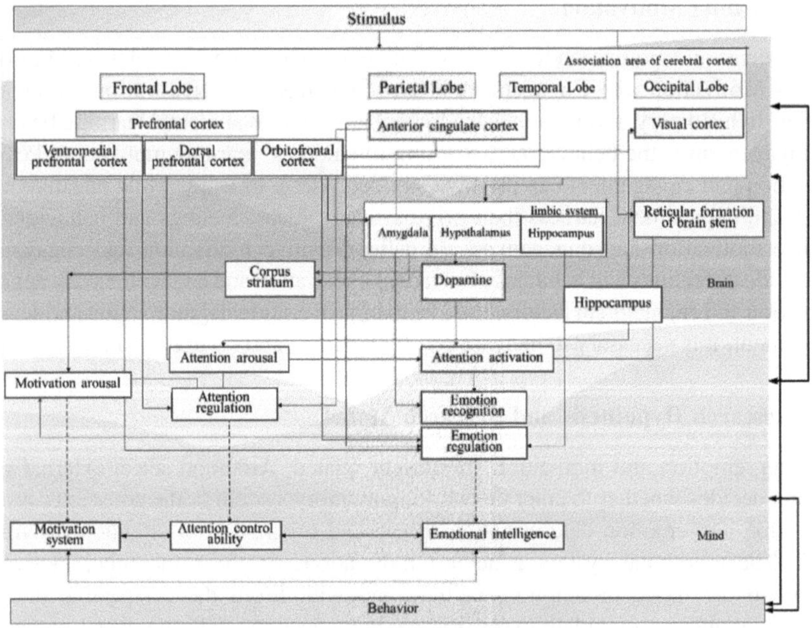

Fig. 1. Research model

Attentional control ability and emotional intelligence are relatively trait feature, consequently, we propose the following hypotheses:

H1: There's a significant positive correlation between attention control ability and emotion intelligence;

H2: Attention control ability has a significant impact on motivation;
H2.1: Attention control ability has a significant positive impact on positive motivation and engagement;
H2.2: Attention control ability has a negative impact on negative motivation and engagement;
H3: Emotion intelligence has a significant impact on motivation;
H3.1: Emotion intelligence has a significant positive impact on positive motivation and engagement;
H3.2: Emotion intelligence has a significant negative impact on negative motivation and engagement; Research method.

2.5 Data Collection

Using multistage cluster sampling method, we selected two primary schools in Beijing, China to conduct a full sample survey of students in grade 4, 5 and 6 (age from 9.5–12.5 years). 1860 valid student questionnaires were obtained, and the efficiency of the questionnaires was 92.86%. Individual missing values are replaced by linear trend at points method.

There are 694 fourth-grade students, covering 36.5% (360 males, 334 females); 567 fifth-grade students, accounting for 29.8% of the total (292 males, 275 females); 642 sixth-grade students, accounting for 33.7% of the total (340 males, 302 females). The total number of males is 992, accounting for 52.1%, and 911 females, covering 47.9%.

2.6 Instruments

Attention Control Ability
The Attentional Control Scale (Derryberry and Reed 2002) was adopted to measure individual attention control level. The scale can be used to test concentration control, attention shifting control.
Item analysis: Item AC4, 5, 9, 11, 14, 15, 16 and 20 did not meet the requirements in the test of correlation and homogeneity between items and total scores, and were deleted; Reliability analysis: Cronbach's α of the scale in the survey reached 0.727, and the reliability of internal consistency was high; Validity analysis: According to confirmatory factor analysis, the results of constructive validity are all reached the recommended value (CMIN/DF = 1.659 < 2.0, GFI = 0.996 > 0.9, NFI = 0.987 > 0.9, CFI = 0.995 > 0.9, RMSEA = 0.019 < 0.08), indicating that the constructive validity of the Attention Control Scale is good and its structure is reasonable.

Emotional Intelligence
Trait and Emotional Intelligence Questionnaire (Short Form) was adopted to test emotional intelligence, which measures four main factors: well-being, self-control, emotional ability and social ability.
Item analysis: The EQ22, 23, 25, 26 and 30 items of emotional intelligence scale did not meet the requirements in the test of correlation and homogeneity between the items and the total score, and were deleted; Reliability analysis: Cronbach's α of the scale in this survey reach 0.823, and the reliability of internal consistency is very good. Validity

analysis: The results of confirmatory factor analysis reach the recommended values ($CMIN/DF = 1.965 < 2.0$, $GFI = 0.994 > 0.9$, $NFI = 0.987 > 0.9$, $CFI = 0.994 > 0.9$, $RMSEA = 0.023 < 0.08$), which indicates that the constructive validity of the scale is good and its structure is reasonable.

Motivation

Motivation and Engagement Scale- Junior School (MES-JS) was used to test motivation. MES-JS is mainly for elementary school student and junior school student. Including positive motivation and engagement, negative motivation and engagement, and eleven sub-dimensions.

Item analysis: From the item analysis results of each item, it can be seen that the discrimination of item D2 did not reach a significant level and was deleted; Reliability analysis: Cronbach's α was 0.825 (very good, very high). The reliability coefficients of the four dimensions were: positive motivation 0.853, positive engagement 0.883, negative motivation 0.834 and negative engagement 0.709, which all exceeded 0.7, indicating that the internal consistency reliability of all variables was very good; Validity analysis: The constructive validity of MES reached the recommended value, ($CMIN/DF = 1.980 < 2.0$, $GFI = 0.965 > 0.9$, $NFI = 0.952 > 0.9$, $CFI = 0.975 > 0.9$, $RMSEA = 0.023 < 0.08$) which showed that Motivation and Input Scale had good constructive validity in two-dimensional division, four-dimensional division, and eleven-dimensional division.

3 Research Result

3.1 Motivation and Engagement

In order to explore the overall motivation level of domestic students, this paper conducts an overall mean analysis and try to find out what kinds of motivation students can improve. In order to explore group differences, such as motivation differences between boys and girls and motivation differences caused by grades, variance analysis was used to analyze.

Table 1 shows that: On positive motivation and positive engagement, students did not reach rank A and B, while on negative motivation and engagement, students reached grade A. That is to say, on the whole, students' motivation of active pursuit represented by self-efficacy is not good, and they need to be intervened and promoted. The motivation of failure avoidance is better, the motivation represented by perseverance is lower, and the negative behavior investment represented by learned helplessness needs to be improved.

Table 1. Motivation and engagement level (N = 1860)

	Mean	S.E.	S.D.	Rank		Mean	S.E.	S.D.	Rank
Positive motivation	87.805	.244	10.509	C	Negative motivation	56.351	.374	16.144	A
Self-efficacy	87.897	.291	12.532	C	Anxiety	56.773	.411	17.726	A
Mastery goals	87.019	.300	12.951	C	Failure avoidance	60.195	.515	22.210	A
Valuing	88.498	.273	11.755	C	Uncertain control	52.084	.479	20.649	A

(continued)

Table 1. (*continued*)

	Mean	S.E.	S.D.	Rank		Mean	S.E.	S.D.	Rank
Positive engagement	81.701	.306	13.211	D	Negative engagement	45.808	.306	13.186	A
Persistence	82.618	.337	14.547	D	Learned helplessness	33.153	.331	14.287	A
Self-regulation, planning	83.186	.337	14.549	D	Self-handicapping	58.463	.429	18.488	A
Self-regulation, Task management	79.299	.412	17.776	D					

There were significant differences in self-efficacy (F = 3.063, P = 0.047 < 0.05), failure avoidance(F = 4.489, P = 0.011 < 0.05) and learned helplessness (F = 3.175, P = 0.042 < 0.05) when age and gender were taken as independent variables, but there was no significant group difference in other variables.

From Fig. 1, the self-efficacy of boys in grade 4 and 5 is lower than that of girls, and the self-efficacy of boys in Grade 6 is higher than that of girls, all of which show a downward trend with the growth of grade; the avoidance failure of boys shows a downward trend, while that of girls is opposite; the average avoidance failure of girls after grade 5 and 6 is higher than that of boys; with the growth of grade, the acquisition helplessness of boys presents an inverted U-shaped development, and the straight line of girls (Fig. 2).

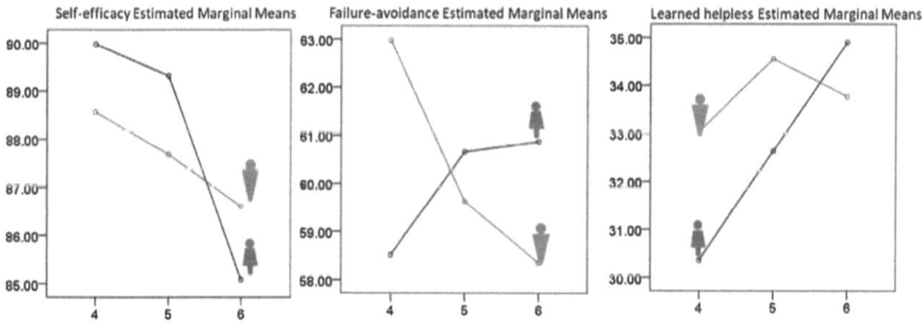

Fig. 2. Average of self-efficacy, failure-avoidance and learned helpless of female and male among grade 4, 5 and 6

3.2 Emotional Intelligence

To explore the differences of emotional intelligence between age and gender, the results of Table 2 show that: well-being (F = 3.995, P = 0.019 < 0.05) and sociability (F = 6.512, P = 0.002 < 0.05) were significantly different under the influence of gender and age. From the perspective of mean and standard deviation, boys' well-being was higher than girls from the fifth grade. On Sociability, girls in the fourth and fifth grade were higher than boys and boys in the sixth grade were higher than girls.

Table 2. Group difference of emotional intelligence (Gender × age)

Variables		Grade4	Grade5	Grade6	Gender × age	
		M ± SD	M ± SD	M ± SD	F	P
Well-being	M	3.565 ± 0.634	3.590 ± 0.667	3.566 ± 0.649	3.995	.019
	F	3.662 ± 0.564	3.502 ± 0.565	3.520 ± 0.573		
Self-control	M	3.424 ± 0.745	3.307 ± 0.750	3.340 ± 0.720	1.261	.284
	F	3.534 ± 0.678	3.309 ± 0.726	3.337 ± 0.683		
Emotionality	M	3.530 ± 0.742	3.446 ± 0.717	3.528 ± 0.725	.677	.508
	F	3.701 ± 0.720	3.568 ± 0.711	3.607 ± 0.678		
Sociability	M	3.402 ± 0.819	3.399 ± 0.812	3.544 ± 0.752	6.512	.002
	F	3.676 ± 0.732	3.482 ± 0.784	3.510 ± 0.779		
Emotional intelligence	M	3.499 ± 0.540	3.455 ± 0.537	3.503 ± 0.547	3.728	.024
	F	3.650 ± 0.479	3.479 ± 0.524	3.507 ± 0.524		

3.3 Attention Control Ability

In order to explore the basic situation of pupils' attention control ability, the scale used in the survey was developed from two dimensions: attention concentration and attention switching. There were significant differences in the ability of attention concentration ($T = -6.486$, $P = 0.000 < 0.05$) and attention switching ($T = 2.668$, $P = 0.008 < 0.05$) between male and female students. The average value of girls' attention switching ability was higher than that of boys, and boys' attention switching ability was higher than that of girls.

There is a significant difference on attention concentrating ability ($F = 3.893$, $P = 0.021 < 0.05$) among three grades. The difference is reflected in the grade 4 and 5. The fourth grade has significantly higher attention control ability and lower standard deviation than the fifth grade. There was no significant difference in attention switching ability between grades. And no significant differences were found with age and gender as co-independent variables.

3.4 Relationship Among Motivation, Attention Control Ability and Emotion Intelligence

Attention level, emotion state, motivation level determines whether the valuable information can be selected into our cognitive system. At meantime Attention control ability, emotional intelligence can both influence whether can student focus on learning and have motivation to learn. The relationship among them facilitate us to better understand the factor that influence our cognition activity. Whether people with higher emotional intelligence have stronger attention control ability? Whether people with stronger attention control abilities have more motivation? In order to answer the above questions, correlation analysis is carried out first, and then structural equation model is used to find the main relationship.

According to Pearson correlation coefficient, significant relationships among all three variables were found. There's significant positive relationship between emotional intelligence and attentional control ability ($r = 0.526$, sig < 0.001), meanwhile positive relationship between emotional intelligence and positive motivation (r = 0.521, sig < 0.001) & engagement (r = 0.543, sig < 0.001) was proved, so as attentional control ability (r = 0.359 & 0.371, sig < 0.001).

Using Amos 21.0 to validate the hypothetical variable relationship model, From Goodness-of-fit data (Table 3), we find that the goodness-of-fit index is completely good, and there is no modification indices appeared.

Table 3. Goodness-of-fit

Goodness-of-fit index	P	Df	CMIN/DF	GFI	AGFI	NFI	CFI	RMSEA
Model vale	0.112	29	1.659	0.999	0.989	0.987	0.995	0.019
Reference value	>0.05		<2.0	>0.9	>0.9	>0.9	>0.9	<0.08

The final model (Fig. 3) of the variable relationship results show that CMIN = 5.998 (P = 0.112 > 0.05). We can clearly find that positive motivation and engagement are positively predicted by attentional control ability and emotional intelligence. On the contrary, negative motivation and engagement are negatively predicted.

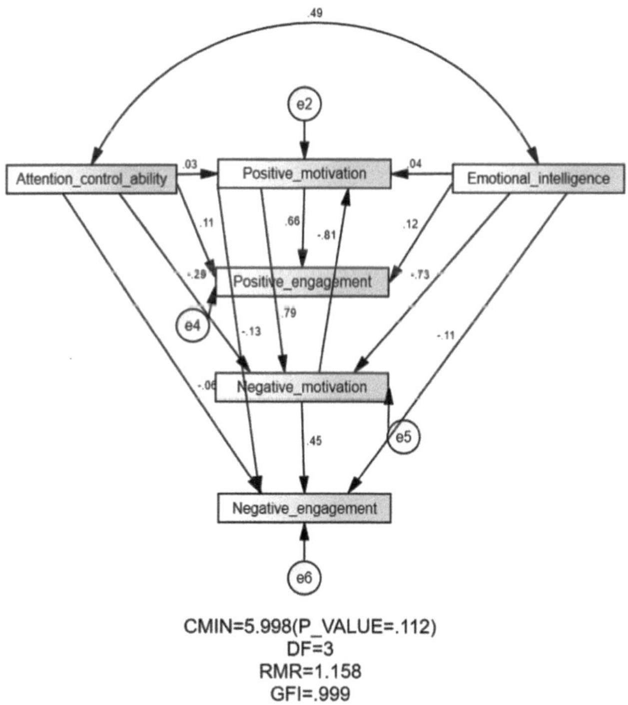

Fig. 3. Relationship of motivation & engagement, attentional control ability and emotional intelligence. Single arrow means the single predictive relationship between variables and the values are standard regression coefficient. Double-head arrow means co-variation between variables. e represent residuals.

According to Table 4 emotional intelligence has a significant positive predictive effect on positive motivation and positive engagement, and a significant negative predictive effect on negative motivation and negative engagement. Attention control ability has a significant positive predictive effect on positive motivation and positive engagement, but a significant negative predictive effect on negative motivation. Only attention control ability had no significant effect on negative engagement in all paths. In addition, the internal relationship between positive and negative motivation and input is similar to other research results (Yin 2018). Positive and negative motivation have significant influence on each other. Positive motivation significantly predicts positive engagement, negative motivation predicts negative engagement, and negative motivation predicts positive input. That is to say, the performance of cognitive motivation level will affect learning input motivation.

Table 4. Optimal matching variables in the model of the relationship

Hypothesis	Relationship	Estimate	C.R.	p
H1	EI ↔ AC	0.184	19.346	***
H2.1	PM ← AC	0.027	20.941	***
H2.1	PE ← AC	0.110	6.496	***
H3.1	PM ← EI	0.043	39.506	***
H3.1	PE ← EI	0.123	6.883	***
H2.2	NM ← AC	−0.286	-9.86	***
H2.2	NE ← AC	−0.060	−2.747	0.006
H3.2	NM ← EI	−0.726	−20.972	***
H3.2	NE ← EI	−0.107	−4.308	***
	PE ← PM	0.656	39.506	***
	NE ← NM	0.455	20.941	***
	NE ← PM	−0.125	−5.918	***
	NM ← PM	0.793	14.671	***
	PM ← NM	−0.805	−15.774	***

P.S. PM = Positive motivation; PE = Positive engagement; NM = Negative motivation; NE = Negative engagement; EI = Emotional intelligence; AC = Attention control ability

By validating the hypothesis above, we find that H1: There's a significant positive correlation between attention control ability and emotion intelligence is completely valid; H2: Attention control ability has a significant impact on motivation is completely valid; H2.1: Attention control ability has a significant positive impact on positive motivation and engagement is completely valid; H2.2: Attention control ability has a negative impact on negative motivation and engagement is partly valid, the reason why such hypothesis isn't supported might because students' negative engagement level is mostly influence by their negative motivation and self-control ability which cover more than attentional control ability; H3: Emotion intelligence has a significant impact on motivation, is completely valid; H3.1: Emotion intelligence has a significant positive impact on positive motivation and engagement is completely valid; H3.2: Emotion intelligence has a significant negative impact on negative motivation and engagement, is completely valid.

4 Discussion and Conclusion

Firstly, according to research result of motivation, attention control ability and emotional intelligence, we find some differences among different groups. Why are there differences between gender and grades?

There is no tendency for Chinese students to abandon themselves and lose interest in school learning, and the anxiety of learning examination is generally low, which is inseparable from taking exams and exercises as the main learning methods. The high-frequency examination in school enhances the threshold of students' anxiety about exams and fear of failure. Learned helplessness is the lowest of all factors. The question like "I lost interest in school" indicates that students' attitude towards school is generally negative, which is inseparable from our ongoing curriculum reform. From the perspective of positive motivation and engagement, we uphold modest education, while family education generally exists comparative psychology, which may lead to low self-efficacy. Compact class schedule, some students do not have enough time to master goals, quick technical assistance or urge, which will lead to more self-abandonment and weaker willpower. However, the lower dimensions of perseverance and self-regulation may be due to the lack of meta-cognition, learning ability and willpower.

Boys' self-acceptance does not show a trend of increasing or decreasing with age, while girls' self-acceptance decreases with age, that is, the older they are, the worse their impression is. This understanding of themselves and their acceptance may affect the 6th grade girls' self-efficacy is lower than that of boys, and the tendency of avoiding failure is higher and higher, while boys are lower and lower. This difference is also influenced by different social evaluation and social expectations of male and female.

Secondly, as for difference in emotional intelligence. With the influence of gender and age, there was a difference in well-being. The downward trend of girls' well-being was much larger than that of boys. This may be further consolidated by the idea of equality between male and female in recent years, girls themselves or their families improve their requirements, so that the increase of pressure leads to the decline of girls' happiness. We generally believe that girls are more sensitive than boys. Sensitivity is one of the dimensions of personality characteristics. People with high sensitivity tend to face positive and negative information more carefully, and are more vulnerable to external information. With the growth of grade, the female students' self-identity decreases, which makes them more easily influenced by their own emotions and others.

Thirdly, emotions will affect cognitive flexibility. Individuals' attention resources will occupy cognitive resources when negative emotions occur, and their thinking falls into passivity. It is difficult to flexibly realize attention switching and task switching. Girls are more susceptible to emotions, which leads to higher attention switching for boys.

Fourthly, Motivation, attention control ability and emotional intelligence are the three core systems of information selection and orientation. Motivation does not exist alone to influence students' information acquisition. Emotion and attention regulation ability play a central role in our brain when receiving external stimuli. The way for students to improve their motivation should take attention control ability and emotional intelligence all into account.

Acknowledgements. This study is based on the project "Studying Game-based Learning from the Perspective of Learning Sciences", which belongs to the 2017 General Projects of Educational Research for the 13th Five-year Plan and was financed by China National Social Science Foundation NO. BCA170072.

References

Derryberry, D., Reed, M.A.: Anxiety-related attentional biases and their regulation by attentional control. J. Abnorm. Psychol. **111**(2), 225–236 (2002)

Um, E."R.", Plass, J.L., Hayward, E.O., Homer, B.D.: Emotional design in multimedia learning. J. Educ. Psychol. **104**(2), 485–498 (2012)

Goleman, D.: An EI-based theory of performance. In: Chemiss, C., Goleman, D. (eds.) The Emotionally Intelligent Workplace: How to Select for, Measure and Improve Emotional Intelligence in Individuals, pp. 27–44. Wiley, New York (2001)

Isen, A.M., Daubman, K.A., Nowicki, G.P.: Positive affect facilitates creative problem solving. J. Pers. Soc. Psychol. **53**(6), 1122 (1987)

Jung, N., Wranke, C., Hamburger, K., Knauff, M.: How emotions affect logical reasoning: evidence from experiments with mood-manipulated participants, spider phobics, and people with exam anxiety. Front. Psychol. **5**, 570 (2014)

Katsuki, F., Constantinidis, C.: Bottom-up and top-down attention: different processes and overlapping neural systems. The Neuroscientist **20**(5), 509–521 (2014)

Müller, N.G., Kleinschmidt, A.: Dynamic interaction of object- and space-based attention in retinotopic visual areas. J. Neurosci. Off. J. Soc. Neurosci. **23**(30), 9812 (2003)

Petersen, S.E., Posner, M.I.: The attention system of the human brain: 20 years after. Annu. Rev. Neurosci. **35**, 73–89 (2012)

Raymond, J.: Interactions of attention, emotion and motivation. Prog. Brain Res. **176**, 293–308 (2009)

Klingberg, T.: The Overloading Brain: Information Overload and the Limits of Working Memory, pp. 1–2. Shanghai Science and Technology Education Publishing Press (2011). (Zhou, J., Zhou D. (Trans.))

Vuilleumier, P.: How brains beware: neural mechanisms of emotional attention. Trends Cogn. Sci. **9**(12), 585–594 (2005)

Yin, H.: What motivates Chinese undergraduates to engage in learning? Insights from a psychological approach to student engagement research. High. Educ. **76**(5), 827–847 (2018)

Hatti, J.: Visible learning: a synthesis of over 800 meta-analyses relating to achievement, pp. 280–281. Educational Science Press (2015). (Peng et al. (Trans.))

Learning Computational Thinking Through Gamification and Collaborative Learning

Lap-Kei Lee[1(✉)], Tsz-Kin Cheung[1], Lok-Tin Ho[1], Wai-Hang Yiu[1], and Nga-In Wu[2]

[1] School of Science and Technology, The Open University of Hong Kong, Ho Man Tin, Kowloon, Hong Kong SAR, China
{lklee, s1201869, s1165683, s1201772}@ouhk.edu.hk

[2] Division of Communication and Social Sciences, Hong Kong Community College, Hong Kong Polytechnic University, Hung Hom, Hong Kong SAR, China
ninwu@hkcc-polyu.edu.hk

Abstract. Computational thinking (CT) is becoming a growing field in educational research and practice. CT is not only related to coding or programming, but also a fundamental skill for everyone to solve problems effectively and efficiently with solutions that are reusable in different contexts, which helps to improve our analytical ability for different tasks. Therefore, parents are eager to enroll their children in children programming courses. This paper presents the design of a web-based game for learning computational thinking anywhere and anytime. It has a visual programming environment for programming virtual robot to complete specific tasks. Our game levels are designed to cover the following five core elements of CT: reformulation, recursion, decomposition, abstraction and systematic testing. The game also supports collaborative learning, in which some game levels involve multiple robots to be programmed by multiple players at the same time. A survey on twenty undergraduate computer science students showed that our game requires the application of the above five core elements of CT to complete, and is likely to be an attractive learning tool for learners including primary students.

Keywords: Computational Thinking · Gamification · Collaborative learning · Visual programming

1 Introduction

The past decade has witnessed an increasing number of research and practice on computational thinking (CT) education (see the survey paper by Shute et al. [1] and the references therein). Education researchers, practitioners and parents found that CT, which originates from computer science, can be applied to domains other than programming [2], and is correlated with success in college and life [3]. CT is a fundamental skill for everyone to solve problems effectively and efficiently; it allows ones to acquire the analytical ability to come up with efficient and effective solutions that are reusable for different tasks in different contexts [4]. Therefore, parents are eager to enroll their children in computer programming classes [5, 6], and the

S. K. S. Cheung et al. (Eds.): ICBL 2019, LNCS 11546, pp. 339–349, 2019.
https://doi.org/10.1007/978-3-030-21562-0_28

number of such kid coding classes has been rapidly increasing, for example, in Hong Kong [7].

The term "Computational Thinking" was coined in the seminal article by Wing [4], who argued that CT is not only referring to thinking like a computer, but also involves the following five core elements in solving problems efficiently and creatively [1]:

1. *Problem reformulation*: Reformulate a seemingly difficult problem into a problem with existing solution. For example, consider the problem of course selection in a university programme. Courses often have prerequisite, which requires the completion of other courses. Finding a feasible order of courses to complete the programme can be reduced to a well-known problem in graph theory of computer science called topological sort.
2. *Recursion*: Construct a system incrementally based on preceding information. This core element involves identifying repetitive patterns in the problem and solve the problem using solutions of the smaller pattern. Note that this definition is broader than the usual definition of "recursion" in computer science, where a problem is solved by using solutions to smaller instances of the same problem.
3. *Problem decomposition*: Break a large complex task into smaller manageable units. There are usually existing solutions to the manageable units. Problem decomposition allows these solutions to be reusable in different complex tasks. The difficulty of solving the task is also reduced due to the lower complexity in solving the smaller tasks.
4. *Abstraction*: Choose an appropriate representation to model the core aspects of the problem to make it tractable (i.e., solvable efficiently). Taking the previous course selection problem as an example. Courses can be modelled as vertices of a graph and the course prerequisite relations can be modelled as edges of the graph. With such problem abstraction, the course selection can be reduced to topological sort.
5. *Systematic testing*: Take purposeful actions to derive solutions. This core element involves finding and fixing errors in the solutions, which is referred to as *debugging* in programming.

The above five core elements of CT can be applied to not only computer programming, but also everyday activities and problems.

This paper presents the design of a web-based game for learning computational thinking anywhere and anytime. In the game, players are asked to program virtual robots to complete specific tasks in a kitchen, e.g., preparing food by moving around, picking up ingredients, chopping in "cutting zone", and putting the deliverables in "delivery zone". The kitchen setting is closely related to everyday activities and is suitable for players with limited or no programming experience. The game contains a sequence of game levels with increasing difficulty. The problem solving for these game levels helps the players to develop the CT skills for the above five core elements. To motivate players to strive for a better solution, they are rewarded different number of "stars" depending on the tasks completed in a game level, and players can earn different in-game titles with these stars.

Our game has a visual programming environment where actions of the virtual robots are shown as action block and programming can be done by drag-and-drop of the action blocks. Such programming interface design can be found in existing programming learning tools like Scratch [8] and Alice [9] (see Sect. 2 for more details), which is suitable for kindergarten and primary students.

Our game also supports *collaborative learning*, which involves a group of students working together to solve a problem, in which students learn through talking among themselves [10]. Some game levels require multiple players to program multiple robots to collaborate on completing the tasks. Denner et al. [11] found that collaborative learning is particularly beneficial to students with minimal programming experience in CT learning; their experiment on 320 middle school students showed that students working collaboratively on Alice tasks achieved significantly better performance than students working alone.

We surveyed twenty undergraduate computer science students; most of them agreed that our game requires the application of the above five core elements of CT, and is likely to be an attractive learning tool for junior learners like primary students.

Organization of the Paper. Section 2 reviews common existing programming tools for CT learning. Section 3 presents the design details of our web-based game. Section 4 gives the preliminary evaluation result. Section 5 discusses the evaluation result and concludes the paper.

2 Existing Programming Tools for CT Learning

Different existing programming tools have been used in CT learning and research studies (see the survey paper [1]). This section reviews three of them that are commonly used and are closely related to our game design.

Fig. 1. User interface of Scratch [8].

Scratch [8] is also a block-based programming environment that allows users to create interactive stories, games and animations by drag-and-drop of the code blocks. Block-based programming environment enables teaching CT without the complex semantics of programming languages like Java and C++, which is particularly suitable for students without prior programming experience. Scratch is a web-based application that can be run anywhere and anytime on the Internet. Users can share their products in its online community. It does not come with a tutorial for CT learning, but users can create their own tutorials. As Scratch provides lots of functions, it would be an overkill for CT learning and the complicated user interface (Fig. 1) may hinder the learning of junior users like primary students.

Alice [9] is a block-based programming environment that allows users to create computer animations using virtual 3D models. Users can place 3D models/objects into the virtual worlds and program their actions using the code blocks. Yet Alice is a standalone application that requires installation on a computer, and does not provide a tutorial with organized topics of CT.

Lego Mindstorms (www.lego.com/en-us/mindstorms) has a block-based programming environment (on a mobile application) for programming physical robots composed of programmable bricks, motors and sensors. The complexity of assembling the physical robot makes it not suitable for primary students without assistance from adults. The high cost of the hardware is also a concern to some users.

3 Our Web-Based Game

This section presents the detailed design of our web-based game for CT learning. Our game is a web application deployed on a web server. Players can connect to the web application using common web browsers, e.g., Google Chrome, Mozilla Firefox (see Fig. 2 for the user interface of our game on Mozilla Firefox). When a player connects to the web application for the first time, he/she is asked to provide a user name, then a user account will be created automatically and the login information will be kept in the player's browser such that he/she will be automatically logged in when returning to the game later.

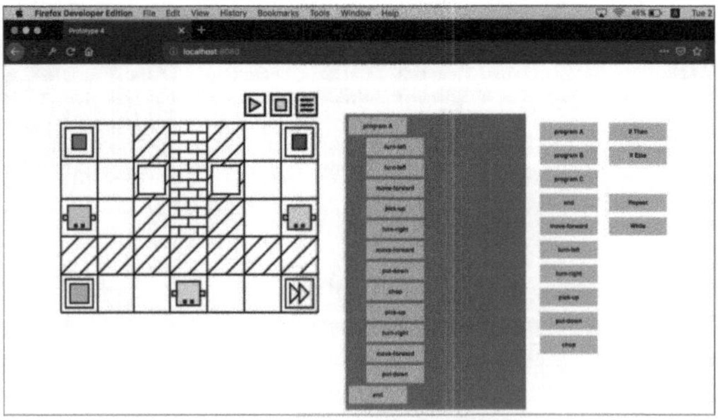

Fig. 2. Our web-based game on the web browser Mozilla Firefox.

3.1 User Interface of the Game

There are two main components in the user interface of a game level (Fig. 3): the *robot action environment* (left) and the *visual block-based programming environment* (right).

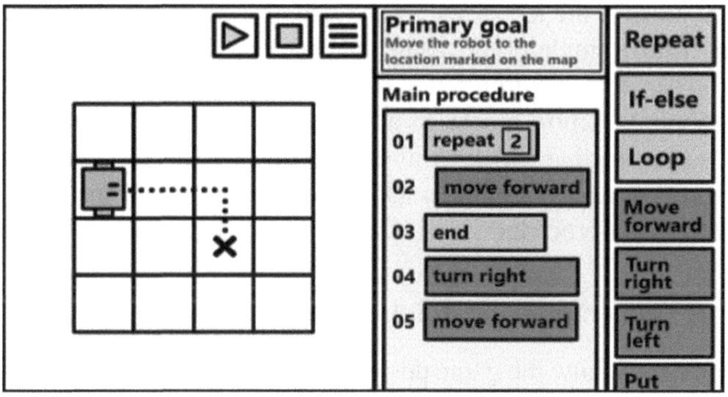

Fig. 3. Design of the user interface of our web-based game (single player game).

Robot Action Environment. The robot action environment is a 2D grid board of blocks arranging in rows and columns that represents the layout of a kitchen. The board contains one robot (for a single player) or multiple robots (for multiplayers) in some blocks of the board (see Fig. 3), which need to complete some specific tasks (e.g., the primary goal shown on the top of Fig. 3).

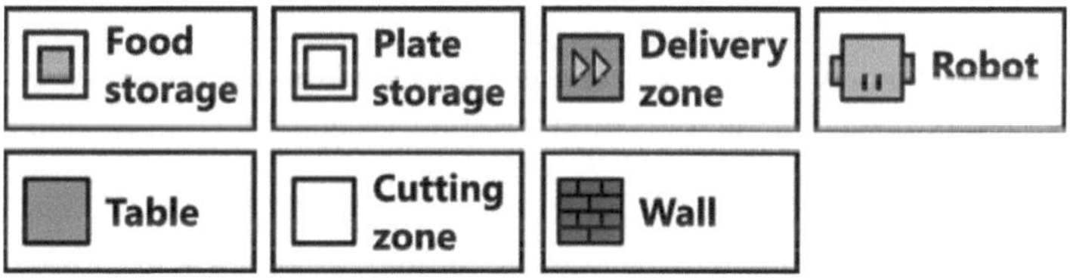

Fig. 4. Function tiles and robot for the robot action environment.

Each robot can be programmed to move around the board and perform some actions when it is next to the following function tiles (Fig. 4):

- *Food storage*: A robot can pick up some food from a food storage.
- *Plate storage:* A robot can pick up a plate for keeping processed food (i.e., chopped food in our game).
- *Delivery zone:* A robot can put down a plate of processed food to the delivery zone, which is usually the primary goal for a game level.
- *Table*: Chopped food can be put down there and later be picked up again (possibly by another robot).

- *Cutting zone*: A robot can put down some food there, chop it and then pick it up again.
- *Wall*: A robot cannot walk through a wall tile.

Visual Block-Based Programming Environment. This environment shows one or more main procedure areas in the left, where each main procedure is for the action of a single robot (see Fig. 3 for a single player game, and see Fig. 7 shown later for a multiplayer game). Player(s) can drag and drop action blocks in the right to the procedure area so as to program the robot(s). Action blocks in a procedure can be removed by dragging and dropping the corresponding block to anywhere outside the procedure area. Our programming environment also supports sub-procedure and allow the creation of a new procedure area for a sub-procedure next to the main procedure area (see Fig. 6 shown later).

3.2 Design of Game Levels for CT Learning

This subsection details how the game design is related to the previously introduced five core elements of CT, namely, problem reformulation, recursion, problem decomposition, abstraction, and systematic testing.

CT Element – Abstraction. Abstraction is applied in every game level. The player is required to model the specific tasks in a step-by-step solution using the action blocks. Sometimes, there is a subtask that concerns efficiency of the solution and the player needs to complete the procedure in limited number of action blocks. Abstract thinking in the player's mind is necessary for such subtask.

CT Element – Systematic Testing. Systematic testing is also applied in every game level, which can be obviously observed. When a player completes the programming of the robot(s) in the visual block-based programming environment, he/she can press the "play" button (the button with a triangle) on top of the robot action environment. The sequence of action blocks in the procedure (and sub-procedures) will be sent to the web server, which will then update the player's browser to show the robot action in a step-by-step manner. The second button with a square allows a user to stop in the middle of the execution. The third button with three strips is the setting button, which allows configuring the display speed of the step-by-step execution in the browser. Such step-by-step execution allows the players to easily spot the errors in their procedure such that debugging of the procedure can be performed.

The game design contains three types of game levels: *tutorial*, *single player game*, and *multiplayer game*.

Tutorial. The game levels in the tutorial aim to let the players get familiar with the robot action environment and the visual block-based programming environments. Figure 3 is a tutorial game level that let the players to understand the orientation of a robot, i.e., the robot can face to one of the four directions: up, down, left, and right. Figure 5 below is another tutorial game level that requires the robot to pick up the counter block and move forward according to the number shown in the counter block. Note that the number on the counter block is randomly chosen from the set {3, 4, 5}, and the "decrement" action block will decrease this number.

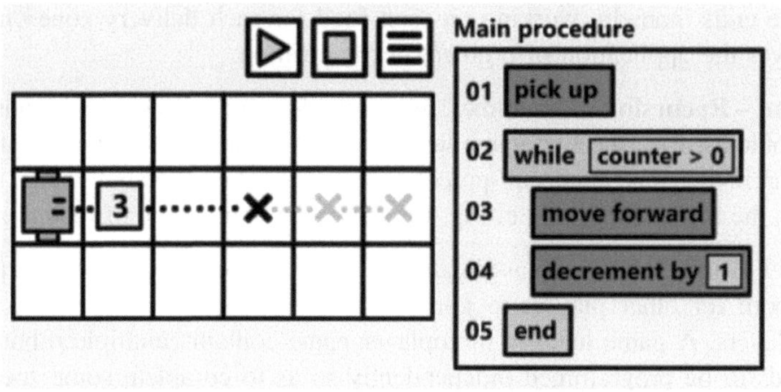

Fig. 5. Tutorial game level involving a counter block and a while-loop.

Single Player Game. It contains four chapters on the following topics of programming: (1) Sequence, (2) Branching, (3) Iteration, and (4) Variable. Each chapter contains six game levels with increasing difficulty. Figure 6 shows two game levels in the chapter of "Iteration", where the player is required to prepare food in different colors for different delivery zones. Two different robot orientation systems are used in these two game levels: The orientation system in the left is relative to the player's screen, and thus arrow is used to indicate the facing direction of the robots, which is easier to program; while the orientation system in the right is relative to the facing direction of the robots, which is harder to program.

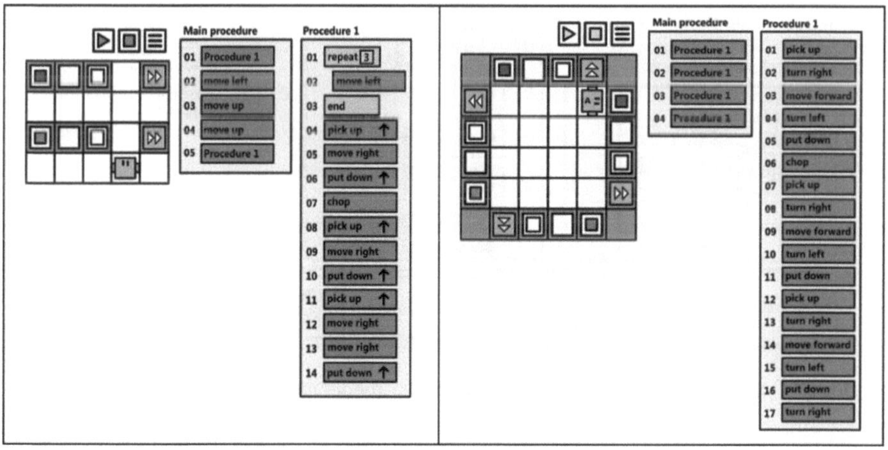

Fig. 6. Two single player game levels on Iteration.

CT Element – Problem Decomposition. The game levels shown in Fig. 6 have a large and complex task of preparing food in different colors for different delivery zones. To solve the game levels, the player needs to break the large task into smaller manageable units, namely, working on each food for each delivery zone one by one. This involves the application of problem decomposition.

CT Element – Recursion. Sometimes, the result of problem decomposition is identical smaller problems, e.g., the two game levels in Fig. 6. Once the player identifies such repeated part in the game level, sub-procedure can be applied repeatedly (e.g., Procedure 1 shown in the two game levels in Fig. 6). This is an application of recursion in CT.

Multiplayer Game. Our web-based game provides a room feature, where a player can create a room for other players to join and play together on some game levels for multiple players. A game level in multiplayer game contains multiple robots, each of which needs to be programmed independently so as to complete some specific task. Figure 7 shows a multiplayer game level, in which two players need to collaborate to deliver the cookie to the delivery zone. Note that our current implementation of the game does not provide communication tools between players, so players are supposed to communicate with each other using their own means. Note also that there is no rule how the players should collaborate. They may work together on the programming of all robots, or they may work independently on different robots. It is a must for the players to solve the problem and learn through communication among themselves, which is the feature of *collaborative learning* [10].

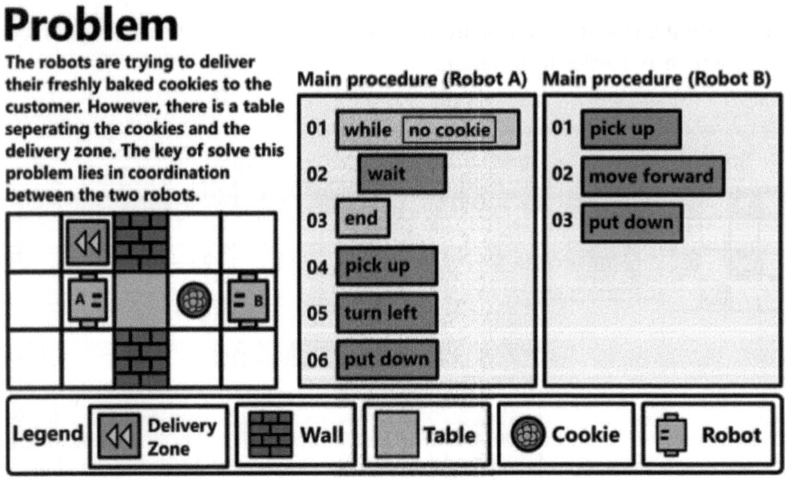

Fig. 7. A multiplayer game level involving two robots and a special item "Cookie".

CT Element – Problem Reformulation. Figure 8 below shows a complex multi-player game level for three robots that requires the application of all the five core elements of CT. The game level requires the robots to prepare a plate of mixture of chopped food (in red and green) and deliver to the delivery zone. Given the wall and table restriction, the problem can be easily reformulated and decomposed into three separate actions for the three robots, where robots A and B were supposed to act in a symmetric way. This is an example of problem reformulation.

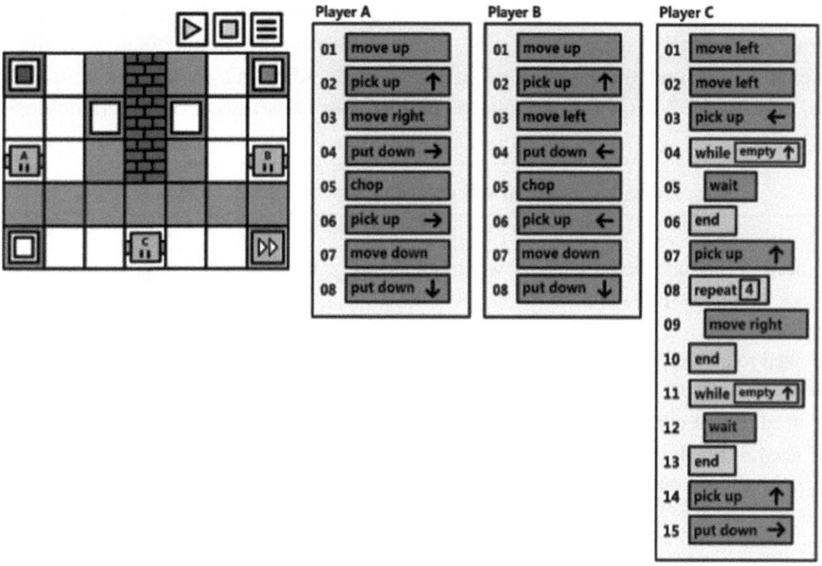

Fig. 8. A multiplayer game level involving three robots. (Color figure online)

Reward System. Reward system is a gamification technique to motivate users to keep playing in the game [12]. In our game, players can earn "stars" by completing specific tasks in a game level (see Fig. 9 for an example). A player earns different in-game title with different number of stars: Total Beginner (less than 20 stars), Apprentice Programmer (at least 20 and less than 150 stars), and Code Master (at least 150 stars).

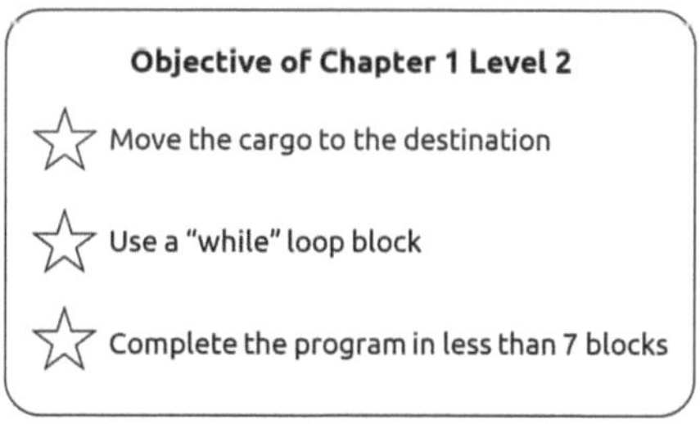

Fig. 9. A multiplayer game level involving three robots.

4 Preliminary Evaluation

Participants and Setting. To confirm that our designed game requires the application of the five core elements of CT, we invited 20 undergraduate students studying Computer Science (who have knowledge on computer programming and CT skills) to play our game in pairs and then complete a survey individually.

Result. The survey used a 5-point Likert scale (1: disagree, 2: partially disagree, 3: neutral, 4: partially agree, 5: agree). Table 1 shows the items related to the core elements of CT and the percentage of participants selecting each point in the Likert scale, and Table 2 shows the results related to user satisfaction on the game design.

Table 1. Survey result on core elements of CT elements.

Item	1	2	3	4	5
(1) I need to simulate the problem answer in mind and abstract the core aspects when I try to solve the problem	0%	0%	15%	65%	20%
(2) I need to convert a problem in a level to a simpler problem in order to complete the level	0%	5%	25%	30%	40%
(3) I need to find out a pattern to construct a solution	0%	0%	10%	40%	50%
(4) I need to break down the problem into small pieces, it is more manageable to solve the problem	0%	0%	25%	25%	50%

Table 2. Survey result on user satisfaction.

Item	1	2	3	4	5
(5) The game can motivate student's interest in improving computational thinking skills	0%	0%	35%	25%	40%
(6) The gameplay is attractive and fun	0%	0%	25%	40%	35%
(7) The game can encourage students to collaborate with each other	0%	0%	15%	50%	35%
(8) The game level is suitable for primary students	0%	0%	20%	30%	50%
(9) The coding interface is easy to use for editing commands	0%	0%	5%	50%	45%

5 Discussion and Conclusion

In the preliminary evaluation, survey items 1 to 4 correspond to the CT elements abstraction, problem reformulation, recursion, and problem decomposition, respectively.

Table 1 shows that the majority of the Computer Science major respondents agreed that our game requires the application of these four CT core elements. As the step-by-step execution requires systematic testing obviously, there is no survey item about this core element of CT. Table 2 also shows that the majority of respondents are satisfied with the game design and user interface, and found that our game can promote CT learning and collaborative learning.

This paper presented the design of a web-based game for gamifying CT learning with the support of collaborative learning. We hope that it can provide insights for other researchers and education practitioners how CT learning can be promoted with gamification and how collaborative learning can be integrated in the process.

Limitations and Future Work. One of the target users of our game is the primary students, who may encounter difficulties that undergraduate students do not have. Our current study did not involve the engagement of primary students and thus the evaluation result provides only limited information on the usability and user satisfaction of our web-based game. A future work is to perform an evaluation on these target users. We are working on improving our game to allow both mobile client and web client (i.e., browsers) to work together, which should greatly increase the usability due to the popularity of mobile devices nowadays. Communication tool will also be added to facilitate collaborative learning inside our game.

References

1. Shute, V.J., Sun, C., Asbell-Clarke, J.: Demystifying computational thinking. Educ. Res. Rev. **22**, 142–158 (2017)
2. Berland, M., Wilensky, U.: Comparing virtual and physical robotics environments for supporting complex systems and computational thinking. J. Sci. Educ. Technol. **24**(5), 628–647 (2015)
3. Friedman, T.L.: The two codes your kids need to know. The New York Times. https://www.nytimes.com/2019/02/12/opinion/college-board-sat-ap.html. Accessed 13 Feb 2019
4. Wing, J.M.: Computational thinking. Commun. ACM **49**(3), 33–35 (2006)
5. Xiang, B.: Computer programming education goes viral in China. XinhuaNet. http://www.xinhuanet.com/english/2018-04/14/c_137110920.htm. Accessed 29 Mar 2019
6. Sun, J.: Get with the program: China's coding kids. Sixth Tone. https://www.sixthtone.com/news/1002642/get-with-the-program-chinas-coding-kids. Accessed 29 Mar 2019
7. Cremer, J.: Does your child need to learn coding? South China Morning Post. https://www.scmp.com/news/hong-kong/education/article/2142622/does-your-child-need-learn-coding. Accessed 13 Feb 2019
8. Resnick, M., et al.: Scratch: programming for all. Commun. ACM **52**(11), 60–67 (2009)
9. Cooper, S., Dann, W., Pausch, R.: Alice: a 3-D tool for introductory programming concepts. J. Comput. Sci. Coll. **15**(5), 107–116 (2000)
10. Gerlach, J.M.: Is this collaboration? In: Bosworth, K., Hamilton, S.J. (eds.) Collaborative Learning: Underlying Processes and Effective Techniques, New Directions for Teaching and Learning no. 59 (1994)
11. Denner, J., Werner, L., Campe, S., Ortiz, E.: Pair programming: under what conditions is it advantageous for middle school students? J. Res. Technol. Educ. **46**(3), 277–296 (2014)
12. Nicholson, S.: A RECIPE for meaningful gamification. In: Reiners, T., Wood, L. (eds.) Gamification in Education and Business. Springer, Cham (2015). https://doi.org/10.1007/978-3-319-10208-5_1

Author Index

MIX
Papier aus verantwortungsvollen Quellen
Paper from responsible sources
FSC® C105338

If you have any concerns about our products,
you can contact us on
ProductSafety@springernature.com

In case Publisher is established outside the EU,
the EU authorized representative is:
Springer Nature Customer Service Center GmbH
Europaplatz 3, 69115 Heidelberg, Germany

Printed by Libri Plureos GmbH
in Hamburg, Germany